Harcourt
Language

SENIOR AUTHORS
Roger C. Farr ◆ Dorothy S. Strickland

AUTHORS
Helen Brown ◆ Karen S. Kutiper ◆ Hallie Kay Yopp

SENIOR CONSULTANT
Asa G. Hilliard III

CONSULTANT
Diane L. Lowe

Orlando   Boston   Dallas   Chicago   San Diego

Visit *The Learning Site!*
www.harcourtschool.com

Contents

Introduction 18

Unit 1

Art/Creativity

Grammar: Sentences
Writing: Expressive Writing   22

CHAPTER 1 Sentences

Sentences 24
Kinds of Sentences 26
Punctuating Sentences 28
Extra Practice 30
Chapter Review 32
■ **Viewing:** Being a Good Viewer 33

CHAPTER 2 Subjects/Nouns

Complete and Simple Subjects 34
Nouns in Subjects 36
Combining Sentences: Compound Subjects 38
Extra Practice 40
Chapter Review 42
■ **Listening and Speaking:** Being a Good Listener and Speaker 43

CHAPTER 3 Writer's Craft: Personal Voice

Literature Model: from *Dancing with the Indians*
     by Angela Shelf Medearis 44
Using Colorful Words 46
Writer's Viewpoint 47
Writing a Descriptive Paragraph 48
     Prewriting and Drafting • Editing • Sharing and Reflecting
■ **Vocabulary:** Colorful Words 51

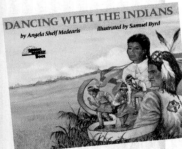

CHAPTER 4 Predicates/Verbs

Complete and Simple Predicates **52**

Verbs in Predicates **54**

Combining Sentences: Compound Predicates **56**

Extra Practice **58**

Chapter Review **60**

Vocabulary: Words from Many Places **61**

CHAPTER 5 Simple and Compound Sentences

Complete Sentences **62**

Simple and Compound Sentences **64**

Combining Sentences **66**

Extra Practice **68**

Chapter Review **70**

Study Skills: Being a Good Reader **71**

CHAPTER 6 Writing Workshop: Personal Narrative

Literature Model: from *My First American Friend*
by Sarunna Jin **72**

Prewriting • Drafting • Revising • Proofreading • Publishing **78**

Listening and Speaking: Acting Out a Story **83**

Unit Grammar Review **84**

Unit Wrap-Up

Writing Across the Curriculum **88**

Books to Read **89**

Unit 2

Health

Grammar: More About Nouns and Verbs
Writing: Informative Writing: Explanation

90

CHAPTER 7 More About Nouns

Nouns. 92
Common and Proper Nouns 94
Abbreviations and Titles. 96
Extra Practice. 98
Chapter Review 100
■ **Study Skills:** Understanding Charts 101

CHAPTER 8 Singular and Plural Nouns

Singular and Plural Nouns 102
Plural Nouns with *es* and *ies* 104
Nouns with Irregular Plurals 106
Extra Practice. 108
Chapter Review 110
■ **Study Skills:** Reading Special Maps 111

CHAPTER 9 Writer's Craft: Paragraphing

Literature Model: from *Baseball: How to Play the All-Star Way*
    by Mark Alan Teirstein. 112
Identifying the Topic. 114
Using Details 114
Using Sequence Words 115
Writing Directions. 116
    Prewriting and Drafting • Editing • Sharing and Reflecting
■ **Listening and Speaking:** Giving Spoken Directions 119

CHAPTER 10   Possessive Nouns

Singular Possessive Nouns **120**
Plural Possessive Nouns **122**
Revising Sentences Using Possessive Nouns **124**
Extra Practice **126**
Chapter Review **128**
■ **Technology:** Writing on the Computer **129**

CHAPTER 11   Action Verbs and the Verb *Be*

Verbs **130**
Action Verbs **132**
The Verb *Be* **134**
Extra Practice **136**
Chapter Review **138**
■ **Vocabulary:** Categorizing Words **139**

CHAPTER 12   Writing Workshop: How-to Essay

Literature Model: from *How to Be a Friend*
    by Laurie Krasny Brown and Marc Brown **140**
    Prewriting • Drafting • Revising • Proofreading • Publishing **148**
■ **Listening and Speaking:** Making an Oral Presentation **153**

Unit Grammar Review **154**

Unit Wrap-Up

Writing Across the Curriculum **158**
Books to Read **159**

Cumulative Review: Units 1–2 . . . . **160**

Unit 3

Social Studies

Grammar: More About Verbs
Writing: Persuasive Writing 164

CHAPTER 13 Main Verbs and Helping Verbs

Main Verbs and Helping Verbs. **166**

More About Helping Verbs **168**

Contractions with *Not* **170**

Extra Practice **172**

Chapter Review. **174**

■ **Study Skills:** Using a Dictionary **175**

CHAPTER 14 Present-Tense Verbs

Verb Tenses **176**

Present-Tense Verbs **178**

Subject-Verb Agreement **180**

Extra Practice **182**

Chapter Review **184**

■ **Vocabulary:** Prefixes and Suffixes **185**

CHAPTER 15 Writer's Craft: Word Choice

Literature Model: from *Ramona and Her Mother*
    by Beverly Cleary **186**

Vivid Verbs. **188**

Specific Nouns **189**

Writing a Friendly Letter. **190**

    Prewriting and Drafting • Editing • Sharing and Reflecting

■ **Vocabulary:** General and Specific Nouns **193**

CHAPTER 16 Past-Tense and Future-Tense Verbs

Past-Tense and Future-Tense Verbs **194**

More About Past-Tense and Future-Tense Verbs **196**

Choosing the Correct Tense **198**

Extra Practice **200**

Chapter Review **202**

■ **Listening and Speaking:** Listening for Facts and Opinions **203**

CHAPTER 17 Irregular Verbs

Irregular Verbs **204**

More Irregular Verbs **206**

Commonly Misused Irregular Verbs **208**

Extra Practice **210**

Chapter Review **212**

■ **Study Skills:** Using a Thesaurus **213**

CHAPTER 18 Writing Workshop: Persuasive Paragraph

Literature Model: from *Coaching Ms. Parker*
by Carla Heymsfeld **214**

Prewriting • Drafting • Revising • Proofreading • Publishing **220**

■ **Listening and Speaking:** Giving an Oral Presentation **225**

Unit Grammar Review **226**

Unit Wrap-Up

Writing Across the Curriculum **230**

Books to Read **231**

Unit 4

Grammar: Pronouns and Adjectives
Writing: Informative Writing: Classification

232

CHAPTER 19 Pronouns

Pronouns 234
Singular and Plural Pronouns 236
Pronoun-Antecedent Agreement 238
Extra Practice 240
Chapter Review 242
■ **Study Skills:** Parts of a Book 243

CHAPTER 20 Subject and Object Pronouns

Subject Pronouns 244
Object Pronouns 246
Using *I* and *Me* 248
Extra Practice 250
Chapter Review 252
■ **Technology:** Exploring Websites 253

CHAPTER 21 Writer's Craft: Effective Sentences

Literature Model: from *A Log's Life* by Wendy Pfeffer 254
Identifying Sentence Variety 256
Combining Sentences 257
Writing a Paragraph That Compares 258
    Prewriting and Drafting • Editing • Sharing and Reflecting
■ **Listening and Speaking:** Comparing Writing and Speaking 261

CHAPTER 22   More About Pronouns

Possessive Pronouns **262**

More Possessive Pronouns **264**

Contractions with Pronouns **266**

Extra Practice **268**

Chapter Review **270**

■ **Vocabulary:** Using Context Clues **271**

CHAPTER 23   Adjectives

Adjectives **272**

Adjectives for *How Many* **274**

Adjectives for *What Kind* **276**

Extra Practice **278**

Chapter Review **280**

■ **Listening and Speaking:** Guest Speakers **281**

CHAPTER 24   Writing Workshop: Advantages and Disadvantages Essay

Literature Model: from "Weird Leaves"
by Deborah Churchman **282**

Prewriting • Drafting • Revising • Proofreading • Publishing **288**

■ **Technology:** Making a Video **293**

Unit Grammar Review **294**

Unit Wrap-Up

Writing Across the Curriculum **298**

Books to Read **299**

Cumulative Review: Units 1–4 . . . . **300**

Unit 5

Social Studies

Grammar: Articles, Adjectives, and Adverbs
Writing: Informative Writing: Research Report   **306**

CHAPTER 25 **More About Adjectives**

Articles 308
Adjectives That Compare 310
Avoiding Incorrect Comparisons 312
Extra Practice 314
Chapter Review 316
■ **Vocabulary:** Synonyms and Antonyms 317

CHAPTER 26 **Adverbs**

Adverbs 318
More About Adverbs 320
Comparing with Adverbs 322
Extra Practice 324
Chapter Review 326
■ **Study Skills:** Taking Notes and Making an Outline 327

Writer's Craft:
CHAPTER 27 **Organizing Information**

Literature Model: from *Horsepower: The Wonder of Draft Horses* by Cris Peterson 328
Making an Outline 330
Matching Audience and Purpose 331
Writing a Paragraph of Information 332
   Prewriting and Drafting • Editing • Sharing and Reflecting
■ **Study Skills:** Taking Notes 335

CHAPTER 28 More About Adverbs and Adjectives

Adjective or Adverb? **336**
Adverb Placement in Sentences **338**
Using *Good* and *Well, Bad* and *Badly* **340**
Extra Practice **342**
Chapter Review **344**
■ **Technology:** Interviewing to Learn About Your Community **345**

CHAPTER 29 Easily Confused Words

Homophones **346**
More Homophones **348**
Homographs and Other Homophones **350**
Extra Practice **352**
Chapter Review **354**
■ **Vocabulary:** Troublesome Words **355**

CHAPTER 30 Writing Workshop: Research Report

Literature Model: from *Beacons of Light, Lighthouses*
    by Gail Gibbons **356**
    Prewriting • Drafting • Revising • Proofreading • Publishing **364**
■ **Technology:** Giving a Multimedia Presentation **369**

Unit Grammar Review **370**

Unit Wrap-Up

Writing Across the Curriculum **374**
Books to Read **375**

Unit 6

Science

Grammar: Usage and Mechanics
Writing: Expressive Writing

376

CHAPTER 31   Negatives

Negatives with *No* and *Not* 378
Other Negatives 380
Avoiding Double Negatives 382
Extra Practice 384
Chapter Review 386
■ **Viewing:** Comparing Images 387

CHAPTER 32   Commas

Commas 388
More About Commas 390
Combining Sentences with Commas 392
Extra Practice 394
Chapter Review 396
■ **Listening and Speaking:** Listening Outside the Classroom 397

CHAPTER 33   Writer's Craft: Elaboration

Literature Model: from *Back Home* by Gloria Jean Pinkney 398
Using Figurative Language 400
Using Exact Words 401
Writing a Character Study 402
    Prewriting and Drafting • Editing • Sharing and Reflecting
■ **Viewing:** Looking at Fine Art 405

CHAPTER 34 Quotation Marks

Direct Quotations **406**
More About Quotation Marks **408**
Punctuating Dialogue **410**
Extra Practice **412**
Chapter Review **414**
■ **Study Skills:** Test-Taking Strategies **415**

CHAPTER 35 Titles

Underlining Titles **416**
Quotation Marks with Titles **418**
Capitalizing Words in Titles **420**
Extra Practice **422**
Chapter Review **424**
■ **Viewing:** Interpreting a Picture **425**

CHAPTER 36 Writing Workshop: Story

Literature Model: from *Half-Chicken* by Alma Flor Ada **426**
  Prewriting • Drafting • Revising • Proofreading • Publishing **434**
■ **Listening and Speaking:** Teamwork **439**

Unit Grammar Review **440**

Unit Wrap-Up

  Writing Across the Curriculum **444**

  Books to Read **445**

Cumulative Review: Units 1–6 . . . . **446**

Extra Practice **454**

Handbook

. . . . **478**

Writing Models

Personal Narrative. **480**

How-to Essay **481**

Persuasive Essay **482**

Advantages and Disadvantages Essay. **483**

Research Report. **484**

Short Story. **486**

Descriptive Paragraph **488**

Book Review **489**

Paragraph That Compares **490**

Paragraph That Contrasts **491**

Friendly Letter with Envelope. **492**

Poems: Rhymed and Unrhymed **494**

Writing Unrhymed Poems **495**

Writing Rubrics

. . . . **496**

Study Skills and Reading Strategies

Skimming and Scanning **502**

Using Book Parts. **504**

Using a Dictionary. **505**

Using the Internet **506**

Using an Encyclopedia **507**

Using Periodicals and Newspapers. **508**

Using an Atlas. **509**

Using an Almanac **510**

Using a Map **511**

Using Graphs **512**

Using Tables **513**

Using Charts **514**

Note-Taking **516**

Summarizing **518**

Outlining **520**

Test-Taking Strategies

   Multiple-Choice Tests **522**

   Essay Tests **523**

Spelling Strategies **524**

Commonly Misspelled Words **527**

Handwriting Models **528**

Thesaurus **530**

Glossary **548**

Vocabulary Power **560**

Index **562**

At a Glance

Grammar

Adjectives 272–280, 308–316, 336–337, 340–344, 469–470, 472

Adverbs . 318–326, 336–344, 471–472

Nouns ... 36–37, 40, 92–100, 102–110, 120–128, 187, 189, 193, 455, 458–460

Pronouns 234–242, 244–252, 262–270, 466–468

Sentences 24–32, 38–39, 41, 56–57, 59–60, 62–70, 254–257, 392–393, 454–457

   commands 26–31

   compound sentences.. 64–65, 68, 70, 392–393, 457

   exclamations 26–32

   predicates 52–60, 456

   questions 26–32, 454

   sentence variety 255–256

   simple sentences 64–65, 68–70, 457

   statements......... 26–32, 454

   subjects 34–42, 52, 62–63, 178–181, 455

Verbs 52–60, 130–138, 166–174, 176–184, 194–202, 204–212, 456, 461–465

Usage and Mechanics

Abbreviations 96–100

Apostrophes 120–128, 170–174, 266–270

Be 134–138, 461

Combining Sentence Parts 38–42, 56–60, 66–70, 255, 257, 392–396

Commas 38–42, 56–60, 64–70, 388–396, 408–414, 475

Contractions .. 170–174, 266–270, 378–380, 384–386

Easily Confused Words 346–354, 473

Exclamation Point 28–32

Negatives 378–386, 474

Periods 24–32, 96–100, 408–414

Pronoun-Antecedent Agreement 238–242

Question Marks 28–32, 408–414

Quotation Marks 406–414, 418–419, 422–424, 476

Subject-Verb Agreement ... 134–138, 180–184

Titles 96–100, 416–424, 477

Writing Forms

Advantages and Disadvantages 282–292, 483, 499

Book Review 489

Character Study 398–404

Comparison/Contrast Writing 254–260, 490–491

Descriptive Writing 44–50, 488

Dialogue 410–414

Directions 112–118

E-mail Message 199, 506

Envelope 492–493

Expressive Writing 44–50, 72–82,
398–404, 426–438,
480, 486–487, 496, 501

Friendly Letter 190–192,
492–493

How-to Writing 140–152,
481, 497

Informative Writing 112–118, 140–152,
254–260, 282–292, 328–334,
356–368, 497, 499–500

Interview Questions 345

Journal Writing . . . 39, 47, 50, 57,
63, 93, 105, 115, 125, 137, 171, 177, 189, 195,
235, 245, 257, 279, 313, 331, 337, 351, 379,
389, 401, 409, 419

Note-taking 327, 335, 516–517

Outline 327, 328–330, 520–521

Personal Narrative 72–82, 480, 496

Persuasive Writing 186–192,
214–224, 482, 498

Poem 494–495

Quotation 406–414

Reflective Writing 50, 82,
115, 118, 152, 189, 192, 224,
257, 292, 331, 334, 368, 401, 404, 438

Research Report . . . 356–368, 484–485, 500

Story 426–438, 486–487, 501

Summary 518–519

Thank-you Note 492–493

Listening and Speaking

Acting Out a Story 83

Being a Good Listener and Speaker 43

Comparing Writing and Speaking 261

Giving an Oral Presentation 225

Giving Spoken Directions 119

Guest Speakers 281

Listening for Facts and Opinions 203

Listening Outside the Classroom 397

Listening for Purpose and Main Idea 281

Making an Oral Presentation 153

Teamwork 439

Grammar: How Language Works

We all learn to speak without thinking about how words work. For example, children who grow up speaking English learn to say *the big dog* instead of *the dog big* before they learn about adjectives and nouns. Later, we study grammar to learn about how words work. Learning about grammar helps us become better writers.

The Building Blocks of Language

Words in English can be grouped into different parts of speech. These are the building blocks of language.

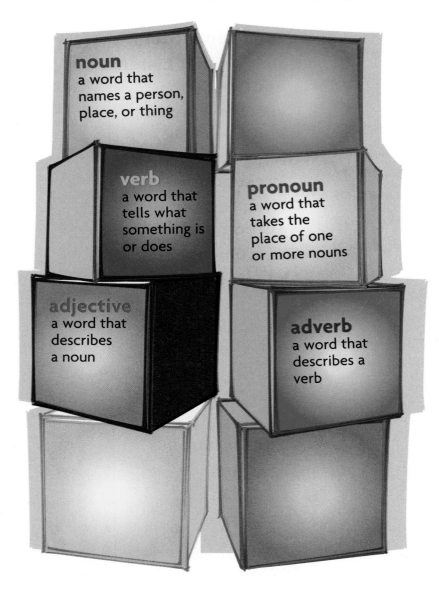

noun
a word that names a person, place, or thing

verb
a word that tells what something is or does

pronoun
a word that takes the place of one or more nouns

adjective
a word that describes a noun

adverb
a word that describes a verb

When you read a book, you do not see the steps the writer took to write it. What you see in a book might be different from the writer's first idea. The writer might have written parts of the book over and over many times.

The writing process can be divided into five steps. Most writers go back and forth through these steps. There is no one correct way to write.

Prewriting

In this step, you plan what you will write. You choose a topic, decide on your audience and purpose, brainstorm ideas, and organize information.

Drafting

In this step, you write out your ideas in sentences and paragraphs. Follow your prewriting plan to write a first draft.

Revising

This step is the first part of editing your writing. You may work by yourself or with a partner or a group. Make changes to make your writing better.

Proofreading

In this step, you finish your editing. Check for errors in grammar, spelling, capitalization, and punctuation. Make a final copy of your writing.

Publishing

Finally, you choose a way to share your work. You may want to add pictures or read your writing aloud to others.

Using Writing Strategies

A **strategy** is a plan for doing something well. Using strategies can help you become a better writer. Read the list of strategies below. You will learn about these and other strategies in this book. As you write, look back at this list to remind yourself of the **strategies good writers use**.

Strategies Good Writers Use

- Set a purpose for your writing.
- Focus on your audience.
- List or draw your main ideas.
- Use an organization that makes sense.
- Use your own personal voice.
- Choose exact, vivid words.
- Use a variety of effective sentences.
- Elaborate with facts and details.
- Group your ideas in paragraphs.
- Proofread to check for errors.

Keeping a Writer's Journal

Many writers keep journals. You can use a journal to make notes and try out new ideas. It is not a place to keep final work. A journal is a place to practice and have fun with writing.

You can keep your own writer's journal. Choose a notebook that you like. Draw pictures on the cover. Then start filling the pages with your notes and ideas.

Vocabulary Power

You can also keep a "word bank" of different kinds of words to use in your writing. Look for the Vocabulary Power word in each chapter. You can also list other new words that you find interesting.

Keeping a Portfolio

A portfolio is a place to keep your writing. You can also use it to show your work.

Student writers often keep two types of portfolios. **Working portfolios** include writings on which you are still working. **Show portfolios** have writings that you are finished with and want to show to others. You can move writings from your working portfolio into your show portfolio.

You can use your portfolios in meetings with your teacher. In meetings, talk about your work. Tell what you are doing and what you like doing. Set goals for yourself as a writer.

Unit 1

Grammar Sentences

Writing Expressive Writing

CHAPTER 1
Sentences 24

CHAPTER 2
Subjects/Nouns 34

CHAPTER 3
Writer's Craft: Personal Voice
Writing a
Descriptive Paragraph. 44

CHAPTER 4
Predicates/Verbs 52

CHAPTER 5
Simple and
    Compound Sentences 62

CHAPTER 6
Writing Workshop
Personal Narrative. 72

Dear Uncle Andy,
   Today I saw a very large sculpture outdoors. It was taller than the trees!

Mr. Andrew Jones
75 Oak Street
Lincoln, TX

USA H
First-Class Rate

23

Sentences

A sentence is a group of words that tells a complete thought.

One part of a sentence tells who or what. This part is called the **subject**. The other part of the sentence tells what the subject is or does. This part is called the **predicate**.

Example:

┌subject┐ ┌─────── predicate ───────┐
An artist carves the horse from wood.

The words in a sentence are in an order that makes sense. Begin every sentence with a capital letter, and end it with an end mark.

Guided Practice

A. Tell whether each group of words is or is not a sentence. Be able to tell how you know.

Example: We went to a folk art museum. *sentence*
Many kinds of art. *not a sentence*

1. Beautiful quilts with many colors.
2. We saw toys from long ago.
3. Made from wood.
4. Liked the spinning top best.
5. They could spin very fast.

Vocabulary Power

an·i·ma·ted film
[an′ə·mā·təd film] *n.*
A series of drawings shown as a motion picture with moving figures. Each picture is slightly changed from the one before to make the drawing seem to move.

Independent Practice

B. For each group of words, write *sentence* if the words make a sentence. Write *not a sentence* if the words do not make a sentence.

Example: Some quilts are folk art. *sentence*

6. Made designs on their quilts.
7. Some quilt designs tell stories.
8. Pictures of people, animals, and plants.
9. Many quilters use well-known patterns.
10. Other quilters make up their own patterns.

C. Make a sentence using each group of words. Put the words in an order that makes sense.

Example: scraps of cloth quilters use
　　　　　Quilters use scraps of cloth.

11. the scraps different are colors
12. pieces cut and sew quilters
13. together can quilters work
14. stories quilts tell
15. quilt this animal has designs

Writing Connection

Real-Life Connection: Greeting Card Fold paper to make a greeting card. Draw a picture of a favorite place on the front. Inside, write a message. On the back, write at least three sentences to tell about the place you drew on the front. Remember that a sentence must tell a complete thought. Start your sentences with capital letters and end them with end marks.

Kinds of Sentences

Statements, questions, commands, and exclamations are different kinds of sentences.

A statement is a sentence that tells something.

A question is a sentence that asks something.

A command is a sentence that gives an order or a direction.

An exclamation is a sentence that shows strong feeling.

Examples:

Statement: We are going to the art museum.

Question: Do you like this picture?

Command: Look at the bright colors.

Exclamation: Wow, this picture is outstanding!

Guided Practice

A. Tell if each sentence is a statement, a question, a command, or an exclamation. Be sure you can explain your answers.

Example: Bring your crayons again tomorrow.
command

1. I saw your picture.
2. Oh, it looks great!
3. Will you show me how to do it?
4. Rub over the paper with many colors.
5. What do I do next?

Independent Practice

B. Write whether each sentence is a statement, a question, a command, or an exclamation.

> **Example:** Do you know that a mural is a big painting?
> *question*

6. Shall we paint a mural?
7. That's such a great idea!
8. What do you want me to do?
9. Help me think of an idea.
10. I like to draw people.
11. How well can you draw plants?
12. We will do a good job together.
13. I just can't wait to get started!
14. Buy several different colors of paint.
15. I will buy the brushes.
16. Where shall we paint our mural?
17. Listen to this idea.
18. Can we paint it on the wall over there?
19. We should ask if it is okay to paint the wall.
20. Hooray, we can do it!

Writing Connection

Writer's Craft: Kinds of Sentences Suppose that you and your friends are planning an art fair at your school. When will the fair be held? What kinds of art will you show? Write an announcement for the fair. Be sure to use each kind of sentence at least once in your announcement.

Kind of Sentence	End Mark
Statement	.
Question	?
Command	.
Exclamation	!

Punctuating Sentences

Using punctuation is one way for a writer to make his or her meaning clear.

You know that a sentence tells a complete thought. Every sentence begins with a capital letter. Each kind of sentence must also end with the correct end mark. A statement and a command end with a period. A question ends with a question mark. An exclamation ends with an exclamation point.

Notice the end mark in each kind of sentence below.

Examples:

Statement: Diego Rivera's art shows history.

Question: How does art show history?

Command: Find out more about Rivera.

Exclamation: Wow, that is amazing!

Guided Practice

A. Tell what mark you would use at the end of each sentence. Be ready to explain how you know.

Example: Do you like murals   ?

1. The ancient Mayans painted murals
2. Aren't they very old murals
3. Study to learn more about them
4. Some were painted 1,200 years ago
5. Wow, that's really old

Independent Practice

B. **Write each sentence. Add the correct end mark.**

Example: How does animation work
How does animation work?

6. You can try animation for yourself

7. Choose a character to draw

8. What do you want your character to do

9. Draw ten slightly different pictures of your character

10. What a great cartoon you drew

C. **Look at the end mark for each sentence. If it is correct, write *correct*. If it is not, rewrite the sentence with the correct end mark.**

Examples: You can change the character's face?
You can change the character's face.

11. Staple your pages together.

12. What happens when you flip the pages.

13. Does the character seem to move.

14. Can we do more!

15. Animation is fun?

Writing Connection

Art Think about a piece of art that interests you. Do some research to find out about the person who created it. Then imagine that you are going to meet this person. Write the conversation you might have with him or her. Be sure you use different types of sentences and punctuate them correctly.

Extra Practice

A. Write whether each sentence is a statement, a question, a command, or an exclamation.
pages 26–27

Example: What is your favorite tool for drawing?
question

1. Jeremy always uses colored markers.
2. Why does he like them?
3. He likes the bright colors.
4. He says they help him draw better.
5. Does Jeremy draw a lot?
6. He always has a marker in his pocket.
7. Once he forgot to put the cap back on.
8. Guess what happened.
9. Oops, the marker made a stain!
10. What do you think he did then?

B. Write each sentence. Add the correct end mark. *pages 28–29*

Example: Does anyone still use crayons
Does anyone still use crayons?

11. Carrie uses crayons to do rubbings
12. What a great idea she had
13. How do you do it
14. Place a piece of paper on something rough
15. Rub over the paper with the side of a crayon

For more activities
with sentences, visit
The Learning Site:
www.harcourtschool.com

C. Read each group of words. Put the words in an order that makes sense. Make the kind of sentence shown. Use correct end marks.

pages 24–29

Example: Question – is a planning puppet Peter show
Is Peter planning a puppet show?

16. Statement – puppets have show will the
17. Command – puppets the help make
18. Exclamation – from a puppet that sock made is
19. Statement – television saw I on puppets
20. Question – is a that finger puppet
21. Statement – puppet it finger looks a like
22. Question – you can puppets where buy
23. Statement – rather them make would I
24. Statement – already you what have you need
25. Exclamation – puppets making fun is such

Writing Connection

Technology Using a computer, write a review of a music concert you heard at your school. What type of music was played? What did you enjoy about the concert? Include each of the four kinds of sentences in your review. Then choose a different font and type size for each kind of sentence. Print your review and share it with your class.

For additional test preparation, visit *The Learning Site:* www.harcourtschool.com

Chapter Review

Some of the sentences in this paragraph are underlined. Choose the best way to correct each numbered sentence. Mark the letter for your answer.

(1) Alexander Calder an artist. (2) Have you ever seen his work. (3) Hanging parts that move he made mobiles with. *Mobile* means "able to move." (4) Can you guess why he called these pieces *mobiles* (5) Also made pieces with no moving parts He called those *stabiles*. Most of Calder's artwork is huge and brightly colored. (6) The work is such fun to look at!

1 A Alexander Calder was an artist.

B Alexander Calder was an artist?

C An artist Alexander was Calder.

D Correct as is

2 F Seen his work.

G Work his have you ever?

H Have you ever seen his work?

J Correct as is

3 A He made mobiles with hanging parts that move?

B He made mobiles with hanging parts that move.

C Made mobiles with hanging parts that move.

D Correct as is

4 F Why he called these pieces *mobiles.*

G Why he called these pieces *mobiles* can you guess.

H Can you guess why he called these pieces *mobiles?*

J Correct as is

5 A Also made pieces with no moving parts?

B He also made pieces with no moving parts.

C Pieces with no moving parts!

D Correct as is

6 F The work is fun to look at?

G Fun to look at.

H The work fun to look at is.

J Correct as is

Being a Good Viewer

Looking at something carefully will help you understand it better. Here are some strategies for being a good viewer.

A good viewer:

- looks closely at the art.

- takes time to describe it.

- looks at what is happening in the art.

- thinks about what the artist is trying to say.

- forms personal opinions about the artwork.

- discusses thoughts with others.

YOUR TURN

Find a picture, an illustration, or another artwork to discuss with a partner. Use some of the tips above to view the artwork carefully.

1. **Decide on the work of art.**

2. **Tell each other what you see.**

3. **Pay attention to details. Notice colors and the material from which the artwork is made. What do you see first?**

4. **Talk with each other about the meaning or message of the artwork.**

5. **After thinking about the piece, present your ideas to the class.**

TIP Imagine what questions your classmates might ask about the artwork you chose. Be sure you are ready to answer these questions.

Complete and Simple Subjects

Every complete sentence has a subject and a predicate.

The person, place, or thing the sentence is about is called the simple subject. The complete subject of a sentence includes the simple subject and all the other words in the subject that describe it. Ask yourself whom or what the sentence is about, and this will tell you the subject.

In the examples below, the simple subject is circled and the complete subject is underlined.

Examples:
My friend (Jared) loves music.
The (family) next door to us plays many instruments.

Vocabulary Power

in•stru•ment
[in′strə•mənt] *n.* A tool for making music.

Guided Practice

A. Find the simple and complete subjects in each sentence.

Example: Your friend can play with us.
friend|simple, Your friend|complete

1. Jared's family makes music together.
2. Each member of the family plays an instrument.
3. His brother plays the banjo.
4. That flute belongs to his sister.
5. His mom is a drummer.

Independent Practice

B. Read each sentence. Write the simple subject in each sentence.

Example: People all over the world have their own music.
People

6. African music uses many drums.
7. Some drums are made from hollow logs.
8. Animal skins are used in some instruments.
9. Some African instruments have strings.
10. Musicians in Africa play flutes, too.

C. Write the complete subject in each sentence.

Example: The silver flute sounds very pretty.
The silver flute

11. People from other countries play flutes as well.
12. Some people found a 9,000-year-old flute in China.
13. The very old flute was made from a bone.
14. The musician next door plays a flute.
15. The old Chinese flute can still make pretty music.

Remember that the complete subject is made up of the simple subject and any words that help describe it.

Writing Connection

Music Imagine you have been asked to plan a musical show. Make an invitation. Draw the musicians and their instruments on the stage. Write a few sentences that describe your show. Underline the simple subjects in your sentences.

Nouns in Subjects

The subject of a sentence names someone or something. A noun can be the most important word in the subject. A noun is a word that names a person, place, or thing.

You know that the subject of a sentence may be more than one word. The simple subject is often a noun. Words that can name whom or what the sentence is about are nouns.

In the sentences below, the complete subject is underlined. Notice that the main word in the complete subject is a noun.

Examples:

Many **people** play music in their homes.

The entire **school** could hear someone singing.

Some **students** knew the song.

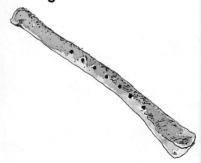

Guided Practice

A. Identify the complete subject in each sentence. Then tell the noun that is the simple subject.

Example: Some music is very important to people.
Some music|complete subject, music|noun

1. Most people enjoy music.
2. The children hear music everywhere.
3. My family enjoys listening to the radio.
4. The television plays a lot of music too.
5. Many stores play music on speakers.

Independent Practice

B. Write each sentence. Underline the complete subject and circle the noun that is the simple subject.

> **Example:** That (song) has a fast beat.

6. That music has a pretty sound.
7. The drummer in the band beats his drum with drumsticks.
8. Our whole class listened to the marching band.
9. The flute player plays very well.
10. Our parents dance to this music.
11. Your neighbor likes to write songs.
12. The boys next door practice their music every day.
13. The audience claps while you sing.
14. Luisa's brother listens to music on the radio.
15. Our teacher plays the guitar for us.

> **Remember** that who or what every sentence tells about is the subject. A noun is often the simple subject.

Writing Connection

Real-Life Writing: Conversation Talk with a partner about an instrument you play or would like to play. Would you like to play alone or in a group? How much time would you spend practicing? Write four sentences that describe your instrument. Then underline the complete subject in each sentence.

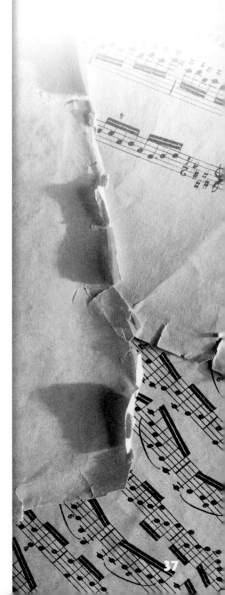

GRAMMAR-WRITING CONNECTION

Combining Sentences: Compound Subjects

Sentences with compound subjects have two or more subjects.

The subjects in a compound subject share the same predicate. The words *and* and *or* are usually used to join the subjects. Use commas to separate three or more subjects.

Examples:

Guitars and violins are stringed instruments.

Ali, Lupe, and Paul play the guitar.

You can combine two sentences that have the same predicate by joining the two simple subjects with *and*.

Examples:

A banjo has strings. **A cello** has strings.

A banjo and a cello have strings.

Guided Practice

A. Find the compound subject in each sentence.

Example: Diego and Eli play the banjo.
Diego and Eli

1. Yuki, Reta, and Sam play in the band.
2. The boys and the girls enjoy the music.
3. Brianna and Max play the trumpet.
4. Fred or Reta sits next to the drummer.
5. My violin case and your violin case are black.

Independent Practice

Remember that compound subjects combine two or more subjects into one sentence using *and* or *or*.

B. Write the sentence. Underline the compound subject in the sentence.

Example: <u>Our band and their band</u> play.

6. Kim and Ray are members of the band.
7. Kim, Ray, and José wear red uniforms.
8. Kim's dad or Ray's mom helps the band.
9. Kim's tuba and Ray's trumpet are new.
10. Two vans or the school bus will take the band.

C. Combine each group of sentences into one sentence that has a compound subject.

Example: The team waits. The band waits.
The team and the band wait.

11. The Alamo School band plays well. Our band plays well.
12. Our school band is in the contest. Her school band is in the contest.
13. The fans cheer for the teams. The band members cheer for the teams.
14. The teams have fun. The bands have fun. The fans have fun.
15. Gina will play in the band next year. Yoko will play in the band next year.

Writing Connection

Writer's Journal: Recording Ideas
List as many kinds of music as you can. Choose one kind of music, and write six sentences describing this kind of music. Combine at least two sentences that share a predicate into one sentence.

Remember

that every sentence has a **subject** and a **predicate**. The **complete subject** is made up of the **simple subject** and all the other words that help describe it.

Extra Practice

A. Write each sentence. Underline the complete subject in each one. Then circle the noun that is the simple subject. *pages 34–37*

Example: (Mozart) was a famous composer.

1. Mozart was born more than 200 years ago.
2. His parents named him Wolfgang.
3. Wolfgang Mozart learned to play music at age four.
4. The young composer started writing his own music at age five.
5. The boy played music in many cities.

Mozart

B. Write the subject in each sentence. Write whether the subject is a simple subject or a compound subject. *pages 36–39*

Example: June is a famous singer.
June | simple

6. Liberty Elementary School has a chorus that performs.
7. Students and teachers are members.
8. Some boys and girls in my class are in chorus.
9. Hannah and her sisters like singing.
10. The girl with red hair and the boy next to her sing in a group.
11. Richard practices on Wednesdays.
12. Sissy gave a concert at the mall.
13. The youngest singer and the oldest singer in the group are best friends.
14. Hannah, Madison, and Liah sing a song together.
15. Everybody should be quiet when they play.

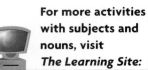

For more activities with subjects and nouns, visit *The Learning Site:* www.harcourtschool.com

C. Combine each group of sentences into one sentence that has a compound subject. Write the new sentence. *pages 38–39*

Example: John picked the wedding music.
Ana picked the wedding music.
John and Ana picked the wedding music.

16. The bride danced to the music.
The groom danced to the music.
17. Her cousin played in the band.
His brother played in the band.
18. The bride wanted louder music.
The guests wanted louder music.
19. Family members asked for a special song.
Friends asked for a special song.
20. The families sang along.
The couple sang along.
All their friends sang along.

Remember
that compound subjects combine two or more subjects into one sentence using *and* or *or*.

Writing Connection

Writer's Craft: Rhyming Words Work with a partner to write a song about something you love to do. List some rhyming words about your topic. Use some of the words as subjects in the sentences of your song. Perform the song for the class.

Chapter Review

Read the paragraph. Choose the complete subject for each numbered sentence.

(1) My friend Michael likes to make music. (2) Michael can make music with almost anything. (3) Boxes, jars, and even rocks can be drums. (4) Flutes can be made from straws and plastic pipes. (5) Michael's friend made maracas from oatmeal boxes filled with dried beans. (6) My favorite instrument is a guitar made from rubber bands stretched over a box.

TIP Be sure to read all the answers for a multiple-choice question. Then choose the best answer.

1 A My friend Michael
  B Michael
  C Michael likes
  D music

2 F Michael says
  G you can make music
  H Michael
  J almost anything

3 A Boxes
  B Boxes, jars, and even rocks
  C rocks can be
  D drums

4 F Flutes can be made
  G straws
  H straws and plastic pipes
  J Flutes

5 A Michael's friend made
  B Michael's friend
  C oatmeal boxes
  D filled with dried beans

6 F My favorite instrument
  G My
  H a guitar made from rubber bands
  J a box

For more activities with subjects and nouns, visit
The Learning Site:
www.harcourtschool.com

Being a Good Listener and Speaker

Listening is one of the best ways to learn things. Speaking is a way of sharing ideas and feelings with others. Here are some tips. They will help you become a better listener and speaker.

If you are listening …

- Pay attention to the speaker.
- Don't disturb the listeners.
- Ask questions when the speaker is finished.
- Take notes about what the speaker said.

If you are speaking …

- Speak clearly and correctly.
- Take your time and don't talk too fast.
- Look at your audience.
- Use hand and body movements to illustrate your point.
- Ask your audience for questions.

YOUR TURN

Form small groups and play a guessing game. Pretend that you are a certain type of artist. Introduce yourself to the group, but don't say what you do. The group should ask you questions and guess what you are. Practice the speaking and listening skills you have learned as you play the game.

Writer's Craft

Personal Voice

When you describe something, you might tell what you see, hear, smell, or taste. You might tell how something feels when you touch it.

In the following lines, a young girl describes a dance that is performed at the Seminole Indian camp she and her family visit each year.

LITERATURE MODEL

The Ribbon Dance is first. The women gather
    around.
Shells on wrists and ankles make a tinkling
    sound.
Shimmering satin ribbons float from head to toe,
    shining human rainbows in the firelight's glow.
Moccasins of dancers make gentle raindrop
    sounds.
Satin ribbons spin around, around, around.

—from *Dancing with the Indians*
by Angela Shelf Medearis

Analyze THE Model

1. What words does the girl use that help you see a picture in your mind?

2. What words does the girl use to describe sounds?

3. What feelings do you think the girl has as she watches the dancers? How can you tell?

Vocabulary Power

shim•mer•ing
[shim′ər•ing] *adj*.
Shining with a faint,
unsteady light.

Using Personal Voice

When you write, you use your personal voice, your own special way of expressing yourself. It means that you use your own words and ideas. Study the chart on the next page.

Strategies for Using Personal Voice	How to Use Strategies	Examples
Use colorful words.	• Use interesting words that help your reader picture the thing you are describing.	• Use words like *skipped* or *tiptoed* instead of *went*. Use words like *huge* or *giant* instead of *big*.
Express your own viewpoint.	• Let your reader know how you feel about the subject.	• Suppose you are describing a lizard. If you think it is ugly and scary, say so. If you think it is beautiful and fascinating, say so.

YOUR TURN

THINK ABOUT DESCRIPTIVE WRITING Work with one or two classmates. Look back at stories or poems that you have read. In each one, find parts in which the writer has described something. Take turns reading these parts aloud.

Answer these questions:

1. What is the writer describing?

2. What colorful words does the writer use?

3. How do these words help you see a picture in your mind?

4. How does the writer feel about the subject? How can you tell?

Using Colorful Words

A. Choose a colorful word from the box to complete each sentence. Write the sentence on your paper.

yelled	wrinkled	huge	muddy	scurried

1. The elephant had _____ gray skin.
2. It was drinking some _____ water.
3. It lifted its _____ trunk.
4. "Oh, it's going to spray us!" Timmy _____.
5. Everyone _____ out of the way.

B. Read the sentences. Think of colorful words you can add to create a clear picture for the reader. Write the revised sentences on your paper.

6. Look at that bike.
7. She ate the apple.
8. Sara heard a sound.
9. Hector picked up the box.
10. Did you see that bird?
11. What a beautiful sunset!
12. Henry has a dog.
13. We played outside.
14. Do you like these shoes?
15. I will wear a dress to the party.

Writer's Viewpoint

C. Read each description and the questions that follow it. Write the answer to each question on your paper.

Description 1: There were three plump peaches in the bowl. I could imagine how sweet and juicy they would taste.

16. Does the writer like or dislike peaches?
17. How do you know the writer's viewpoint?

Description 2: The old house was a terrible mess. Everything was dusty and dirty.

18. What is the writer's viewpoint about the house?
19. How do you know how the writer feels?

Description 3: The little bug darted across the floor. It had pretty yellow stripes that seemed to glow in the sunshine.

20. How does the writer feel about the bug?
21. How do you know the writer's viewpoint?

Writing AND Thinking

Writer's Journal

Write to Record Reflections Many writers have favorite subjects that they write about often. In your Writer's Journal, list two or three of your favorite subjects. Then explain your viewpoint on each of these subjects, and tell why you like to write about them.

Writing a Descriptive Paragraph

In the lines from *Dancing with the Indians*, a girl describes a beautiful dance she saw on a trip with her family. When Darryl went to the park with his family, he saw swans swimming on a pond. Read this descriptive paragraph that Darryl wrote about the swans. Look for colorful words.

MODEL

colorful words

writer's viewpoint

> Some large white birds were swimming on the pond. My dad said they were swans. I watched them skim silently across the water like skaters on ice. Their long necks curved gently from side to side. Suddenly there was a huge splash! The biggest swan rose up, beating the water with its enormous wings. I jumped, and then I laughed. Those swans weren't so gentle and quiet after all!

Analyze THE Model

1. What colorful words does Darryl use to tell what he saw and heard?

2. What words in Darryl's paragraph do you like? Why do you like them?

3. What is Darryl's viewpoint about the swans? How do you know?

4. Does the paragraph give you a clear picture of what Darryl saw and heard? Why or why not?

WRITING PROMPT Look around your classroom. Find an interesting object that you would like to describe. You might choose something that you especially like or dislike. Write a paragraph to tell about the object. Use colorful words to help your reader picture the object you are describing. Express your feelings and viewpoint in your writing.

STUDY THE PROMPT Ask yourself these questions:

1. How will you choose a subject to write about?

2. What is your purpose for writing?

3. What will you include in your paragraph?

Prewriting and Drafting

Plan Your Descriptive Paragraph Make a web like this one to help you get started. Write the name of the object in the center of your web.

USING YOUR
Handbook

• Use the Writer's Thesaurus to find colorful words that will help you describe your object.

colorful words that tell what the object looks like

colorful words that tell what sound the object might make

what the object does or what you do with it

Name of Object

colorful words that tell how the object feels when you touch it

your viewpoint about the object

colorful words that tell about any smell or taste the object might have

Editing

Read over the draft of your paragraph. Do you want to change or add anything? Use this checklist to help you revise your paragraph:

☑ **Do you think your reader will be able to picture the object?**
☑ **Can you use more colorful words to describe the object?**
☑ **Did you express your viewpoint?**
☑ **How did you use your personal voice in your paragraph?**

Use this checklist as you proofread your paragraph:

☑ **I have begun my sentences with capital letters.**
☑ **I have used the correct end marks for my sentences.**
☑ **I have checked to see that each sentence has a subject and a predicate.**
☑ **I have used a dictionary to check spelling.**

Editor's Marks

✂ take out text
∧ add text
ᗒ move text
¶ new paragraph
≡ capitalize
/ lowercase
◯ correct spelling

Sharing and Reflecting

Writer's Journal

Make a final copy of your paragraph. Then read it to two of your classmates. Listen as they read their paragraphs. Tell what you like best about their descriptions. Share ideas about how you can improve your writing by using colorful words and by expressing your viewpoint. Write your reflections in your Writer's Journal.

Colorful Words

A group of third graders thought of colorful words they could use to describe something that shines. Look at the words in the web they made.

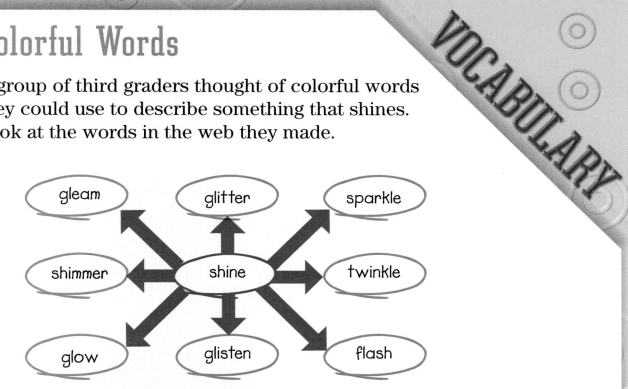

YOUR TURN

Play a game with colorful words. Follow these steps:

STEP 1 Sit in a circle with two or three classmates.

STEP 2 Take turns picking a word from the web.

STEP 3 Challenge the person on your left to use your word in a sentence.

STEP 4 Then that person has a turn to choose a word and challenge the next person. When you make up a sentence, think about the exact meaning of the word. For example, you might say that a star shines, but you probably wouldn't say it flashes.

STEP 5 Continue until you have used all the words.

After you play the game, your group can try making a web of your own. You might brainstorm words that you can use to describe something cold or to describe a sound the wind makes.

Complete and Simple Predicates

Every sentence has a subject and a predicate.

The complete predicate is all the words that tell what the subject of the sentence is or does. The predicate usually follows the subject of a sentence.

The simple predicate is the main word in the complete predicate.

The bold words in the sentences below are the complete predicates. The underlined words are the simple predicates.

Examples:

Houses, schools, and stores **<u>are</u> buildings**.

A building **<u>has</u> many parts**.

The roof **<u>covers</u> the building**.

Vocabulary Power

car·pen·ter
[kär′pən·tər] *n.*
A person who makes, builds, or repairs things, often using wood.

Guided Practice

A. Read each sentence. Name the complete predicate. Then tell which word is the simple predicate.

Example: The builder makes a plan for a new building.
makes a plan for a new building|makes

1. Mr. Thompson built our new house.
2. He drew a plan for the house.
3. The plan is a blueprint.
4. The blueprint shows all the floors and rooms.
5. My bedroom is the big room upstairs.

Independent Practice

B. Write each sentence. Underline the complete predicate.

Example: The carpenter told us about building a house.
The carpenter <u>told us about building a house.</u>

6. Carpenters follow a blueprint.
7. The frame is wood or steel.
8. The floors in our house have carpets.
9. The walls of my room are blue.
10. This wall has a big picture window.

C. Write each sentence. Underline the simple predicate.

11. The new front door squeaks sometimes.
12. The carpenter planned the house well.
13. This house looks beautiful.
14. Someone built Sasha's home 100 years ago.
15. Our house is new.

Remember that the complete predicate tells what the subject is or does.

Writing Connection

Technology When do you think the place you live in was built? How do you think it was built? Talk to your family members or neighbors about the place you live. Then use a computer or books from the library to find out more about building homes. Write some sentences about what you learn. Then underline the complete predicate in each sentence. Circle the simple predicate.

Remember

that every
predicate has a
verb that tells
what the subject
is or does.

Verbs in Predicates

The verb is the main word in the predicate of a sentence.

Every predicate has a verb that tells what the subject is or does. The verb is the same word as the simple predicate. The other words in the predicate tell more about the verb.

The bold words in the sentences below are the complete predicates. The underlined words are the verbs.

Examples:
Jack's father **builds tall buildings in New York**.

The Empire State Building **is steel**.

We **run up the stairs**.

Guided Practice

A. Read each sentence. Find the verb in the underlined predicate.

Example: Some tall buildings *rise more than 100 stories*. rise

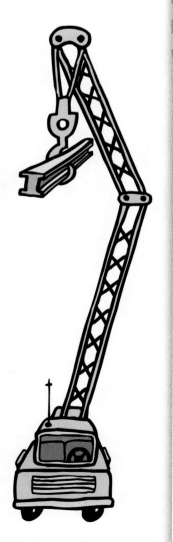

1. Construction of these tall buildings <u>takes a year or more</u>.
2. The carpenters <u>build the lower floors first</u>.
3. Cranes <u>lift large pieces of steel</u>.
4. The workers <u>construct the stairs</u>.
5. Some office buildings <u>have glass walls</u>.
6. The workers <u>connect the pipes</u>.
7. José <u>starts the electric power</u>.
8. Large buildings <u>have rooms of many sizes</u>.
9. Tommy's mom <u>has a new desk</u>.
10. Tommy <u>sees a pattern in the wallpaper</u>.

Independent Practice

B. Write each sentence. Underline the complete predicate once. Underline the verb twice.

> **Example:** Mrs. Venegas draws plans for many kinds of buildings.
>
> *Mrs. Venegas <u>draws plans for many kinds of buildings.</u>*

11. She designs schools, hospitals, and hotels.
12. Mrs. Venegas studies pictures of old buildings.
13. She gets ideas from the pictures.
14. The Venegas Company built the new mall near my house.
15. They made the mall a good shopping place.
16. We shop at the department stores.
17. I like stores with bright lights and soft carpets.
18. The newspaper printed ads for the new mall.
19. Food stands fill the center of the mall.
20. Mrs. Venegas won an award for her design.

DID YOU KNOW?
The glass walls of some buildings let in the warmth of the sun. This helps heat the buildings.

Writing Connection

Writer's Craft: Vivid Verbs Think of a place where you like to go. What can you do there? Write about that place, using interesting verbs in your predicates. Then underline the verbs you use.

GRAMMAR—WRITING CONNECTION

Combining Sentences: Compound Predicates

A **compound predicate** is two or more predicates that have the same subject. Each predicate has its own verb. The predicates in a compound predicate are joined by *and* or *or*.

Use commas to separate three or more predicates in a compound predicate.

Example:
Sarita **draws** pictures *and* **reads** books.
Every afternoon, Sarita **sleeps, studies,** *or* **plays**.

Combine two or more sentences with the same subject into one with a compound predicate.

Example:
Mrs. Liang **picked flowers**.
Mrs. Liang **painted**.
Mrs. Liang **picked flowers and painted.**

Guided Practice

A. Read each sentence. Name the simple predicates in each compound predicate.

Example: We eat dinner inside and relax on the porch. *eat, relax*

1. Tim plants seeds and waters the garden.
2. We painted the walls and hung drapes.
3. They study books and read magazines.
4. In our yard, we jump rope and play ball.
5. In the kitchen, they cook food and eat lunch.

Independent Practice

B. Read the sentence pairs. Then write one sentence with a compound predicate.

Example: Painting can be easy. Painting is fun.
Painting can be easy and is fun.

6. Some people buy old furniture. Some people save lots of money.

7. People paint the furniture. People fix broken parts.

8. This lamp is broken. This lamp needs a new shade.

9. These floors look dirty. These floors need carpet.

10. The yellow room seems bigger. The yellow room makes people feel happy.

11. Bright colors are fun to use. Bright colors look good in children's rooms.

12. Pictures hang on walls. Pictures make a room more interesting.

13. Mark likes to paint rooms. Mark is good at it.

14. Alma picks out paint. Alma buys furniture.

15. Mrs. Young decorates homes. Mrs. Young chooses furniture.

Remember
that a compound predicate is two or more predicates with the same subject.

Writing Connection

Writer's Journal: Describe a Room
Draw a picture of a room that you would like to have. Write eight sentences about it. Then combine some of your sentences by using compound predicates.

Extra Practice

A. Write each sentence. Underline the complete predicate once. Underline the simple predicate twice. *pages 52–53*

Example: Most cities have several government buildings.
Most cities <u>have several government buildings</u>.

1. These buildings are a city hall, a post office, and a firehouse.
2. Carpenters used wood on many of these buildings.
3. Some people plan parks.
4. Some parks have playgrounds and ball fields.
5. People use a park for many purposes.

B. Read each sentence. Write the verb in each sentence. *pages 54–55*

Example: The park planner studies the needs of the people in our town. *studies*

6. People in a small town travel to the park by car or on foot.
7. People in a city sometimes ride a bus to the park.
8. The town park has a parking lot.
9. The city park is near bus and train stops.
10. Young children play on the playground.
11. People water-ski on the lake.
12. The baseball fields need seats.
13. A designer chooses plants for the park.
14. Trees and bushes offer shelter for birds and animals.
15. Ducks and swans swim in the pond.

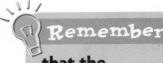

Remember

that the predicate of a sentence tells what the subject of the sentence is or does. A simple predicate is the main word in the complete predicate.

For additional activities using predicates, visit *The Learning Site:*

www.harcourtschool.com

C. Read the sentences in each group. Then write one sentence with a compound predicate.

pages 56–57

Remember

that a compound predicate is two or more predicates that share the same subject.

Example: Sun Lee designs schools.
Sun Lee plans libraries.
Sun Lee designs schools and plans libraries.

16. Decorators pick bright colors for classrooms.
Decorators choose soft colors for the school library.

17. Our school cafeteria looks cheerful.
Our school cafeteria has sturdy tables.

18. Gyms and cafeterias hold many students.
Gyms and cafeterias are noisy places.

19. Students often work in groups in classrooms.
Students need lots of space.

20. Sun Lee gave the computer area good lighting.
Sun Lee chose comfortable chairs.
Sun Lee showed the workers where to put electrical outlets.

Writing Connection

Technology Work with a partner to plan a park, school, or store. First, draw your plan by hand. Then use a computer to draw your plan. How is drawing by hand different from drawing by computer? Write five sentences about the differences. Trade sentences with your partner. Circle the complete predicates in the sentences.

Chapter Review

Follow the directions for each question. Write the letter of your answer.

For Numbers 1–4, find the simple predicate, or verb, in each sentence.

1 Our class learned about castles.
   A   B   C   D

2 Castles were beautiful and sturdy.
     A   B   C   D

3 People made castles from stone.
    A   B   C   D

4 An army of soldiers lived in the castle.
     A   B   C   D

5 Find the sentence that is complete and is written correctly.
A Many castles by high walls.
B Surrounded many castles high walls.
C Many castles were surrounded by high walls.
D Surrounded by high walls.

6 Find the sentence that best combines these two sentences into one.

Our class took a trip to a castle.
Our class visited all its rooms.

A Our class and our teacher took a trip.
B Took a trip to a castle and visited.
C Our class took a trip to a castle and its rooms.
D Our class took a trip to a castle and visited all its rooms.

STANDARDIZED TEST PREP

TIP Remember to read all the answer choices carefully. Then make your decision.

For additional test preparation, visit *The Learning Site:*
www.harcourtschool.com

Words from Many Places

Suppose you are traveling to Mexico, Japan, and Hawaii. When you get there, you want to be able to say hello to people you meet. Here are some ways to say hello in each place.

In Mexico and most other countries in Central and South America, people speak Spanish. This is how they say hello:

Ho′la [ō′lä]

Say hello in Spanish to a partner. Shake your partner's hand.

In Japan, people speak Japanese. This is one way to say hello:

Ko•ni•chi•wa [kō•nē•chē•wä]

Say hello in Japanese to a partner.

In the state of Hawaii, people speak English most of the time. However, they still use many Hawaiian words. The Hawaiian language uses the same word for *hello* and *good-bye*. This is how to greet someone in Hawaiian:

A•lo•ha [ə•lō′hä]

A person may welcome a visitor to Hawaii by putting a necklace of flowers around the visitor's neck. The necklace is called a lei [lā]. Try greeting a partner in Hawaiian. Pretend to place a lei on your partner.

YOUR TURN

Find France and China on a map. With a partner, use a computer or the school library to learn about these countries. What languages do people in France and in China speak? Find out how to say hello in these languages.

Complete Sentences

A **complete sentence** is a group of words that
has a subject and a predicate. It expresses a
complete thought.

A group of words that does not express a
complete thought and does not have a subject and a
predicate is not a complete sentence.

Examples:

Complete Sentence	Not a Complete Sentence
I like to read stories.	To read stories.
What kind of stories do you like to read?	What kind of stories?
Mary enjoys reading adventure stories.	Reading adventure stories.

Guided Practice

**A. Tell whether each group of words is a
complete sentence. Explain how you know.**

Examples: Children's literature includes many
imaginary stories.
complete sentence

Some imaginary stories are.
not a complete sentence

1. About animals who talk.
2. The animals talk like people.
3. Literature can make children laugh.
4. Speaking English very well.
5. Characters in some very popular stories.

Vocabulary Power

fan•ta•sy
[fan′tə•sē] *n.* A
story about things
and people that
could not be real.

Independent Practice

B. Read each sentence. Write *complete sentence* if the group of words is a complete sentence. If it is not a complete sentence, rewrite the group of words to make it a complete sentence.

Example: Writes short poems.
She writes short poems.

6. Sometimes funny and simple.
7. Children's literature may rhyme.
8. Mother Goose poems are very old.
9. "Little Jack Horner" a nursery rhyme.
10. The word *Horner* rhymes with *corner*.
11. Some poems are fun to read many times.
12. Poems can tell stories.
13. Do not have to rhyme.
14. Good poems a long time to write.
15. Some poets very long poems.

Writing Connection

Writer's Journal: Evaluating Writing
Think of an animal character in a story you have read. Write a poem that describes this character. Then trade your poem with a partner, and write two complete sentences in your journals about each other's poems. Tell something you liked about your partner's poem. Share your sentences with each other.

Simple and Compound Sentences

A sentence that expresses one complete thought is a **simple sentence**. Two or more simple sentences can be combined to make a **compound sentence**.

The words *and*, *but*, and *or* are usually used to combine the sentences. A comma (,) goes before the combining word.

Examples:
Simple Sentences A fable tells a story. It teaches a lesson.
Compound Sentence A fable tells a story, and it teaches a lesson.

Guided Practice

A. Tell whether each sentence is a simple sentence or a compound sentence.

Example: Aesop's Fables are classic literature.
simple sentence

1. Fables are imaginary stories about animals.
2. Animal fables can teach the difference between right and wrong.
3. Today fables are written down, and adults read them to children.
4. Long ago, people told fables aloud.
5. "Little Red Riding Hood" is an old fable, but children still like to read it.

Independent Practice

B. Read each sentence. Write whether it is a simple sentence or a compound sentence.

Example: She writes books, and she draws pictures.
compound sentence

6. Children's books often have pictures.
7. An artist reads the children's story, and then the artist imagines the characters in the book.
8. An artist's imagination makes the characters come to life.
9. Pictures can be in black and white, or they may be in color.
10. Some writers draw their own pictures, but it takes a long time to draw pictures for a book.
11. Sometimes authors write about things that have happened.
12. A real-life story might include characters that seem real.
13. Some real-life stories are happy, but some are sad.
14. I enjoy reading these stories.
15. I tell my friends about books, and they share books with me.

Remember

that a simple sentence expresses one complete thought. A compound sentence is two or more simple sentences combined with a comma (,) and a joining word.

Writing Connection

Writer's Craft: Personal Voice Think about something funny that has happened to you. Using simple and compound sentences, tell about the funny thing that happened to you.

GRAMMAR–WRITING CONNECTION

Combining Sentences

When you write, it is a good idea to combine sentences.

Too many short sentences can make your writing seem choppy. Combining sentences can make your writing more lively and interesting.

Example:
Simple Sentences Yolanda might write a mystery story. She might write a science fiction story.

Compound Sentence Yolanda might write a mystery story, or she might write a science fiction story.

Guided Practice

A. Use the combining word shown to combine each pair of sentences.

Example: Science fiction stories are about science. They are imaginary. *and*
Science fiction stories are about science, and they are imaginary.

1. Science fiction is one kind of literature. It is not the only kind. *but*
2. Some science fiction stories are about outer space. Others take place on Earth. *and*
3. One famous story is about the sea. It is set at the bottom of the ocean. *and*
4. A science fiction story may be about computers. It may be about spaceships. *or*
5. I like science fiction stories. My brother does not like them. *but*

Independent Practice

B. Rewrite the following sentences. Use the combining word shown to combine them.

> **Example:** I like to read. She likes to read. *and*
> *I like to read, and she likes to read.*

6. Some of the characters in historical stories are real. Some are made up. *but*

7. A story might tell how people dressed long ago. It might tell what they ate. *or*

8. Some historical stories include maps. They also may have pictures. *and*

9. The maps show where people lived. Sometimes they show where people traveled. *or*

10. Some people do not like to read about the past. I enjoy historical stories. *but*

11. *Little House on the Prairie* is set in the late 1800s. It tells about pioneer life. *and*

12. Laura Ingalls Wilder is the author. There are nine books in the series. *and*

13. The books tell about real events. The story is told by one of the characters. *but*

14. The facts in a historical story should be true. The story should be fun to read. *but*

15. Students may learn to write stories like this. They may read them in social studies. *or*

Writing Connection

Real-Life Writing: News Report With a partner, write a news report about an upcoming event at your school. Then revise your report by combining sentences that go together.

Remember

that combining sentences can make your writing easier to read and more interesting. You can use the words *and, but,* and *or* to combine sentences. Be sure to use a comma (,) before the combining word.

Extra Practice

A. Write *complete sentence* if the group of words is a complete sentence. If it is not a complete sentence, rewrite the group of words to make a complete sentence.
pages 62–63

 1. Some magazines about science.
 2. Other children's magazines are about history.
 3. Not have to read every story in the magazine.
 4. You can learn a lot from magazines.
 5. Magazines for computer users.

B. Write whether each sentence is a simple sentence or a compound sentence. *pages 64–65*

Examples: Now and then I read an adventure story.
simple sentence

The story was about a dangerous trip, and it scared me. *compound sentence*

 6. Usually, children love adventure stories.
 7. The children in the story are brave, and they have many adventures.
 8. Some adventure stories are set in faraway places, but others take place near home.
 9. A child in the story was in danger, but his dog saved him.
10. Characters in adventure stories hike up mountains, sail boats, and explore caves.

C. Use the word shown to combine each pair of sentences. *pages 66–67*

Example: Writers of children's stories work hard. They enjoy what they do. *and*
Writers of children's stories work hard, and they enjoy what they do.

11. Some children like to read aloud. They like to listen to stories. *or*

12. Many people write children's books. They must understand children. *and*

13. Some writers know what children like to read. They know how to make children laugh. *and*

14. Writers must have good ideas. They need good imaginations, too. *and*

15. Pictures can help children understand a story. Words are important, too. *but*

16–20. Think about a book or story you have enjoyed. Write five compound sentences that tell about the setting, the characters, and the events of the story. *pages 64–65*

Writing Connection

Writer's Craft: Write a Summary Imagine that you are planning a TV show about your class. Work with a small group of classmates to write a summary of your show. Write at least ten sentences. Then revise your summary. Look for ways you can join sentences.

Chapter Review

Choose the best way to write the underlined section of each sentence. Write the letter of your answer. If there is no mistake, choose "Correct as is."

TIP Read the directions first. Try to put them into your own words to be sure you understand what you are supposed to do.

1 Most libraries have a <u>children's room or they have special</u> places for children's books.

   A children's room they have special

   B children's room. Have special

   C children's room, or they have special

   D Correct as is

2 <u>Workers in a children's library.</u>

   F The workers in a children's library.

   G Workers in a children's library know children.

   H In a children's library know children.

   J Correct as is

3 Librarians know what children <u>like to read they buy books</u> that children love.

   A like to read, and they buy books

   B like to read buying books

   C like to read, never buy books

   D Correct as is

4 <u>They may read a picture book.</u>

   F Reading a picture book.

   G They may picture book.

   H They may read book.

   J Correct as is

For additional test preparations, visit *The Learning Site:* www.harcourtschool.com

Being a Good Reader

Good readers read for a purpose. They make sure they understand what they are reading. Being a good reader takes practice. Here are some strategies you can use as you read:

Preview the selection to get an idea of the subject.

Set a Purpose for reading the selection. Are you reading to get information or to be entertained?

Make and Confirm Predictions as you read. Make predictions about what you will learn or what will happen next. Were your predictions correct? You can change your predictions as you read more details about the subject or story.

Use Graphic Organizers to help you focus on your reading purpose. You can use Story Maps for fiction selections. K-W-L Charts are useful when you read nonfiction selections.

Summarize what you have learned as you read parts of the selection. If you are unsure about what you just read, go back and **reread** that part.

YOUR TURN

Choose a short article or story you would like to read. Read the selection once and then summarize what you read. Read the selection again using the strategies you learned above. Write a few sentences comparing how the second reading was different from the first.

Writing Workshop

In Chapter 3, you learned about personal voice. In this chapter, you will use what you learned as you write a personal narrative, a story about yourself. Before you begin, you will read a personal narrative written by a Chinese girl after she came to the United States. As you read, think about the writer's viewpoint and what this story tells about her.

My First American Friend

story by Sarunna Jin
illustrated by Stacey Schuett

Sarunna Jin left her home in China when she was just six years old. As a third-grader, she wrote this narrative about her experience with a special friend when she first came to the United States.

Soon after I got to America, I started first grade. I didn't know any English. That made it difficult for me to do everything. I tried to talk with the other children, but we could not understand each other.

No one played with me. Oh, how sad and lonely I was for my friends that I had left behind! I felt especially sad when my mom read a letter from my grandmother. It said that one of my friends in China had knocked on my grandmother's door and asked, "Is Sarunna back yet?" That made me sadder. Then something happened to make me feel better.

I was sitting at my desk during playtime when a girl named Ali came over to play with me. Ali had blue eyes, a pretty smile, and beautiful blonde hair. I had never seen such pretty hair before. Even though I could only speak a little bit of English, Ali and I had lots of fun together. She let me touch her pretty hair.

From that day on, we always played together at school. Sometimes we played on the swings. Sometimes we played on the slide.

In the classroom, we built blocks and painted together. Ali and I became best friends and were very happy.

At the end of the school year, Ali told me that she was moving to another school. I was sad again because my very best friend was leaving. On the last day of school, we hugged and said good-bye.

In second grade, my English improved a lot. I still had some problems with the language, but I made many new friends.

This year, I am in the third grade, and my English is perfect! I have many friends now. I'm very happy, but I'll always remember Ali, my first American friend.

Vocabulary Power

ex•pe•ri•ence
[ik•spir´ē•əns] *n.*
Something one has gone through; knowledge or skill gained by doing something.

Analyze THE Model

1. Name some colorful words Sarunna uses to help you imagine the events in her personal narrative.

2. What do the beginning, middle, and ending of a personal narrative do?

3. Think about what Sarunna learned. What would you say if a friend said, "I'm scared about making friends at my new school"?

READING — WRITING CONNECTION

Parts of a Personal Narrative

In her personal narrative, Sarunna Jin described an important event in her life. Study this personal narrative, written by a student named Marty. Pay attention to the parts of a personal narrative.

MODEL

Practice Makes Perfect

writer's viewpoint

beginning

I have always loved to play the trumpet. When I was in first grade, everyone told me how talented I was, and I believed them. I practiced only the music I liked.

dialogue/ using *I*

I was in the school band. One day my director said, "Marty, here's a solo. I want you to play it at the fall concert. It's not easy, so make sure you practice it."

"I can play it with my eyes closed!" I said.

using *my*

middle

The final rehearsal came. I hadn't practiced my solo one bit. The director raised his baton, and we began to play. Everything went fine until my solo. My tone was clear, but the notes and rhythm were all wrong. By the end of the solo, I was almost in tears.

Luckily, I still had one week before our performance. I spent every night that week practicing my solo. I stayed up as late as my parents would let me, trying to play the solo as well as I could.

The night of the concert, I played my solo okay, but I did not play my best. My experience taught me that practice is very important. I knew I would certainly be better prepared for our next concert!

details / using *me*

end / writer's viewpoint

Analyze THE Model

1. Why does Marty begin by writing about his love for playing the trumpet?

2. What details does Marty use to help you picture the events of his personal narrative?

3. What can you learn from Marty's story?

Summarize THE Model

Use a flowchart like the one shown here to help you identify the main events in Marty's personal narrative. Then use your flowchart to write a summary of his personal narrative. Be sure to include all the important points. Leave out the details.

Beginning

↓

Middle

↓

End

Writer's Craft

Personal Voice Find words and sentences in Marty's personal narrative that express his thoughts and feelings. Then tell why Marty includes these words and sentences in his personal narrative.

Prewriting

Purpose and Audience

Marty wrote a true story about the importance of practicing his trumpet. What is something you love to do? Have you learned anything about yourself by doing this activity? In this chapter, you will tell your classmates about an activity that is important to you by writing a personal narrative.

WRITING PROMPT Write a personal narrative for your classmates about an activity you love. Describe an event that happened when you did this activity. Then tell something that this event taught you about yourself. Organize your story so that it has a clear beginning, middle, and end.

Before you begin, think about your audience and purpose. For whom are you writing? What are you supposed to tell them?

MODEL

Marty made a story map to plan his personal narrative:

I love playing the trumpet.

Beginning (Activity)

I did not practice my solo, and I played poorly at our last rehearsal.

Middle (Important Event)

Practice is important.

End (What I Learned)

YOUR TURN

Choose an activity to write about. Then use a story map like Marty's to plan your personal narrative.

Strategies Good Writers Use

- Decide on your purpose and audience.
- Map out the beginning, middle, and end of your narrative.

Organization and Elaboration

Before you begin your draft, read through these steps:

STEP 1 Begin by describing the activity. Tell readers why you like this activity.

STEP 2 Use details to describe something that happened when you did this activity.

STEP 3 Use the strategies for personal voice you learned in Chapter 3.

STEP 4 End by telling readers what you have learned about yourself as a result of doing this activity.

MODEL

Here is the beginning of Marty's personal narrative. What activity will he describe? How do you know? What clues does Marty give about the lesson he will learn?

> I have always loved to play the trumpet. When I was in first grade, everyone told me how talented I was, and I believed them. I practiced only the music I liked.

YOUR TURN

Write a draft of your personal narrative. Use your story map as a guide. Tell about the event and explain what you learned about yourself. Remember to use your personal voice.

Strategies Good Writers Use

- Use vivid descriptive words.
- Use personal voice to describe your thoughts and feelings.

 Use a computer to draft your essay. You can use the Spell-check feature to double-check your spelling.

Revising

Organization and Elaboration

Read your draft carefully. Think about these questions:

- How can I make my beginning, middle, and end stronger?
- Where should I add information or details?
- Is there any information I don't need?
- How can I explain what I learned more clearly?

MODEL

See how Marty revised his personal narrative. What information did he add? Find a sentence that he cut. Look at the last sentence. See how he changed the sentence to "show" instead of "tell" about himself.

> I was in the school band.
> ∧One day my director said, "~~That's all for today, everyone~~. Marty, here's a solo. I want you to play it at the fall concert. It's not easy, so make sure you practice it."
> "I can play it with my eyes closed!" I said.
> ∧~~But I was a bragger, and I thought I never needed to practice.~~

YOUR TURN

Revise your personal narrative. Add more details to help your reader clearly understand the events. Remove details you do not need. If you would like, you and a partner can trade essays and give each other suggestions.

Checking Your Language

When you proofread, you look for mistakes in grammar, spelling, punctuation, and capitalization. If you do not fix these mistakes, your writing may not be clear for your readers.

MODEL

Here's how Marty's work continued. After he revised it, he proofread his story. Look at the punctuation he added. What other errors did he fix?

> The final rehearsal. I hadn't practiced my solo one bit. The director raised his baton. We began to play Everything went fine until my solo. my tone was clere but the notes and rhythm were all wrong. By the end of the solo, was almost in taers.

Strategies Good Writers Use

- Use complete sentences.
- Put a punctuation mark at the end of each sentence.
- Make sure all words are spelled correctly.

YOUR TURN

Proofread your story. Make sure that you:

- **use complete sentences.**
- **start each sentence with a capital letter.**
- **end each sentence with a punctuation mark.**
- **use correct spelling.**

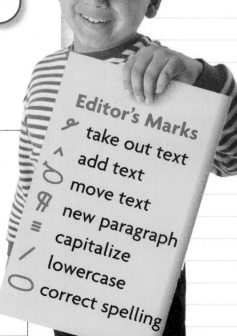

Editor's Marks

- ℘ take out text
- ∧ add text
- ⟳ move text
- ¶ new paragraph
- ≡ capitalize
- / lowercase
- ○ correct spelling

Publishing

Sharing Your Work

Now you will publish your personal narrative. Answer these questions to help you decide on the best way to share your work:

1. Who is your audience? How can you publish your personal narrative so that your audience can read and enjoy it?

2. Should you include pictures with your personal narrative to help your readers better imagine the events you're describing?

3. Should you present your personal narrative aloud? To act out your story, use the information on page 83.

USING YOUR
Handbook

Use the rubric on page 496 to evaluate your personal narrative.

Reflecting on Your Writing

 Using Your Portfolio What did you learn about your writing in this chapter? Write your answer to each question below.

1. Did your writing meet its purpose?

2. Using the rubric from your Handbook, how would you score your own writing?

Add your answers to your portfolio. Then review your personal narrative. Make a checklist of ways to improve your writing. Add your checklist and your personal narrative to your portfolio.

Acting Out a Story

Marty decided to act out his personal narrative. He played his trumpet to act out some parts of it. If you want to act out your personal narrative, follow these steps:

STEP 1 Plan how the people in your personal narrative should look and sound to the audience. Do they use certain hand motions? What are their voices like?

STEP 2 Find props for your narrative. Since your narrative is about something you like doing, find a prop related to that activity. You can use different kinds of clothing, pictures, and other items.

STEP 3 Decide how you want to present your personal narrative. Do you want to read it just as it is written, or do you want to set aside your writing and present it more dramatically? You could even ask your friends in class to help you present your personal narrative as a play.

Oral Presentations

Here are some ways you can improve your oral presentation:

- Find the voice that is right for each person in your narrative. Experiment with your voice. Try using loud voices, soft voices, slow-speaking voices, and so on.
- Imitate the actions and hand motions of people in your narrative.
- Practice presenting your narrative so you do not have to look at the words all the time.

Unit 1
Grammar Review
CHAPTER 1

Sentences
pages 24–33

Sentences pages 24–25

A. Write *sentence* if the group of words is a complete sentence. Write *not a sentence* if the group of words is not a complete sentence.

1. I love folk art.
2. Made drawings on clay pots.
3. Pots of many different colors.
4. Some artists drew animals on the pots.
5. Want to make some folk art.

Kinds of Sentences pages 26–27

B. Write whether each sentence is a statement, a question, a command, or an exclamation.

6. Look at my quilt.
7. It's so beautiful!
8. Was it made by a folk artist?
9. My father bought it at an art show.
10. Do you like it?

Punctuating Sentences pages 28–29

C. Write each sentence correctly. Make a capital letter at the beginning. Use the correct end mark.

11. did you see the quilts at the county fair
12. tell me how the quilts were made
13. many scraps of cloth were sewn together
14. how beautiful that quilt is
15. it has a very colorful pattern

Complete and Simple Subjects *pages 34–35*

A. Write each sentence. Draw one line under the complete subject. Draw two lines under the simple subject.

1. My sister Neela sang my favorite song.
2. Our mother taught it to us years ago.
3. The beautiful song has many high notes.
4. Our music teacher taught Neela how to sing well.
5. Our dog likes to sing along, too.

Nouns in Subjects *pages 36–37*

B. Write the complete subject in each sentence. Then write the noun that is the simple subject.

6. The students in my class brought music to school.
7. My best friend brought a book of folk songs.
8. Carla's favorite music is jazz.
9. The boy next to me brought an old record.
10. The teacher shared some of his favorite songs.

Combining Sentences: Compound Subjects *pages 38–39*

C. Combine each pair of sentences into one sentence that has a compound subject.

11. Karen studied the piano. Jamal studied the piano.
12. Their parents were very pleased. Their grandparents were very pleased.
13. Their grandmother bought them a piano. Their grandfather bought them a piano.
14. Their friends came to hear them play. Their neighbors came to hear them play.
15. The music rang through the house. The laughter rang through the house.

Unit 1
Grammar Review

CHAPTER 2

Subjects/
Nouns
pages 34–43

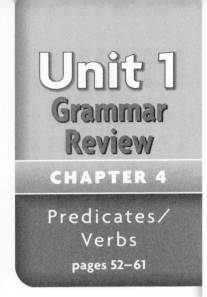

Unit 1
Grammar Review

CHAPTER 4

Predicates/
Verbs

pages 52–61

Complete and Simple Predicates *pages 52–53*

A. Write each sentence. Draw one line under the complete predicate. Draw two lines under the simple predicate.

1. Some families buy new houses.
2. Other families build new houses.
3. Some build houses themselves.
4. Others hire a builder.
5. A builder made this house for us.

Verbs in Predicates *pages 54–55*

B. Write each sentence. Underline the verb that is the simple predicate.

6. Larry is a good builder.
7. He knows about building.
8. He hires good workers.
9. He and his builders work as a team.
10. They all do their jobs well.

Combining Sentences: Compound Predicates *pages 56–57*

C. Combine each pair of sentences into one sentence with a compound predicate.

11. Tamika bought an old house. Tamika fixed it up.
12. She chose colors for the kitchen. She bought the paint.
13. She painted the kitchen. She let the paint dry.
14. The sink was old. The sink needed new pipes.
15. Tamika took out the old pipes. Tamika put in new ones.

Complete Sentences *pages 62–63*

A. Write *sentence* if the group of words is a complete sentence. Write *not a sentence* if the group of words is not a complete sentence.

1. Folktale like this one.
2. What are folktales?
3. They are very old stories.
4. Around for thousands of years.
5. One person told a tale to another.

Simple and Compound Sentences *pages 64–65*

B. Write whether each sentence is a simple sentence or a compound sentence.

6. Often the good characters win in folktales.
7. Bad characters do mean things, and they are punished.
8. Good deeds are often rewarded.
9. Some people did not know why something happened, and they made up a story to explain it.
10. Some people did not understand thunder, and they told stories to explain what causes it.

Combining Sentences *pages 66–67*

C. Use the combining word in parentheses ( ) to combine each pair of sentences. Be sure to use a comma.

11. This story is a little sad. I like it anyway. (but)
12. I wrote it myself. I drew a picture. (and)
13. A son grows up. He moves far away from his family. (and)
14. He marries the girl he loves. She lives far away. (but)
15. I may change the ending. I may leave it as it is. (or)

Unit 1
Wrap-Up

Writing Across
the Curriculum:
Art and
Creativity

Once Upon a Time . . .

Stories can be told in many ways. Sometimes stories are written, but they can also be told through pictures, songs, and movement. Pick a story that you know well. Then tell it in different ways. Here are some steps to help you do this.

Pick a Story

With a group of classmates, pick a story that all of you know. Read the story again, and answer the following questions:

- Who are the characters? Describe them.

- What are the story's main events? List them.

- Where does the story take place? Describe the setting.

- How does the story make you feel? Explain your answer.

Tell the Story in New Ways

- Tell the story through pictures. Plan scenes from the story to illustrate and have each group member draw a scene. Put the pictures on a poster in sequence. Add to or revise the pictures if the story is hard to understand. Display your poster.

- Write a song that tells your story. Assign different parts of the song to each group member. Perform the song for classmates.

- Assign roles to group members, and act out the actions of the story with movement only.

Compare Your Stories

- With your group, discuss the new ways you told the story. What was easy to tell and difficult to tell through pictures, singing, and movement?

- Write a short essay comparing the different ways you told the story. Share your essay with classmates.

Books to Read

Click! A Book About Cameras and Taking Pictures
by Gail Gibbons
NONFICTION
Discover fun facts and helpful hints, as well as how photographs are made and other historical information about the camera.
Award-Winning Author

Arthur Writes a Story
by Marc Brown
FICTION
While trying to outdo the other students in his class, Arthur learns that the best stories come from real life.
Children's Choice

Unit 2

| Grammar | More About Nouns and Verbs |
| Writing | Informative Writing: Explanation |

CHAPTER 7
More About Nouns 92

CHAPTER 8
Singular and Plural Nouns 102

CHAPTER 9
Writer's Craft: Paragraphing
Writing Directions. 112

CHAPTER 10
Possessive Nouns 120

CHAPTER 11
Action Verbs and the Verb *Be* . . . 130

CHAPTER 12
Writing Workshop
Writing a How-to Essay. 140

Nancy's Fruit Salad

apple
orange   melons
strawberries   kiwi
                          grapes

• Cut up fruit into bite-size pieces.
• Mix together in a large bowl.

Nouns

**A noun is a word that names a person, an
animal, a place, or a thing.**

You can make your writing clearer and more
interesting to read by carefully choosing the nouns
you use.

Examples:

person: Stay safe by getting an **adult** to help you
with cooking.

animal: I keep my **dog** on a leash.

place: Don't run in the **hallways.**

thing: Sometimes we wear **goggles** in science class.

Vocabulary Power

pre•cau•tion
[pri•kô′ shən] *n.*
Care taken ahead of
time; a measure
taken to avoid
possible harm or
danger.

Guided Practice

A. Identify each noun in the sentence.

Example: Keep safe in the lab by cleaning up spills.
lab, spills

  1. Check with an adult before eating strange
     foods.
  2. Put away your toys.
  3. Don't leave toys on the stairs.
  4. Use a mat in the tub.
  5. Make sure the water is not too hot.
  6. Never touch a hot stove.
  7. Ask adults to help you with tools.
  8. Using electricity near water is unsafe.
  9. Be careful around a dog you don't know.
  10. Let adults clean up broken glass.

Independent Practice

B. Write the sentence. Underline each noun.

Example: Never run in the hallways at school.
Never run in the <u>hallways</u> at <u>school</u>.

11. Listen to directions from your teacher.
12. Stay seated in your chair.
13. Handle scissors carefully.
14. Take turns on the playground.
15. Keep the floor clean so you don't trip or slip.

C. For each underlined noun, write *person*, *place*, or *thing*.

Example: Sit down on the school <u>bus</u>.   *thing*

16. Keep your <u>arms</u> inside the bus.
17. Pay attention to the <u>driver</u>.
18. Talk softly with a <u>friend</u>.
19. Be careful when you get to your <u>stop</u>.
20. Look both ways for <u>cars</u>.

Writing Connection

Writer's Journal

Writer's Journal: Word Bank Writers must be able to choose the right nouns to explain their ideas. Good writers are always adding words to their personal word banks. On a sheet of paper, make three lists labeled *People/Animals*, *Places*, and *Things*. Write as many safety-related words as you can think of in each list. Choose ten words that you might use in your writing. Copy them into your word bank.

People/Animals	Places	Things
firefighter guide dog	police station	fire alarm traffic light

Common and Proper Nouns

A **common noun** names any person, place, or thing. A **proper noun** is the name of a particular person, place, or thing.

A common noun begins with a lowercase letter. People's titles, names of holidays, days of the week, and months are proper nouns. Begin each important word of a proper noun with a capital letter.

> **Example:**
>
> **Common nouns**
>
> For safety, **children** must look before crossing a **street**.
>
> **Proper nouns**
>
> **Carmen** and **Maria** looked both ways before crossing **East First Street**.
>
> The **Fourth of July** is my favorite holiday.

Guided Practice

A. Tell whether each underlined noun is a common noun or a proper noun.

Example: "Don't run across <u>Main Street</u>," reminded <u>Maria</u>. *proper, proper*

1. The <u>girls</u> stopped at the <u>curb</u>.
2. <u>Maria</u> looked both <u>ways</u>.
3. The <u>children</u> waited for the <u>bus</u> in front of <u>Rike's Department Store</u>.
4. Use your <u>eyes</u> and <u>ears</u> to look for <u>cars</u>.
5. We taught our dog <u>Mandy</u> to sit at the <u>curb</u>.

Independent Practice

B. Write each sentence. Capitalize each proper noun.

Example: carmen puts on her seat belt when she rides in the car with grandma.
Carmen puts on her seat belt when she rides in the car with Grandma.

6. Her cat elsa will ride safely in a cat carrier.
7. The people in the garcia family use seat belts on long trips to see uncle alan.
8. They also wear seat belts on short trips to los angeles.
9. mom tells maria not to wave her hands out the window.
10. The children behave so dad can drive safely on their trip to texas.
11. mr. clancy taught us to ride our bikes on safe roads.
12. Ask aunt mary to help you check your brakes.
13. Get your bike fixed at main street fix-it shop.
14. I always bicycle with jamie.
15. It is the law in maryland to wear a helmet.

Writing Connection

Technology Search the World Wide Web for information about safety topics. Print out the information you find. Work with a group to make a list of safety topics from your searches. Organize the topics by listing them under the labels *People, Places,* and *Things.* When you list proper nouns, be sure to use capital letters.

More Abbreviations

before noon	A.M.
after noon	P.M.
Street	St.
Avenue	Ave.
Road	Rd.
minutes	min.
seconds	sec.
inches	in.
feet	ft.
yards	yd.
a man	Mr.
a woman	Ms.
a married woman	Mrs.

USAGE AND MECHANICS

Abbreviations and Titles

An abbreviation is a short way to write a word.

Use a period after most abbreviations. An abbreviation for a proper noun begins with a capital letter. The **title** of a person, such as *Mr.*, *Mrs.*, *Ms.*, and *Dr.*, begins with a capital letter.

Example:

Ms. Ram told us to take swimming lessons.

The names of days and months may be abbreviated.

Some Common Abbreviations			
Days		**Months**	
Sunday	Sun.	January	Jan.
Monday	Mon.	February	Feb.
Tuesday	Tues.	August	Aug.
Wednesday	Wed.	September	Sept.
Thursday	Thurs.	October	Oct.
Friday	Fri.	November	Nov.
Saturday	Sat.	December	Dec.

Guided Practice

A. Tell the abbreviation for the underlined word or words.

Example: (a man) Marks teaches swimming.   *Mr.*

  1. In January, take a class at an indoor pool.
  2. Can you swim in several feet of water?
  3. My class is at 10:00 (before noon).
  4. (a woman) Wong is the lifeguard.
  5. The pool is 50 yards long.

Independent Practice

B. Write each sentence. Write out the word for each underlined abbreviation.

> **Example:** I use the equipment carefully on Park <u>St.</u> Playground.   *Street*

6. A precaution I take is to talk only to people I know when I go to the <u>Ave.</u> Mall.

7. I keep safe by dressing warmly when I play outside in <u>Feb.</u>

8. I skate on ice only if it is many <u>in.</u> thick.

9. I skate at 11:00 <u>A.M.</u>

10. If I stay outside ten <u>min.</u> without sunscreen, I might get burned.

11. Do not ride in <u>Dec.</u> if it is icy.

12. Use a light and go with an adult if you have to ride after 8:00 <u>P.M.</u>

13. <u>Mr.</u> Naito said to check your tires.

14. It may take many <u>sec.</u> to stop your bike.

15. Do not ride on High <u>Rd.</u>

Remember

that an abbreviation is a short way to write a word. Many abbreviations end with a period. Abbreviations for proper nouns begin with a capital letter.

Writing Connection

Real-Life Writing: Safety Poster Use books or the World Wide Web to make a safety poster. Put a safety tip for each day of the week on your poster. Start by writing the abbreviations for the days of the week on your poster paper. Then write a tip after each one. Use colorful drawings to make your poster interesting.

This Week's Tips

Mon. Don't run in the halls.
Tues. Wear a helmet when you ride a bike.
Wed. Take stairs one at a time.
Thurs. Clean up messes.
Fri. Cross the street carefully.
Sat. Take turns on the playground.
Sun. Wear a seat belt in the car.

Remember

that a common
noun begins with
a lowercase letter.
A proper noun
begins with a
capital letter. An
abbreviation ends
with a period.
Abbreviations for
proper nouns and
titles for people
begin with capital
letters.

Extra Practice

A. Write each noun in the sentence.
pages 92–93

Example: Never play with matches or candles.
matches, candles

1. Keep paper away from heaters.
2. Only adults should start fires in fireplaces.
3. Your family should get the chimney cleaned.
4. Never use the stove without an adult present.
5. Have a plan for getting out if there is a fire.

B. Write each sentence. Capitalize each proper noun. *pages 94–95*

Example: Skate on the sidewalk, not on main street.
Skate on the sidewalk, not on Main Street.

6. Mr. diaz says we should always wear a
   helmet and guards when we skate.
7. Dr. rahim says to warm up your body before
   skating.
8. Skate in lakewood park, where it is safe.
9. jan stays to the right and felix to the left.
10. You can buy safety equipment at tommy's
    super skateland.

C. Write the abbreviation for each underlined word. *pages 96–97*

Example: Skate fifty <u>feet</u>, and then stop.   *ft.*

11. It is safe to skate at 9:00 (<u>before noon</u>).
12. At 9:00 (<u>after noon</u>) it is too dark to skate.
13. Wear a wool cap in <u>January</u>.
14. Do not let your attention wander for even
    one <u>minute</u>.
15. You may have only one <u>second</u> to get out of
    the way of another skater.

For more activities
with nouns and
abbreviations, visit
The Learning Site:
www.harcourtschool.com

D. **If a sentence is capitalized correctly, write *correct*. If there is a mistake, write the sentence correctly.** *pages 94–97*

Example: "Wear guards whenever you skate," said mr. Bell. *Mr.*

16. Wear tape that will shine in the dark if you skate at 9:00 P.M.
17. I need to buy a bandage for my sore foot at max's super value drugs.
18. mr. Day says it's best to point your skates to the side when you go down stairs.
19. Do not skate in chung park or anywhere there is a sign that says not to skate.
20. Watch out for twigs or pebbles in your path.
21. Take a trip on our boat, the lucky duck.
22. Please remember these safety tips from our teacher, ms. ashley.
23. Do not sail without Mom or dad.
24. Wear the waterworld Boat Company life jacket.
25. Mr. yoon and I look forward to our boat trip.

Writing Connection

Writer's Craft: Giving Reasons Ask several people to tell their reasons for following a certain safety tip. Use the list of ideas to write a paragraph telling why the tip is important for everyone to follow. Then trade papers with a partner. Underline each common noun. Then circle each proper noun.

STANDARDIZED
TEST PREP

Chapter Review

Read the passage. Some sections are underlined. Choose the best way to write each underlined section and mark the letter for your answer. If the underlined section needs no change, mark the choice "No mistake."

---

(1) <u>Wonder park</u> has a sign to help you be a safe hiker. (2) The sign says "Beginner Trail 500 <u>yds"</u> (3) The ranger, <u>Kendra Monty,</u> says to be sure you know the weather before you hike. (4) It is not safe to leave in a <u>Jan</u> snowstorm. (5) It also would not be smart to start a long hike at <u>7:00 P.M.</u> (6) <u>Ms Rivera</u> says you should always hike with an adult.

TIP Read the entire passage first to be sure you understand it. Then reread it to decide on answers.

1 A wonder park
   B Wonder Park
   C Wonder Pk
   D No mistake

2 F yds."
   G yrd"
   H yrd."
   J No mistake

3 A Kendra monty
   B Ms. Kendra monty
   C kendra Monty
   D No mistake

4 F january
   G Janry.
   H January
   J No mistake

5 A 7:00.
   B 7:00 A.M.
   C 7 A.M.
   D No mistake

6 F Ms. Rivera
   G Ms. rivera
   H ms. Rivera
   J No mistake

For additional test preparation, visit *The Learning Site:*
www.harcourtschool.com

Understanding Charts

This chart helps you stay safe while swimming. It is important to know how to read charts.

Safe Swimming Conditions				
Number of Swimmers	1–10	11–25	26–35	36–50
Number of Lifeguards	1	1	2	2
Number of Watchers	1	2	3	4

Use the chart to answer these questions.

1. What does the middle row of numbers tell you?
2. How many lifeguards are needed if ten people are swimming?
3. How many watchers are needed if thirty people are swimming?
4. How many people are needed altogether if forty people are swimming?

YOUR TURN

Work with a partner to make your own chart that shows how many people follow safety tips. Here are the steps you should follow:

1. Decide on three tips you will use. Ask children and adults whether they use each tip. Keep track of their answers.

2. Along the top of your chart write the kinds of people you asked : Adults, Children.

3. Write the tips along the left side of your chart.

4. Fill in the information you collected to show how many children and how many adults use each of the tips.

Singular and Plural Nouns

A <mark>singular noun</mark> names one person, animal, place, or thing. A <mark>plural noun</mark> names more than one person, animal, place, or thing.

Nouns can be singular or plural. Add *s* to most singular nouns to form the plural.

Singular Nouns	Plural Nouns
apple	apples
food	foods
plant	plants

Vocabulary Power

nu•tri•ent
[n(y)o͞oʹtrē·ənt] *n.*
Something in food
that helps people,
animals, and plants
stay healthy.

Guided Practice

A. Tell whether the underlined word in each sentence is a singular noun or a plural noun.

Example: Our food comes from <u>plants</u> and animals.
plural noun

  1. People eat different kinds of <u>foods</u>.
  2. Some foods come from <u>plants</u>.
  3. Some foods come from <u>animals</u>.
  4. Think about a <u>lasagna</u>.
  5. The <u>noodle</u> is made of flour.
  6. <u>Grains</u> come from plants.
  7. The tomato <u>sauce</u> comes from plants, too.
  8. The <u>cheese</u> is made of milk from cows.
  9. <u>Spices</u> come from many plants.
  10. Foods from both plants and <u>animals</u> are in lasagna.

Independent Practice

B. Write whether the underlined word in each sentence is a singular noun or a plural noun.

> **Example:** A <u>food</u> can come from a plant.
> *singular noun*

11. Think about the <u>meals</u> you eat.
12. It is easy to recognize each <u>type</u> of food.
13. Broccoli and <u>cabbages</u> are plants.
14. <u>Carrots</u> and parsnips are roots.
15. A <u>peach</u> grows on a tree.

C. Write the plural noun or nouns in each sentence. Then write the singular form of the noun.

> **Example:** Grains come from plants.
> *Grains, Grain; plants, plant*

16. We eat these plants in different ways.
17. Breakfast cereals are made from grain.
18. Noodles, dinner rolls, and crackers are also made from grain.
19. Eggs, steaks, and cheeses come from animals.
20. Nuts are covered with shells.

Writing Connection

Science Make a list of foods that come from plants. Then make a list of foods that come from animals. Review your two lists with a partner. Point out the singular and plural nouns in your lists.

Plural Nouns with *es* and *ies*

Some nouns end with *es* or *ies* in the plural form.

Remember that you can make most singular nouns plural by adding *s*. Some nouns end with *s*, *x*, *ch*, or *sh*. Add *es* to form the plural of these nouns. To form the plural of a noun that ends with a consonant and *y*, change the *y* to *i* and add *es*. Look at the examples in the chart below.

Singular Nouns	Plural Nouns
glass	glasses
box	boxes
peach	peaches
radish	radishes
baby	babies
berry	berries
puppy	puppies

Guided Practice

A. Give the plural form of the nouns in parentheses ( ).

Example: Estelle eats healthful (lunch).
lunches

1. Estelle likes to eat vegetable (sandwich).
2. She makes one with lettuce and (radish).
3. She eats little (box) of raisins with her lunch.
4. Estelle enjoys fresh (strawberry).
5. She mixes them with (blueberry).

Independent Practice

B. Write each sentence. Correct the spelling of the underlined plural noun.

Example: Our <u>bodys</u> need vitamins.
Our bodies need vitamins.

6. <u>Studys</u> show that people should eat vegetables.
7. There are different vegetable <u>familyes</u>.
8. Cabbage can help prevent many <u>illnessies</u>.
9. <u>Carrotes</u> are rich in vitamin A.
10. <u>Radishs</u> are fat-free and tasty in salads.

C. Write the plural form of the nouns in parentheses ( ).

Example: Leafy green vegetables have large (quantity) of nutrients. *quantities*

11. Drink at least three (glass) of milk each day.
12. Some (berry) have vitamin C.
13. Vitamin C also comes from fruits like oranges and (peach).
14. Our (body) make vitamin D from sunlight.
15. Fish such as salmon and (anchovy) are good sources of protein.

Writing Connection

Writer's Journal

Writer's Journal: Listing Nouns Do you think you are eating a balanced diet? Make a list of foods you need to add to your diet. Then make a list of unhealthful foods you are eating. Use the correct plural forms for these foods.

Nouns with Irregular Plurals: Spelling Changes	
Singular	Plural
child	children
foot	feet
goose	geese
man	men
mouse	mice
tooth	teeth
woman	women

Nouns with Irregular Plurals: No Spelling Changes	
Singular	Plural
deer	deer
fish	fish
salmon	salmon
sheep	sheep
trout	trout

USAGE AND MECHANICS

Nouns with Irregular Plurals

Some nouns change their spelling in the plural form. Other nouns have the same spelling in the singular and the plural forms.

Not all nouns are made plural by adding *s* or *es*. Some nouns change their spelling. Some do not change at all. These nouns have irregular plurals. Look at the examples of nouns with irregular plurals in the charts.

Guided Practice

A. Give the plural form of each noun in parentheses ( ).

Example: (Trout) are a type of fish.
Trout

1. Adults and (child) need protein in their diets.
2. Chickens, turkeys, and (goose) are good sources of protein.
3. (Fish) are also rich in protein.
4. (Salmon) have special fatty acids.
5. These fatty acids are found in sardines and (trout), too.
6. They can help (man) have healthy hearts.
7. Cheese has calcium that builds strong bones and (tooth).
8. Cheese is made from the milk of cows, goats, or (sheep).
9. (Child) need calcium to build strong bones.
10. (Woman) also need calcium for their bones.

Independent Practice

B. Write each sentence. Use the correct plural form of the noun in parentheses ().

> **Example:** Growing (child) need to eat the right foods.
> *Growing children need to eat the right foods.*

11. Marta's skirt is made out of wool from (sheep).
12. Her shoes do not fit her (foot).
13. Marta is growing as fast as other healthy (child) do.
14. Marta is almost four (foot) tall.
15. She drinks milk for strong bones and (tooth).
16. Marta and her family eat lots of different (fish).
17. They ate three (trout) last night.
18. Tonight, they will eat four (salmon).
19. Marta and her sisters will need the proper nutrients to be healthy (woman).
20. Her brothers will be strong and healthy (man).

Remember that some nouns change their spelling in the plural form. Some nouns have the same spelling in the singular and the plural forms.

Writing Connection

Real-Life Writing: Advertisement Pretend that a new seafood restaurant is coming to your community. Write an advertisement for the restaurant. Include the restaurant's name and some of its special dishes. Use at least three irregular plural nouns in your advertisement.

Remember

that singular
nouns name one
person, animal,
place, or thing,
and plural nouns
name more than
one. Form the
plural of most
nouns by adding *s*
or *es*.

Extra Practice

**A. Write the plural noun or nouns in each
sentence.** *pages 102–103*

Example: The Food Guide Pyramid helps you plan
balanced meals.
meals

1. At the bottom of the pyramid are foods made
with grains.
2. These foods are full of nutrients.
3. Next come vegetables and fruits, which have
vitamins and minerals.
4. Protein comes from meats and dairy
products.
5. Nuts and dried peas and beans are also rich
in protein.

**B. Form a plural noun from the underlined
singular noun.** *pages 102–105*

Example: Alicia poured two glass of orange juice.
glasses

6. Then she put cereal in two <u>bowl</u>.
7. The cereal came from two different <u>box</u>.
8. She put <u>strawberry</u> on the cereal in one bowl.
9. She put sliced <u>peach</u> on the cereal in the
other bowl.
10. Then she toasted <u>slice</u> of whole-grain bread.

**For more activities
with singular and
plural nouns, visit
The Learning Site:
www.harcourtschool.com**

C. Write the plural noun or nouns in each sentence. Then write the singular form of each. *pages 106–107*

Example: Mom called the children to breakfast.
children, child

11. Tim came to the kitchen with bare feet.
12. He saw two deer outside the window.
13. He heard a flock of geese fly overhead.
14. Mom reminded Tom to brush his teeth.
15. She also reminded him to feed his three fish.

D. Write each sentence. Change each underlined singular noun to a plural noun. *pages 102–107*

Example: The two <u>boy</u> were in a hurry.
The two boys were in a hurry.

16. They left their <u>lunch</u> on the table.
17. They would be hungry without their <u>sandwich</u>.
18. They would not have <u>vitamin</u> from the fruit.
19. They also forgot their <u>boot</u>.
20. Their <u>foot</u> would get cold and wet.
21. Dad ran after the <u>child</u>.
22. He gave them their <u>shoe</u>.
23. He also gave them <u>hug</u>.
24. The <u>boy</u> ran to catch the school bus.
25. They left their <u>book</u> on the table.

> ### Remember
> that some irregular nouns change their spelling in the plural form. Other irregular nouns keep the same spelling in the plural form.

DID YOU KNOW?
In general, fruits and vegetables with dark colors are more nutritious than light-colored ones.

Writing Connection

Writer's Craft: Clear Explanations Write a paragraph that explains how to have a balanced diet. Mention at least six healthful foods in your paragraph. Use the correct plural forms for these foods.

Chapter Review

Look for mistakes in noun usage in the sentences below. Write the letter of your answer.

STANDARDIZED
TEST PREP

1 A Fruits and
   B vegetables are grown
   C in many stateses.
   D *(No mistakes)*

2 J Oranges and
   K lemons are grown
   L in Florida.
   M *(No mistakes)*

TIP Read each
answer choice
before you decide
on your answer.

3 A Fruits like
   B apples and cherrys grow
   C on trees in Michigan.
   D *(No mistakes)*

4 J Wherever childs live,
   K they can grow fruits
   L and vegetables.
   M *(No mistakes)*

5 A Carrots and
   B radishies are also good
   C plants to grow.
   D *(No mistakes)*

6 J My favorite
   K vegetables are corn
   L and peases.
   M *(No mistakes)*

**For additional test
preparation, visit
*The Learning Site:***
www.harcourtschool.com

Reading Special Maps

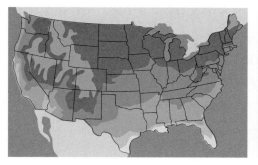 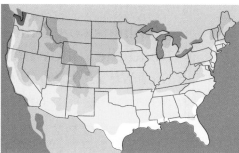

Average Dates of Last Spring Frost

- June 1-June 30
- May 1-May 31
- April 1-April 30
- March 1-March 31
- February 1-February 28
- January 1-January 31

Average Dates of First Fall Frost

- July 1-July 31
- August 1-August 31
- September 1-September 30
- October 1-October 31
- November 1-November 30
- December 1-December 31

Most parts of the country have frost. The map on the left shows when the last frost happens in those places. It helps you figure out when the growing season for fruits and vegetables begins. The map on the right shows when the first frost happens. It helps you figure out when the growing season ends.

Choose a state on each map. Then check the dates. You can grow a garden after the last frost happens and before the first frost happens.

YOUR TURN

Map Reading Choose a partner. Look at the two maps together. Talk about what you see on the maps. Then use the maps to answer the questions below.

1. **In what parts of the country does the growing season last almost all year?**

2. **Which New England state has the shortest growing season?**

3. **If you lived in Minnesota, what would be the best month for planting a vegetable garden?**

4. **When might you plant a garden if you lived in central Florida?**

TIP Make sure that you understand all the words and symbols or pictures on a map. The key is the box that explains the pictures.

Writer's Craft

Paragraphing

Informative writing is writing that gives information, or explains something.

Read the following batting directions from *Baseball: How to Play the All-Star Way*. As you read, notice the order of the steps.

LITERATURE MODEL

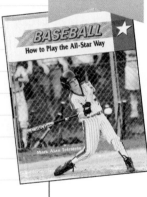

"First, you should pick up a bat you can handle, one that's not too heavy," says Mattingly. "… Next, take a shoulder-width stance. Your feet should be a comfortable distance apart, not too wide and not too close together."

Raise the bat. Your hands should be even with your back shoulder. You must always swing level or down on the ball. Never swing up.

—from *Baseball: How to Play the All-Star Way* by Mark Alan Teirstein

Analyze THE Model

1. What do these directions tell you how to do?

2. What words tell you the order of the steps?

3. How are the first and second paragraphs different?

Forming Paragraphs

Each sentence in a paragraph tells about one main idea. Putting information into paragraphs is called paragraphing. Look at the chart on the next page to learn more about paragraphing.

Vocabulary Power

il•lu•mi•nate
[i•loo′mə•nāt′] *v.*
To light up.

Strategies for Paragraphing	Applying the Strategies	Examples
Identify your topic.	• Begin each paragraph with a **topic sentence** that states the main idea.	• Fruit is a good snack.
Include details.	• Give **details** about the main idea in other sentences.	• Most fruits taste sweet. Fruit is nutritious.
Use sequence words.	• Use words that show sequence, such as **first**, **next**, and **last**.	• First, you pick a ripe banana. Next, you peel the banana.

YOUR TURN

THINK ABOUT INFORMATIVE WRITING
Work with two classmates. Find magazine articles that give information or explain something. Talk about how the writers used paragraphing.

Answer these questions:
1. What information does the writer give you?
2. What is the main idea of the first paragraph?
3. What details does the writer include?

Identifying the Topic

A. Read the three topic sentences. Choose the best one for the passage that follows. Write the complete paragraph on your paper. Remember to indent the first line.

TOPIC SENTENCES:

- Dogs and cats are good pets.
- Dogs need people to take care of them.
- Pets are not a lot of work.
- Someone has to feed the dog every day.

Someone has to be sure the dog has enough water to drink. Dogs need to be walked, bathed, and brushed. Some long-haired dogs even get haircuts! All dogs, especially puppies, need someone to play with them.

Using Details

B. Read the topic sentence. Choose three details that fit that topic sentence. Write the complete paragraph on your paper. Remember to indent the first line.

TOPIC SENTENCE:

It is important to keep your teeth clean.

DETAILS:

- Try to brush your teeth after every meal.
- Keep your hands clean by washing them often.
- Use a small, soft toothbrush and toothpaste.
- Brush both the front and back of your teeth.
- Most animals also use their teeth to chew.

Using Sequence Words

C. Write the paragraph on your paper. Choose the best sequence word from the box to fill each blank so that the paragraph makes sense.

Next	Last	After	First

Here is how I made a leaf print. _____ I put the leaf on a sheet of newspaper. _____ I used a small roller to roll paint all over the leaf. _____ that, I placed the leaf on white paper, with the paint side down. I covered the leaf with clean newspaper. _____, I rubbed the newspaper gently to make the print.

Writing AND Thinking

Writer's Journal

Write to Record Reflections Sometimes you have to read directions. Maybe you are playing a new game, making a craft, or taking a test in school. Some directions are easy to follow, but others are not. What makes directions easy or hard to understand? Write your reflections in your Writer's Journal.

Writing Directions

The passage you read explained how to hit a baseball. Tina wanted to tell her classmates how to make a garden sculpture. Read the directions that Tina wrote. Look at the topic sentence and the details in each paragraph. Notice how Tina used signal words to help you understand the sequence.

MODEL

topic sentence

Making a garden sculpture is fun and easy. First you take a clay saucer, the kind used under flowerpots. Use crayons to decorate the outside of the saucer. Then fill it about 3/4 of the way with potting soil. Spray the soil with water to make it moist. Next, sprinkle on a layer of grass seed. Cover the seeds with a thin layer of soil and spray again with water.

signal words/details

topic sentence

signal words/ details

Now you are ready to enjoy your garden! Place the saucer in a sunny window. Once a day, spray the soil with water. After your garden sprouts, you can add other decorations like twigs, pebbles, shells, or small toys.

Analyze the Model

1. What do these directions tell you how to do?

2. What is the main idea of the first paragraph? How do you know?

3. What sequence words does Tina use? Why are they important?

YOUR TURN

WRITING PROMPT Do you know how to make a sandwich, tacos, or other dish? Write at least two paragraphs describing the directions. Share them with your classmates. Each paragraph should have a topic sentence, details, and sequence words.

STUDY THE PROMPT Ask yourself these questions:

1. Who is your audience?

2. What is your purpose for writing?

3. What information will you give your readers?

4. What writing form will you use?

Prewriting and Drafting

Organize Your Ideas Write down the steps for your directions. Then use a chart like this one to plan your paragraphs.

FIRST PARAGRAPH
Begin with a topic sentence that tells what the reader will learn to do. Give details.

OTHER PARAGRAPHS
Explain the steps in order. Write a topic sentence for each paragraph. Use sequence words.

USING YOUR
Handbook

• Use the Writer's Thesaurus to find signal words to show the order of the steps.

Editor's Marks

𝒫 take out text

∧ add text

↻ move text

¶ new paragraph

≡ capitalize

/ lowercase

◯ correct spelling

Editing

Read over the draft of your directions. Can you make them easier for your reader to understand? Use this checklist to help you revise the directions.

☑ **Will your reader be able to follow the directions easily?**

☑ **Are the steps in the right order?**

☑ **Have you used sequence words to help your reader understand the order?**

☑ **Will your reader understand what each paragraph is about?**

Use this checklist as you proofread your paragraph.

☑ **I have begun my sentences with capital letters.**

☑ **I have used the correct end marks for sentences.**

☑ **I have capitalized proper nouns.**

☑ **I have used plural nouns correctly.**

☑ **I have indented the first line of each paragraph.**

☑ **I have used a dictionary to check spelling.**

Sharing and Reflecting

Writer's Journal

Make a final copy of your directions. Share them by trading with a partner. Read each other's work and role-play following the directions. Talk about what you liked best and what you might do better next time. Write your reflections in your Writer's Journal.

Giving Spoken Directions

You don't always write down the directions you give. Many times you just tell the directions to someone. When you give directions by speaking instead of in writing, you are giving spoken directions.

In some ways, spoken directions and written directions are the same. In other ways, they are different. Look at the Venn diagram to find out how.

Written Directions
reader can go back and read them over
divided into paragraphs

Both
give steps in time order; use signal words for time order

Spoken Directions
listener needs to remember them or ask speaker to repeat them

YOUR TURN

Practice giving spoken directions with one or two classmates. Follow these steps:

STEP 1 Decide what the directions will be about. You might give directions for doing a job on your classroom job chart.

STEP 2 Give the directions out loud. Don't write them down. Each member of your group should take a turn giving directions.

STEP 3 As each person speaks, the others should listen carefully. Then role-play carrying out the directions.

STEP 4 Afterward, discuss what you have learned about giving good spoken directions and why it is important.

Strategies for Listening and Speaking

Use these strategies to give, as well as understand and follow, spoken directions:

- Speakers should use a rate, volume, pitch, and tone that fit their audience and purpose.
- Listeners should listen carefully and remember the order of the steps.

Singular Possessive Nouns

A possessive noun shows that a person or thing owns or has something.

You have learned that a singular noun names one person, place, animal, or thing. A singular possessive noun shows ownership by one person or thing. Add an apostrophe (') and an *s* to most singular nouns to form a possessive noun. You can use possessive nouns to make sentences shorter and easier to understand.

Example:
Rita went into the office <u>belonging to the dentist</u>.
Rita went into the <u>dentist's</u> office.

Vocabulary Power

cav•i•ty [kavʹə•tē]
n. A small hole in a tooth, caused by decay.

Guided Practice

A. Tell another way to say each word group, using a singular possessive noun.

Example: the office of Dr. Reno
   Dr. Reno's office

1. the dentist of Kerry
2. the toothbrush belonging to her sister
3. the bristles of the toothbrush
4. the health of a tooth
5. the teeth of a person
6. the mouthwash belonging to Kerry
7. the dental floss belonging to Dad
8. the class of Yoko
9. the mouth of a student
10. the tooth of a child

Independent Practice

B. Write each group of words in a different way, using a singular possessive noun.

Example: the father of Jamal
Jamal's father

11. the dental floss belonging to the boy
12. the health of a mouth
13. the store belonging to Mr. Lee
14. the owner of the store
15. the medicine chest of the bathroom

C. Write the possessive form of each underlined singular noun.

Example: My <u>friend</u> dentist gives each patient a new toothbrush.
friend's

16. My <u>dentist</u> office has a chart on the wall.
17. It tells about a <u>food</u> effect on dental health.
18. <u>Candy</u> sugar can cause a cavity in a tooth.
19. The <u>chart</u> pictures show foods that are good for your teeth.
20. I will put the foods on my <u>family</u> shopping list.

> **Remember**
> that a possessive noun shows ownership. Add an apostrophe (') and an *s* to a singular noun to form a singular possessive noun.

Writing Connection

Writer's Craft: Topic Sentence and Details
Write a paragraph about a person who takes good care of his or her teeth and gums. Include at least three possessive nouns in your paragraph, as in "Lia's brother visits the dentist twice a year."

Plural Possessive Nouns

A possessive noun can be plural.

Remember that a plural noun names more than one person, place, or thing. A plural possessive noun shows ownership by more than one person, place, or thing. To form a plural possessive noun, add only an apostrophe (') to a plural noun that ends with *s*.

Examples:

All the <u>students'</u> eyes were closed.

Your <u>eyelids'</u> job is to protect your eyes.

A plural possessive noun and a plural noun ending with *s* are pronounced exactly the same way.

Guided Practice

A. Tell how to write the possessive form of each plural noun.

Example: eyes *eyes'*

1. books
2. teachers
3. friends
4. neighbors
5. doctors
6. parents
7. lenses
8. irises
9. days
10. eyes

Independent Practice

B. Write the possessive form of each underlined plural noun.

Example: two <u>boys</u> eyes
boys'

11. two <u>builders</u> strong hands
12. six <u>nurses</u> office
13. three <u>teachers</u> eyesight
14. the <u>babies</u> eyebrows
15. two <u>girls</u> cavities

C. Write each sentence, using the possessive form of the plural noun in parentheses.

Example: The (eyes) health should be protected.
The eyes' health should be protected.

16. Nico and Karen are (builders) helpers.
17. They don't use the (workers) saws.
18. The (saws) edges are very sharp.
19. Dust flies from the (builders) work.
20. The (helpers) eyes are covered by special glasses.

Writing Connection

Science Think about items your friends or family members use to care for their eyes. Then write several sentences about how these items are helpful. Use at least three plural possessive nouns, as in "My two sisters' desk lights help them not to strain their eyes." Make sure each possessive noun is written correctly.

USAGE AND MECHANICS

Revising Sentences Using Possessive Nouns

You learned that you can sometimes shorten a sentence by using a possessive noun.

A noun and the phrase *belonging to* or the word *of* can be replaced by a possessive noun.

Example:

The <u>shirts of the players</u> were blue.

The <u>players' shirts</u> were blue.

Be careful to form the possessive forms of singular and plural nouns correctly. An apostrophe in the wrong place can change a word's meaning.

Guided Practice

A. Tell how you could write each sentence, using a possessive noun.

Example: Running is the favorite sport of Corey.
Running is Corey's favorite sport.

1. Exercise is good for the health of your body.
2. It improves the strength of your muscles.
3. It can also make blood belonging to a person flow better.
4. Bicycling is the favorite exercise of one child.
5. Baseball is the favorite sport of many girls.

Independent Practice

B. Write each sentence, using a possessive noun.

Example: The team of my brother practices hard.
My brother's team practices hard.

6. The practice time of the swimmers is in the morning.
7. The parents of the athletes make sure they get enough rest.
8. The bedtime of Davon is early.
9. He arrives at the swimming pool belonging to the town at 7:00 A.M.
10. The coach of the boys makes sure they swim safely.
11. The children of my neighbor exercise together.
12. The parents of Brittany enjoy walking.
13. The first walk of her parents was only a few blocks.
14. The Hermans walk on the streets of their neighborhood.
15. The sneakers of the Hermans are bright red.

Remember
that you can sometimes shorten a sentence by using a possessive noun to replace the words *belonging to* or *of* and a noun.

Writing Connection

Writer's Journal

Writer's Journal: Recording Ideas

Think about the kinds of exercise you have gotten this week. List them in your journal. Write how each kind of exercise helps the different parts of your body. For example, you might write, "Bicycling strengthens my legs' muscles." Write all possessive nouns correctly.

Remember

that a possessive
noun shows that
a person or thing
owns or has
something. Add
an apostrophe (')
and an *s* to most
singular nouns to
form the
possessive. Add
only an
apostrophe to
form the
possessive of a
plural noun that
ends with *s*.

For more activities
with possessive
nouns, visit
The Learning Site:
www.harcourtschool.com

Extra Practice

A. Write the possessive form of each singular or plural noun. *pages 120–123*

Example: teacher   *teacher's*

1. Elena
2. minutes
3. school
4. friend
5. workouts

B. Write whether the underlined possessive noun is singular or plural. *pages 120–123*

Example: Summer is <u>Elena's</u> favorite season.
singular

6. The <u>summer's</u> weather is hot.
7. The <u>sun's</u> rays can cause sunburn.
8. Sunblock protects skin from the <u>rays'</u> power.
9. It stops the sun from burning a <u>person's</u> skin.
10. The <u>friends'</u> sunblock prevented sunburn.

C. Complete each sentence, using the correct word in parentheses ( ). *pages 120–123*

Example: Bobby went to a (doctors, doctor's) office.
Bobby went to a doctor's office.

11. The family took Bobby to (Dr. Sindy's, Dr. Sindys) office.
12. (Bobbys', Bobby's) doctor gave him a checkup.
13. The doctor looked in the (childs', child's) ears.
14. She took the (boys, boy's) temperature.
15. The doctor answered his (parents', parents) questions.

D. Write each sentence, using a possessive noun. *pages 124–125*

Example: The doctor looked at the chart belonging to Bobby.

The doctor looked at Bobby's chart.

16. He said that rest and exercise are important to the health of a body.
17. Exercise builds up the strength of the muscles.
18. The sleep time of a person is also important.
19. The need for rest of an individual cannot be ignored.
20. Even just the rest of an hour can give you more energy.

Remember that you can sometimes shorten a sentence by using a possessive noun.

DID YOU KNOW? People who begin exercising when they are young will usually be active all their lives. People who exercise feel better and are healthier than people who do not exercise.

Writing Connection

Real-Life Writing: Letter Write a letter to a friend, describing the things you do during the day to take care of your body. Include several sequence words and at least three possessive nouns. For example, you could write, "First, I floss to protect my gums' health."

STANDARDIZED
TEST PREP

Chapter Review

Read the paragraph. Choose the correct possessive noun for each numbered space. Write the letter of your answer.

> My school wants to improve the __(1)__ physical fitness. The school is testing __(2)__ eyesight, hearing, and strength. Each class will go to the __(3)__ office. A nurse will check each __(4)__ health. All the __(5)__ results will be collected. The __(6)__ students will get any help they need. My science __(7)__ next lesson will teach us about eating right. Each __(8)__ health is important.

TIP Read all of the answer choices before deciding on your answer.

1 A student
   B students
   C students'
   D students's

2 F everyone's
   G everyones
   H everyones'
   J everyones's

3 A principals
   B principals'
   C principals's
   D principal's

4 F child's
   G child
   H childs's
   J childs

5 A tests's
   B tests
   C tests'
   D test'

6 F schools's
   G school
   H school's
   J schools

7 A teachers
   B teacher's
   C teacher'
   D teachers's

8 F person's
   G persons
   H person'
   J persons's

For additional test preparation, visit *The Learning Site*:
www.harcourtschool.com

Writing on the Computer

Most computers have a word processing program that makes writing and revising easier. To use a word processing program, begin typing. If you make mistakes or errors, you can edit, or change, your writing easily on the computer.

To move words, groups of words, sentences, or paragraphs, highlight the words you want to move. Then, click CUT. Move the cursor to the place where you want the words. Then click PASTE.

- To add words or punctuation marks, place the cursor where you want the new parts, and just type.

- To remove words or punctuation marks, first highlight them. Then, press the DELETE key.

- You can check your spelling by clicking on the SPELL CHECK button. If a word is spelled incorrectly, the program will give you suggestions for the correct spelling.

YOUR TURN

1. Write six to ten simple sentences by using a word processing program.

2. Use CUT and PASTE to combine pairs of sentences to make compound sentences.

3. Add commas and combining words, and use DELETE to remove any unnecessary words.

4. Use the SPELL CHECK to check your spelling.

If you do not have a computer in your school, do this activity on pieces of paper.

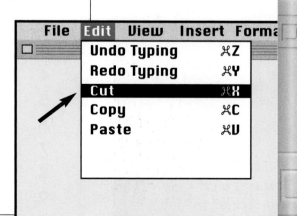

Verbs

A verb is the main word in the predicate of a sentence.

You know that a sentence has a subject and a predicate. The predicate tells what the subject is or does. The verb is the main word in the predicate of a sentence.

Examples:

Predicate

Lola and Lily **sleep** eight hours each night.

Predicate

I **feel** better today.

Predicate

Everyone in my family **drinks** juice in the morning.

Predicate

We **eat** an apple every day.

Predicate

Lily **brushes** her teeth.

Guided Practice

A. Find the verb in each sentence.

Example: Lola is sick.   *is*

1. My sister has the flu.
2. Her forehead seems hot.
3. Lola feels sleepy and weak.
4. The doctor listens to her heart.
5. I bring her medicine.
6. She rests in bed.
7. Dad puts extra blankets on her bed.
8. Mom gives her juice.
9. Lola's energy comes back.
10. She is better.

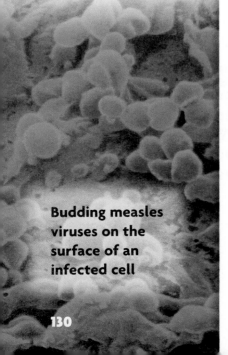

Budding measles viruses on the surface of an infected cell

Independent Practice

B. **Write the sentences. Underline the verb in each sentence.**

Example: Skin covers the whole body.
Skin <u>covers</u> the whole body.

11. Our skin protects us.
12. Skin keeps germs out of our bodies.
13. Germs are small and alive.
14. We all carry germs on our bodies.
15. Germs travel on our hands.

C. **Choose the verb in the box that best completes each sentence. Write the sentence.**

are	fights	wins	cause	wash	make

Example: Not all germs _____ sickness.
Not all germs cause sickness.

16. Some germs _____ in your home.
17. Sometimes germs _____ a person sick.
18. Your body _____ them, though.
19. Usually the body _____ the fight.
20. I _____ the germs off my hands.

Writing Connection

Real-Life Writing: Reminder List Work with a partner. Make a list of ways to stop the spread of disease. Underline the verbs in your list. Place your list somewhere at home where family members can see it.

Remember that a verb is the main word in the predicate of a sentence.

Action Verbs

**An action verb is a word that tells what the
subject of a sentence does.**

You know that the subject of a sentence is often
a noun. An action verb tells what the subject does.
To find an action verb in a sentence, look for words
that tell about an action.

Examples:

Juan **opens** his eyes wide for the doctor.

The doctor **shows** him the eye chart.

Juan **sees** better with glasses.

Guided Practice

A. Find the action verb in each sentence.

Example: Anna takes a shower every day.
takes

1. Joel enjoys his bath.
2. They use mild soap and water.
3. They wash their hair every day, too.
4. A bath or shower removes germs.
5. Vaccines prevent disease.
6. Marta and Luis play outside.
7. They scrub their hands before lunch.
8. They wear clean clothes every day.
9. Thomas eats healthful foods.
10. Monica drinks eight glasses of water each
    day.

Independent Practice

B. Write each sentence. Underline the action verb.

Example: I visit my doctor today.
I <u>visit</u> my doctor today.

11. Dr. Ellen Brown lives down the street.
12. She knows about the human body.
13. Dr. Brown works at the hospital.
14. She smiles at her patients.
15. She makes me well again.

C. Choose the action verb from the box that best completes each sentence. Write the sentence.

like listens opens examines gives looks

Example: Irma _____ her own doctor's office today.
Irma opens her own doctor's office today.

16. Now Irma _____ sick children.
17. She _____ to their hearts.
18. She _____ in their mouths and ears.
19. She sometimes _____ vaccines to children.
20. The children _____ Dr. Irma.

Writing Connection

Writer's Craft: Strong Verbs In a paragraph, record your ideas about what you can do to keep yourself healthy. Use strong action verbs in your sentences. Then trade paragraphs with a partner. Have your partner circle the action verbs in the paragraph.

> **Remember** that an action verb tells what the subject of a sentence does.

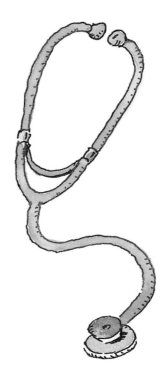

Subject	Form of *Be*
Singular	
I	am
you	are
he, she, it	is
Plural	
we	are
you	are
they	are

USAGE AND MECHANICS
The Verb *Be*

Forms of the verb *be* link the subject to a word or words in the predicate.

You know that an action verb names what the subject of a sentence does. The verb *be* does not show action.

Examples:

Julia **is** strong.

You **are** better now.

I **am** at the nurse's office.

The verb *be* has several different forms. The subject of the sentence and the form of the verb *be* must agree. The chart shows how the forms of *be* agree with singular and plural subjects.

Guided Practice

A. For each sentence, choose the correct form of the verb *be* in parentheses ( ).

Example: The clinic (is|are) now ready for an emergency.   *is*

1. Sean's knee (is|are) hurt.
2. A first-aid kit (are|is) in my bathroom.
3. First-aid kits (are|is) important.
4. Bandages (am|are) good for small cuts.
5. Cleaning the cut (am|is) a type of first aid.
6. Sean's knee (is|are) dirty.
7. My hands (is|are) clean.
8. I (am|is) gentle with his knee.
9. He (is|are) better now.
10. We (am|are) both happy again.

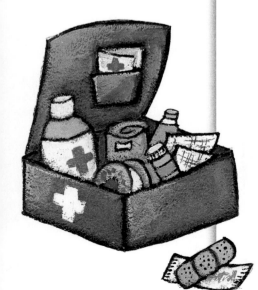

Independent Practice

B. Complete each sentence, using the correct form of the verb be. Write the sentence.

Example: Vaccines _____ available to us.
Vaccines are available to us.

11. Vaccines _____ tools for fighting disease.
12. I _____ now vaccinated against illness.
13. Today, the doctor _____ in charge of the vaccines.
14. They _____ over there in his cabinet.
15. This vaccine _____ in pill form.

C. For each sentence, choose the correct form of the verb be in parentheses ( ). Write each sentence.

Example: Most vaccines (is, are) shots.
Most vaccines are shots.

16. You (am, are) the first in line.
17. I (are, am) scared of vaccines.
18. However, I (am, is) thankful for them.
19. My sister (are, is) afraid of getting a shot.
20. Now we both (is, are) brave.

Remember
that forms of the verb *be* link the subject to a word or words in the predicate.

Writing Connection

Art Make a poster showing what you know about being healthy. Draw some things a person might do to stay well. Then write three or four sentences that describe your drawings.

Extra Practice

A. Write each sentence. Underline the verb in each sentence. *pages 130–131*

Example: Scientists study disease.
Scientists <u>study</u> disease.

1. They learn the causes of disease.
2. It is hard work.
3. Often, scientists find new cures.
4. Sometimes it takes many years.
5. I am interested in medicine and science.

B. Write each sentence. Underline the action verb in each sentence. *pages 132–133*

Example: Some diseases spread between people.
Some diseases <u>spread</u> between people.

6. Doctors know about many diseases.
7. Doctors keep their patients healthy.
8. Some illnesses strike during the summer.
9. One vaccine prevents flu.
10. Family members give each other colds.

C. Write the verb in each sentence. Tell whether it is an action verb or a form of the verb *be*. *pages 132–135*

Example: My mother is a scientist.
is; form of be

11. Some scientists collect information about disease.
12. You are good at science.
13. Scientists give the information to the public.
14. Sasha's father examines germs through a powerful lens.
15. We are careful about germs on our hands.

Remember

that a verb is the main word in the predicate of a sentence. An action verb tells what the subject of a sentence does. Forms of the verb *be* link the subject to a word or words in the predicate.

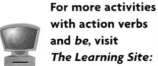

For more activities with action verbs and *be*, visit *The Learning Site:*
www.harcourtschool.com

D. Rewrite each sentence, using the correct form of the verb *be* in parentheses (). *pages 134–135*

Example: I (are, am) out in the rain with only an umbrella. *am*

16. You (am, are) dry.
17. I (is, am) sick today.
18. Mom (is, am) home with me.
19. I (is, am) at the doctor's office this morning.
20. Maggie (is, are) much better now.

E. Rewrite each sentence, using the correct form of the verb *be*. *pages 134–135*

21. When they _____ sick, people need to be careful about spreading their germs to others.
22. Here _____ some good ideas.
23. You _____ at risk for disease if you drink from another person's glass.
24. I _____ always careful about washing my hands before I eat.
25. It _____ a good idea to cover your mouth when you cough.

Writing Connection

Writer's Journal: Reflections on Health Imagine that you are showing someone ways to stay healthy. Choose one of these actions: washing hands, brushing teeth, getting enough sleep, getting vaccinations. Write a paragraph that tells how to do the action you chose. Remember to use words like *first, next,* and *then* in your paragraph.

Chapter Review

Read the paragraph and choose the word that belongs in each space. Write the letter of your answer.

> Most of my classmates (1) a cold. Germs (2) this sickness. No one (3) outside for a while. Some students in my class (4) home. Now they (5) better. It (6) back-to-school time for everyone. We (7) all healthy again. I (8) happy to go back to school.

TIP Be sure you read the directions before you answer any questions.

1 A plays
 B are
 C have
 D am

2 F am
 G is
 H cause
 J write

3 A are
 B plays
 C am
 D becomes

4 F am
 G feels
 H gives
 J stay

5 A is
 B have
 C are
 D am

6 F is
 G am
 H run
 J are

7 A are
 B have
 C am
 D is

8 F is
 G has
 H am
 J are

For more test preparation, visit *The Learning Site:*
www.harcourtschool.com

Categorizing Words

Sorting Words into Categories

Knowing how to sort things is an important skill. Sorting helps us group things that are alike into categories. When we sort, we are able to see how things are alike and how they are different.

For example, when you think of a healthful lifestyle, you may think of diet and exercise. Notice how the words below are sorted into these two categories.

Diet	Exercise
fruits	walking
vegetables	running
low-fat foods	biking

YOUR TURN

1. **How would you describe yourself? Make a list of four categories you belong in, such as sister, friend, student, and so on.**

2. **Look at your list of categories. What words would you use to describe yourself in each category? Sort some of these words into each category.**

You know that how-to writing tries to explain how to do something. In this helpful guide, the authors explain how to be a friend and how to solve an argument. As you read, think about how the authors organize their advice to make it clear.

HOW TO BE A FRIEND

A Guide to Making Friends and Keeping Them

by Laurie Krasny Brown and Marc Brown

Ways To Be A Friend

There are many ways to show that you like someone and want to be a friend.

Heads or tails?

You can play fair. Flip a coin with a friend to see who goes first.
You can share toys and other things.

You can protect a friend if someone starts bothering him.

You can stand up for friends, even when other kids complain about them or make fun of them.
You can invite them to play with you.

You can listen to your friends and pay attention to what they say.

You can try to cheer up a friend who's feeling sad.

You can cooperate. Go along with *your friend's* ideas sometimes.

Okay, what do *you* want to play?

This math is hard. I don't get it!

Try it this way.

You can offer help to friends when they need it.

You can keep your word. Then friends will know that they can trust you.
You can do things for friends, like making them special presents.

You can compliment your friend, even when she wins and you lose. That's being a good sport.

Talking Out an Argument

Here are some steps to help you talk out an argument:

1 Stop arguing.

2 Calm down. Take deep breaths, count backwards, relax your muscles, or leave the group for a minute.

3 Agree to talk it out.

4 Everyone gets a turn to tell, not yell, their story and be listened to without interruptions.

5 Think up lots of ideas for solving the problem.

6 Try to choose the best solution, the one everyone agrees on and thinks will work.

7 Decide how to go about carrying out this plan.

8 Do it!

9 Remember, arguments are allowed, but meanness is not!

Remember:
In order to please everyone at least a little, you may not get exactly what you want.

Vocabulary Power

co•op•er•ate
[kō•op′ə•rāt′] *v.* To work with another person or persons for a common purpose.

Analyze THE Model

1. The authors describe many ways to be a friend. Name three ways.

2. How do the pictures help give information in this how-to guide?

3. Why do the authors number their advice about talking out an argument?

READING-WRITING CONNECTION

Parts of a How-to Essay

Laurie Krasny Brown and Marc Brown tell the reader how to be a friend and settle an argument. Read the how-to essay below, written by a student named Mario. Notice the parts of the essay.

MODEL

How to Put a Puzzle Together

Putting a puzzle together can be a challenge, but when you are done, the reward is a great picture. Here are some steps that can help you when you put a puzzle together.

materials needed

You will need to find a large table. Spread out all the puzzle pieces on the table with the color side up.

steps in order

sequence words

First, find all the pieces with straight edges. Those pieces will form the outside edge of the puzzle. Then, sort the rest of the pieces by colors or images. For example, you may look for blue pieces for a blue sky or green pieces for green grass. Use the picture on the cover of the puzzle box as a guide.

Next, begin putting the edge of the puzzle together, connecting the pieces with straight edges. It may take several tries to find which pieces fit together, but don't give up. Soon the outer edge of the puzzle will be put together.

Finally, you can begin putting the inside of the puzzle together by matching shapes of pieces with common colors. Eventually, you will have many large sections that will fit together to make the big picture.

sequence words

details to explain the step

Analyze THE Model

1. **What is the purpose of Mario's essay?**

2. **What step does Mario describe first? Next? Finally?**

3. **Why is the order of the steps important?**

Summarize THE Model

Use a flowchart like this one to tell the steps Mario described in his essay. Then use your notes to write a summary of his how-to essay. Remember to include only the important points.

How-to Topic

Step 1

Step 2

Step 3

Step 4

Writer's Craft

Paragraphing Mario used paragraphs to organize his how-to essay. List the topic sentences he used. Then, list the details he included in each paragraph. Tell how the signal/sequence words help you follow the steps in Mario's essay.

Prewriting

Purpose and Audience

In this chapter, you will write a how-to essay about something you do well.

Write a how-to essay explaining to your classmates how to do an activity that you do well. Tell what materials are needed. Then describe each step, using sequence words. Remember that each paragraph should have a topic sentence and details.

Strategies Good Writers Use

- Decide on your purpose and audience.
- Brainstorm the steps that are needed to do something.

MODEL

Mario began by thinking of things he enjoys doing. He decided to tell how to put a puzzle together. He made this flowchart to organize his ideas:

How-to Topic:
Putting a Puzzle Together

1. Find all the pieces with straight edges.

2. Sort the rest of the pieces by color.

3. Connect the pieces with straight edges.

4. Connect pieces with common colors for the inside.

YOUR TURN

Choose an activity that you do well. Use a flowchart to organize the steps needed to do the activity.

Organization and Elaboration

Follow these steps to help you draft your essay:

STEP 1 **List Materials**

List all the materials needed to complete the activity.

STEP 2 **Describe Each Step**

Give the steps to follow in order.

STEP 3 **Use Sequence Words**

Use details and words such as *first*, *next*, and *last* to help your readers follow the steps.

MODEL

Read the beginning of Mario's essay. What does he think about the activity he is describing?

> Putting a puzzle together can be a challenge, but when you are done, the reward is a great picture. Here are some steps that can help you when you put a puzzle together.
>
> You will need to find a large table. Spread out all the puzzle pieces on the table with the color side up.

YOUR TURN

Follow the steps above to write your draft. Look at the ideas on your flowchart from prewriting. Use Mario's how-to essay as a model.

Strategies Good Writers Use

- List all the materials needed.
- Use a signal/sequence word with each step.
- Use details that help describe each step.

You may want to use a computer to write your draft. Then you can type over words you want to change.

Revising

Organization and Elaboration

Begin by carefully rereading your draft.

- How well have I organized the steps? Are any steps missing?
- What words did I use to make the order of the steps clear? Do I need to add a sequence word to any step?
- Have I used topic sentences and details?

Strategies Good Writers Use

- Add sequence words to make the order clear.
- Add details to make the information more interesting.
- Use topic sentences.

Save a copy of your first draft before you revise it. That way you can go back to your original if you don't like your revisions.

MODEL

Look at the changes Mario made to a part of his draft. Notice that he added sequence words to make the order of steps more clear. What other changes did he make? Were his changes helpful?

It is important to make sure none of the pieces of the puzzle are missing. First, Find all the pieces with straight edges. Those pieces will form the outside edge of the puzzle. Then, Sort the rest of the pieces by colors or images. For example, you may look for blue pieces for a blue sky or green pieces for green grass. Use the picture on the cover of the puzzle box as a guide.

YOUR TURN

Reread your how-to essay to see if the order of your steps makes sense. Check that you used signal/sequence words.

Checking Your Language

It is important to proofread your writing for mistakes in grammar, spelling, punctuation, and capitalization. Mistakes may make it hard for your readers to understand your steps.

MODEL

Mario revised his essay. Then he proofread it. Look at another part of his essay. Notice how he corrected spelling mistakes. What grammar mistake did he correct? What other mistakes did he correct?

> Next
> ~~Now~~, begin putting the edge of the puzzle
> together, connecting the p~~ei~~ces with straight straite
> edges. it may take several tries trys to find which
> pieces fit ~~go~~ together, but don't give up. Soon
> the outer edge of the puzzle will be put
> together.

YOUR TURN

Proofread your revised how-to essay. Read it three times:
- **The first time, check your spelling.**
- **Next, check for grammar mistakes.**
- **Last, check for mistakes in capitalization and punctuation.**

Strategies Good Writers Use

- Check for the correct forms of verbs.
- Use a dictionary to check the spelling of hard words.
- Check that each sentence begins with a capital letter.
- Be sure each sentence ends with a punctuation mark.

Editor's Marks
- ✐ delete text
- ∧ insert text
- ◯ move text
- ¶ new paragraph
- ≡ capitalize
- / lowercase
- ◯ correct spelling

Publishing

Sharing Your Work

Now you will share your essay. Use the following questions to help you decide how to publish it:

1. Who is your audience?

2. Should you type your essay on a computer or write it by hand? Should you write in manuscript or cursive? Think about which form would be the best one for your audience.

3. Should you present your essay orally? To give an oral presentation, follow the steps on page 153.

USING YOUR
Handbook

• Use the rubric on page 497 to evaluate your paragraph.

Reflecting on Your Writing

 Using Your Portfolio Think about what you learned about writing from this chapter. Write your answer to each of these questions in your portfolio:

1. Which stage of writing did you do the best: prewriting, drafting, or revising? Explain why. Which stage was the most difficult? Why?

2. Using the rubric from your Handbook, how would you score your own writing? Explain your answer.

Add your answers and your essay to your portfolio. Then look at the writing in your portfolio. Which piece is your best writing? Tell why you think so.

Making an Oral Presentation

Mario decided to share his how-to essay with his classmates in an oral presentation. You can also present your how-to essay orally. Follow these steps:

STEP 1 Write on note cards in big print
- the materials needed.
- the steps in order.
- the reason to do the activity.

STEP 2 When you speak, use your notes, but look at the audience some of the time. Looking at your audience will help keep them interested in your presentation.

STEP 3 Speak in a loud, clear voice so that everyone can hear and understand you.

STEP 4 After you finish, ask if anyone has questions about your how-to essay. Then answer your classmates' questions.

Strategies
for
Listening *and* Speaking

Listen carefully to the presentations of your classmates. Use these strategies to better understand their ideas:
- Listen for the materials you need to do the activity.
- Listen for the order of the steps.
- Decide whether you want to do the activity.

153

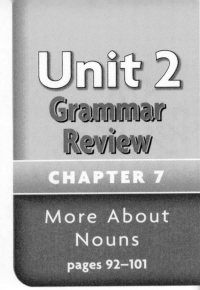

Unit 2
Grammar Review

CHAPTER 7

More About Nouns
pages 92–101

Nouns   pages 92–93

A. Write each sentence. Then underline the nouns in each.

1. My sister made a salad.
2. My friend asked her mother to cut the vegetables.
3. Children are not supposed to use sharp knives.
4. Some dressing spilled on the floor.
5. My father cleaned up the dressing so that we would not slip.

Common and Proper Nouns   pages 94–95

B. Write each sentence. Capitalize each proper noun.

6. The moreno family is planning a trip to san diego.
7. carlos will ask his mother to help him pack.
8. rita and carlos will ride in the back seat of the car.
9. Their dog, happy, will stay home.
10. They're going to visit the san diego zoo.

Abbreviations and Titles   pages 96–97

C. Write the abbreviation for the underlined word.

11. (a man) Wu believes in being careful.
12. He has a pool behind his house on Maple <u>Street</u>.
13. Next <u>Wednesday</u> he will build a fence around his pool.
14. The fence will be six <u>feet</u> high.
15. It will be finished before his son's party on <u>September</u> 1.

Singular and Plural Nouns *pages 102–103*

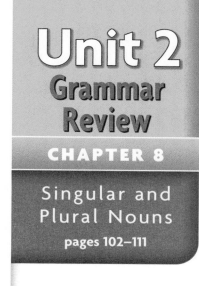

A. Write the common and proper nouns in each sentence. Then write whether each noun is singular or plural.

1. On some mornings Joyce wants doughnuts.
2. Her parents say cereal is more healthful.
3. My brother likes eggs.
4. He eats two pieces of whole wheat toast.
5. He also likes fresh apples in the morning.

Plural Nouns with *es* and *ies* *pages 104–105*

B. Write the plural form of each noun in parentheses ( ).

6. Stella likes fruit in her (lunch).
7. Sometimes she brings (bunch) of grapes.
8. On other days she eats a handful of (cherry).
9. She and Pablo ate two (box) of (berry).
10. She gave him some of her (peach).

Nouns with Irregular Plurals *pages 106–107*

C. Write the plural form of each noun in parentheses ( ).

11. Ahmed caught five (trout) for dinner.
12. Max cooked mutton, which comes from (sheep).
13. Uncle Victor cooked three (salmon) last week.
14. The two (woman) at the fish market sold us some tuna.
15. The (child) in my family like meat and fish.

Unit 2
Grammar Review

CHAPTER 10

Possessive
Nouns
pages 120–129

Singular Possessive Nouns *pages 120–121*

A. Write the possessive form of each underlined singular noun.

1. Eric listens to his <u>mother</u> words.
2. She cares about <u>Eric</u> health.
3. Eric looks at the cans on the <u>store</u> shelves.
4. Eric reads a soup <u>can</u> label.
5. All the <u>soup</u> contents are listed on the label.

Plural Possessive Nouns *pages 122–123*

B. Write the possessive form of each underlined plural noun.

6. Learning to read is part of all <u>students</u> education.
7. It's important to read all <u>products</u> labels.
8. Labels tell how well a food meets our <u>bodies</u> needs.
9. It is the food <u>companies</u> job to label their products.
10. Labels also warn buyers about <u>foods</u> bad effects.

Revising Sentences Using Possessive Nouns *pages 124–125*

C. Rewrite each sentence, using a possessive noun.

11. Jo looked at the lunches belonging to her two friends.
12. The lunch of Ali looked healthful.
13. The lunch of another girl was full of raw vegetables.
14. The lunch belonging to Jo contained two packages of snacks.
15. The labels of the two packages showed that the snacks were healthful.

Verbs   *pages 130–131*

A. Write each sentence. Underline the verb in each sentence.

1. Marta stays home from school.
2. She protects her classmates from her flu germs.
3. Sometimes she catches colds at school.
4. Her mother warns her about germs.
5. Marta's family cares for her.

Action Verbs   *pages 132–133*

B. Write each sentence. Underline the action verb in each sentence.

6. Marta eats a good breakfast.
7. She dresses for school.
8. Her mother hands her warm clothes.
9. Usually Marta walks to school.
10. Today her father drives her.

The Verb *Be*   *pages 134–135*

C. For each sentence, choose the correct form of the verb *be* in parentheses (). Write each sentence.

11. Len (is, are) nice and warm.
12. I (is, am) taking care of him.
13. He (is, am) almost over the flu.
14. You (am, are) nice to bring him his homework.
15. We (is, are) very thankful.

You Are What You Eat

What foods do you eat every day? Could your diet be more healthful? Here are some steps to help you decide.

Make a Menu Calendar

- Make a calendar of the next seven days. Start with tomorrow.

- Divide each day into four sections.

- Label the sections *Breakfast, Lunch, Dinner,* and *Snacks.*

Watch What You Eat

- Beginning tomorrow, notice what foods you eat.

- Write the foods in the right sections of your chart.

- Go to the school library to research the foods you ate.

Revise Your Menu Calendar

- Study your chart and circle the healthful foods. Draw a line through the foods that are not.

- List on your menu calendar healthful foods that you could have eaten. Put them next to the foods you crossed out.

- Add to your menu calendar healthful foods that you plan to eat.

Report on Your Diet

- Use your menu calendar to prepare a report. How can you make your diet more healthful?

- Decorate your menu calendar. Draw pictures of foods you want to add to your diet.

- Share your report and menu calendar with your classmates.

Books to Read

Dinosaurs Alive and Well: A Guide to Good Health
by Laurie Krasny Brown
NONFICTION
The dinosaurs offer tips on good food, exercise, and other hints that help teach healthful habits for everyone.
Award-Winning Author

What Food Is This?
by Rosemarie Hausher
NONFICTION
Find interesting facts about fruits, vegetables, and many other types of food.
Award-Winning Author

159

Sentences pages 24–27

Write each sentence. Label it *statement, command, question,* or *exclamation*.

1. The Oakwood School band has many instruments.
2. Have you ever heard a piccolo?
3. How heavy the tuba is!
4. Don't drop the drum.
5. All the students want to play in the band.

Subjects and Predicates

pages 34–37, 52–55

Write each sentence. Draw one line under the complete subject and two lines under the complete predicate. Circle the simple subject and the simple predicate.

6. A children's book writer visited our school.
7. The writer read her picture books to us.
8. Our class looked at all her different books.
9. The author wrote on many different subjects.
10. The audience asked the writer a lot of questions.

Simple and Compound Sentences pages 64–65

Write each sentence. If the sentence is a simple sentence, write *simple sentence* after it. If it is a compound sentence, write the word that joins the two simple sentences.

11. The city built a new park near our house.
12. The park is small, but it is really beautiful.
13. It has jogging paths, and it has a little pond.
14. Fish and ducks swim in the pond.
15. We can sail toy boats, or we can feed the ducks.

Common and Proper Nouns

pages 92–95

**Write each sentence. Underline the common nouns.
Circle the proper nouns.**

1. The swimmers learned about safety.
2. Mr. Abernathy taught the boys and girls to swim.
3. The lifeguards posted signs with rules on them.
4. Carlos Diaz was the lifeguard.
5. He saved a life last summer.

Possessive Nouns *pages 120–123*

**Write the possessive noun or nouns in each
sentence. Then write whether each possessive noun
is *singular* or *plural*.**

6. Clara's eyes were giving her trouble.
7. She had trouble reading the teacher's writing on
   the board.
8. Tests showed her eyes' weakness.
9. Her classmates' faces showed that they liked her
   glasses.
10. Tonya's glasses are smaller than Clara's glasses.

Action Verbs *pages 132–133*

Write the sentences. Underline the action verbs.

11. Some mosquitoes carry disease.
12. Ticks bite animals and people.
13. People get Lyme disease from ticks.
14. Lyme disease makes people tired.
15. Their muscles ache badly.

Language Use

Read the passage, and decide which type of mistake, if any, appears in each underlined section. Mark the letter for your answer.

Ms. <u>hopkins</u>, a nurse, spoke to our class about
(1)
nutrition. She knows a lot <u>about childrens health.</u> She
(2)
said that we should <u>eat whole grains, drink lowfat
(3)
milk, and avoid</u> sugary snacks. <u>Even peanut butter
(4)
sandwichs</u> can be <u>good for you?</u> She brought us some
(5)
whole-wheat <u>crackers to try and they</u> were delicious.
(6)

---

1 A Spelling
   B Capitalization
   C Punctuation
   D No mistake

2 F Spelling
   G Capitalization
   H Punctuation
   J No mistake

3 A Spelling
   B Capitalization
   C Punctuation
   D No mistake

4 F Spelling
   G Capitalization
   H Punctuation
   J No mistake

5 A Spelling
   B Capitalization
   C Punctuation
   D No mistake

6 F Spelling
   G Capitalization
   H Punctuation
   J No mistake

Written Expression

Use this paragraph to answer questions 1–4.

Before you begin to jog, you should stretch gently for several minutes. Increase your jogging speed and your time gradually. You should be able to speak while jogging. If you cannot speak, you are going too fast. Some people don't like to jog. First, be sure your shoes fit comfortably.

1 Choose the best opening sentence for this paragraph.

   A You should begin a jogging program slowly.

   B Never jog alone at night.

   C I used to jog, but now I walk instead.

   D Joggers sometimes suffer from shin splints.

2 Which sentence should be left out of this paragraph?

   F You should be able to speak while jogging.

   G If you cannot speak, you are going too fast.

   H Some people don't like to jog.

   J First, be sure your shoes fit comfortably.

3 Where should the last sentence in the paragraph be?

   A Where it is now

   B Before sentence 1

   C Between sentences 4 and 5

   D Between sentences 5 and 6

4 Choose the best closing sentence for the paragraph.

   F Be careful when you are crossing streets.

   G If you use caution, jogging can be good exercise.

   H You can also jog on a treadmill.

   J People jog in all sorts of weather.

Unit 3

Grammar More About Verbs

Writing Persuasive Writing

CHAPTER 13
Main Verbs and Helping Verbs . 166

CHAPTER 14
Present-Tense Verbs 176

CHAPTER 15
Writer's Craft: Word Choice
Writing a Friendly Letter 186

CHAPTER 16
Past-Tense and
   Future-Tense Verbs 194

CHAPTER 17
Irregular Verbs 204

CHAPTER 18
Writing Workshop
Writing a Persuasive
   Paragraph 214

Vote for
José Lopez
for
Class President
Election Day
is
November 14.

Main Verbs and Helping Verbs

Sometimes the predicate of a sentence has two or more verb parts that work together.

Example:

Kimi **may eat** fish, black beans, and noodles.

A main verb is the most important verb in the predicate. A helping verb can work with the main verb to tell about the action.

Example:

        helping   main
        verb   verb

She and her family **are celebrating** the New Year.

Sometimes other words come between the helping verb and the main verb.

Example:

Her parents **have** often **talked** about life in Japan.

Guided Practice

A. For each sentence, tell which underlined verb is the main verb and which is the helping verb.

Example: Kimi's parents <u>are working</u> in the United States now.
are: helping verb; working: main verb

1. They <u>are teaching</u> Kimi Japanese ways.
2. Kimi <u>has</u> already <u>learned</u> about Japanese traditions for New Year's Day.
3. "I <u>can get</u> new clothes!" Kimi announces.
4. <u>Did</u> the family <u>clean</u> the house yesterday?
5. Kimi's parents <u>have prepared</u> special dishes.

Independent Practice

B. For each sentence, write which underlined verb is the main verb and which is the helping verb.

> **Example:** Chim's parents <u>are</u> no longer <u>living</u> in Vietnam.
>
> *are: helping verb; living: main verb*

6. They <u>have built</u> a home in New York.
7. Chim's family <u>can</u> still <u>follow</u> traditions from Vietnam, too.
8. His family <u>has prepared</u> special foods for New Year's Day.
9. Chim and his parents <u>are wearing</u> new clothes.
10. They <u>will give</u> Chim a red envelope.
11. He <u>should act</u> delighted to get an envelope.
12. His parents <u>have put</u> money in it!
13. His father <u>is</u> now <u>handing</u> him the red envelope.
14. "I <u>was waiting</u> until we had eaten our rice cakes," he says.
15. "<u>May</u> I <u>count</u> my money?" asks Chim.

> **Remember**
> that the main verb is the most important verb in the predicate. The helping verb works with the main verb to tell about the action.

Writing Connection

Social Studies Talk with a partner about some reasons people move from one country to another. Using a main verb and a helping verb in each sentence, write three to five sentences recording your ideas.

Some Forms of Be, Have, and Do

be	have
am	has
are	had
is	do
was	does
were	did

More About Helping Verbs

There are many verbs that can be helping verbs.

Some common helping verbs are forms of *be*, *have*, and *do*.

Examples:

DeShay and her family **are observing** Kwanzaa.

DeShay **does** not **want** the celebration to end.

Some other common helping verbs are *may, might, can, could, will, would,* and *should.*

Examples:

The family **will celebrate** for seven days.

They **should enjoy** their time together.

Guided Practice

A. Identify the helping verb in each sentence.

Example: Kwanzaa has always lasted seven days.
has

1. DeShay can enjoy honoring her African American traditions.
2. Kwanzaa is ending on New Year's Day.
3. DeShay has lit a candle on each day of Kwanzaa.
4. She will light the last candle today.
5. DeShay and her brother have already helped prepare the feast.

Independent Practice

B. Write each sentence. Underline the helping verb once. Underline the main verb twice.

Example: *Tom is staying up late tonight.*

6. Tom has lived in New York City all his life.
7. People in New York do love New Year's Eve!
8. Tom and his parents will go to Times Square this New Year's Eve.
9. Tom might not enjoy the long ride there.
10. They are celebrating the same way next year.
11. Tom's family have now joined the huge crowd at Times Square.
12. Moving lights on a huge sign are telling the exact time.
13. The crowd should count down the seconds to midnight.
14. Everyone will happily celebrate at midnight!
15. They can make a lot of noise!

Writing Connection

Writer's Craft: Vivid Verbs Think about a holiday that your family observes. List some interesting verbs that you might use to describe what your family does at this special time, such as *feast* and *celebrate.* Then choose four of these verbs and use them in sentences about the holiday. These sentences may describe what you have done in the past or what you expect to do. Use helping verbs with your main verbs in the sentences.

USAGE AND MECHANICS

Contractions with *Not*

A **contraction** is a shortened form of two words.

Often, the word *not* is added to a verb or a helping verb to form a contraction. An **apostrophe (')** takes the place of the *o* in *not*.

Examples:

is + not = isn't	have + not = haven't
are + not = aren't	do + not = don't
was + not = wasn't	could + not = couldn't
were + not = weren't	should + not = shouldn't

Guided Practice

A. Name the two words used to make each contraction.

Example: don't   *do not*

1. isn't
2. wasn't
3. shouldn't
4. hasn't
5. doesn't

B. Name the contraction for each word pair.

Example: do not   *don't*

6. have not
7. are not
8. were not
9. had not
10. could not

Independent Practice

C. **Write a contraction for the underlined words in each sentence.**

> **Example:** Some people <u>would not</u> like to travel.
> *wouldn't*

11. However, some people <u>are not</u> happy to stay in one place.

12. "Life <u>is not</u> fun without adventure," they say.

13. They <u>do not</u> seem to fear new experiences.

14. Life in one country <u>does not</u> excite them.

15. Some people <u>would not</u> be able to follow their dreams where they live.

16. My neighbor <u>could not</u> find a medical school where she lived before.

17. She <u>does not</u> want to give up her dream of becoming a doctor.

18. She <u>is not</u> a person who gives up easily.

19. She <u>was not</u> afraid to move.

20. She <u>has not</u> let anything stop her.

Writing Connection

Writer's Journal

Writer's Journal: Reflecting on Writing List two suggestions you might give to a newcomer in your community. Use contractions with *not* to write your suggestions. Then rewrite your sentences, spelling out the helping verb and *not*. With a partner, read both sets of sentences aloud. Which set of sentences sounds more friendly? Would you rather hear suggestions with or without contractions? Why?

Extra Practice

A. Write the helping verb in each sentence.
pages 166–169

Example: People have come to America from all
over the world.
have

1. The Statue of Liberty has welcomed many of
them.
2. It is still standing in New York harbor.
3. You may see pictures of it.
4. Many people are already planning to visit the
Statue of Liberty next year.
5. They will not forget the experience.

**B. Make a chart with two columns. Label the
first column *Helping Verbs* and the second
column *Main Verbs*. Write each underlined
verb in the correct column.** *pages 166–169*

Example: Yen <u>did</u> not <u>see</u> the Statue of Liberty.

Helping Verbs	Main Verbs
did	see

6. She <u>can remember</u> the Golden Gate Bridge,
though.
7. She <u>had traveled</u> from China on a jet.
8. "We <u>were landing</u> in San Francisco," Yen
explains.
9. "I <u>was sitting</u> in a window seat."
10. "Hundreds of cars <u>were crossing</u> the bridge."

C. Write the two words that make up each underlined contraction. *pages 170–171*

Example: Flora thought moving to a new country <u>wasn't</u> going to be easy.
was not

11. Los Angeles <u>didn't</u> feel like home right away.
12. She <u>couldn't</u> speak much English yet.
13. Her old friends <u>weren't</u> there.
14. Flora discovered that she <u>wasn't</u> alone, though.
15. "<u>Don't</u> worry," said Maria. "I am new here, too!"

D. Write each sentence, using a contraction for the underlined words. *pages 170–171*

Example: People <u>do not</u> always stay in the same place.
People don't always stay in the same place.

16. Sita <u>was not</u> born in the United States.
17. Her family <u>did not</u> leave India until last year.
18. Sita <u>has not</u> stopped writing to her friends and family in India.
19. They <u>do not</u> forget to send e-mail to Sita.
20. Sita and her family <u>could not</u> forget their traditions and customs.

Remember
that the word *not* is often added to a verb or a helping verb to form a contraction.

DID YOU KNOW?
In 1884 the people of France gave the Statue of Liberty to the people of the United States.

Writing Connection

Real-Life Writing: Make a Poster Work with a partner to list suggestions you might give to someone who has come to the United States for the first time. Use at least two helping verbs and two contractions. On notebook paper, make a poster listing these suggestions. Then illustrate your poster.

Chapter Review

Read the passage and choose the word or group of words that belongs in each space. Write the word that best completes the sentence.

> Harry (1) "Hi" to his best friend. He always smiles at his friends. He may also (2). That is the way he lets them know he likes them. He (3) the tradition in his community. Carlita (4) people by saying "Hi!" She and her family have always (5) "Buenos Dias!" to one another. (6) it amazing how many ways there are to say "Hello"?

TIP Remember to read all answer choices before making your selection.

1 A had shouting
  B does shouting
  C can shouting
  D is shouting

4 F isn't greet
  G haven't greet
  H doesn't greet
  J hasn't greet

2 F wave
  G waving
  H waved
  J will wave

5 A say
  B said
  C says
  D sayed

3 A did following
  B has following
  C is following
  D might following

6 F Isn't
  G Weren't
  H Hasn't
  J Doesn't

For additional test preparation, visit _The Learning Site:_
www.harcourtschool.com

Using a Dictionary

Dictionaries are very useful study tools. A dictionary entry lets you know how to pronounce a word. It also gives the part of speech and the definitions of a word.

You know that words in a dictionary are arranged in alphabetical order. You will find **guide words** at the top of every page in the dictionary. Guide words show the first and last entry word on each page. For example, if you were looking for the word *culture*, you would know to look for it on a page with the guide words *cue* and *cumulate*, since it comes alphabetically between these words. Do you think you would find the word *custom* on the same page?

guide word   part of speech   definitions   entry word   pronunciation

cue 187 **cumulate**

cue [kyōō] *n., v.* **cued, cu·ing** 1 *n.* In theatrical performances, something, as an action or word, that serves as a signal or reminder to another actor: Wait for your *cue* before you start your speech. 2 *v.* To give a cue to (a performer). 3 *n.* Any signal to begin: The conductor gave the *cue* to the orchestra. 4 *n.* A helpful hint or indication, as when one is uncertain what to do.
cuff [kuf] *n.* 1 A band or fold at the wrist of a sleeve. 2 A folded piece at the bottom of a trouser leg. 3 A handcuff.
cuff link One of a pair of fasteners that hold together buttonless shirt cuffs.
cu ft or **cu. ft.** 1 cubic foot. 2 cubic feet.
cui·rass [kwi·ras´] *n.* A piece of armor worn to protect the upper part of the body.
cui·sine [kwi·zēn´] *n.* 1 A style or type of cooking: French *cuisine.* 2 The food prepared: The *cuisine* is excellent.

cul·tur·al [kul´chər·əl] *adj.* Having to do with or resulting in culture: *cultural* traditions. —**cul´tur·al·ly** *adv.*
cul·ture [kul´chər] *n., v.* **cul·tured, cul·tur·ing** 1 *n.* The entire way of life of a particular people, including its customs, religions, ideas, inventions, and tools: ancient Egyptian *culture.* 2 *n.* The training or care of the mind or body: physical *culture.* 3 *n.* The knowledge, refinement, and good taste acquired through training the mind and faculties: a person of *culture.* 4 *n.* The growing or improvement of animals or plants: the *culture* of bees. 5 *n.* A colony or growth, as of bacteria or viruses, in a prepared medium, as for study. 6 *v.* To grow and improve; cultivate: to *culture* roses.
cul·tured [kul´chərd] *adj.* 1 Having or showing culture or refinement: a *cultured* person. 2 Produced by special methods: *cultured* bacteria.

C

YOUR TURN

Look up each word below in a dictionary. Write the page number of the page where you find each word. Then write the guide words that are on the page.

1. adventure   4. observe

2. heritage   5. traditions

3. welcome   6. celebrate

TIP Before you begin looking for a word, decide whether it will most likely be in the front, the middle, or the back of the dictionary.

Verb Tenses

The tense of a verb tells the time of the action.

You know that every predicate has a verb that tells what the subject is or does. The verb also tells whether the action is happening now, has happened in the past, or will happen in the future.

Examples:

Today Juan **works** at the library.

Takesha **helped** at her town's library last week.

Anna **will volunteer** there tomorrow.

Guided Practice

A. Tell whether the underlined verb shows action that is happening in the present, has happened in the past, or will happen in the future.

Example: Only citizens <u>vote</u> in United States elections.   *present*

1. People <u>make</u> important decisions by voting.
2. Every four years citizens <u>will choose</u> the President of the United States.
3. Congress <u>changed</u> the voting age to eighteen in 1971.
4. Adults <u>register</u>, or sign up, to vote.
5. Many people <u>will decide</u> for whom to vote.
6. People <u>shouted</u> out their votes in colonial times.
7. Later, citizens <u>recorded</u> their votes on paper.
8. Some people still <u>write</u> paper votes.
9. Most voters <u>use</u> voting machines now.
10. Soon people <u>will vote</u> on home computers.

Vocabulary Power

reg•is•ter
[rej′is•tər] *v.* To enter the name or names of in an official list.

Independent Practice

Remember

that the tense of a verb tells the time of the action.

B. Write each sentence, and underline the verb. Write whether the verb shows action that is happening in the present, has happened in the past, or will happen in the future.

Example: Voting machines keep votes secret.
Voting machines keep votes secret.
present

11. Early voting machines weighed 700 pounds.
12. Today's voting machines use computers.
13. Machines check the votes.
14. They will read 1,000 votes a minute.
15. Voting machines improve over time.
16. An election allows people to make choices.
17. States will make voting easier next year.
18. Some states will register voters on election day.
19. For years people away from home mailed their votes.
20. A person's vote stays a secret.

DID YOU KNOW?
The famous inventor Thomas Alva Edison created the first voting machine that recorded votes in 1868. Congress members did not like it. They said it moved the process of voting along too fast!

Writing Connection

Writer's Journal: Writing Idea
Citizens must follow many rules. Rules help keep us safe. What is one important rule that you follow? In a paragraph, explain why you think it is important to follow this rule. Since you are writing about something you do now, remember to use present tense.

Present-Tense Verbs

A **present-tense verb** tells about action that is happening now.

To form present-tense verbs, follow these rules:

- If the subject of the sentence is *he*, *she*, *it*, or a singular noun, add *s* or *es* to most verbs.

- If the subject of the sentence is *I*, *you*, *we*, *they*, or a plural noun, do not add *s* or *es* to most verbs.

Examples:

Mrs. Sanchez **leads** her class to the empty lot.

They **plant** a garden.

Spelling Present-Tense Verbs

For most verbs, add *s*.

For verbs that end with *s, sh, ch,* or *x*, add *es*.

For verbs that end with a consonant plus *y*, change the *y* to *i* and add *es*.

Guided Practice

A. For each sentence, choose the correct present-tense verb in parentheses ( ).

Example: Children (work, works) to improve their communities.   *work*

1. Some children (join, joins) groups to help.
2. Others (start, starts) their own groups.
3. Some students (volunteers, volunteer).
4. They (collect, collects) toys for sick children.
5. They also (draw, draws) pictures.
6. Reka (pick, picks) up trash in the park.
7. Two friends (help, helps) her on Saturdays.
8. One person (push, pushes) a cart.
9. The other (toss, tosses) the trash into the cart.
10. The people in the neighborhood (recognize, recognizes) the children's hard work.

Independent Practice

B. Choose the correct present-tense verb in parentheses ( ). Write each sentence.

> **Example:** Community volunteers (makes, make) a difference.
> *Community volunteers make a difference.*

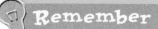
Remember that present-tense verbs show action that is happening now.

11. They (decide, decides) what they want to do.
12. A person (find, finds) out who needs help.
13. Sometimes a community group (asks, ask) for help from people.
14. Some children (starts, start) their own project.
15. Adults often (help, helps) them.
16. Shamonda and four other girls (visit, visits) a nursing home.
17. One of the girls (play, plays) the piano.
18. The girls (take, takes) gifts to their friends at the nursing home.
19. A gift (make, makes) life more fun for the people who live there.
20. How can you (act, acts) to improve your community?

Writing Connection

Writer's Craft: Giving Reasons Write a paragraph about a rule you would like to make. Why is your rule important? Exchange paragraphs with a partner. Circle any present-tense verbs. Think about the reasons your partner gave for making the rule. How could the reasons be expressed more clearly? Give feedback to help your partner make his or her paragraph clearer.

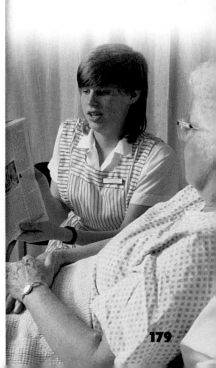

USAGE AND MECHANICS

Subject-Verb Agreement

The correct form of the verb depends on the subject of the sentence. A verb must agree with the subject.

You know that a present-tense verb has different forms for singular and plural subjects. The subject and the verb must always match, or agree. A singular subject is usually followed by a verb that ends with *s*. *I, you,* or a plural subject is usually followed by a verb that does not end with *s*.

Examples:
Each citizen **works** to improve the community.

You can **volunteer**, too.

Guided Practice

A. Tell whether the subject of each sentence is singular or plural. Choose the verb in parentheses ( ) that agrees with the subject.

Example: A citizen (need, needs) to give something to the community.   *singular, needs*

1. Many citizens (attend, attends) government meetings.
2. Some citizens (interest, interests) other people in important projects.
3. They (put, puts) up announcements.
4. The announcement (tell, tells) why the project is important.
5. I (write, writes) letters to the newspaper.

Independent Practice

B. If the verb in the sentence agrees with the subject, write *correct*. If the verb does not agree with the subject, write the sentence, using the correct verb.

Remember
that a verb must agree with the subject of the sentence.

Example: Television give a lot of information about community matters.
Television gives a lot of information about community matters.

6. Interested citizens writes to Congress.
7. Children learns about important events by reading.
8. A librarian shows them books about government matters.
9. Newspapers also tells what is happening.
10. A member of Congress listens to people.
11. Some students help people running for public office.
12. They addresses envelopes.
13. An active student hand out papers.
14. He or she makes phone calls.
15. Some students decides to run for office someday.

Writing Connection

Real-Life Writing: Announcement With a partner, think of a group activity that could make your community a better place. Together, write an announcement telling why the project is important. You may want to ask the whole school or community to be part of the project.

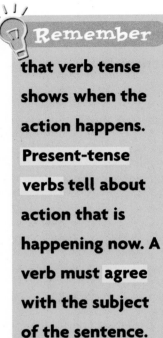

Remember

that verb tense
shows when the
action happens.
Present-tense
verbs tell about
action that is
happening now. A
verb must agree
with the subject
of the sentence.

Extra Practice

A. Write each sentence, and underline the verb. Tell whether it shows action that is happening in the present, happened in the past, or will happen in the future. *pages 176–177*

Example: Isis collects food for hungry people.
Isis <u>collects</u> food for hungry people.
present

1. She started when she was four.
2. Isis and her grandmother get food from neighbors.
3. They will gather thousands of items.
4. They helped many people with the food.
5. Isis will help many more people.

B. Write the correct present-tense verb in parentheses ( ). *pages 178–179*

Example: Chris (make, makes) his community better by helping animals. *makes*

6. He (work, works) in a shelter, a place for stray animals.
7. The people at the shelter (takes, take) care of many cats.
8. Chris (raise, raises) money for the shelter.
9. He (feed, feeds) the cats.
10. The cats (play, plays) with Chris, too.
11. Laws (protect, protects) animals.
12. Laws (make, makes) the community safe.
13. Sometimes a citizen (want, wants) a new rule.
14. I (think, thinks) about rules.
15. Everyone (decide, decides) whether to make rules into laws.

C. For each sentence, tell whether the subject is singular or plural. Then write the sentence, using the correct verb in parentheses ().

pages 180–181

Example: Volunteers (help, helps) build homes for people who need them.
plural, help
Volunteers help build homes for people who need them.

16. First, they (create, creates) a plan of action.

17. Then the volunteers (choose, chooses) a lot on which to build.

18. Each person (put, puts) effort into making the plan work.

19. Another group (work, works) to place a family in the house.

20. Community groups (take, takes) pride in their work.

Writing Connection

Technology Using a computer, type an announcement of an upcoming community event. Computers have different fonts, or styles of letters. Just as subjects and verbs must agree in your writing, your message and your font should match. Try several fonts. Do some look old-fashioned? Do others look modern? If you cannot use a computer, write your announcement in different colors and types of lettering. Think about which colors and types of lettering go best with your message.

For more activities with present-tense verbs and subject-verb agreement, visit *The Learning Site:*

www.harcourtschool.com

Chapter Review

Read the passage and choose the present-tense verb that belongs in each space. Mark the letter for your answer.

STANDARDIZED
TEST PREP

> Passing good laws is one way people __(1)__ the nation. Congress __(2)__ laws. Members of Congress __(3)__ to ideas for laws. They __(4)__ these ideas into bills. Members __(5)__ for or against each bill. Finally, they __(6)__ on whether to make the bill a law. The President also __(7)__ to agree or disagree with the bills. After a bill __(8)__ a law, people have to obey it.

TIP Remember to read all the answer choices before making your selection.

1 A improved
  B improve
  C improves
  D will improve

2 F pass
  G will pass
  H passes
  J passed

3 A listen
  B listened
  C listens
  D will listen

4 F writed
  G wrote
  H writes
  J write

5 A speak
  B will speak
  C spoke
  D speaks

6 F votes
  G voted
  H vote
  J will vote

7 A got
  B gets
  C will get
  D get

8 F will become
  G become
  H became
  J becomes

For additional test preparations, visit *The Learning Site:*
www.harcourtschool.com

Prefixes and Suffixes

A **prefix** is a word part added to the beginning of a root word. A prefix changes the meaning of the word. A **suffix** is a word part added to the end of a root word. A suffix also changes the meaning of the word.

Combining prefixes and suffixes with root words such as *view* and *fix* creates new words with new meanings.

$$re- + view = review \text{ (view again)}$$

$$fix + -able = fixable \text{ (able to be fixed)}$$

Prefixes	
re-	again *or* back
dis-	not *or* absence of
un-	not *or* do the opposite of
mis-	bad, badly, wrong, *or* wrongly

Suffixes	
-able	can be
-less	without
-ment	result *or* condition
-ful	full of

YOUR TURN

Experiment with adding prefixes and suffixes to root words to make new words.

1. **Pick a root word from the box below.**

2. **Look at the list of prefixes. Choose a prefix to combine with the root word.**

3. **Choose another root word, and add a suffix from the list.**

4. **Continue adding prefixes and suffixes until you have used each root word in the box.**

TIP Check to make sure that your combinations are real words by looking them up in a dictionary.

Some Root Words
honor   adjust   agree   play
comfort   do   place

Writer's Craft

Word Choice

Persuasion means trying to get someone to agree with your ideas. For example, you might persuade your friend to try your idea for a class project.

Read the following passage from the book *Ramona and Her Mother*. In this paragraph, Beezus persuades her mother to let her get her hair cut.

LITERATURE MODEL

BEVERLY CLEARY
RAMONA
AND HER
MOTHER
Illustrated by Alan Tiegreen

"Some of the girls at school get their hair cut at Robert's School of Hair Design. People who are learning to cut hair do the work, but a teacher watches to see that they do it right. It doesn't cost as much as a regular beauty shop. I've saved my allowance, and there's this lady named Dawna who is really good. She can cut hair so it looks like that girl who ice skates on TV, the one with the hair that sort of floats when she twirls around and then falls in place when she stops."

—from *Ramona and Her Mother*
by Beverly Cleary

Analyze THE Model

1. What does Beezus want her mother to do?

2. How does she try to persuade her mother?

3. Why did Beezus describe the girl who ice skates?

Vocabulary Power

ad•ver•tise•ments
[ad•vûr•tīz′mənts]
n. Ideas that are made known to the public, especially by paid announcement.

To persuade someone, you need to choose your words carefully. Your words may change the person's feelings about your ideas. To learn more about word choice, study the chart on the next page.

Word Choice Strategies	How to Use Strategies	Examples
Use vivid verbs.	• Choose verbs that describe actions in an interesting way.	• A car **whizzes** by. • The puppy **tumbled** down the hill.
Use specific nouns.	• Choose nouns that name one thing instead of nouns that name a whole group. Use the most specific noun for your purpose.	• Jon loves **fruit**. • Jon loves **apples** and **peaches**.

YOUR TURN

THINK ABOUT WORD CHOICE Work with one or two classmates. Look in your classroom for examples of writing that tries to persuade you. For example, you might look at posters, fliers, notices, and advertisements. Talk about each of the examples you find.

Answer these questions:

1. What do the writers try to persuade you to do?
2. What vivid verbs do the writers use?
3. What specific nouns do the writers use?
4. Do the writers' words succeed in persuading you? Why or why not?

Vivid Verbs

A. Choose a vivid verb from the box to replace the underlined word in each sentence. Write the revised sentence on your paper.

> **flapped   perches   whispered**
> **jingled   skips**

 1. Annie <u>goes</u> down the street.
 2. The bird <u>moved</u> its wings.
 3. Jerry <u>sits</u> on the edge of the chair.
 4. The telephone <u>rang</u>.
 5. "Please be quiet," Kate <u>said</u>.

B. Read the paragraph. Think of vivid verbs you can use to fill in the blanks. Write the completed paragraph on your paper.

As the storm came closer, the children _____ across the fields. Soon, the rain began to _____ down from the sky. The wind _____ in their faces. The huge raindrops _____ their clothes. Still the children _____ outside. The thunder _____. At last the children _____ into a small shed. "Oh no," Matthew _____, "the roof _____!" The children _____.

Specific Nouns

C. Choose a specific noun from the box to replace the general noun that is underlined in each sentence. Write the revised sentence on your paper.

barn   disk   table   cabin   papers

1. Put this <u>thing</u> in the slot in the computer.
2. That <u>furniture</u> is too heavy to carry.
3. Can you move that pile of <u>stuff</u>?
4. Cows live in a <u>building</u>.
5. Abraham Lincoln lived in a log <u>building</u>.

D. Look at each pair of nouns. Decide which noun is more specific. Write that noun on your paper.

1. book, textbook
2. jacket, clothing
3. machine, computer
4. checkers, game
5. instrument, piano

Writing AND *Thinking*

Writer's Journal

Write to Record Reflections Sometimes advertisements persuade you to buy things you really don't need. How can you decide whether or not you ought to buy what someone is trying to persuade you to buy? Write your reflections in your Writer's Journal.

Friendly Letter

Beezus tried to persuade her mother to let her get her hair cut at a beauty school. Carmen wants to get her hair cut, too, but she isn't sure about the style. She sent a picture to her friend Teresa. Read this **friendly letter** that Teresa wrote to persuade Carmen to get her hair cut.

MODEL

heading

> 22 Tower Street
> City, State ZIP
> Date

greeting

Dear Carmen,

body of letter

I am looking at the photograph you sent me. I think this haircut would look great on you. It's so pretty the way it ripples over the head and flares out just below the ears.

I imagine your hair swaying to the music as you dance. It would bounce and swing as you leap high and then swoop down.

I have not forgotten your ballet recital next weekend. My mom promised to take me. I'll see you there, and I hope I will see your new haircut, too!

closing
signature

> Your friend,
> Teresa

1. What is Teresa persuading Carmen to do?

2. What vivid verbs does Teresa use?

3. Why was it a good idea for Teresa to use specific nouns instead of more general nouns like *thing*?

4. Do you think Teresa's letter will succeed in persuading Carmen? Why or why not?

YOUR TURN

WRITING PROMPT Write a friendly letter to persuade your friend who lives in the next town to come to the science fair with you. Use vivid verbs and specific nouns.

STUDY THE PROMPT Ask yourself these questions:

1. What is your purpose for writing?

2. Who is your audience?

3. What reasons will persuade your reader?

USING YOUR Handbook

- Use the Writer's Thesaurus to find vivid verbs and specific nouns to use in your letter.

Prewriting and Drafting

Plan Your Friendly Letter Use a chart like this one to help you plan your letter.

Tell your friend about your idea.

Give reasons to persuade your friend to agree with your idea. Choose your words carefully.

End your letter in a friendly way.

Editor's Marks

𝒫 take out text

∧ add text

↶ move text

¶ new paragraph

≡ capitalize

/ lowercase

◯ correct spelling

Editing

Read over the draft of your friendly letter. Do you want to make any changes? Use this checklist to help you revise your letter.

☑ Have you made it clear what you want your reader to do?

☑ Have you given good reasons to persuade your reader?

☑ Did you use enough vivid verbs?

☑ Are there places where you can use more specific nouns?

☑ Did you use the correct form?

Use this checklist as you proofread your paragraph.

☑ I have begun my sentences with capital letters.

☑ I have used the correct end marks for my sentences.

☑ I have used helping verbs correctly.

☑ I have checked for subject-verb agreement.

☑ I have used a dictionary to check my spelling.

Sharing and Reflecting

Writer's Journal

Exchange letters with a partner. Share ideas about how you can improve your persuasive writing by using vivid verbs and specific nouns. Write your reflections in your Writer's Journal.

General and Specific Nouns

General nouns, like **vehicle,** name large groups of things. More specific nouns, like **truck,** name smaller groups of things. Some nouns, like **dump truck,** are even more specific.

Vehicle (General)

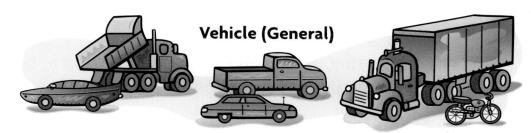

Truck (More Specific)

Dump Truck (Most Specific)

YOUR TURN

Work with a partner to create your own diagram like the one on this page. You can draw the pictures or write the words. Use one of the following general nouns to begin your diagram, or think of an idea of your own.

General Nouns	
furniture	animal
plant	person
place	food

Past-Tense and Future-Tense Verbs

A past-tense verb shows that an action happened earlier. **A future-tense verb** shows that an action will happen later.

You know that present-tense verbs describe action that is happening now. To tell about something that happened earlier or that will happen later, use the past tense or the future tense.

Examples:

Present tense The people **vote** for the President today.

Past tense The people **voted** for the President yesterday.

Future tense The people **will vote** for the President tomorrow.

Vocabulary Power

fed·er·al [fed′ər·əl] *adj.* Having to do with the central government of the United States.

Guided Practice

A. Find the verb in each sentence. Tell whether it is a *past-tense* verb or *future-tense* verb.

Example: All the states decided to elect governors.
decided; past tense

1. Governors will discuss laws for their states.
2. The state lawmakers will vote on the laws.
3. They provided money for schools last year.
4. They helped state parks.
5. They discussed state roads.

Independent Practice

B. Write the verb in each sentence. Tell whether the verb is *past tense* or *future tense*.

Example: Kerry presented a report.
presented; past tense

6. She explained about the President's many jobs.
7. The President will talk on television to the nation tonight.
8. The President will approve new laws.
9. Presidents visited other countries in the past.
10. Our President will greet other world leaders at the dinner next week.
11. Americans elected John F. Kennedy President in 1960.
12. The most people voted for Richard Nixon in 1968.
13. They will elect a new President every four years.
14. Past Presidents studied federal issues.
15. Our next President will listen to citizens, too.

Remember

that a past-tense verb tells what happened in the past. A future-tense verb tells what will happen later.

James Carter, Jr., 39th President of the U.S., 1977–1981.

Ronald Reagan, 40th President of the U.S., 1981–1989.

Writing Connection

Writer's Journal

Writer's Journal: Thinking About Quotations Find an interesting quotation from a speech by a President. Copy the quotation in your journal. Look for vivid verbs that the President used. Circle these words. Then underline any past-tense and future-tense verbs.

More About Past-Tense and Future-Tense Verbs

To form the **past tense** of most verbs, add *ed* or *d* to the present-tense verbs.

The spellings of some verbs change when you add *ed*. To form the **future tense** of a verb, use the helping verb *will* with the main verb.

Present Tense	Past Tense
talk	talked
save	saved
cry	cried
clap	clapped

Examples:

Past tense

Last spring our class **visited** the Congress.

Another senator **stopped** by to ask a question.

Future tense

Our class **will visit** the Library of Congress.

Guided Practice

A. Give the correct form of the verb in parentheses ( ).

Example: The Constitution was (accept) in 1787. (past tense)   *accepted*

1. We (want) a national capital. (past tense)
2. George Washington (locate) the capital on a river. (past tense)
3. Many people (plan) the new city. (past tense)
4. We (visit) our nation's capital next fall. (future tense)
5. The capital (rest) in the nation's center in 1791. (past tense)

Independent Practice

B. Write each sentence, using the verb in parentheses ( ). Form the tense that is given.

Example: The first Congress (form) in 1789. (past tense) *formed*

6. The first House of Representatives (include) only 59 members. (past tense)
7. We (elect) new representatives next year. (future tense)
8. The number of representatives (depend) on our state's population. (future tense)
9. California (occupy) 52 Congressional seats in 1995. (past tense)
10. Lois and Jill (study) the Congress. (past tense)
11. The senators (work) in the Capitol Building last month. (past tense)
12. Voters (select) a senator in the next election. (future tense)
13. Congress (pick) a leader soon. (future tense)
14. Members of Congress (work) hard in the coming months. (future tense)
15. Congress (pass) new laws. (past tense)

Remember to add *ed* or *d* to most present-tense verbs to show past tense. Use the helping verb *will* with a main verb to show future tense.

Writing Connection

Writer's Craft: Using Powerful Words With a partner, brainstorm an idea for making an improvement in your community. Make a list of words you might use to urge people in government to act on your idea. Use your list of words to write a paragraph about your idea. Check to be sure you have used past-tense and future-tense verbs correctly.

USAGE AND MECHANICS

Choosing the Correct Tense

When you write a sentence, you must choose the correct tense of a verb.

If the action of a sentence takes place now, choose a present-tense verb. If the action took place in the past, choose a past-tense verb. If the action will take place later, choose a future-tense verb.

Examples:

The senator **opens** the letter.
(present tense)

The senator **opened** the letter.
(past tense)

The senator **will open** the letter.
(future tense)

Guided Practice

A. Choose the correct form of the verb in parentheses ( ) for each sentence.

Example: Senators (listened, will listen) to voters last year.   *listened*

1. Senators (received, will receive) hundreds of letters last week.
2. They (opened, will open) each letter later.
3. They (responded, will respond) to each writer tomorrow.
4. One senator (decided, will decide) to answer all her letters last week.
5. She (finished, will finish) yesterday.

Independent Practice

B. Write the correct form of the verb in parentheses ( ) for each sentence.

Example: Nine people now (serve, served, will serve) on the United States Supreme Court.
serve

6. The Constitution (created, create, will create) the Supreme Court many years ago.
7. The Supreme Court still (will decide, decided, decides) important issues.
8. The President (select, selected, will select) a new Supreme Court judge in the future.
9. The Senate (vote, voted, will vote) on the President's choice next week.
10. Judge Sandra Day O'Connor (lives, lived, will live) in Arizona in the 1980s.
11. The President (watched, will watch, watches) her work as a judge for many years.
12. No women (serve, serves, served) on the Supreme Court at that time.
13. Next month the judges (decided, will decide, decide) many cases.
14. Two women now (served, will serve, serve) on the Supreme Court.
15. Future Presidents (appoints, will appoint, appointed) more women.

Writing Connection

Technology Write an e-mail message to an official about an issue that is important to your community. Use correct verb tenses in your e-mail as you explain the importance of the issue.

Extra Practice

A. Identify the verb in each sentence. Label each verb *past tense* or *future tense*.
pages 194–195

Example: Lawmakers will pass many laws this year.
will pass; future tense

 1. Congress passed laws to protect workers in the early 1900s.
 2. These laws changed workers' lives.
 3. Workers will need more help in the future.
 4. Workers will want new laws.
 5. Lawmakers will help them.

B. Write each sentence by using the verb in parentheses ( ). Form the tense that is given at the end of the sentence. *pages 196–197*

Example: Local governments (provide) services for their citizens. (future tense)
will provide

 6. Tax money (finance) the services. (future tense)
 7. Local governments (use) some of the taxes to buy fire trucks. (past tense)
 8. Firefighters (hurry) to fires in their new trucks. (past tense)
 9. We (purchase) books for the library with the money next year. (future tense)
10. Our local government also (need) money for streetlights. (past tense)

For more activities
with past-tense
and future-tense
verbs, visit
The Learning Site:
www.harcourtschool.com

C. Write the verb from the box that best fits each sentence. *pages 198–199*

> **will open   changed   arrive**
> **arrived   asked   allows   waited**

Example: Yesterday's vote _____ a school rule.
changed

11. Last year, many students _____ at school early.
12. They _____ outside.
13. The students _____ to wait inside the building.
14. The rule now _____ them to go inside early.
15. Next year, a teacher _____ the building early.

D. Rewrite each sentence, correcting any errors.
pages 198–199

Example: We returned our library books tomorrow.
We will return our library books tomorrow.

16. I return my books to the library tomorrow.
17. Then I pay a fine for my overdue book.
18. Last year, my community add more books to the library.
19. Have you decide what to read next?
20. I help you choose a good book later.

Writing Connection

Real-Life Writing: Writing a Want Ad Pretend that you need to hire someone for a government job, such as a police officer or a governor's secretary. With a partner, write a want ad for the job. Use words that will make people want the job. Be sure to use correct verb tenses.

DID YOU KNOW?
In the United States, more than 22 million people work for federal, state, and local governments.

Chapter Review

Choose the correct verb form for each underlined word. If the underlined word needs no change, choose "No mistake."

> (1) In the past, people <u>construct</u> dirt roads. (2) Horses <u>walk</u> along the roads in those days. (3) Automobiles <u>create</u> big mud holes in the roads. (4) To help keep the town cleaner, people back then <u>design</u> stronger roads made of brick. (5) These days, our town <u>raises</u> money for new roads with taxes. (6) Next year, we <u>complete</u> a new highway.

TIP Read each sentence carefully to determine when the action of the sentence takes place.

1 A will construct
  B constructs
  C constructed
  D No mistake

2 F walked
  G walks
  H will walk
  J No mistake

3 A will create
  B created
  C creates
  D No mistake

4 F will design
  G designs
  H designed
  J No mistake

5 A will raise
  B raised
  C raise
  D No mistake

6 F completes
  G will complete
  H completed
  J No mistake

For additional test preparation, visit *The Learning Site:*
www.harcourtschool.com

Listening for Facts and Opinions

A **fact** is a statement that can be proved true. If you say, "Our nation's capital is in Washington, D.C.," you have stated a fact. You can prove that Washington, D.C., is the capital of the United States.

An **opinion** is a statement that cannot be proved. An opinion is a person's feeling or belief. "Dogs are better pets than cats" is an opinion. People can discuss the statement, but no one can prove it is true or false.

As you listen to a speaker, listen for judgment words such as *better*, *best*, *worst*, *always*, *never*, and *should*. These words often signal an opinion.

Examples:

Fact	Opinion
I voted for the mayor.	The mayor is a nice person.
Tomorrow is Election Day.	Elections are exciting events.

YOUR TURN

FACT AND OPINION Find three ads in magazines or newspapers. Read them to a partner. Have your partner tell which statements in the ads are facts and which are opinions. Then switch ads and tell whether the statements in your partner's ad are facts or opinions.

TIP Notice how people look and sound when they say things. Many times, people sound and look serious when they are stating facts. They often show more feeling when they are giving opinions.

Irregular Verbs	
Verb	**Past Tense**
come	came
do	did
have	had
say	said
see	saw

Irregular Verbs

**An irregular verb is a verb that does not end
with *ed* to show past tense.**

You know that past tense is the form of a verb
that tells about action that happened in the past.
You can make most verbs past tense by adding *ed*,
but irregular verbs have different endings. Some
also have different spellings.

> **Examples:**
>
> I **came** to this school last year. (past tense of the
> verb *come*)
>
> My father **said** the school has changed since he was
> a student. (past tense of the verb *say*)

Guided Practice

**A. Choose the verb in parentheses ( ) that
correctly completes each sentence.**

Example: Last year I (see, saw) many old schools on
our trip to the coast.
saw

   1. Mr. Anderson (see, saw) many different
schools on his trip to China last summer.
   2. He (come, came) to our school yesterday.
   3. Mr. Anderson (have, had) pictures of
different schools in China.
   4. One community (had, have) a special festival.
   5. The people (did, done) a play about their
past.

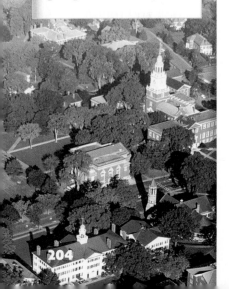

Independent Practice

Remember that an irregular **verb** does not use an *ed* ending to show past tense.

B. Write each sentence. Use the past tense of the verb in parentheses () to complete the sentence.

Example: I _____ a new student in our school. (see)
I saw a new student in our school.

6. Many new people _____ to live here last year. (come)
7. Community leaders _____ we needed a new school. (say)
8. They _____ a study about our community. (do)
9. I _____ workers building our new school. (see)
10. The workers _____ a good job. (do)
11. Our teacher _____ the old school was very different. (say)
12. We _____ photographs of the old school. (see)
13. I _____ a drawing of our new school. (do)
14. Mika _____ she liked my drawing. (say)
15. Yesterday I _____ a great idea for how to decorate our school lunchroom. (have)

Writing Connection

Art Design a poster showing what a place in your community looked like in the past and what it looks like today. Write captions for your pictures. Use present-tense verbs to tell about your community today. Use past-tense verbs to tell about your community in the past.

More Irregular Verbs

Some irregular verbs end with *n* or *en* to show past tense with helping verbs.

You know that irregular verbs change spelling in the past tense. Most irregular verbs change forms again when they are used with helping verbs.

Examples:

I **took** a trip to the mayor's office.

I **have taken** many trips to the mayor's office.

More Irregular Verbs		
Verb	Past Tense	Past Tense with Have, Has, Had
eat	ate	eaten
give	gave	given
grow	grew	grown
ride	rode	ridden
write	wrote	written

Guided Practice

A. Choose the correct word or words in parentheses ( ) to complete each sentence.

Example: It (has took, has taken) years to build our new library. *has taken*

1. I (ridden, rode) over to see it on opening day.
2. The library (has grown, has grew) in size.
3. Library helpers (given, gave) many new books to the library.
4. Everyone (have eaten, ate) a big dinner to celebrate.
5. The mayor (written, wrote) a speech.

Independent Practice

B. Write each sentence, using the correct past-tense verb in parentheses ().

Example: Charlotte has (grew, grown) over the years.
Charlotte has grown over the years.

6. Charlotte's factories have (gave, given) many people jobs.
7. Some people in the city have (rode, ridden) bicycles to work.
8. Many people have (ate, eaten) in the city's restaurants.
9. Food critics (gave, given) them good reviews.
10. Many cities (grew, grown) quickly in the past ten years.
11. I (wrote, has written) about my trip to North Carolina.
12. I had (rode, ridden) the train before.
13. Charlotte has (grew, grown) quite steadily.
14. Our class (wrote, written) a letter to the city's mayor.
15. Ms. Taylor had (gave, given) us the address.

Remember

that some irregular verbs use *n* or *en* to form the past tense with helping verbs.

Writing Connection

Real-Life Writing: Interview Talk with a person who has lived in your community for a long time. Ask him or her questions about how the community has changed over the years. Then write four sentences telling what you learned from your interview. Use present-tense and past-tense verbs in your sentences. Include at least two irregular verbs.

USAGE AND MECHANICS

Commonly Misused Irregular Verbs

Some verbs are commonly misused.

Certain verbs look or sound alike but have different meanings. Others seem to tell the same idea but are used differently.

Commonly Misused Verbs	
Verbs	**Definitions**
lie, lay	to recline; to place something
rise, raise	to go up; to lift or push something up
teach, learn	to give knowledge; to get knowledge

Examples:

Let's **lie** down on the grass.

A balloon **rises** from the crowd.

My sister **teaches** people how to play tennis.

Guided Practice

A. Identify the verb in parentheses ( ) that completes the sentence correctly.

Example: Students (teach, learn) about rules in school.
learn

1. We (raise, rise) for "The Star-Spangled Banner."
2. The song (teaches, learns) us about our flag.
3. (Lie, Lay) your coat on the chair.
4. (Raise, Rise) your hand to salute the flag.
5. A plaque (lies, lays) next to the flagpole.

Independent Practice

B. Write the verb in parentheses ( ) that completes each sentence correctly.

Example: Some communities (teach, learn) from the changes made in other communities.
learn

6. The sun (raises, rises) each morning over the buildings downtown.
7. I mustn't (lie, lay) in bed and miss the sunrise.
8. Let's (lie, lay) flowers in the community park.
9. I hope they let me (raise, rise) the banner at the new art gallery.
10. I will (teach, learn) you where to look for information about our city's history.
11. When the temperature (raises, rises), businesses turn on their air conditioners.
12. Workers (lay, lie) the bricks for the school's new sidewalk.
13. Leaves will soon (lay, lie) all over the ground.
14. (Raise, Rise) your hand if you want to rake.
15. I will (teach, learn) you about the different kinds of leaves.

Remember

that some verbs may be easily confused. To choose the correct verb, think about the meaning of the sentence.

Writing Connection

Writer's Craft: Choosing a Form Write a paragraph, poem, or letter about how your school is different from schools of the past. Use at least three irregular or commonly misused verbs. Exchange paragraphs with a partner. Correct any sentences that have incorrect irregular or commonly misused verbs.

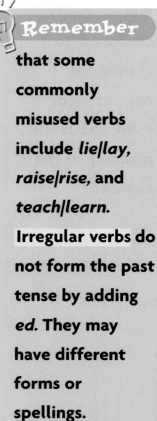

Remember that some commonly misused verbs include *lie/lay*, *raise/rise*, and *teach/learn*. Irregular verbs do not form the past tense by adding *ed*. They may have different forms or spellings.

Extra Practice

A. Write each sentence. Choose the correct verb in parentheses ( ) to complete it. *pages 204–207*

> **Example:** Our city planners (has, had) a design for our city park.
> *Our city planners had a design for our city park.*

1. They (saw, seen) parks in other cities.
2. They had (wrote, written) letters to our mayor.
3. Our city planners (gave, given) plans to the mayor, too.
4. They (come, came) to a town meeting last week.
5. The people of the town (says, said) they liked the ideas.

B. Write the correct present-tense verb in parentheses ( ) to complete each sentence. *pages 208–209*

> **Example:** Hopes (raise, rise) among the farmers in the community as they begin to plant corn.
> *rise*

6. They (raise, rise) their voices and sing while they work together.
7. Some new farmers (teach, learn) ways to grow corn.
8. Others (teach, learn) one another how to grow new crops.
9. The farmers (lie, lay) the seeds in rows.
10. They watch the new plants (raise, rise) from the ground.

C. Write each sentence. Choose a verb from the box and use its correct past-tense form to fill in the blank. Use each verb once. *pages 204–207*

give   write   come   grow   say

11. Mr. Bergen _____ to talk to our class.

12. He has _____ us a new plan for our town.

13. He explained how our town has _____.

14. We _____ down his ideas as he spoke.

15. Our teacher _____ Mr. Bergen wanted our ideas, too.

D. Rewrite the sentences below, correcting each error. *pages 204–207*

16. Our class has gave the mayor some ideas for a new recreation center.

17. We have wrote down our plan.

18. We have went to Cedar City.

19. We seen a huge recreation center there.

20. Our city has have the same playground for a long time.

Writing Connection

Social Studies Work in a small group to find out what your community was like in the past. Where did people live? What were the schools like? How did people travel to work and school? What did people in your community do for recreation? Write a paragraph that describes your community in the past. Use the past-tense forms of irregular verbs correctly.

Chapter Review

Read the paragraph. Choose the correct verb for each sentence.

> Our class has __(1)__ a report about city planning. Our city's planner, Ms. Love, __(2)__ to our class. She has __(3)__ many drawings of plans for a new mall. We __(4)__ our hands to ask questions. We studied all of the plans. We __(5)__ her some ideas of our own. Projects like this __(6)__ us about our community.

TIP Read the entire paragraph first to get an idea of its whole meaning. Then read the sentences one at a time.

1 A wrote
   B written
   C write
   D writed

2 F come
   G had came
   H comed
   J came

3 A do
   B does
   C done
   D did

4 F raised
   G rised
   H risen
   J rose

5 A gived
   B gives
   C gave
   D given

6 F learns
   G teach
   H teaches
   J learn

For additional test preparation, visit _The Learning Site:_
www.harcourtschool.com

Using a Thesaurus

Understanding the Thesaurus

A **thesaurus** is a writer's tool. It is a book that lists words and their synonyms and antonyms. **Synonyms** are words that have similar meanings. **Antonyms** are words with opposite meanings. Entry words are listed in alphabetical order. Two guide words at the top of each page show the first and last words on that page. Some entries may also suggest another word that you can look up for more synonyms and antonyms.

Using the Thesaurus

Suppose you are writing a report. You notice that some words do not mean exactly what you want to say. You also see that you have used the same word over and over again. You can use a thesaurus to find different words to use. First, look up the entry word in the index. Use the index to find the page on which the word appears. Turn to that page, and read the synonyms. Find the synonym that most closely matches the meaning you want.

the <u>nice</u> box
the <u>colorful</u> box
the <u>pretty</u> box

YOUR TURN

Read a paragraph that you wrote for an earlier assignment. Circle any words that you have used more than once. Circle any words that do not mean exactly what you want to say. Use your thesaurus to replace these words with synonyms. Underline the new words.

TIP Make sure that your new word makes sense in the sentence. Use a dictionary to check the word's meaning.

WESTBEND

HOME

r

You know that when you try to persuade someone of something, you are trying to get that person to believe something or do something. In this story, the students in Ms. Parker's class are trying to persuade their teacher to let them coach her. As you read this story, think about the reasons the students use to support their opinions.

Coaching Ms. Parker

by Carla Heymsfeld
illustrated by Steve Royal

Ms. Parker does not want to play in Westbend Elementary's yearly baseball game between the teachers and the sixth graders. She has no confidence in her baseball skills. Her students think they should start coaching her after school to get her ready for the big game. Can they convince Ms. Parker that this is a good idea?

"Is something wrong?" Ms. Parker asked.

Several seconds passed. Mike swallowed hard. He couldn't seem to get started. Elizabeth gave him a little shove. "Mike has something to tell you," she said to Ms. Parker.

215

Mike wondered why Elizabeth, if she was so eager, didn't tell Ms. Parker herself. He looked at Elizabeth, who looked right back at him. It was like being trapped in a rundown. He took a deep breath. "Ms. Parker," he said, "we were wondering . . ." His voice trailed off helplessly. What *were* they wondering?

"Yes?" Ms. Parker lifted her eyebrows.

"We wondered . . . uh . . . if you'd like to come out after school and . . . er . . . play baseball with us. You know, practice a little for the . . . uh . . . game." There. He'd said it. He held his breath.

Ms. Parker nodded just a little. "That's very nice of you, Mike," she said kindly. "I understand what you are trying to do, but it won't work."

"Mike's a good teacher," Ho-Pu chimed in loyally.

Ms. Parker stared glumly at Mike. She did not seem convinced.

"All you need is a little practice," Kathy assured her.

"Wouldn't you help us if we couldn't do something?" Elizabeth demanded.

"Yeees," Ms. Parker dragged the word out. Clearly, she was not an eager student. "I guess if you are willing to teach me, I ought to try to learn."

"Can you start this afternoon?" It was Elizabeth again. At least, Mike thought, she's persistent.

"I don't know. I don't have any sneakers with me." Ms. Parker looked down at her white suede sandals. "Don't you need to let your parents know if you are going to stay after school?"

"We could start tomorrow," Frank suggested. It was amazing what a little team spirit could do.

"I . . . I suppose that will be okay." Ms. Parker hesitated.

"Great!" Yussif cried. Then, before she could change her mind, they all ran back to the baseball diamond for the few minutes left of recess.

Vocabulary Power

con•fi•dence
[kon′fə•dəns] *n.* Firm belief or trust.

Analyze THE *Model*

1. Why do you think Ms. Parker's students want to coach her?

2. What reasons do the students give to convince Ms. Parker?

3. What reason do you think is the strongest?

Persuasive Paragraph

READING — WRITING CONNECTION

Parts of a Persuasive Paragraph

The students tried to persuade Ms. Parker to let them coach her so she could become a better baseball player. Read this persuasive paragraph written by a student named Ben. Notice the different parts of his paragraph. Also, watch for his use of vivid verbs and specific nouns.

MODEL

statement of opinion

first reason

second reason

supporting details
third reason

restatement of opinion/call to action

Some people think you can play the piano without practicing, but it can't be done. There are many things you have to learn and practice. You have to figure out how to use the right fingers on the right keys. It sounds simple, but it takes a lot of work. Then you have to learn to read music. Reading music is like learning a new language, and it's a challenge! You also have to discover how to play with feeling. This is a skill that comes only with a lot of practice. If you really want to play the piano well, you have to focus on your lessons and practice playing as much as you can.

1. What is Ben's purpose? Who do you think is his audience? Explain your answers.

2. What are Ben's reasons for practicing the piano?

3. What details does Ben give to support his reasons?

Summarize THE *Model*

Use a web like the one below to help you identify Ben's reasons and supporting details. Then use the web to write a summary of his persuasive paragraph. Remember that you should include the important reasons and leave out the details. Be sure to write what Ben's opinion is at the beginning of your summary.

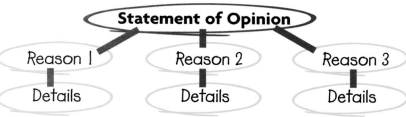

Writer's Craft

Vivid Verbs and Specific Nouns Ben used vivid verbs and specific nouns in his persuasive paragraph. They help make his writing more persuasive. When you use vivid and specific words, your reasons will be clearer for your readers. Reread Ben's paragraph. Make a list of the words he uses that are vivid and specific. Tell why you think they make his paragraph more persuasive.

CHAPTER 18
Persuasive Paragraph

Purpose and Audience

You probably have strong opinions about many things. In this chapter, you will share an opinion with your classmates by writing a persuasive paragraph.

WRITING PROMPT Write a paragraph that persuades your classmates that regular practice will help them improve a skill. You can write about any skill you choose. State your opinion. Then give reasons that support your opinion. At the end of the paragraph, encourage your classmates to take action.

Before you begin, think about your audience and purpose. For whom are you writing the paragraph? What opinion will you persuade them to share?

MODEL

Ben wanted to convince his classmates that it is important to practice in order to play the piano. He used this web to organize his ideas:

Strategies Good Writers Use

- Decide on your purpose and audience.
- Think of strong reasons that will persuade your readers to share your opinion.
- Think of details that can help explain your reasons.

Statement of Opinion: You can't become a good piano player without practicing.

Reason 3
You have to learn to play with feeling.

Reason 1
You have to learn how to place your fingers.

Reason 2
You have to learn to read music.

YOUR TURN

Choose the topic for your paragraph. Use a web to organize your ideas.

Organization and Elaboration

Follow these steps to help you organize your paragraph:

STEP 1 Get Your Audience's Attention
Write a strong statement of opinion that will make readers want to read more.

STEP 2 State Your Reasons
Write at least two reasons that support your opinion.

STEP 3 Add Details
Think of details that will make each reason clear.

STEP 4 Call Your Readers to Action
Restate your opinion. Then urge your readers to take action.

MODEL

Here is the beginning of Ben's draft of his paragraph. What is his statement of opinion? How does this statement make you want to read more?

> Some people think you can play the piano without practicing, but it can't be done. There are many things you have to learn and practice.

YOUR TURN

Write a draft of your paragraph. Use the steps above to help you get started. You can also use your chart for ideas.

Strategies Good Writers Use

- Begin by stating your opinion.
- Include at least two reasons that support your opinion.
- Use details that tell more about your reasons.

Use a computer to write your draft. You can use the delete feature to fix mistakes.

Revising

Strategies Good Writers Use

- Include details to support reasons.
- Replace common verbs with vivid verbs.
- Use specific nouns.

Organization and Elaboration

Reread your draft carefully. Think about these questions as you read:

- Did I clearly state my opinion at the beginning?
- Did I use good details to help strengthen my reasons?
- Can I change any of my verbs to more vivid verbs?
- Can I make any of my nouns more specific?

MODEL

Here is part of the draft of Ben's paragraph. Notice that he changed the order of his reasons. He also changed a verb and a noun.

> You have to ~~learn~~ figure out how to use the right fingers on the right keys. It sounds simple, but it takes a lot of work. You also have to discover how to play with feeling. Then you have to learn to read music. Reading music is like learning a new language ~~thing~~, and it's a challenge!

YOUR TURN

Revise your persuasive paragraph to include good details that support your reasons. What vivid verbs and specific nouns can you add to make your paragraph more interesting and persuasive?

Proofreading

Checking Your Language

When you proofread, you check for mistakes in grammar, spelling, punctuation, and capitalization. Correcting these mistakes can make your paragraph clearer and more persuasive.

MODEL

Here is the last part of Ben's paragraph. He has proofread to correct his punctuation mistakes. What other mistakes did he correct?

> This is a skill that comes only with a lot of ~~practise~~ practice⊙ if you really want to play the piano well, you ~~has~~ have to focus on your lessons and practice playing as much as you can.

Strategies Good Writers Use

- Check for subject-verb agreement.
- Check the dictionary if you are unsure how a word is spelled.
- Check sentences for correct punctuation and capitalization.

YOUR TURN

Proofread your revised paragraph by reading it several times. Each time you read, check for one of these kinds of mistakes:

- **grammar errors**
- **spelling errors**
- **punctuation errors**
- **capitalization errors**

Editor's Marks

ℐ	take out text
∧	add text
↻	move text
ℋ	new paragraph
≡	capitalize
/	lowercase
◯	correct spelling

Persuasive Paragraph

Publishing

Sharing Your Work

Now you can share your persuasive paragraph with an audience. Answering these questions can help you discover the best way to share your work:

1. Who is your audience? How can you share your persuasive paragraph so your audience will see or hear it?

2. Should you write your paragraph by hand or type it on the computer? Can you illustrate it with drawings or clip art?

3. Can your audience read your paragraph, or would it be better to read the paragraph to them? To give an oral presentation, use the information on page 225.

Use the rubric on page 498 to evaluate your persuasive paragraph.

USING YOUR
Handbook

Reflecting on Your Writing

 Using Your Portfolio What did you learn about your writing in this chapter? Write your answer to each question below.

1. Did your writing meet its purpose?

2. Using the rubric from your Handbook, how would you score your writing?

Add your answers and your paragraph to your portfolio. Then look through your portfolio. Find one piece of writing you like best, and write a few sentences explaining why you like it.

Giving an Oral Presentation

Ben decided the best way to share his paragraph was to present it orally. You can also give an oral presentation of your persuasive paragraph. Follow these steps:

STEP 1 Decide on your audience and purpose.

STEP 2 Use note cards to write your statement of opinion and your reasons. Number your note cards so you don't lose track of the order.

STEP 3 Use props if they will help you make your point. Charts, pictures, and objects can help you explain your reasons.

STEP 4 Speak in a loud, clear voice. Make eye contact with people in the audience, and use small hand movements to emphasize your points.

STEP 5 Take time at the end to ask for questions from your audience. Answer the questions clearly.

Strategies for Listening and Speaking

- Use details, vivid verbs, and specific nouns to describe your ideas, feelings, and experiences.
- Don't distract your listeners by moving too much or saying "um."
- If someone in the audience interrupts you, ask him or her to wait until the end of the presentation.

Unit 3
Grammar Review
CHAPTER 13

Main Verbs and
Helping Verbs
pages 166–175

Main Verbs and Helping Verbs

pages 166–167

A. **Write each sentence and underline the main verb. Then circle the helping verb.**

  1. Julia's ninth birthday is arriving tomorrow.
  2. Her parents have secretly prepared for it.
  3. Yesterday they were shopping for gifts.
  4. The kitchen is smelling like chocolate cake.
  5. Julia's parents do enjoy these birthday traditions.

More About Helping Verbs

pages 168–169

B. **Write each sentence. Underline the helping verb once. Underline the main verb twice.**

  6. Did they create these old customs?
  7. Many of their customs were learned from their parents.
  8. Julia's grandmother has always served chocolate birthday cakes.
  9. Some customs have come from her dad.
  10. How many candles will be on Julia's cake?

Contractions with *Not* pages 170–171

C. **Write each sentence using a contraction to replace the underlined words.**

  11. We <u>have not</u> been to the Memorial Day parade before.
  12. We <u>do not</u> forget the birthdays of Presidents Lincoln and Washington.
  13. <u>Is not</u> the Fourth of July a special holiday here?
  14. <u>Does not</u> your family have a picnic on Labor Day ?
  15. You <u>are not</u> allowed to vote until you are eighteen.

Verb Tenses   *pages 176–177*

A. Write whether the underlined verb shows action that is happening in the present, happened in the past, or will happen in the future.

1. Tree Musketeers <u>is</u> a group run by boys and girls in El Segundo, California.
2. The children hope their actions <u>will keep</u> Earth clean.
3. They <u>started</u> their city's first recycling program.
4. They <u>serve</u> their city in many ways.
5. Their example <u>will encourage</u> other children.

Present-Tense Verbs   *pages 178–179*

B. Choose the correct present-tense form of the verb in parentheses ( ) for each sentence.

6. Members of Tree Musketeers (plant, plants) trees.
7. Sometimes a citizen of El Segundo (ask, asks) them to plant a special tree.
8. Perhaps a family (want, wants) a tree to honor a special person.
9. Tree Musketeers (dig, digs) holes for the trees.
10. People (call, calls) these trees Memory Trees.

Subject-Verb Agreement   *pages 180–181*

C. If the verb in the sentence agrees with the subject, write *correct*. If the verb does not agree with the subject, write the verb correctly.

11. Tree Musketeers' first tree stand near Memory Row.
12. The group call it Marcie the Marvelous Tree.
13. They all feel very proud of Marcie.
14. Marcie grows taller every year.
15. Every year Marcie have more new trees nearby.

Unit 3
Grammar Review

CHAPTER 16

Past-Tense and
Future-Tense
Verbs

pages 194–203

Past-Tense and Future-Tense Verbs   *pages 194–195*

A. Write the verb or verb phrase in each sentence. Label each verb *past tense* or *future tense*.

1. Allison will run for class president.
2. She served as secretary for two years in a row.
3. She will speak to the class on Thursday afternoon.
4. She will explain her plans to the class.
5. Allison planned her speech carefully.

More About Past-Tense and Future-Tense Verbs   *pages 196–197*

B. Write the correct form of the verb, using the tense in parentheses ( ) for each sentence.

6. As president, Allison run (future) class meetings.
7. Last year, Carlos act (past) as president.
8. The class decide (past) several important issues.
9. They vote (past) for a field trip to the state capital.
10. They visit (future) the capital this spring.

Choosing the Correct Tense

pages 198–199

C. Write the correct form of the verb in parentheses ( ) for each sentence.

11. Next summer, our member of Congress (traveled, will travel) to Washington, D.C.
12. Two senators from this county (represented, will represent) our state next year.
13. Tomorrow the voting polls (opened, will open) at seven in the morning.
14. My father (studied, will study) the issues last week.
15. He (planned, will plan) all of his choices then.

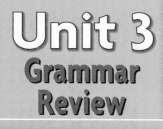
Irregular Verbs *pages 204–205*

A. Write the past tense of the verb in parentheses () to complete each sentence.

1. The City Council _____ plans for a new park. (has)
2. Community members _____ to meetings for three months. (come)
3. The planners _____ nothing for a long time. (do)
4. Then we _____ the workers beside the road. (see)
5. People _____ they were excited. (say)

More Irregular Verbs *pages 206–207*

B. Choose the correct past-tense verb in parentheses () to complete each sentence.

6. Mr. Rivel had (drawn, drew) plans for a bike path.
7. We had (ate, eaten) at Rachel's Diner.
8. Then we (rode, ridden) home safely on our bikes.
9. Some people had (gave, given) up on the project.
10. Others (wrote, written) letters to the mayor.
11. The support has (grew, grown) over the past year.
12. It has (took, taken) a big community effort.
13. Mrs. Shammil (took, taken) notes at the meeting.
14. She (grew, grown) up in our town.
15. People (ate, eaten) cookies after the meeting.

Commonly Misused Irregular Verbs *pages 208–209*

C. Choose the correct verb in parentheses () to complete each sentence.

16. Mrs. Lenz (learns, teaches) gardening to me.
17. She (rises, raises) corn and tomatoes.
18. She (lies, lays) her tools down after gardening.
19. She (lies, lays) down in the afternoon for an hour.
20. She (rises, raises) before her husband comes home.

Make a Difference

Have you ever had a good idea about how to help your community? Why not share your idea? Write a letter to someone who can help you make a difference. Follow the steps below.

Pick Your Best Idea

- Make a list of ideas that you have for helping your community.

- Read the list to three classmates. Pick the best idea on your list.

Research Your Idea

- Learn more about your topic. Check online or in recent newspapers for information.

- Gather facts to support your idea.

- Revise your idea based on your research.

Draft a Letter

- Think about the best audience for your idea.

- Write a letter describing your idea for helping your community and why it is important.

- Explain why your audience should agree with your idea.

- Exchange letters with a classmate. Ask for suggestions on how to improve it.

Publish Your Letter

- Mail your letter.

- With classmates, photocopy all the letters and staple them together in a packet.

Wanda's Roses
by Pat Brisson
REALISTIC FICTION
Wanda's care of a thorn bush in an abandoned lot brings her neighbors together as they work to improve their neighborhood.
Award-Winning Author

Recycle! A Handbook for Kids
by Gail Gibbons
NONFICTION
Hints and facts about the benefits of recycling and how to reduce the amount of garbage thrown away every day.
**Notable Social Studies Trade Book;
Outstanding Science Trade Book**

A Picture Book of Benjamin Franklin
by David A. Adler
BIOGRAPHY
Benjamin Franklin used his ideas to make a difference in his community and for his country.
Award-Winning Author

Unit 4

Grammar Pronouns and Adjectives

Writing Informative Writing: Classification

CHAPTER 19
Pronouns 234

CHAPTER 20
Subject and Object Pronouns . . 244

CHAPTER 21
Writer's Craft: Effective Sentences
Writing a Paragraph
That Compares 254

CHAPTER 22
More About Pronouns 262

CHAPTER 23
Adjectives 272

CHAPTER 24
Writing Workshop
Writing an Advantages and
    Disadvantages Essay 282

Categorize... To Do... Reply... Reply To All... Forward...

To: Michael
From: Lee
Subject: Re: Living near the mountains

Michael,
You asked what I like best about living near the mountains. The thing I like best is the view.

Pronouns

A **pronoun** is a word that takes the place of one or more nouns.

Examples:

Silvia bought a telescope. *She* looked at the sky.

There are many stars and planets. Silvia saw *them* with the telescope.

Pronouns					
I	we	you	he	she	it
they	me	us	him	her	them

Guided Practice

A. Read each pair of sentences. Find the pronoun in the second sentence. Then tell which noun in the first sentence was replaced by the pronoun.

Example: The sun is important. It is the center of the solar system. *It|sun*

1. Nine planets move in our sky. They move around the sun.
2. Earth is a planet. It moves around the sun.
3. Silvia and Todd know that the planets are different sizes. They know that some planets are quite large.
4. Venus and Mars are the closest planets to Earth. Silvia saw them without a telescope.
5. Silvia's brother looked for the smallest planet. He saw Mercury with Silvia's telescope.

Vocabulary Power

as·tron·o·my
[ə·stro′nə·mē] *n.*
The study of stars, planets, and other objects in the sky.

Independent Practice

B. Rewrite each sentence. Use a pronoun in place of the underlined word or words.

> **Example:** The children looked at the sky.
> *They*

6. "Anna can see Mercury," said Anna.
7. "Point out Mercury to Will," said Will.
8. Anna showed Will where to look.
9. Then Will could see the planet, too.
10. Later the children saw Jupiter and Mars.
11. Will saw those planets first.
12. My friends and I used to think the planets were stars.
13. Jane knows the difference between stars and planets.
14. Jane told my friends and me that stars make light and heat.
15. A planet gets light and heat from the sun.

Remember

that a pronoun is a word that takes the place of one or more nouns.

Writing Connection

Writer's Journal: Writing Idea Earth is the third planet from the sun, and Mars is the fourth. Someday, people may be able to travel to Mars. Suppose that you were the first person to walk on Mars. Using pronouns in place of some nouns, write a paragraph telling what you think walking on Mars would be like.

Singular and Plural Pronouns

Pronouns	
Singular	Plural
I	we
me	us
you	you
he, she, it	they
him, her, it	them

A **singular pronoun** takes the place of a singular noun. A **plural pronoun** takes the place of a plural noun.

Always capitalize the pronoun *I*.

The pronoun *you* is both singular and plural.

Examples:
I like learning about the planets.
I; singular

Earth is neither too hot nor too cold for us.
us; plural

Guided Practice

A. Find the pronoun in each sentence. Tell if it is a singular pronoun or a plural pronoun.

Example: One night I saw Mars.
I; singular

1. Emily, what do you know about astronomy? Have you ever seen Mars?
2. Mars looks like a red star, but it does not twinkle.
3. We are learning about the planets in school.
4. The class made a chart about them.
5. Uncle James gave me a telescope for looking at the planets.

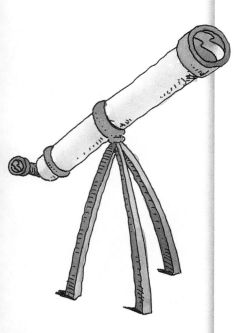

Independent Practice

B. Write a pronoun to take the place of the underlined word or words in each sentence. Then write *S* if the pronoun is singular or *P* if the pronoun is plural.

> **Example:** Mr. Hernandez taught us about the planets.
> *He; S*

6. My classmates and I made a model of our solar system.
7. The model showed the sun and the planets.
8. Nancy wanted to make the model of Jupiter.
9. Jupiter is the biggest planet, so Mark helped Nancy.
10. Ben made the model of Saturn, and I helped Ben.
11. Ben and I did not know how to make Saturn's rings.
12. We worked on the rings for a long time.
13. Finally, the rings were finished.
14. "That Saturn looks great!" Mr. Hernandez told Ben and me.
15. "Nancy and Mark, did Nancy and Mark have fun?" asked the teacher.

Remember that a singular pronoun takes the place of a singular noun. A plural pronoun takes the place of a plural noun.

Writing Connection

Real-Life Writing: Conversation Suppose you could travel through the solar system on a space shuttle. With a partner, discuss and then write about living conditions inside the shuttle. Pay attention to each other's statements, checking to make sure that singular and plural pronouns are used correctly.

Antecedent	Pronoun
Kelly	she, her
Andy	he, him
star	it
stars	they, them
Kelly and Andy	they, them
children	they, them
Kelly and I	we, us

USAGE AND MECHANICS

Pronoun-Antecedent Agreement

The **antecedent** of a pronoun is the noun or nouns the pronoun replaces.

Example:
The **stars** were bright, and **they** were far away.
(*Stars* is the antecedent of *they*.)

You have learned that a singular pronoun replaces a singular noun, and a plural pronoun replaces a plural noun. This is one part of pronoun-antecedent agreement. A pronoun must agree with its antecedent in both number and gender.

Guided Practice

A. Read each pair of sentences. Find the antecedent of each underlined pronoun.

Example: No one knows the exact number of stars. There are too many of <u>them</u> to count.
stars

1. Kelly saw lights in the sky.
   <u>She</u> knew they were stars.
2. Stars look tiny in the night sky.
   However, <u>they</u> are really huge.
3. The sun is a star.
   <u>It</u> is the nearest star to Earth.
4. The sun warms and lights Earth.
   <u>It</u> is the source of life on our planet.
5. Kelly and I wore special glasses to view the solar eclipse.
   <u>It</u> made Earth go dark.

Independent Practice

B. Read each pair of sentences. Write the antecedent of each underlined pronoun.

Example: A few stars have names. <u>They</u> are the brightest stars that we see from Earth.   *stars*

6. Kelly saw what looked like a falling star.
   Andy told <u>her</u> it was a meteor.
7. Andy and I have seen meteors before.
   <u>We</u> learned about <u>them</u> in class.
8. Meteors are pieces of rock or metal.
   <u>They</u> burn up as <u>they</u> travel through the air.
9. Sailors can use the North Star as a guide.
   <u>It</u> tells <u>them</u> which direction is north.
10. Mom asked, "Do stars move?"
    Andy and Kelly told <u>her</u> that <u>they</u> do.
11. Antares and Sirius are two stars.
    Andy wanted to learn about <u>them</u>.
12. The librarian gave Andy and Kelly a book.
    <u>They</u> thanked <u>her</u> for the help.
13. Antares is a red supergiant star.
    <u>It</u> is more than 300 times as large as the sun.
14. Kelly read about Sirius.
    <u>She</u> found out that <u>it</u> is really a double star.
15. The sun is a medium-size star.
    <u>It</u> is part of the Milky Way.

Remember that the antecedent of a pronoun is the noun or nouns the pronoun replaces.

Writing Connection

Writer's Craft: Summarize Write ten sentences about Earth. Use a science book to help you. Summarize the characteristics of the planet. Be sure the pronouns you use agree with their antecedents.

Extra Practice

A. Write the pronouns in each sentence.

pages 234–235

1. Marcie's parents gave her a telescope.
2. It was something she had always wanted.
3. Marcie called Angel and told him about it.
4. He said, "Now you can see Neptune and Uranus."
5. She said, "I could never see them before."

B. Write the pronoun that can take the place of the underlined noun or nouns. *pages 236–237*

6. <u>Mercury and Venus</u> are closest to the sun.
7. You do not need a telescope to see <u>Venus and Mars</u>.
8. You do not need <u>a telescope</u> to see Saturn or Jupiter either.
9. <u>Saturn and Jupiter</u> are both very big planets.
10. <u>Jupiter</u> is the largest planet in our solar system.

C. Write the antecedent for each underlined pronoun. *pages 238–239*

11. Look at the moon every night and see how <u>it</u> changes.
12. The moon has eight phases, and you can see <u>them</u> all.
13. Look at a calendar. <u>It</u> tells when each phase begins.
14. Marcie and Kevin looked at the moon. <u>They</u> realized <u>it</u> was a full moon.
15. Marcie saw the moon an hour later, and <u>she</u> thought <u>it</u> had moved.

For more activities with pronouns, visit *The Learning Site:*

www.harcourtschool.com

D. Write a pronoun in place of each noun in parentheses (). Use a pronoun that agrees in number and gender with the antecedent.

pages 238–239

16. Scientists who study the planets in astronomy have learned much about (the planets).

17. The planet farthest from the sun is Pluto. People need telescopes to see (Pluto).

18. The planet closest to the sun is Mercury. (Mercury) moves around the sun faster than any other planet.

19. The other planets are farther from the sun. (The other planets) have farther to travel around the sun than Mercury does.

20. Mercury goes around the sun in 88 Earth-days. Earth takes 365 Earth-days to travel around (the sun).

Writing Connection

Technology Suppose you could live on another planet. Which planet would you choose? Use an electronic encyclopedia or another online reference work to find out about that planet. Then write several sentences supporting your choice. Check your sentences, and if possible, replace some nouns with pronouns.

Chapter Review

Read the passage. Some words are missing. Choose the pronoun to fit in each blank space, and mark the letter for your answer.

Demarcus asked us to study the moon with him. __(1)__ looked at __(2)__ every night at the same time. Every night we drew a picture to show what __(3)__ looked like. After a few weeks, Demarcus got all the pictures together. __(4)__ asked his older sister to put __(5)__ in a book. __(6)__ made a flip book. Demarcus thanked __(7)__ for __(8)__ .

TIP Be careful to match your answer choices to the numbers in the paragraph.

1 A She
  B They
  C We
  D You

2 F him
  G it
  H them
  J he

3 A they
  B it
  C he
  D she

4 F They
  G It
  H He
  J She

5 A she
  B he
  C them
  D they

6 F It
  G She
  H Her
  J Him

7 A I
  B they
  C her
  D it

8 F he
  G I
  H they
  J it

For additional test preparations, visit *The Learning Site:* **www.harcourtschool.com**

Parts of a Book

Books have special parts that tell how to use them.

The Front of the Book

- The title page tells the name of the book.

- The copyright page tells when the book was published.

- The table of contents tells the name of each chapter or section and the page on which it begins.

The Back of the Book

- The glossary lists important words in alphabetical order and tells you their meanings.

- The index tells what page or pages in the book to find a certain topic.

- The bibliography tells the names of other books on the same subject.

YOUR TURN

WORK WITH A PARTNER Choose a book that has all the features mentioned above. Then follow the numbered directions.

1. **Find the table of contents. Tell your partner the title of the first chapter in the book.**

2. **Tell your partner the page number on which the chapter begins.**

3. **Go to the glossary. Read to your partner the first word and its definition.**

4. **Find the last topic listed in the index. Go to the page or pages cited and see what the book says about the topic.**

TIP
Nonfiction books about history or science will probably include most of these parts.

Subject Pronouns	
I	we
you	you
he, she, it	they

Subject Pronouns

A subject pronoun takes the place of one or more nouns in the subject of a sentence.

Remember that the subject is the part of the sentence that names someone or something. Always capitalize the pronoun *I*.

Examples:

I love the spring.

She felt the cold air outside.

You go camping every summer.

They like to splash through the puddles.

Guided Practice

A. Name the subject pronoun in each sentence.

Example: They know what the temperature is.
They

1. I see a thermometer on the wall.
2. It is a tool that measures temperature.
3. It has numbers along the side.
4. They tell what the exact temperature is.
5. He owns nine thermometers.
6. They are all different sizes.
7. We used a thermometer to measure water temperature.
8. She was sick and needed to use a thermometer.
9. You can borrow a thermometer.
10. It is very useful.

Vocabulary Power

Fahr·en·heit
[far′ən·hīt′] scale: *n.*
A temperature scale showing 32 degrees at the freezing point of water and 212 degrees at the boiling point of water.

Independent Practice

B. Write the subject pronoun in each sentence.

Example: You are learning about weather.
You

11. You can feel the temperature.
12. It can be measured in degrees Fahrenheit.
13. We know that winter is cold in some parts of the country.
14. They have warmer winters in the South.
15. He asked why the temperature changes.
16. She talked about how the sun's rays hit Earth.
17. They don't seem as hot in the winter.
18. I drew a picture of the sun and Earth.
19. We understand temperature better now.
20. To learn more, you could read a book about temperature.

Remember
that a subject pronoun takes the place of one or more nouns in the subject of a sentence.

Writing Connection

Writer's Journal

Writer's Journal: Thinking About the Weather Choose a season, and write three sentences telling what you like about it. Record your ideas about why you like these things. Try to express your thoughts by using at least three subject pronouns in your sentences.

Object Pronouns	
me	us
you	you
him, her, it	them

Object Pronouns

An **object pronoun** follows an action verb or a word such as *about, around, at, for, from, near, of, to,* or *with.*

Object pronouns are usually in the predicate of a sentence.

Examples:

The wind hit **us** hard.

The summer was too hot for **him**.

Nate told **her** about the Fahrenheit scale.

A fan cooled **me**.

Guided Practice

A. Name the object pronoun in each sentence.

Example: The teacher taught us about the weather.
us

1. Mr. Rivera told me about the air.
2. A blanket of air covers us.
3. The sun heats it.
4. The sun keeps us warm.
5. Wind is air that blows around you.
6. Wind can chill you.
7. The teacher told her about the water in air.
8. Mr. Rivera told him that water high up in the air forms clouds.
9. A weather forecaster watches the clouds and studies them.
10. Leah will tell you about the weather.

Independent Practice

B. Write the object pronoun in each sentence.

Example: Molly showed them a snowball.
them

11. The snowstorm caught us by surprise.
12. Paco and Vicki were not expecting it.
13. The sidewalks had a thick layer of snow on them.
14. Luis handed him a snow shovel.
15. The snow made us cold and wet.
16. Kim's father made them some hot chocolate.
17. The hills had snow on top of them.
18. Tom wanted to go sledding with her.
19. Tommeka made a snowman with me.
20. I hope the sun doesn't melt it.

Remember

that object pronouns follow action verbs and words such as *about, around, at, for, from, near, of, to,* and *with.*

Writing Connection

Writer's Craft: Clear Pronouns Think about your favorite season. Using the correct forms of pronouns, record your thoughts about what you and your friends do during that season.

USAGE AND MECHANICS

Using *I* and *Me*

The word *I* is a **subject pronoun**. The word *me* is an **object pronoun**.

Remember that *I* is used in the subject of a sentence. The word *I* is always capitalized. The word *me* is used in the predicate of a sentence.

Examples:

I am delighted by the weather.

The sun feels good to **me**.

When you talk about yourself and another person, always name the other person first.

Examples:

Tasha and I raked the leaves.

Dad asked Kevin and **me** to shovel the snow.

Guided Practice

A. Use *I* or *me* to complete each sentence.

Example: _____ saw a rainbow today. *I*

1. _____ drink water to stay cool.
2. The sun shines down on Julie and _____.
3. _____ drink a lot of water in the summer.
4. The sun's rays can give _____ a bad sunburn.
5. _____ shiver with cold in the winter.
6. Wearing layers of clothing keeps _____ warm.
7. Chad and _____ saw the storm clouds.
8. _____ feel chilly when I get wet.
9. Hot drinks make _____ feel warm.
10. Pedro and _____ use an umbrella in the rain.

Independent Practice

B. Choose the correct words in parentheses ( ) to complete each sentence. Write each completed sentence.

> **Example:** (Sis and I, Sis and me) like rainy days.
> *Sis and I like rainy days.*

11. The newspaper told (Ann and I, Ann and me) what weather was coming.
12. (Mom and I, Mom and me) expected snow.
13. (I, Me) thought the temperature was 32 degrees Fahrenheit.
14. The fog may make (me and you, you and me) late.
15. (The animals and I, The animals and me) waited for the rain to stop.
16. (My sister and I, I and my sister) play baseball in the summer.
17. The Smiths took (me, I) to the beach.
18. The heat made (I, me) sleepy.
19. (My friends and me, My friends and I) like to swim.
20. (I, Me) am hungry after swimming.

Remember
that *I* is a subject pronoun and *me* is an object pronoun. When you talk about yourself and another person, always name the other person first.

Writing Connection

Art Draw a picture of yourself and a friend outside enjoying the weather. Write a caption that describes the weather and tells what you and your friend are doing. Be sure to use *I* and *me* correctly in your caption.

Remember

that a subject
pronoun takes
the place of one
or more nouns in
the subject of a
sentence. An
object pronoun
follows an action
verb or a word
such as *about,
around, at, for,
from, near, of, to,*
or *with.*

For more activities
with subject
and object
pronouns, visit
The Learning Site:
www.harcourtschool.com

250

Extra Practice

A. Write each sentence, using the correct pronoun. *pages 244–247*

Example: The raindrops fell on (them, they).
The raindrops fell on them.

1. (I, Me) had never been in a big storm.
2. The storm shook (she, her) and the boat.
3. (He, Him) thinks it is safer to be indoors.
4. The rain soaked (we, us) to the skin.
5. (They, Them) cleaned up the mess from the storm.

B. Write *subject pronoun* or *object pronoun* to name the underlined word in each sentence. *pages 244–247*

Example: <u>We</u> shook the water from our shoes.
subject pronoun

6. <u>He</u> found the umbrella.
7. The road was too muddy for <u>us</u>.
8. <u>You</u> ran to the house to stay dry.
9. <u>She</u> found a lost cat during the storm.
10. Marvin brought raincoats for <u>them</u>.

C. Rewrite each sentence. Replace the underlined words with a pronoun. *pages 244–247*

Example: <u>Terry and Jeff</u> saw a flash in the sky.
They saw a flash in the sky.

11. The lightning scared <u>Yoko and Pat</u>.
12. <u>The car</u> got stuck in the flood.
13. There were extra coats for <u>Aldo and me</u>.
14. <u>Rishi and I</u> watched the wind bend the trees.
15. <u>Seth</u> helped Nia clean off the mud.

D. Write the object pronoun in each sentence.

pages 246–247

Example: Juan told us that the rain would end soon.
us

16. The teacher told him about fog.
17. The fog made them late to school.
18. Sometimes the fog scares her.
19. Morning fog can make you cold.
20. It's hard to see me through thick fog.

E. Rewrite each sentence to correct the errors.

pages 244–249

21. Scientists tell we the temperature in degrees Fahrenheit.
22. Them study the weather every day.
23. Now me can prepare.
24. Me and Tisha wore coats today.
25. The boots are for Rudy and I, and the scarf is for Eva.

Remember that *I* is a subject pronoun and *me* is an object pronoun. When you talk about yourself and another person, always name the other person first.

DID YOU KNOW? In very powerful storms called hurricanes, winds sometimes blow at speeds of 150 miles per hour.

Writing Connection

Real-Life Writing: Make a List With some classmates, describe today's weather. Then make a list to record what you like or dislike about it. Include subject and object pronouns in your list.

Chapter Review

Read the paragraph and choose the word that belongs in each space. Write the letter for your answer.

__(1)__ can see the changes that autumn brings to our family. Father knows that the cool air will bring __(2)__ vegetables ready for picking. __(3)__ must gather all the crops before the winter snows. __(4)__ miss summer's hot, dry days. I am sorry to say good-bye to __(5)__ , but autumn must come. __(6)__ puts a chill in the air. Mother says the autumn winds make __(7)__ feel good. __(8)__ just make me want to play football.

TIP Choose the answer you think is correct. Then read the sentence with your answer in place to make sure it is correct.

1 A You
   B Them
   C Her
   D Me

2 F he
   G I
   H him
   J she

3 A Her
   B He
   C Me
   D Them

4 F Them
   G Him
   H I
   J Her

5 A them
   B she
   C I
   D he

6 F It
   G Her
   H Them
   J Me

7 A she
   B they
   C I
   D her

8 F Me
   G They
   H Them
   J Him

For additional test preparation, visit *The Learning Site:*
www.harcourtschool.com

Exploring Websites

Before Going Online

• Think of a question you have about a topic.

• Choose words in your question that are important. These words will become the key words for your search.

While Online

1. Use a search engine.
2. In the search box, type your key words. You can use the words *and* or *or* between key words. Press **Enter**.
3. Look at the names of the Websites that are listed. Click on the site that seems to describe the information you want.
4. Read what is at the Website.
5. Compare the information you found on the Web with information from another source, such as an encyclopedia, to make sure it is correct.
6. Print any information that interests you or that may be useful. Then write the Web address that is in the address box. You may want to return to this Website again.

YOUR TURN

You can use the Internet to find information about weather. First, think of a question to ask about weather. Then, follow the directions above to start your Web search. When you are finished, trade Website addresses with your classmates. When you have time, visit the sites they found.

Writer's Craft

Effective Sentences

You know that you give information when you explain something or give directions. You might also compare things, or tell how they are alike.

Read these verses from the book *A Log's Life*.

LITERATURE MODEL

A thunderous crack startles the porcupine
    sleeping nearby.
  The tall oak begins to topple.
    Squirrels feel the trembling,
      and they scramble out of their hole.

One strong gust of blustery wind
  tears the great oak's roots from the ground.
    The tree crashes down, shaking the forest
      floor.
    Branches break. Limbs splinter. Leaves
      scatter.

—from *A Log's Life*
by Wendy Pfeffer

Analyze THE Model

1. How are the effects of lightning and wind alike?

2. Why do you think the writer uses some long sentences and some short ones?

3. Can you find a compound sentence in the first verse? How do you know it is compound?

Using Effective Sentences

When you use effective sentences, you give information in a clear and interesting way. Study the chart on the next page.

Vocabulary Power

blus•ter•y
[blus′tər•y] *adj.*
Noisy; forceful.

Strategies for Writing Effective Sentences

How to Use the Strategies

Write a variety of sentences.

- Don't make all your sentences alike. Use long sentences and short sentences. Use different kinds of sentences — statements, questions, exclamations.

Combine sentences.

- Look for places where you can use compound subjects and compound predicates. Combine simple sentences to write compound sentences.

YOUR TURN

ANALYZE INFORMATIVE WRITING **Work with one or two classmates. Read several paragraphs from your science textbook or from a magazine article on a science topic. Look at the kinds of sentences the writer uses. Talk with your group about which sentences are most effective.**

Answer these questions:

1. What is the writer's subject?
2. What is the writer's purpose?
3. What different kinds of sentences does the writer use?
4. Can you find sentences in which the writer compares things or tells how different things are alike?

Identifying Sentence Variety

A. Read each pair of sentences. If both sentences are the same kind, write *Same* on your paper. If the sentences are a different kind, write *Different* on your paper.

1. What a big oak tree!
   It is so tall!
2. What kind of tree is this?
   It has needles instead of leaves.
3. Look at this leaf.
   On which tree did it grow?
4. I saw a chestnut, but I did not see a walnut.
   There are twigs and branches lying on the ground.
5. The trunk is thick.
   Its bark is peeling because many forest animals have used it to sharpen their claws.

B. Read the two passages. One passage has a variety of sentences. The other passage does not. On your paper, tell which passage you think has more effective sentences. Then tell why you think so.

1. Some dinosaurs ate meat. Some dinosaurs ate plants. Some dinosaurs ate both meat and plants. Some dinosaurs probably ate the eggs of other dinosaurs.
2. How big were dinosaurs? You probably know that some dinosaurs were very large. Other types of dinosaurs were small. Some of them may have been smaller than you are!

Combining Sentences

C. Read each pair of sentences. Combine the two sentences into one sentence. Write the new sentence on your paper.

1. Birds make nests. Birds lay eggs.
2. Lightning flashed. Thunder boomed.
3. Fish live in this pond. Turtles live in this pond.
4. Frogs hop. Snakes slither on the ground.
5. Daffodils bloom in spring. Tulips bloom in spring.

D. Read the paragraph. Then revise it, using a variety of sentences without changing the meaning of the paragraph. Write a final draft of the paragraph.

Winter is fun. Lakes are frozen. We ice skate. Our noses get cold. Spring is nice. It is warm. Gardens grow. We plant flowers. Summer is hot. The sun shines brightly. We swim in the lake.

Writing AND Thinking

Writer's Journal

Write to Record Reflections Reread some pages in your Writer's Journal. Think about the sentences you used. Are they mostly short, or are there longer sentences, too? How else are the sentences alike or different? Now write a paragraph in your Writer's Journal. Tell how you might write more effective sentences in the future.

Paragraph That Compares

You can compare the lightning and the wind in *A Log's Life* by telling how they are alike. They both shake the tree and make it fall down. They both are powerful forces of nature.

Jake wrote a paragraph to share with his classmates. He wanted to compare horses and cows. Read the paragraph that Jake wrote. Look at the different kinds of sentences he used.

MODEL

simple sentences

compound sentence

question

Horses and cows are a lot alike. They are both raised on either farms or ranches. Both are quite large. Also, they both like to eat grass. Horses and cows are important to humans, too. We get milk from cows, and we can ride horses. Can you think of other ways they are alike?

Analyze THE *Model*

1. What is Jake's purpose for writing this paragraph?

2. What comparisons does Jake make in the paragraph?

3. Has Jake written effective sentences? Explain your answer.

WRITING PROMPT Think of two different things in nature that you can compare because they are alike in some ways. For example, you might compare a frog and a toad, or a butterfly and a bird. Write a paragraph for your teacher that compares the two things. Tell how they are alike. Use effective sentences to make your paragraph interesting to read.

STUDY THE PROMPT Ask yourself these questions.

1. Who is your audience?
2. What is your purpose for writing?
3. What two things will you compare?
4. What writing form will you use?

Prewriting and Drafting

Plan Your Paragraph Choose two things that you want to compare. Create a chart like this one to help you decide which common traits you will include in your paragraph.

Traits	First Subject	Second Subject
Choose traits that will be common to both subjects, such as color, feel, age, or size.	Write a describing word for each trait.	Write a describing word for each trait.

Which traits have describing words that are alike? Describe those traits in your paragraph.

USING YOUR
Handbook

Use the Writer's Thesaurus to find words that will help you explain how the subjects are alike.

Editing

Reread the draft of your paragraph that compares. Use this checklist to help you revise it.

☑ Do you give your reader enough information about the things you are comparing?

☑ Will your reader understand how the two things are alike?

☑ Are your sentences all the same, or have you used different types?

☑ Can you combine sentences to make them more effective?

Use this checklist as you proofread your paragraph.

☑ I have begun my sentences with capital letters.

☑ I have used the correct end marks for each type of sentence.

☑ I have used singular and plural pronouns correctly.

☑ I have used a dictionary to check my spelling.

Sharing and Reflecting

Writer's Journal

Make a final copy of your paragraph that compares. Then share it with a partner. Tell what you like best about your partner's paragraph. Talk about writing effective sentences. Write your reflections in your Writer's Journal.

Comparing Writing and Speaking

Have you ever made a speech? In some ways, making a speech is like writing. Look at the diagram to see how they are alike.

You plan what you will write or say.

You evaluate and revise before writing your final draft or giving your speech.

How Writing and Making a Speech Are Alike

You think about your purpose and your audience.

You should use effective sentences.

YOUR TURN

Work with a group of three classmates to practice making speeches. Follow these steps:

STEP 1 With your group, brainstorm a list of subjects for short speeches.

STEP 2 Choose a subject from the list. Plan a short speech to give information on that subject.

STEP 3 Practice your speeches. Help each other revise the speeches to use more effective sentences.

STEP 4 Give your speech to the group.

STEP 5 Listen to your classmates' speeches. Evaluate the speeches as well as the information.

Strategies for Listening and Speaking

- When you speak to inform, use a rate and volume that fits your audience and purpose.
- Describe ideas clearly.
- When you listen, think about and evaluate what the speaker is saying.
- When you speak to share ideas about classmates' speeches, be courteous and make comments that will be helpful.

Possessive Pronouns

A **possessive pronoun** shows ownership.

You know that a pronoun takes the place of a noun. A possessive pronoun takes the place of a possessive noun. Some possessive pronouns are *my*, *your*, *his*, *her*, *its*, *our*, and *their*.

The noun or pronoun that a possessive pronoun refers to is called its **antecedent**. The antecedents are circled in the sentences below.

Examples:

(Deer) make **their** home in the forest.

(I) clicked **my** camera and scared a deer.

A (deer) stopped eating and raised **its** head.

Vocabulary Power

e•col•o•gy
(i•kol′ə•jē) *n.*
The relationship of plants and animals to each other and their surroundings.

Guided Practice

A. Read each sentence. Name the possessive pronoun and its antecedent.

Example: I saw a deer in my backyard.
my|I

1. If you see a male deer, you will probably notice his antlers.
2. I read in my book that antlers are horns.
3. A male deer uses his antlers for fighting.
4. A female deer is a doe, and her baby is a fawn.
5. The fawns I saw have white fur on their tails.

Independent Practice

B. Write the possessive pronoun in each sentence.

> **Example:** I read in my book about the ecology of the forest.
>
> *my*

6. I hike in the forest during my vacation.
7. I see forest animals in their natural habitats.
8. A squirrel uses its sharp teeth to break a nutshell.
9. Squirrels use their claws to hold on to tree branches.
10. A mother squirrel makes a nest for her young.
11. Our footsteps scare the squirrel away.
12. She will probably run to one of her other nests.
13. For their safety, squirrels usually have more than one nest.
14. Jon wants a squirrel for his pet.
15. Keeping a squirrel as your pet is not a good idea.

Writing Connection

Art What kinds of animals do you see where you live? Draw a picture of these animals and their surroundings. Write several sentences about your picture that tell what the animals are doing. Use possessive pronouns in your sentences.

More Possessive Pronouns

Some possessive pronouns can stand alone.

These possessive pronouns take the place of other possessive pronouns and the things being owned. They are *mine, yours, his, hers, ours,* and *theirs.*

Notice how the possessive pronouns *hers* and *his* stand alone in the sentences below. *His* can stand alone or be used with a noun.

Examples:
That coat is <u>her coat</u>. That coat is **hers**.

That book is <u>his book</u>. That book is **his**.

Guided Practice

A. Name the possessive pronoun in each sentence.

Example: The blue suitcase is mine. *mine*

1. The book about South America is hers.
2. Ours is the guide who knows the most about the ecology of the rain forest.
3. The video camera is his.
4. Those three tickets are ours.
5. The eggs in the macaws' nest are theirs.
6. That toucan thinks the passion fruit is his.
7. The monkeys think the bananas are theirs.
8. That monkey's scream sounds a lot like yours.
9. That parrot looks a lot like ours.
10. I wish that toucan could be mine.

Independent Practice

B. Read the sentence pairs. Write the possessive pronoun that belongs in each space.

> **Example:** We took pictures of the animals in the rain forest.
> Those pictures are _____.   *ours*

11. A male orangutan collects some fruit.
The fruit is _____.

12. A mother orangutan feeds a baby orangutan.
The baby is _____.

13. Orangutans find large leaves and use them as umbrellas.
The leaves are _____.

14. I took a photograph of an orangutan that I saw in a tree.
The photograph is _____.

15. Maybe you will visit the rain forest someday.
I will compare my photographs with _____.

Remember that some possessive pronouns can stand alone. They are *mine, yours, his, hers, ours,* and *theirs.*

DID YOU KNOW?
At least half of Earth's plants and animals live in tropical rain forests.

Writing Connection

Writer's Craft: Clear Pronouns Think of three different animals. Make a chart that tells where the animals live, what they look like, and what they eat. Use the information on your chart to write a paragraph that tells how the animals are alike and how they are different. Use correct possessive pronouns in your paragraph.

USAGE AND MECHANICS

Contractions with Pronouns

A **contraction** can sometimes be formed by joining a pronoun and a verb.

Remember that a contraction is a short way to write two words. Many contractions are made by joining a pronoun and a verb. In a contraction, one or more letters are left out, and an apostrophe (') takes the place of the missing letters.

Examples		
I am = I'm	I would = I'd	I have = I've
it is = it's	he would = he'd	she has = she's
you are = you're	you will = you'll	you have = you've
we are = we're	they will = they'll	they have = they've

Guided Practice

A. Name the pronoun and the verb that were used to make each contraction.

Example: you'll   *you will*

1. I'll
2. they're
3. we've
4. she's
5. you're

6. we'd
7. we'll
8. they've
9. she'd
10. I'm

Independent Practice

B. Find the contraction or contractions in each sentence. Write the words that were used to make each contraction.

Example: When my brother goes to the desert, he'll be searching for bugs.
he will

11. We're hoping to see beetles in the desert.
12. They're hard to find during the day.
13. My sister thinks we'll find them with her help.
14. She'll follow the hints she found in a book about desert insects.
15. If you cut open a cactus, you'll see it's full of beetles.
16. They'll scurry away on their long legs.
17. When the sun goes down, you'll see beetles come out for food.
18. I've heard that desert insects have special ways to find water.
19. If they lived in the rain forest, they'd find water more easily.
20. I'd like to know more about desert insects and the ecology of the desert.

Remember that a contraction can sometimes be formed by joining a pronoun and a verb. An apostrophe takes the place of the missing letters.

Writing Connection

Science Suppose that you and your class are on a nature hike in the woods. Write a paragraph describing what you and your friends see and do. Use at least four contractions formed from pronouns and verbs in your paragraph.

Remember

that a possessive pronoun shows ownership and takes the place of a possessive noun. Some possessive pronouns can stand alone.

For more activities on pronouns, visit *The Learning Site:*

www.harcourtschool.com

Extra Practice

A. Rewrite each sentence using a possessive pronoun. *pages 262–263*

Example: Maya enjoys Maya's tropical fish tank.
*Maya enjoys **her** tropical fish tank.*

1. Many tropical fish make fish's homes in coral reefs.
2. Maya loved Maya's first trip to a coral reef.
3. She learned that the coral reef's rocks are formed by tiny animals.
4. Maya used Maya's goggles underwater to look at the animals.
5. Uncle Ray used Uncle Ray's underwater camera to take pictures.

B. Read each sentence. Write the possessive pronoun that belongs in each space.
pages 264–265

Example: Uncle Ray bought the camera, so it is _____.
his

6. These pictures of the reef are _____ because I took them.
7. Maya took the pictures, so they are _____.
8. If we show our pictures to Maya and Uncle Ray, they will show us _____.
9. Whose pictures came out better, theirs or _____?
10. If you take pictures of a coral reef, maybe you will like _____ better than mine.

C. Find the contraction in each sentence. Write the two words that were used to make the contraction. *pages 266–267*

Example: I'm looking forward to our vacation.   *I am*

11. We're visiting Hawaii for the second time.
12. We'll visit a reef in a glass-bottom boat.
13. I'd like to see a clown fish in the reef.
14. Angelfish can swim through narrow spaces because they're very thin.
15. A coral reef is colorful because it's full of different plants and animals.

D. Write a contraction for each underlined word pair. *pages 266–267*

16. <u>You would</u> be amazed to see a desert in springtime.
17. Many plants are blooming, so <u>it is</u> very colorful.
18. Because barrel cacti have large stems to store water, <u>they will</u> survive in the desert.
19. <u>I am</u> curious about some plants called living rocks.
20. <u>I would</u> like to take pictures of these plants.

Remember that a contraction can be made from a pronoun and a verb. Use an apostrophe in place of the missing letters.

Writing Connection

Technology Make up a rhyme about a plant or an animal. Use possessive pronouns and contractions in your rhyme. Type your rhyme on a computer. Use word-processing software to see how your rhyme looks in different type fonts. Choose the font you like best to print your rhyme.

mine
their
her
yours
its
his

Chapter Review

Read the passage and choose the word that belongs in each space. Write the letter for your answer.

---

    (1) science class studied rivers, lakes, and ponds. (2) spent two weeks finding out about animals and plants. On (3) last day, we went on a field trip to a pond.

    Did you know that frogs live underwater as larvae? When they become adults, (4) live out of water. Look for lily pads, and (5) probably see a frog or two! We saw something else near the lily pad. A snapping turtle raised (6) head out of the water!

TIP Remember to read all the answers before making your choice.

1 A It's
  B They're
  C Mine
  D My

2 F My
  G Its
  H Her
  J We

3 A our
  B mine
  C ours
  D yours

4 F they've
  G they'll
  H she'll
  J it

5 A they'll
  B you'll
  C we're
  D their

6 F my
  G their
  H its
  J your

For additional test preparation, visit *The Learning Site:*
www.harcourtschool.com

Using Context Clues

You may find some unfamiliar words as you read. You can use context clues to help you figure out what these new words mean. When you read the words and sentences that are near a new word, you can often find context clues.

Different Kinds of Context Clues

- synonyms and antonyms

- the way the new word is used in the sentence

- other sentences that define or explain the new word

- pictures or captions

In the example below, an unfamiliar word is circled. The context clues are underlined.

Example:

In some northern parts of the United States, there are dense forests. These forests are thick with spruce, pine, and other trees. There is very little room between the trees. (The word *dense* can mean "thick." A dense forest is crowded with trees.)

YOUR TURN

Find a section in your science book that tells about an animal or plant that you want to know more about. Look at one or two paragraphs. Write down any words that are unfamiliar to you. Then go back and read the paragraphs carefully, looking for context clues. List any clues you find, and write what you think the unfamiliar words mean. Then use a dictionary to check your work.

TIP When you come across an unfamiliar word, ask yourself what part this word plays in the sentence. Is it a noun? a verb? the subject? the predicate?

Adjectives

An adjective is a word that describes a noun.

Remember that a noun names a person, a place, an animal, or a thing. An adjective tells more about a noun. An adjective can come before the noun it describes. It can also follow a verb such as *is* or *seems*.

Examples:

Wolves often live in **snowy** places.

They have **thick** hair.

The leader of the pack is **smart**.

Guided Practice

A. Name the adjective that describes the underlined noun in each sentence.

Example: The red <u>fox</u> is related to the wolf.
red

1. Wolves have furry <u>coats</u>.
2. They can make a lot of different <u>sounds</u>.
3. Sometimes they make a sad <u>howl</u>.
4. At times they make a quiet <u>woof</u>.
5. Sometimes <u>wolves</u> are shy.
6. A wolf may have gray <u>fur</u>.
7. Its <u>jaws</u> seem strong.
8. Wolves sometimes eat small <u>animals</u>.
9. Hungry <u>wolves</u> hunt in packs.
10. They are good <u>hunters</u>.

Independent Practice

Remember

that an **adjective** describes a noun. An adjective can come before the noun or after a verb such as *is* or *seems*.

B. Read the sentences below. Then write the adjective in each sentence.

> **Example:** Wolves are social animals.
> *social*

11. A wolf is a canine animal.

12. Wolves have big paws.

13. A wolf may have black fur.

14. It may even have white fur.

15. Sometimes wolves make a loud bark.

16. They have long tails.

17. Wolves are not fierce all the time.

18. Sometimes, wolves seem peaceful.

19. A wolf is a pack animal.

20. Young wolves follow the leader of the pack.

Writing Connection

Writer's Craft: Vivid Adjectives If you could be any animal, what would you be? Think about an animal you might like to be. Write a list of adjectives that describe this animal. Choose three of those adjectives, and use them in sentences that tell why you would like to be this animal.

Adjectives for *How Many*

Some adjectives tell *how many*.

You know that an adjective describes a noun. The adjectives in the following sentences tell *how many*.

Examples:

Two coyotes hunt together.

They may eat **some** berries.

All coyotes are canine animals.

Not all adjectives that tell *how many* give an exact number.

Guided Practice

A. Name the adjective in each sentence that describes the underlined noun.

Example: Most <u>coyotes</u> have bushy tails.
Most

1. Today there are coyotes in many <u>parts</u> of the United States.
2. Most <u>coyotes</u> live in the West.
3. They usually live six <u>years</u>.
4. Some <u>coyotes</u> live in the mountains.
5. Many <u>coyotes</u> live in the desert.
6. Coyotes can weigh thirty <u>pounds</u>.
7. Many <u>coyotes</u> hunt alone.
8. Coyotes eat several <u>foods</u>.
9. Few <u>coyotes</u> come near humans.
10. Coyotes can run more than twenty <u>miles</u> an hour.

Independent Practice

B. Read each sentence. Write the adjective that tells *how many* and the noun it describes.

> **Example:** All coyotes are nocturnal.
> *All|coyotes*

11. A coyote can have six pups.

12. A pup's eyes open after two weeks.

13. Most female coyotes are good mothers.

14. Few coyotes live in groups.

15. Grown pups stay within ten miles of their parents.

16. Coyotes have several types of barks.

17. They can make many sounds.

18. Their barks can travel three miles.

19. They howl during two seasons.

20. There are more coyotes in America today than ever before.

> **Remember**
>
> that some adjectives tell *how many*, but not all give an exact number.

Writing Connection

Science Think of an animal you like. Create a web, using adjectives that describe this animal. Be sure to include adjectives that tell *how many*. Use the web to write a paragraph about the animal. Then read the paragraph to a friend and discuss possible changes.

GRAMMAR-WRITING CONNECTION

Adjectives for *What Kind*

Some adjectives tell *what kind*.

Remember that other adjectives tell *how many*. Adjectives for *what kind* can describe size, shape, or color. They can also tell how something looks, sounds, feels, tastes, or smells.

> **Examples:**
> Frogs have **long** legs.
>
> Some frogs have **round** spots.
>
> Some toads have **green** stripes.

Use adjectives for *what kind* to make sentences more interesting and more specific.

Guided Practice

A. Identify the noun that each underlined adjective describes.

> **Example:** Frogs have <u>flat</u> heads.
> *heads*

  1. Frogs like <u>wet</u> places.
  2. Their calls are <u>loud</u>.
  3. Some frogs have <u>yellow</u> bodies.
  4. Many frogs are <u>green</u>.
  5. Frogs have <u>smooth</u> skin.
  6. Frogs use their <u>long</u> tongues to catch food.
  7. A frog has <u>webbed</u> feet.
  8. Frogs can live in <u>cold</u> weather.
  9. Toads like <u>rainy</u> days.
  10. Some toads are <u>brown</u>.

Independent Practice

B. For each of the sentences below, write the adjective that tells what kind.

> **Example:** Fish can be _____ pets. (good, canine)
>
> *good*

11. Goldfish have _____ skin. (scaly, more)
12. Compared to adult cats, kittens are _____. (small, few)
13. Cats usually have _____ coats. (three, soft)
14. Puppies are _____ dogs. (young, some)
15. A beagle is a _____ animal. (most, canine)

C. For each of the sentences below, write the adjective and the noun that each adjective describes.

> **Example:** Dogs like to chew on rubber balls.
>
> *rubber|balls*

16. Saint Bernards are considered friendly dogs.
17. Poodles have curly hair.
18. Dalmatians have black spots.
19. A greyhound is a tall dog.
20. Dogs may have pointed ears.

Remember that some adjectives tell *what kind.* They can describe size, shape, or color. They can tell how something looks, sounds, feels, tastes, or smells.

Writing Connection

Real-Life Writing: Conversation With a partner, discuss two different animals, using adjectives that tell *what kind.* Then use the adjectives to create a chart that shows how those animals are different and alike.

Remember

that an adjective is a word that describes a noun. It can tell *how many* or *what kind.*

Extra Practice

A. Read each sentence. Then write the adjective that tells *how many*. *pages 274–275*

Example: Eagles live in many areas.
many

1. Most eagles stay away from people.
2. In some places, eagles nest on the ground.
3. Their feathers have several shapes.
4. Eagles have few enemies.
5. They can live for fifty years.

B. Write an adjective that tells *how many* to complete each sentence. The adjective may or may not be an exact number. *pages 274–275*

Example: Eagles have _____ feathers.
many

6. Eagles have _____ wings.
7. They have _____ strong beak.
8. _____ kinds of eagles, the bald eagle and the golden eagle, live in North America.
9. _____ other kinds live in the tropical regions of Asia and Africa.
10. _____ eagles eat meat.

C. Read each sentence. Write the adjective that tells *what kind*. *pages 276–277*

Example: Eagles are powerful.
powerful

11. Eagles have a large wingspan.
12. Stiff feathers allow them to glide.
13. An eagle has good eyesight.
14. Eagles look for small animals for food.
15. They can eat rabbits, birds, and young deer.

For more activities with adjectives, visit *The Learning Site:*
www.harcourtschool.com

D. Read each sentence and choose the adjective that best describes the noun. Then write the completed sentence. *pages 272–277*

Example: _____ eagles hunt during the day. (All, Red)
All eagles hunt during the day.

16. Eagles have _____ legs and feet. (strong, more)

17. They use their _____ claws to catch food. (purple, sharp)

18. Eagles use their _____ beaks for tearing. (some, hooked)

19. Eagles build nests in _____ trees. (tall, glass)

20. _____ eggs are cared for by the mother and the father. (Most, Happy)

21. _____ eagles are called eaglets. (Red, Young)

22. Eaglets are covered with _____ fuzz called down. (gray, any)

23. _____ feathers will grow within weeks. (Plastic, Regular)

24. Eaglets are not _____ flyers. (many, good)

25. _____ eaglets stay near their nest at first. (Many, None)

Writing Connection

Writer's Journal: Reflecting on Writing

Think about an animal book you have read. What was it about? What did you like or dislike about it? Write a paragraph about the book, and include the title of the book as well as your answers to these questions. Be sure to include at least four adjectives that tell *how many* and *what kind*.

Chapter Review

Read the paragraph. Some words are missing. Choose the word that belongs in each space. Then write the letter of your answer.

> (1) Lemon trees are _____ trees. (2) They grow in _____ countries. (3) The flowers on a lemon tree have a _____ smell. (4) People use lemons in _____ ways. (5) _____ people use lemon juice for baking. (6) By themselves, lemons have a _____ taste. (7) Lemons are a _____ source of vitamin C. (8) Lemons are an _____ crop in the United States.

TIP Read all directions carefully before you begin.

1 A sad
  B flower
  C one
  D fruit

2 F one
  G each
  H none
  J many

3 A seven
  B any
  C sweet
  D several

4 F several
  G none
  H trees
  J like

5 A None
  B Every
  C Some
  D Tree

6 F quick
  G all
  H many
  J sour

7 A none
  B round
  C good
  D square

8 F few
  G eight
  H important
  J many

For additional test preparations, visit *The Learning Site:*
www.harcourtschool.com

Guest Speakers

Have you ever had a guest speaker in your classroom? If so, you know how important it is to be a good listener. Here are some guidelines to follow before, during, and after a guest speaker's talk.

Before the Talk

- Think of what you already know about the guest speaker's topic.

- Predict what the speaker might say.

During the Talk

- Listen *carefully* to the speaker.

- Listen for ideas that the speaker *repeats*.

- Listen for *reasons* or *opinions*.

- Listen for *more information* that the speaker tells about an idea.

After the Talk

- Raise your hand to ask questions.

- Think about what you learned.

- Discuss your thoughts with someone else who heard the talk.

YOUR TURN

With a partner, take turns reading aloud the paragraphs that you wrote for the activity on page 279. After you listen to your partner's paragraph, write down the following information:

1. The title of the book that your partner read.

2. Two things your partner said about the book.

3. Whether your partner liked the book.

4. Why you want or don't want to read the book.

Advantages
and
Disadvantages
Essay

Writing Workshop

poinsettia

silversword

You know that one reason for writing is to give information. This selection is about different kinds of leaves. As you read, think about the kinds of information the author gives.

Weird Leaves

by Deborah Churchman
(from *Ranger Rick,* Oct. 1999)

When you imagine a leaf, do you see a flat, green thing that soaks up the sun in summer and then turns bright colors and flutters to the ground in the fall?

You're right. That's what many leaves are like. Some kinds of leaves are really *weird*, though.

Take the Christmasy-looking *poinsettia* in the photo, for example. Did you know that the "petals" of the flower are really special kinds of leaves called *bracts*?

Many other leaves are not what you'd imagine either. Here are just a few of the not-so-leafy, just-plain-weird leaves!

starfish plant

Advantages and Disadvantages Essay

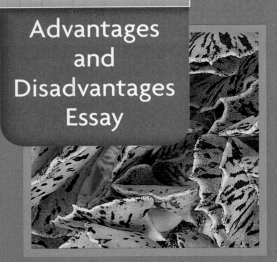

kalanchoe

Swiss cheese plant

string-of-beads plant

Weird Color

Most leaves are green. They get their color from a special pigment called *chlorophyll* [klôr′ə•fil]. The leaves use that pigment to make food. Leaves have red, yellow, or other pigments too. (The pigments do different jobs for the plant.) Those weird colors are easy to see in plants like the *kalanchoe* [kal′ən•kō′ē] and the *starfish plant*.

Then there's the *silversword*. Its color comes from a blanket of hairs on its leaves. The hairs help keep the plant from drying out.

Weird Shape

Some leaf shapes are real surprises. One leaf, for example, is full of holes. These holey leaves grow on a rainforest vine with a perfect name. It's called the *Swiss cheese plant*.

The *string-of-beads* plant grows in the hot, dry Namib Desert in southwestern Africa. The round leaves on this plant act just like little bottles, storing up water after a rare desert rain. They slowly supply water to the plant during the hottest, driest times.

Then there are the needles of many *evergreen trees*. Guess what? Needles are leaves too! Thin leaves like these survive better in drying winds than flat, broad leaves do.

Weird Feel

Most leaves have a waxy coating, which makes them feel smooth. (The waxy coating helps to keep moisture in.) Some other leaves feel hairy, prickly, sticky, or bumpy.

Take the leaves of one kind of *echeveria* [ech′ə•və•rē′ə]. They're lumpy and bumpy. Like the string-of-beads leaves, echeveria leaves store water for the plant to use during dry times. So those leaves are really thick.

Another kind of *echeveria* feels downright *furry!* The furry feel comes from thousands of tiny, soft hairs. As in the silversword, they help keep the plant from drying out. That's a good thing for a plant that grows in dry or windy places, such as deserts and mountains.

Now that you know about weird leaves, why not go outside and look for some?

echeveria

Vocabulary Power

ev•er•green
[ev′ər•grēn] *adj.* Having leaves that stay green throughout the year.

Analyze THE Model

1. What does Deborah Churchman do in the first sentence to help you imagine a leaf?

2. How does she vary her first three sentences to make the beginning of her article effective?

3. Into what sections does she divide her article?

4. Why does she divide her article into sections?

echeveria

READING — WRITING CONNECTION

Parts of an Advantages and Disadvantages Essay

Deborah Churchman used details to describe different kinds of leaves. Study the essay, written by a student named Jon. Notice the details he uses to describe the advantages and disadvantages of summer.

MODEL

Summer

by Jon Yee

Sometimes, I dislike summer. Other times, I like it. How can I have both feelings? The reason is that summer has some disadvantages and some advantages.

There are some things I don't like about summer. One problem with summer is the hot, humid weather. If that isn't bad enough, summer insects bite my skin and make me itch. One more disadvantage of summer is that there is no school, so I do not get to see all of my friends.

There are a lot of good things about summer, though. I love the long, sunny days. I also like to go to the pool with my

topic
sentence

disadvantages
and details
about them

advantages
and details
about them

friends. We play water games and have races. Summer treats are great, too. Sometimes, Mom makes us glasses of icy lemonade, or Dad buys us ice cream.

Summer has many advantages and disadvantages. It seems to me that summer is wonderful and terrible at the same time!

advantages and details about them

conclusion

Analyze THE Model

1. **What is the purpose of Jon's essay?**

2. **What audience might be interested in this essay? Why do you think so?**

3. **Why do you think Jon writes about the disadvantages of summer first?**

Summarize THE Model

Create a web like the one shown to help you identify the advantages and disadvantages of summer in Jon's essay. Then use your graphic organizer to write a summary of Jon's essay.

Summer

Advantages

Disadvantages

Writer's Craft

Sentence Variety Jon used a variety of sentences to make his writing interesting. Find one short, direct sentence and one long, descriptive sentence. What are the different kinds of sentences that he used?

Prewriting

Purpose and Audience

There are two sides to many situations. In this chapter, you will write an advantages and disadvantages essay about living in a certain place.

WRITING PROMPT Write an essay for your classmates, telling the advantages and disadvantages of living in a certain place. Choose a place, and write about why people might like to live there and why they might not. Include details that support your ideas.

Before you begin, think about your audience and purpose. Who will your readers be? What should your essay tell them?

MODEL

Jon got ready to write his essay by listing the main disadvantages and advantages of summer. Then he thought of details to go with each idea. He used this list to organize his thoughts.

Advantages
- *Long days*
  Detail: sunny
- *Treats*
  Details: icy lemonade, ice cream
- *Pool fun*
  Details: water games, races

Disadvantages
- *No School*
  Detail: miss friends
- *Weather*
  Details: hot and humid
- *Insect bites*
  Detail: make me itch

YOUR TURN

Choose a place to write about. Think about the disadvantages and advantages of living there. Use a chart to plan your essay.

Drafting

Organization and Elaboration

Follow these steps to help you organize your essay:

STEP 1 **Grab Your Reader's Interest**
Make the opening interesting to your readers.

STEP 2 **Decide How to Organize Your Essay**
Look at your prewriting chart. Decide whether to start with the advantages or the disadvantages.

STEP 3 **Use Descriptive Details**
As you write, explain each idea with descriptive details.

STEP 4 **Finish with a Summary Thought**
Summarize your thoughts in an interesting way.

MODEL

Here is the beginning of Jon's essay. How does he get his readers' attention?

> Sometimes, I dislike summer. Other times, I like it. How can I have both feelings? The reason is that summer has some disadvantages and some advantages.

YOUR TURN

Now write a draft of your essay. Use your organizer and the steps above as a guide. Remember to include details that support your ideas.

Strategies Good Writers Use

- Make your beginning and ending interesting.
- Include details and examples to support your ideas.

Use a computer to draft your essay. You can use the cut and paste feature to move paragraphs.

SUMMER
by
Jon Yee

Advantages and Disadvantages Essay

Revising

- Organize your ideas into paragraphs.
- Include enough examples and details to make ideas clear.

Use the thesaurus feature to get ideas for vivid words.

Organization and Elaboration

As you read your draft, think about these questions:

- Will my opening interest readers?
- Will readers be able to tell which ideas are advantages and which are disadvantages?
- What supporting details did I use?
- Did I end my essay with a summary thought?

MODEL

Here is a draft of the next part of Jon's essay. How did he make the topic of this paragraph clearer? What details did he add to make his writing stronger?

¶ There are some things I don't like about summer. One problem with summer is the
hot, humid
weather. If that isn't bad enough, summer insects bite my skin and make me itch. One more disadvantage of summer is that There is no school, so I do not get to see ~~people.~~
all of my friends.

YOUR TURN

Revise your essay. Make sure that you have a strong beginning and ending. Be sure that the ideas about advantages are together and the ideas about disadvantages are together.

Proofreading

Checking Your Language

When you proofread, you look for mistakes in grammar, spelling, punctuation, and capitalization. It is important to correct these mistakes so that your writing will be clear and easy to read.

MODEL

After Jon revised his essay, he proofread it. Here is the next part of Jon's draft. Look at how he fixed his grammar mistakes. What other mistakes did Jon correct?

> There are
> A lot of good things about summer, though I love the long, sunny days. I also liked to go to the pool with my me friends. We play water games and have races. Summer treats are grate, too. sometimes, Mom makes made us glasses of icy lemonaid or Dad buys us ice cream.

Strategies **Good Writers Use**

- Check for noun, verb, and pronoun mistakes.
- Circle misspelled words and find out how to spell them.

YOUR TURN

Proofread your essay. Make sure that you
- **check grammar.**
- **check spelling.**
- **check punctuation and capitalization.**

Editor's Marks

ℐ	take out text
∧	add text
ᗞ	move text
¶	new paragraph
≡	capitalize
/	lowercase
◯	correct spelling

Publishing

Sharing Your Work

Now you will publish your essay. Answer these questions to help you decide how to share your work:

1. Who is your audience? How can you publish your essay so they will see it?

2. What can you do to make sure your handwriting will be easy for your audience to read?

3. Could you present your essay as a video? To make a video, use the information on page 293.

USING YOUR
Handbook

• Use the rubric on page 499 to evaluate your essay.

Reflecting on Your Writing

Using Your Portfolio Think about what you learned in this chapter. Write and explain your answer to each question below:

1. Which stage of writing was the most difficult?

2. Using the rubric from your Handbook, how would you score your own writing?

3. The next time you write an advantages and disadvantages essay, what will you do differently?

Put your answers and your essay in your portfolio. Then write a paragraph that explains a goal for improving your writing.

Making a Video

Jon presented his essay as a video. He videotaped the events in his essay and used his essay as the spoken part of the video. You can do the same. Follow these steps:

STEP 1 Think about what your audience will hear in your video. Should your essay be read as the spoken part? Should you use music in the background?

STEP 2 Think about what your audience will see. Can you videotape the subject of your essay live? If not, find photos or draw pictures to videotape.

STEP 3 Make sketches of each scene you will show in your video. Use your essay to write captions for your sketches. This step will help you decide what should be said as you film each scene.

STEP 4 Film your video. Read or have someone else read the spoken part of the video as you film the scenes.

STEP 5 Show your video to your class. Ask what they liked about it. What could you have done differently?

Strategies for Video Producers

- Hold the video camera steady.
- Stop the camera between shots.
- Speak slowly and clearly. Do not rush.

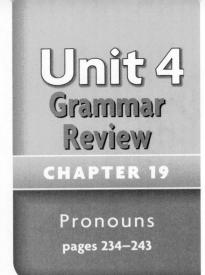

Unit 4
Grammar Review
CHAPTER 19

Pronouns
pages 234–243

Pronouns   pages 234–235

A. Rewrite each sentence. Use a pronoun in the place of the underlined word or words.

1. <u>The moon</u> lies between earth and the sun.
2. <u>Mark and I</u> watched a solar eclipse.
3. <u>Elena and her dad</u> watched it in the mountains.
4. <u>People</u> should watch the eclipse through a special lens.
5. <u>The sun</u> looked like it had a bite out of it.

Singular and Plural Pronouns

pages 236–237

B. Write a pronoun to take the place of the underlined words in each sentence. Then write *S* if the pronoun is singular or *P* if it is plural.

6. <u>Jamie and his family</u> watched a lunar eclipse.
7. Earth moved between <u>the sun and the moon</u>.
8. <u>Sunlight</u> could not reach the moon.
9. <u>People everywhere</u> saw the dim, reddish moon.
10. <u>Elena and I</u> could see the shadow of earth.

Pronoun-Antecedent Agreement   pages 238–239

C. Write the correct pronoun to replace the words in parentheses ( ).

11. Jon would like to travel in space. (Jon) says the distances are too far.
12. The closest star to our sun is nine light-years away. (The closest star to our sun) is named Sirius.
13. Venus and Mars are millions of miles away. It would take months to reach (Venus and Mars).
14. I told Elena that she is good at science. I told (Elena) to think about being an astronaut.
15. Elena said that (Elena) would like to see space.

Unit 4
Grammar Review
CHAPTER 20

Subject and
Object
Pronouns
pages 244–253

Subject Pronouns *pages 244–245*

A. Write the subject pronoun in each sentence.

1. He watched the news last night.

2. They predicted our first winter storm.

3. It will bring nearly two inches of rain.

4. We measured the rainfall in a beaker.

5. You can see that there is more rain than last year.

Object Pronouns *pages 246–247*

B. Write the object pronoun in each sentence.

6. Every day the weather affects us.

7. Tomorrow it may snow on you.

8. Please tell me when ski season begins.

9. I want to go with them to Colorado.

10. An instructor can teach her how to snowboard.

Using *I* and *Me* *pages 248–249*

C. Use *I* or *me* to complete each sentence. Write each sentence.

11. _____ see rain clouds gathering over the hills.

12. The rain is pouring down on _____ .

13. Hold the umbrella over _____ , please.

14. _____ like to walk on a rainy day.

15. _____ do not mind getting damp.

16. The wind whips around Carlos and _____ .

17. _____ wrap my raincoat tighter.

18. Thunder and lightning scare _____ a little.

19. _____ will run into the house to watch the rest of the storm.

20. My sister and _____ enjoy a good storm.

Unit 4
Grammar Review

CHAPTER 22

More About
Pronouns
pages 262–271

Possessive Pronouns

pages 262–263

A. Write the possessive pronoun in each sentence.

1. Marie loves to visit the forest near her house.
2. Marie said, "I can see the forest from my window."
3. Many animals make their homes there.
4. Each animal must find all its food in the forest.
5. The male deer depends on plants for his meals.

More Possessive Pronouns

pages 264–265

B. Write the possessive pronoun that belongs on each line.

6. Marie sometimes thinks of the forest as _____, even though it does not belong to her.
7. Near the stream is the perfect place for a picnic, and Marie's family thinks of it as _____.
8. Marie's dad likes tuna sandwiches, so he knows that one is _____.
9. The fresh fruit is mom's favorite, so it is _____.
10. "I will eat the peanut butter sandwich, because it is _____," Marie said.

Contractions with Pronouns

pages 266–267

C. Write a contraction for each word pair in parentheses ( ).

11. Marie said to Manuel, "(I am) going to the park."
12. "I hope (you will) come with me," she said.
13. (They had) been there many times before.
14. (I would) love to go to the park," said Manuel.
15. "(We have) always had fun there," he added.

Adjectives *pages 272–273*

A. For each sentence below, write the adjective or adjectives that describe the underlined noun.

1. There are several <u>kinds</u> of cats near my house.
2. The calico has orange and brown <u>spots</u>.
3. One old tomcat has six <u>toes</u> .
4. The Persian <u>cat</u> has long soft fur.
5. A Siamese cat has blue <u>eyes</u>.
6. Lions and lionesses are big <u>cats</u>.
7. They live in wild <u>places</u> in Africa.
8. Tigers live in the Indian <u>jungles</u>.
9. Panthers can have black or spotted <u>fur</u>.
10. Big and little <u>cats</u> like to sleep and eat.

Adjectives for *How Many*

pages 274–275

B. For each sentence, write the adjective that tells *how many*.

11. A lagoon is one place birds stop for water.
12. Many birds migrate from the north.
13. They stop in several places on their journey.
14. Some birds migrate very far.
15. We saw twenty Canada geese flying.

Adjectives for *What Kind*

pages 276–277

C. For each sentence, write the adjective that tells *what kind*.

16. The geese have wide wings.
17. Small birds migrate also.
18. You can see big flocks resting on the water.
19. How do migrating birds know where to fly?
20. They always return to their summer homes.

Friend or Foe?

Some types of plants and animals are called "weeds" or "pests." We call them this because they cause problems or are disliked. Believe it or not, many weeds and pests can be helpful to people. The steps below will help you find out how.

Decide on a Weed or Pest

- With a group of classmates, make a list of plants or animals that people dislike.

- With the help of your teacher, select one plant or animal. Choose one that you have heard several people mention.

Research the Plant or Animal

- Why do people complain about this plant or animal?

- What harm does this plant or animal cause humans?

- Can it be used in science or as medicine by doctors?

- How does it help or hurt the environment?

- Does your research show that this plant or animal is helpful to people in some way? If not, go back to your group's list and choose a different plant or animal to research.

Report Your Discoveries

- Write a paragraph that explains how your weed or pest is both helpful and harmful. Paste it onto poster board and illustrate it. Present your poster to classmates.

A Desert Scrapbook
by Virginia Wright-Frierson

NONFICTION

Learn, with the help of watercolor pictures, about the habits of the animals that live in the Sonoran Desert.

Tiger Lilies and Other Beastly Plants
by Elizabeth Ring

NONFICTION

Many flowers and weeds look like animals. Discover when and where these "animals" are found in the wild.

Outstanding Science Trade Book

Cactus Hotel
by Brenda Z. Guiberson

NONFICTION

Many desert creatures find safety in the prickly branches of a saguaro cactus.

Notable Children's Book in the Language Arts

Sentences *pages 24–27*

Write each sentence. Add the correct end mark.

1. Mr. Montero's class visited the art museum
2. Look at that suit of armor
3. Isn't that stained glass window beautiful
4. That painting is so amazing
5. Each student liked something different

Subjects and Predicates

pages 34–37, 52–55

Write each sentence. Draw one line under the complete subject and two lines under the complete predicate. Then circle the simple subject and the simple predicate.

6. Our class held a photography contest.
7. Each student entered a photograph.
8. Reka's photo showed her dog asleep.
9. Tak took a picture of his twin sisters.
10. The winner received a blue ribbon.

Complete Sentences *pages 62–63*

Write *complete sentence* if the group of words is a complete sentence. If it is not a complete sentence, rewrite the group of words to make it a complete sentence.

11. A haiku is a short, simple poem.
12. Most haiku three lines, and many of them are about nature.
13. Are five, seven, and five syllables long.
14. Some haiku poets write about the seasons, but others write about animals.
15. Would like to write a haiku?

Common and Proper Nouns

pages 92–95

Write each sentence. Capitalize each proper noun.

1. mrs. garcia has taught her children safety rules.
2. luis and carmen always cross the street at the light or in a crosswalk.
3. They wait for the crossing guard, mr. harmon.
4. They are especially careful at the corner of main street and pine street.
5. The children walk to patterson elementary school.

Singular and Plural Nouns

pages 102–107

Write the plural noun or nouns in each sentence. Then write the singular form of the noun or nouns.

6. My doctor says I should eat plenty of fruits and vegetables.
7. Sugar isn't very good for your teeth.
8. It is important to get enough vitamins, minerals, and protein.
9. Children need calcium for their bones.
10. Vitamin A is important for eyes.

Verbs *pages 130–135*

Write each sentence. Underline each verb.

11. Linda is in a gymnastics class.
12. The gymnasts perform on mats.
13. Some kids jump over the vaults.
14. Linda does cartwheels.
15. She walks on the balance beam.

Main Verbs and Helping Verbs
pages 166–169

Write each sentence. Underline the main verb. Circle the helping verb.

1. My great-grandfather was born in Norway.
2. He had come to America at the age of eighteen.
3. He did not speak much English.
4. By age twenty, he had learned English very well.
5. Now he is studying Spanish.

Verb Tenses pages 176–179, 194–199

Choose the correct verb in parentheses ( ) to complete each sentence.

6. The first settlers (moved, will move) to my town in 1685.
7. Many more people (followed, will follow) them.
8. Over 6,000 people (live, lived) here now.
9. The town (grew, will grow) larger in the future.
10. We (will need, needed) a new school.

Irregular Verbs pages 204–207

Write the sentences. Change each underlined present-tense irregular verb to the past tense.

11. Our teacher <u>says</u> we should have a feast.
12. Everyone <u>has</u> a dish from a different land.
13. We <u>eat</u> the foods of many cultures.
14. My friends <u>throw</u> a party on Friday.
15. Ms. Morales <u>comes</u> to the party.

Subject and Object Pronouns

pages 234–237, 244–247

Write each sentence. Draw one line under each subject pronoun and two lines under each object pronoun.

1. We were surprised when a snowstorm hit yesterday.
2. We were in school, and the snow started to fall.
3. When the third graders heard that school was closing early, they cheered.
4. The teacher told us to get ready to leave.
5. The children got on the buses that took them home.

Possessive Pronouns *pages 262–265*

Write each sentence. Underline the possessive pronoun.

6. My favorite animals at the zoo are the tapirs.
7. Their noses are long and thick.
8. Each tapir has his own favorite shady spot.
9. That stuffed tapir on the shelf is mine.
10. My sister left hers at Yoko's house.

Adjectives *pages 272–277*

Write each sentence. Underline each adjective.

11. Each fall the geese fly over the town.
12. Their loud honking says that winter is coming.
13. They are on their way to warm southern waters.
14. Bright cheerful chickadees stay here in winter.
15. They hop around on the icy ground.

Language Use

Read the passage and choose the word or group of words that belongs in each space. Mark the letter for your answer.

> Rain (1) fall on the desert very often. When it (2), the whole desert (3) in flowers. The (4) colors are bright and vivid. Desert animals (5) need much water. Desert plants (6) also able to grow with little water. Some plants (7) water in (8) stems.

1 A doesn't
B don't
C do not
D do

2 F do
G does
H will do
J don't

3 A explode
B will exploded
C explodes
D exploded

4 F flowers
G flower's
H flowers'
J flowerses

5 A don't
B doesn't
C does not
D didn't

6 F is
G am
H was
J are

7 A stores
B has stored
C storing
D store

8 F their
G they're
H there
J they

Written Expression

Use this paragraph to answer questions 1–4.

In *My Side of the Mountain*, author Jean Craighead George tells the story of Sam, a boy who runs away to the Catskill Mountains. Sam wants to live on his own for a while. He makes new friends, tames a falcon, and finds a home for himself inside a hollow tree.

1 Which of these sentences would go best after the last sentence in this paragraph?

   A Sam needs to be with his family.

   B The falcon's name is Frightful.

   C Sam learns a lot about nature and about himself.

2 Why was this paragraph written?

   F To persuade you to do something

   G To tell about a book

   H To tell how to do something

3 Which of these sentences would not belong in the paragraph?

   A Jean Craighead George writes many books.

   B Sam learns how to cook and eat wild plants.

   C Sam makes it through a hard winter alone.

4 Choose the best topic sentence for this paragraph.

   F I had never read a book by Jean Craighead George.

   G Living in a tree can be fun.

   H *My Side of the Mountain* is an exciting book.

Unit 5

Grammar	Articles, Adjectives, and Adverbs
Writing	Informative Writing Research Report

CHAPTER 25
More About Adjectives........308

CHAPTER 26
Adverbs......................318

CHAPTER 27
Writer's Craft: Organizing Information
Writing a Paragraph
of Information 328

CHAPTER 28
More About Adverbs
and Adjectives.............336

CHAPTER 29
Easily Confused Words.......346

CHAPTER 30
Writing Workshop
Writing a Research Report....356

Automobiles

The assembly line was improved by Henry Ford. He used the moving assembly line to produce the Model T. The Model T was the most popular car in the United States in the early 1900's.

Articles

The words *a*, *an*, and *the* are called articles.

Articles are a special group of adjectives. You know that an adjective describes a noun or pronoun. Use *a* before singular nouns and adjectives that begin with a consonant sound.

Examples:

A farmer and her family live there.   *A, farmer*

They live in a rural area.   *a, rural*

Use *an* before singular nouns and adjectives that begin with a vowel sound.

Examples:

An orchard is near Centerville.   *An, orchard*

It is an old apple orchard.   *an, old*

Use *the* before singular and plural nouns.

Examples:

The countryside is beautiful.   *The, countryside*

The towns are far from each other.   *The, towns*

Vocabulary Power

ru•ral [rŏŏr′əl] *adj.*
Belonging to or happening in the country rather than in a city.

Guided Practice

A. Read each sentence. Choose the correct article. Be able to explain your choice.

Example: (The, An) farmer raises crops.
The

  1. Her crops are planted in (the, a) spring.
  2. (The, An) crops need rain to grow.
  3. Crops also need (an, a) warm temperature.
  4. There is (a, an) orchard on the farm.
  5. Peaches grow in (a, the) orchard.

Independent Practice

B. Write each sentence. Use the correct article or articles. Be ready to explain your choices.

Example: Turnips are (the, a) root crop.
Turnips are a root crop.

6. Turnips grow well in (the, a) winter.
7. (The, An) turnip once was used as food for animals.
8. Hay is now (a, an) common food for animals.
9. Some hay comes from (an, a) grass called alfalfa.
10. Alfalfa is left on (the, a) ground to dry.
11. Dried alfalfa becomes (the, a) hay.
12. Straw is made from (the, a) stems of wheat.
13. Straw is used for (a, an) animal's bedding.
14. Then some straw is put into (the, a) soil.
15. As (an, a) result, (the, an) soil becomes good for planting crops.

Writing Connection

Art Why might a person from a city want to visit a farm? Make a poster about a rural community. Try to get people from cities to visit that community. Trade posters with a classmate. Circle all the articles in the poster. Make sure your partner used *a, an,* and *the* correctly.

Some Special Forms for Comparing	
good	**bad**
better	worse
best	worst

Adjectives That Compare

Adjectives can be used to compare two or more people, places, or things.

Add *er* to most short adjectives to compare two people, places, or things. Add *est* to most short adjectives to compare more than two people, places, or things. If an adjective ends with a consonant and *y*, change the *y* to *i* and add *er* or *est*.

Examples:

This barn is in a **sunnier** place than the horse stable.

That dairy, though, is in the **sunniest** place of all.

Other adjectives use special forms to compare. *Good* and *bad* are two of these adjectives. Notice their special forms for comparing in the chart.

Guided Practice

A. Read each sentence. Choose the correct adjective.

Example: This farm is (older, oldest) than that one.
older

1. The (newer, newest) farmhouses of all are built with concrete.
2. Many (older, oldest) farmhouses were built with stone.
3. The stable is built in the (brighter, brightest) part of a farm.
4. Horses have (good, better) protection in their stables than out in the fields.
5. (Fewer, Fewest) oxen than tractors plow fields.

Independent Practice

B. Rewrite each sentence, using the correct comparing form of the adjective in parentheses ( ).

Example: (Few) crops grow in winter than in spring.
Fewer crops grow in winter than in spring.

6. Apples can grow in (cool) areas than oranges.
7. Peaches need (warm) climates than pears.
8. Sunny places are the (good) areas to grow grapes.
9. It is hard to farm in the (hot) regions of all.
10. Growing crops is also difficult in the very (dry) regions.
11. Farmers do not deliver their (bad) products to market.
12. Farming is an (easy) job today than it was in the past.
13. Instead of their old equipment, farmers now use (fast) new machinery.
14. Before milking machines were invented, milking was a (hard) chore than it is now.
15. Inventions have brought rural families into (close) contact with the rest of the world.

Writing Connection

Writer's Craft: Vivid Adjectives Talk with a partner about the neighborhood, town, or city where each of you lives. How are these places alike? How are they different? Write several sentences comparing these places. Be sure to use adjectives that compare.

USAGE AND MECHANICS

Avoiding Incorrect Comparisons

Some adjectives need the word *more* or *most* for comparing.

Most adjectives with two or more syllables need the word *more* or the word *most* for comparing nouns. Use *more* when comparing two nouns. Use *most* when comparing more than two nouns.

Examples:

I think that apples are **more delicious** than grapes.

I think that kiwi is the **most delicious** fruit of all.

Never use both *er* and *more* or both *est* and *most* when you compare with adjectives.

DID YOU KNOW?
California produces more food than any other state in the nation. Its leading products include milk, beef, grapes, tomatoes, and lettuce.

Guided Practice

A. Read each sentence. Tell whether the adjective form is correct or incorrect.

Example: The farmer had a more better crop than his neighbor did.
incorrect; more better *should be* better

I. Rice is the most difficult crop to grow.
2. Rice is a plentifuler grain in California than in Texas.
3. Corn is a more ordinarier grain than millet.
4. Winter wheat is grown in more milder climates than other types of wheat.
5. Bread wheat is the most common type of wheat.

millet

Independent Practice

B. Write each sentence, using the correct form of the comparing adjective in parentheses ( ).

Example: This is the (popular) farm animal at the fair.
This is the most popular farm animal at the fair.

6. A foal is (young) than a horse.

7. The (clumsy) horse of all is a newborn foal.

8. Donkeys are (stubborn) than horses are.

9. The (careful) sheepherder of all is the dog.

10. Sheep are (gentle) than most animals and can't protect themselves.

11. Chickens are (friendly) birds than geese are.

12. That rooster's feathers are (colorful) than this chicken's feathers.

13. Animals are the (good) helpers on a farm.

14. That bull is the (fearless) animal on the farm.

15. Of all the animals on a farm, large animals have the (expensive) needs.

Remember
to add *er* or *est* to many short adjectives that compare. Add *more* or *most* to most adjectives with two or more syllables. Never use *er* with *more* or *est* with *most* when you compare with adjectives.

Writing Connection

Writer's Journal: Write a Comparison What do you think is the best thing about living on a farm? What is the best thing about living in a big city? Write a few sentences that compare farm life to city life. Be sure to use the correct adjective forms.

Remember

that *a, an,* and
the are a special
group of
adjectives called
articles. Use
more or *er* with
adjectives that
compare two
nouns. Use *most*
or *est* with
adjectives that
compare more
than two nouns.

For more activities
with articles and
adjectives that
compare, visit
The Learning Site:

www.harcourtschool.com

Extra Practice

**A. Write each sentence. Use the correct article
or articles.** *pages 308–309*

Example: Farmers work hard to make (the, a) living.
Farmers work hard to make a living.

1. There are no farms in (the, an) city.
2. Farms are important to (a, an) rural area.
3. Some people who live in rural areas work on
   (a, an) farm.
4. Some farmers grow (the, a) single crop each
   year.
5. Soybeans are (an, a) popular crop.
6. Soybeans have (a, the) cover called (an, a)
   pod.
7. (An, A) acorn is larger than (an, a) soybean.
8. (A, An) major cooking oil is made from
   soybeans.
9. Soybeans are rich in (a, an) protein.
10. Soybean oil is used as fuel on (an, the) buses
    in some cities.

**B. Write each sentence, using the correct
comparing form of the adjective in
parentheses ( ).** *pages 310–311*

Example: This city is the (grand) place I've seen.
This city is the grandest place I've seen.

11. The (large) farms in the United States are in
    the Midwest.
12. Iowa and Texas have a (great) number of
    farms than other states do.
13. Milk cows are (tame) than some other cattle.
14. The (wild) horses of all do not live on farms.
15. The (strong) horse on a farm is the draft
    horse.

C. Write each sentence. Choose the correct comparing form of the adjective in parentheses (). Be ready to explain your choices. *pages 310–313*

> **Example:** I had the (most wonderful, wonderfulest) time at the county fair.
> *I had the most wonderful time at the county fair.*

16. County fairs are (more rarer, rarer) events in cities than in small towns.

17. Only the (most splendid, most splendidest) animals win prizes at a fair.

18. Prizewinners become the (most valuable, valuablest) animals.

19. The sheepdog is a (skillfuler, more skillful) dog than many other dogs.

20. A donkey is a (more powerful, more powerfuler) worker than a sheepdog.

Writing Connection

Real-Life Writing: Postcard Make a postcard about your community. On the front, draw a picture of your neighborhood or town. Write a sentence about your community that compares it to another place. Use at least one adjective that compares. On the back, write a message inviting a friend to visit.

Chapter Review

Read the sentences. Check the underlined words to see whether they are used correctly. If you find a mistake, choose the answer that could replace the underlined words. If there is no mistake, choose _Correct as is_.

1 <u>An</u> sheep often is raised for its wool.

   A A   **C** More

   B Most   **D** Correct as is

TIP Answer the questions you are sure about first. Then go back and answer the others.

2 In the United States, <u>most</u> sheep are raised in the west than anywhere else.

   F an   **H** a

   G more   **J** Correct as is

3 Some sheep feed on the open range. Others have <u>more controlled</u> feedings in pastures.

   A controlledest   **C** most controlled

   B controlleder   **D** Correct as is

4 As you may know, <u>a</u> wool we use for clothing comes from a sheep's coat.

   F an   **H** more

   G the   **J** Correct as is

5 Many people like <u>the</u> comfort of wool.

   A more   **C** an

   B the   **D** Correct as is

6 A wool sweater is <u>warmest</u> than a cotton sweater.

   F warmer   **H** an

   G warm   **J** Correct as is

For additional test preparation, visit _The Learning Site:_

www.harcourtschool.com

Synonyms and Antonyms

You have learned about many kinds of adjectives. You may have noticed that some adjectives mean almost the same thing. Other pairs of adjectives are opposites.

Words that mean almost the same thing are called **synonyms**. Look at this sentence:

A barn is a **bigger** building than a stable.

You could replace the word *bigger* with *larger* or *more enormous*. These words are synonyms. Look for other synonyms for *bigger* in a thesaurus.

Antonyms are words with opposite meanings. The adjectives in these sentences are antonyms:

The barn is **older** than the stable.

The stable is **newer** than the barn.

Can you think of other adjectives that are antonyms?

YOUR TURN

Write a mystery story. Use words from the list below in your story. Then trade stories with a partner. In your partner's story, underline the adjectives. Rewrite your partner's story, using synonyms and antonyms for the underlined words. Talk about how word choice changes the meaning of the story.

awful	bright	fast	many
beautiful	clean	happy	noisy
brave	empty	heavy	old

TIP You can make your writing more interesting by using more vivid synonyms and antonyms for ordinary words.

317

Adverbs

An **adverb** is a word that describes, or tells about, a verb.

Some adverbs tell *how* an action happens.

Examples:

Firefighters and police officers work **hard** for you.

The librarian asked us to work **quietly** in the library.

The gym teacher said I ran **fast**.

Juan **carefully** crossed the street.

Guided Practice

A. Name the adverb that tells *how*. Then name the verb it describes.

> **Example:** The storyteller closed the book gently.
> *gently, closed*

1. Librarians search the Internet quickly.
2. They happily help people do research.
3. Children listen quietly as librarians read them stories.
4. Librarians carefully replace books on shelves.
5. They work hard to keep the library in order.
6. We must talk softly in the library.
7. Our class easily won the reading contest.
8. People from our neighborhood use the public library regularly.
9. My group finished the book quickly.
10. We must treat the books gently.

Vocabulary Power

ca·reer [kə·rir′] *n.*
A person's lifework or profession.

Independent Practice

B. Write the adverb that tells *how*. Then write the verb it describes.

Remember
that some adverbs tell how an action happens.

Example: The librarian searched the shelves calmly.
calmly, searched

11. She quickly found the book she wanted.
12. The librarian cheerfully offered to show Jeff a good website.
13. Jeff easily found the website.
14. He went to a table and sat quietly.
15. Two girls spoke softly at the next table.
16. Please ask nicely if you need more help.
17. Nikki happily searched the shelves for books on kittens.
18. We watched the librarian's helper put the books back on the shelf correctly.
19. Nikki carefully put her books on the counter.
20. Jeff eagerly searched the website for facts.

Writing Connection

Real-Life Writing: Conversation Brainstorm with a partner a list of people who are helpful in your community. Then discuss with your partner the jobs these people have. After your discussion, write three sentences that describe what one person on your list does. Use adverbs that tell *how* in your description.

More About Adverbs

An **adverb** is a word that describes, or tells about, a verb.

Some adverbs tell *when* or *where* an action happens.

> **Examples:**
>
> I **always** like talking with firefighters about their work. *tells when*
>
> I just saw a firefighter **outside**. *tells where*

Guided Practice

A. Identify the adverb and whether it tells *when* or *where*.

> **Example:** May we visit the police station soon?
> *soon, when*

1. Police officers work there.
2. Heidi often reads books about police officers.
3. May we visit the fire station tomorrow?
4. We sometimes ask the police for information.
5. The police always help people.
6. You can find community helpers everywhere.
7. The firefighters will go anywhere someone needs help.
8. We should stand here until the light changes.
9. The light is green, so let's cross now.
10. Cho is waiting outside for the crossing guard.

Independent Practice

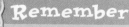
B. Write each sentence. Underline the adverb that tells *where* or *when*.

Example: *Eliott left his house <u>early</u>.*

11. Soon he was at the community center.

12. He opened the door and went inside.

13. Children were playing everywhere.

14. He and his friends are playing basketball today.

15. They practice often.

16. Eliott sometimes helps clean the gym.

17. He swept the floor yesterday.

18. His friends will help out tomorrow.

19. The broom they use is here.

20. I think we should start practicing now.

21. We cannot go outside in the rain.

22. Let's go to the library later.

23. Will you go there with me?

24. I always look for books about basketball.

25. I usually find magazines, too.

Writing Connection

Writer's Craft: Persuasive Words Firefighters help others by keeping people, land, and communities safe. Write four sentences that describe another "helping" career in your community. Use adverbs to help explain *when* and *where* the helping takes place.

Comparing with Adverbs

Adverbs can compare two or more actions.

When comparing two actions, add *er* to most short adverbs. Use *more* before adverbs with two or more syllables. When comparing more than two actions, add *est* to most short adverbs. Use *most* before adverbs with two or more syllables.

Examples:

This fire spread **faster** than last week's fire.

This fire spread the **fastest** of all the fires.

The firefighters came **more rapidly** than the police.

They came the **most rapidly** of all the workers.

Do not use both *er* and *more* or *est* and *most* when you compare with adverbs.

Guided Practice

A. Tell how you would change the underlined adverb to make the sentence correct.

Example: The deer ran <u>quickly</u> from the fire than the turtles did. *more quickly*

1. Some campers act <u>carefully</u> than others.
2. Some fires spread <u>fast</u> than others.
3. We will follow our fire safety plan <u>closely</u> next time.
4. The fire burned <u>long</u> than the firefighters thought it would.
5. The water sprays <u>quickly</u> when it's first turned on than it does later.

Independent Practice

B. Write each sentence using the correct form of the underlined adverb.

> **Example:** The forest fire raced <u>fast</u> than the wind.
> *The forest fire raced faster than the wind.*

6. The flames jumped <u>high</u> than the trees.
7. The top of the fire burned the <u>hot</u>.
8. Of all the grasses, the dry brush burned the <u>rapidly</u>.
9. The wind changed, and the fire burned <u>wildly</u> than ever.
10. As the fire spread, firefighters had to work <u>quickly</u> than before.
11. They dug <u>rapidly</u> than they had in the morning.
12. The fire spread <u>slowly</u> than before.
13. Water from the hoses sprayed <u>hard</u> than a rainstorm.
14. When the fire was out, firefighters stayed <u>long</u> to make sure new fires did not start.
15. No one cheered <u>loudly</u> than the chief after the fire was out.

Remember to add *er* to adverbs to compare two actions. Add *est* when you compare more than two actions. Use *more* or *most* before adverbs that have two or more syllables.

Writing Connection

Social Studies Think of things you can do to help others in your community or at your school. Talk about these ideas with a partner. Together, list your four favorite ideas. Then write a paragraph that compares your ideas. Be sure to use adverbs that compare correctly.

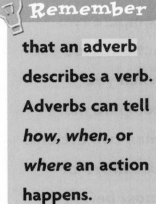

Remember

that an adverb describes a verb. Adverbs can tell *how, when,* or *where* an action happens.

Extra Practice

A. Write the adverb in each sentence.
pages 318–321

Example: Police officers often fight crime. *often*

1. Officers must behave bravely.
2. They act swiftly to protect people.
3. Police officers sometimes call for extra help.
4. The officers visited our school again.
5. Traffic officers drive quickly to catch speeding cars.
6. Their sirens blare loudly.
7. Officers riding horses work outside.
8. Police officers often talk to students.
9. A police captain questions the driver closely.
10. The officers carefully climb the tower.

B. Write the word or words in parentheses ( ) that make the sentence correct. *pages 322–323*

Example: The police officer moved _____ than the criminal. (more fast, faster)
faster

11. Police officers use cars _____ than bicycles. (more often, most often)
12. In bad weather, people should drive _____ than they do in good weather. (more slowly, slowlier)
13. Police helicopters fly _____ than skyscrapers. (more high, higher)
14. Police officers have to work _____ than we imagined. (more carefully, carefuller)
15. The police got to the accident _____ than the firefighters did. (quick, more quickly)

C. Write the adverb in each sentence. Then write whether it tells *how, when,* or *where*.
pages 318–321

Example: Police dogs work well with their police partners.
well, how

16. Officers choose dogs that can be trained easily.
17. The dogs always obey commands.
18. They work hard.
19. Police dogs sometimes guard buildings.
20. The fire station dog may ride somewhere on the fire engine.

D. Write the adverb in each sentence. Then write the verb it describes. *pages 318–323*

Example: Officer Jackson drove carefully down the street.
carefully, drove

21. Suddenly a car passed him.
22. It was going faster than his police car.
23. Officer Jackson quickly started his flashing lights.
24. The siren on his car blared loudly.
25. Finally, the car stopped.

Remember that **adverbs** can be used to compare actions. Add *er* or use *more* to compare two actions. Add *est* or use *most* to compare more than two actions.

Writing Connection

Art Think about something you could do to improve your community. Talk about your idea with a partner. Work with your partner to design a poster that illustrates your idea. Use adverbs to explain *how, when,* and *where* your idea could be used.

STANDARDIZED TEST PREP

Chapter Review

Read each sentence and look at the underlined words. There may be a mistake in word usage. If you find a mistake, choose the answer that shows the correct usage. If there is not a mistake, choose *Correct as is*.

1 Think about the community workers <u>who cheerful help you</u>.

  A who most cheerful help you

  B who cheerfully help you

  C who more cheerful help you

  D Correct as is

2 Police and firefighters <u>work more harder</u> to keep you safe.

  F work most hardest   **H** work hard

  G work better hard   **J** Correct as is

3 Volunteers in the school office or library are <u>the most friendly</u>.

  A the more friendly   **C** the more friendlier

  B the most friendliest   **D** Correct as is

4 Construction crews <u>work inside</u> on roads and bridges.

  F work behind   **H** work over

  G work outside   **J** Correct as is

5 Doctors and nurses always <u>take goodest care</u> of you.

  A take best care   **C** take good care

  B take more gooder care   **D** Correct as is

6 Many people <u>usual work</u> together to make a neighborhood nice.

  F more usual work   **H** most usually

  G usually work   **J** Correct as is

TIP Don't spend too much time on one question. Make sure to save some time to check your answers.

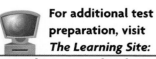
For additional test preparation, visit *The Learning Site:* www.harcourtschool.com

Taking Notes and Making an Outline

Gathering Information

Reading for information is different from reading for fun. When you are reading for information, you should take notes. Write information you find about a subject on separate cards. Include the name of the source where you find the information.

School crossing guards help children safely cross the street. — from newspaper story in the Daily News

Making an Outline

Use your note cards to prepare an outline. Start by listing the main idea in each group of cards. You do not need to use complete sentences in an outline. Number the main ideas. Under each main idea, include some facts or details. Use capital letters to list the facts and details. Here is an outline that organizes information about volunteers.

Volunteers Needed!

I. At schools
   A. Crossing guards
   B. Recess monitors
   C. After-school tutors
II. At hospitals
   A. Flower deliverers
   B. Gift shop helpers
   C. Patient visitors

YOUR TURN

Find a magazine article or newspaper story about something that interests you. As you read, take notes on separate cards. Before you write about the subject, use your notes to make an outline. Use your outline to write four sentences about this subject.

Writer's Craft

Organizing Information

Before you write to inform, you can find out facts about a subject and organize them.

Read the following passage. Look at the different kinds of facts the writer tells about draft horses.

LITERATURE MODEL

HORSEPOWER
The Wonder of Draft Horses

by Cris Peterson
Photographs by Alvis Upitis

A most remarkable horse named Kate has huge black hooves the size of dinner plates. She is as tall as a basketball player and weighs as much as a classroom of third-graders. Kate is a Percheron draft horse.

One hundred years ago, draft horses like Kate pulled carriages full of people and wagons full of milk. Before there were tractors or combines, horses pulled plows through spring sod and corn pickers through fall fields.

—from *Horsepower: The Wonder of Draft Horses*
by Cris Peterson

Analyze THE Model

1. What is the writer's main subject?
2. What facts does the writer give about the size of draft horses?
3. What information does the writer give about the work done by draft horses?

Vocabulary Power

draft [draft] *adj.*
Used for pulling heavy loads.

Using an Outline

Before you write to inform, you must consider your audience and purpose. It is also a good idea to use an outline to help you plan what you will write. An **outline** is like a map for writing and organizing information. Study the examples on the next page.

Strategies for Organizing Information

After you think about your audience and purpose, use an outline to plan the best way to present your information to them.

Percheron Draft Horses

I. Size
  A. Hooves as big as dinner plates
  B. As tall as a basketball player
  C. Weigh as much as a classroom of third-graders
II. Work done by draft horses
  A. Pulled carriages full of people
  B. Pulled wagons full of milk
  C. Pulled plows and corn pickers

YOUR TURN

THINK ABOUT HOW INFORMATION IS ORGANIZED Work with a partner. Choose a chapter in your social studies textbook. Look through the chapter to find heads and subheads. Then use the heads and subheads to make an outline of the chapter.

Making an Outline

A. Read the paragraph. On your paper, make an outline like the one shown below. Write facts from the paragraph to complete the outline.

> Wheat and corn are important crops. Wheat is used mainly to make bread, pastries, cereal, and pasta. Corn is eaten as a vegetable, made into cereal, or used to feed cattle and other livestock.

Important Crops

  I. (name of crop)

      A. _____

      B. _____

      C. _____

      D. _____

  II. (name of crop)

      A. _____

      B. _____

      C. _____

Matching Audience and Purpose

B. On your paper, write the number for each kind of writing. Next to the number, write the letter of the purpose and audience that matches that kind of writing.

Kind of Writing

1. a letter to a magazine asking for more science articles to be printed

2. a science report about frogs

3. an article for your school newspaper about your class trip to the museum

4. a friendly letter to share some facts you learned in social studies

Purpose and Audience

a. to inform classmates about a topic

b. to persuade a magazine editor to do something

c. to inform a friend about a topic

d. to describe something for all the other students in your school

---

Writing AND Thinking

Writer's Journal

Write to Record Reflections If you put on a show, your audience is the people who watch the show. Why do you think the people who read something you write are also called an audience? How is an audience of readers like an audience who watches you dance, sing, give a speech, or put on a play? Write your reflections in your Writer's Journal.

Paragraph of Information

The purpose of the book *Horsepower: The Wonder of Draft Horses* is to inform readers about draft horses. The audience is readers like you. Becky, a third grader, researched the subject of zebras. She made an outline to organize her facts. Then she used the outline to help her write a paragraph of information to share with her classmates. Read the outline and paragraph that Becky wrote.

MODEL

title   Zebras

main idea   I. Size

detail   A. Smaller than a horse

detail   B. 4–5 feet high at shoulders

main idea   II. Appearance

detail   A. White or pale yellow with black stripes

detail   B. Short mane

detail   C. Large ears

Zebras are smaller than horses. Most are four to five feet high at the shoulders. They have white or pale yellow coats with black stripes. Zebras' manes are short, but their ears are large.

Analyze THE *Model*

1. What two main heads did Becky use in her outline?

2. Did Becky follow her outline? How can you tell?

3. Does Becky's paragraph explain the information clearly? Why or why not?

YOUR TURN

WRITING PROMPT Write a paragraph for your classmates about a topic you have learned about in Social Studies. Use your textbook to help you put the facts about your topic in an outline. Then use your outline to write your paragraph.

STUDY THE PROMPT Ask yourself these questions:

1. What is your purpose for writing the paragraph?

2. Who is your audience for the paragraph?

3. What will you do before you begin writing?

Prewriting and Drafting

Organizing Your Information Write down facts that you want to include in your paragraph. Then organize the facts by making an outline.

> **Title of Outline** (your topic)
> **I.** An important idea
>   **A.** Detail about the idea
>   **B.** Another detail
>
> **II.** Another important idea
>   **A.** Detail about this idea
>   **B.** Another detail

Add more main heads and subheads if you need them. When your outline is complete, use it to write a draft of your paragraph.

USING YOUR
Handbook

• Use the Writer's Thesaurus to help you restate information in your own words.

Editing

Read over the draft of your paragraph of information. Is there anything you would like to change or add? Use this checklist to help you revise your paragraph.

☑ **Does your writing fulfill your purpose?**
☑ **Is the information well organized?**
☑ **Will your audience understand the information in your paragraph?**

Use this checklist as you proofread your paragraph.

☑ **I have begun my sentences with capital letters.**
☑ **I have used the correct end marks.**
☑ **I have used adjectives and adverbs correctly.**
☑ **I have used subject and object pronouns correctly.**
☑ **I have used a dictionary to check my spelling.**

Editor's Marks

✗ take out text
∧ add text
⟳ move text
¶ new paragraph
≡ capitalize
/ lowercase
◯ correct spelling

Sharing and Reflecting

Make a final copy of your paragraph, and share it with a partner. Is there any information you don't understand? If there is, talk about how to explain it better. Discuss how organizing information helps you carry out your purpose for writing. Write your reflections in your Writer's Journal.

Taking Notes

You need to write down the facts you find in your research to remember them. You don't need to copy all the words, though. Instead, you can take notes.

Read the encyclopedia article below. Then look at the notes Tammy took when she read the article. Later she used her notes to make an outline.

Encyclopedia Article

Corn Oil
Corn oil is used for cooking and as salad oil. It is also used in the manufacture of products ranging from margarine to paint, soap, and linoleum.

Tammy's Notes

uses for corn oil – cooking, salad oil
also margarine, paint, soap, linoleum

Notice that Tammy's notes are much shorter than the article. Tammy wrote only the words she needed to remember.

YOUR TURN

Now you can practice taking notes. Follow these steps:

STEP 1 Work with a partner. Look up an interesting subject in an encyclopedia.

STEP 2 Choose an article or part of an article. Take notes on the information. You and your partner should each take your own notes.

STEP 3 Now compare your notes with your partner's notes. Talk about why each of you wrote down certain words and left out other words.

STEP 4 Then talk about what you and your partner have learned that will help both of you take better notes next time.

TIP When taking notes from different sources, use a separate note card for each detail. Write the title of the source on the note card.

Adjective	Adverb
soft	softly
slow	slowly
clear	clearly

Adjective or Adverb?

You can tell whether a word is an adjective or an adverb by looking at the word it describes.

Remember that an adjective describes a noun. It tells *what kind* or *how many*. An adverb describes a verb. It tells *where, when,* or *how.*

Examples:
San Antonio is a **peaceful** city. (adjective; tells *what kind*)
People can live **peacefully** in San Antonio. (adverb; tells *how*)

Often, words that end in *ly* are adverbs. Several of these adverbs are in the chart. However, you should always check if a word ending in *ly* describes a noun or a verb.

Guided Practice

A. Tell whether each underlined word is an adjective or an adverb.

Example: We listened <u>quietly</u> to the tour guide.
adverb

1. She told us about the <u>beautiful</u> city of San Antonio.
2. She spoke <u>calmly</u> to our group.
3. I listened <u>carefully</u> for facts about the city.
4. She used a <u>quiet</u> voice when she spoke of the Alamo.
5. The Alamo is the location of a <u>famous</u> battle.

Independent Practice

B. Write whether each underlined word is an adjective or an adverb. Then write the noun or verb it describes.

> **Example:** The birds outside our hotel chirped <u>cheerfully</u>.
> *adverb; chirped*

6. I awoke <u>early</u>.
7. We rode on a <u>new</u> bus to *La Villita*, or Little Village.
8. "Exit <u>carefully</u>!" said the bus driver.
9. *La Villita* takes up a <u>square</u> block.
10. It has beautiful <u>old</u> houses.
11. "Good afternoon!" the tour guide said <u>cheerfully</u>.
12. "<u>Two</u> people are missing from our group today," she said.
13. She gave <u>some</u> directions to the group.
14. We walked <u>rapidly</u> to the riverfront.
15. Soon we were eating lunch <u>happily</u>.

Writing Connection

Writer's Journal: Recording Ideas

Think about your community. What are some places that visitors might enjoy? Record your favorite ideas in a list. Then write several sentences about what you can see and do at the places on your list. Use adjectives and adverbs in your sentences.

Adverb Placement in Sentences

Adverbs can be in different places in a sentence.

You know that adverbs describe verbs. Sometimes, an adverb may come directly before or after the verb in a sentence. Other times, an adverb may be at the beginning or the end of a sentence. Notice that the adverb *eagerly* is in a different place in each sentence below.

Examples:

People **eagerly** travel to Texas.

People travel **eagerly** to Texas.

Eagerly, people travel to Texas.

People travel to Texas **eagerly**.

To vary your writing, try putting the adverbs in different places in your sentences.

Guided Practice

A. Identify the adverb in each sentence.

Example: Early settlers in Texas depended mostly on the land.
mostly

1. Many people farmed successfully.
2. Some people depended mainly on animals.
3. Farmers and ranchers carefully caught wild horses.
4. They tamed the wild horses quickly.
5. Finally, people could ride the horses.

Independent Practice

B. Write each sentence. Put the underlined adverb in a different place.

Example: <u>Once</u>, Texas was the largest state in the United States.
Texas was once the largest state in the United States.

6. Texans <u>proudly</u> show visitors their capital city, Austin.

7. There are parks in Austin <u>everywhere</u>.

8. There are <u>also</u> seven beautiful lakes.

9. Austin's population has increased <u>rapidly</u>.

10. <u>Now</u>, almost a half million people live in the city.

11. Texas was a part of Mexico <u>once</u>.

12. It is <u>now</u> the second largest state in the United States.

13. Some people <u>still</u> wear cowboy boots in Texas.

14. Texas is <u>widely</u> known for its open spaces.

15. However, people <u>usually</u> live in cities.

Remember

that you can put adverbs in different places in a sentence. This is one way to make your writing more interesting.

Writing Connection

Writer's Craft: Main Idea and Details Do some research to find out about a special event from your community's past. Work in a small group, and write a paragraph about the event. Be sure your paragraph includes details about when, how, and where this event took place. Place adverbs in different positions in your sentences.

USAGE AND MECHANICS

Using *Good* and *Well,* *Bad* and *Badly*

**Remember that an adjective describes a noun.
An adverb describes a verb.**

Good is always an adjective that tells *what kind.*
It describes a noun. *Well* is usually an adverb that
tells *how.* It describes a verb.

Examples:

Adjective: Texas is a **good** place to live.

Adverb: You can live **well** there.

Bad is an adjective. It is used to describe a noun.
It is sometimes used after the word *feel* to describe
the subject. *Badly* is an adverb. It is used to
describe a verb.

Examples:

Adjective: San Antonio has **bad** dry spells.

Adverb: Crops grow **badly** in dry spells.

Guided Practice

**A. Tell whether each sentence is correct or
incorrect.**

Example: The Battle of Flowers, an event during
Fiesta San Antonio, had a badly start.
incorrect

1. A battle sounds like a bad thing.
2. The Battle of Flowers is a well event.
3. It rained badly the first year of the event.
4. People felt bad that they had to wait four
   days to start it.
5. The event was held later and went good.

Independent Practice

Remember that *good* and *bad* are adjectives, and *well* and *badly* are adverbs.

B. Write *good* or *well* to complete each sentence.

Example: How _____ do you know your community?
well

6. Name three _____ places to visit in your community.
7. Where can you get more _____ information?
8. What kinds of businesses do _____ in your community?
9. Do any crops grow _____ in your area?
10. Are there any _____ parks where you live?

C. Write *bad* or *badly* to complete each sentence.

Example: Usually San Antonio does not have _____ weather.
bad

TEXAS

San Antonio

11. However, people can feel _____ when the temperature is over 100 degrees.
12. In the heat, people's bodies need water _____.
13. Some people sleep _____ on hot nights.
14. The heat can be _____ during the day.
15. It is not so _____ at night.

Writing Connection

Social Studies What do you like about your community? Are there some things your community should improve? Write several sentences telling what you like and dislike about your community. Use *good, well, bad,* and *badly* in the sentences.

Remember

that an adjective
describes a noun.
An adverb
describes a verb.
You can put
adverbs in
different places
in a sentence.

Extra Practice

A. Write whether the underlined word is an adjective or an adverb. *pages 336–337*

Example: Native Americans settled in Texas <u>first</u>.
adverb

1. Other settlers came more <u>recently</u>.
2. Some <u>brave</u> pioneers came from Mexico.
3. Mexican Texans brought along <u>many</u> customs and traditions.
4. <u>Today</u>, Mexican traditions are common.
5. Traditional Mexican foods are <u>popular</u> dishes in Texas.

B. Add the adverb from the parentheses ( ) to each sentence. Put it in the best place. *pages 338–339*

Example: (today) We learned about the cowhands in early Texas.
Today, we learned about the cowhands in early Texas.

6. (often) They wore hats like the big Mexican hats.
7. (skillfully) They rode their horses.
8. (sometimes) The cattle were frightened by noises.
9. (softly) Cowhands sang to them at night.
10. (usually) Cowhands slept outdoors.

C. Rewrite the sentences below, using the correct word in parentheses (). *pages 340–341*

Example: Crops grow (well, good) in San Antonio.
Crops grow well in San Antonio.

11. Our tour guide said we would like the (good, well) climate in San Antonio.
12. Every community has (badly, bad) weather sometimes, though.
13. The San Antonio Symphony plays (well, good).
14. There are many (well, good) parks in San Antonio.
15. We visited *La Villita*, or Little Village, for a (good, well) look at old San Antonio buildings.
16. Many people in San Antonio speak both English and Spanish (good, well).
17. Unfortunately, our field trip to San Antonio went (bad, badly).
18. The weather was not (good, well).
19. The museum's roof was leaking (badly, bad).
20. Our teacher hopes our next trip will not be so (badly, bad).

DID YOU KNOW?
Fiesta San Antonio is held every April. It celebrates the creation of the Texas Republic in 1836. The festival lasts one week.

Writing Connection

Real-Life Writing: Friendly Letter Think about a fair, festival, or other event in your community or at your school. Write a letter to a friend or family member telling about the special event. Use adjectives and adverbs in your letter. Put the adverbs in different places in your sentences.

STANDARDIZED TEST PREP

For additional test preparation, visit *The Learning Site:* www.harcourtschool.com

Chapter Review

Read the paragraph. Choose the word that belongs in each numbered blank. Mark the letter for your answer.

My grandmother moved to San Antonio, and I miss her (1) _____. Yesterday I felt (2) _____ when I got a letter from her. She wrote that San Antonio has lots of (3) _____ parks and museums. People can eat (4) _____ at many restaurants. She said she likes to shop in the *Paseo del Rio*. There's not a (5) _____ store there. She told me she fell and hurt her arm (6) _____. The doctor at the hospital treated her (7) _____. Sometimes the heat gets pretty (8) _____ in San Antonio. There's lots of sunshine, though, and the climate is (9) _____. I hope the sun is shining (10) _____ when I visit Grandma next month.

1 A good   **C** bad
   B terrible   **D** terribly

2 F happily   **H** happy
   G madly   **J** badly

3 A good   **C** funnest
   B well   **D** badly

4 F good   **H** bad
   G well   **J** happy

5 A swiftly   **C** bad
   B well   **D** badly

6 F good   **H** bad
   G well   **J** badly

7 A good   **C** bad
   B gently   **D** gentle

8 F brightly   **H** bad
   G well   **J** badly

9 A pleasant   **C** nicest
   B well   **D** pleasantly

10 F healthy   **H** badly
   G brightly   **J** healthier

Interviewing to Learn About Your Community

Preparing for an Interview
You will need:
- a videocamera or an audiocassette recorder
- videotape or audiotape

Planning an Interview
- If you will be recording the interview on videotape, think about how you want your interview to look. Where can you conduct your interview? What kind of background do you want to see in the picture?
- Learn something about the subject.
- Make up interesting questions. They should be the kind that need more than *yes* or *no* answers.

After an Interview
- Add music or other interesting sound effects to the videotape or audiotape before and after the interview.
- Write what you will say to introduce your tape to the class.

YOUR TURN

Interview someone in your community who knows about a community event, or ask a partner to act the part of such a person. Record the interview on videotape or audiotape. Be sure you know some facts about the event before you tape the interview. After you have finished the interview, present it to your class.

Homophones

Homophones are words that sound alike but have different meanings and different spellings.

Examples:

   Write a letter.   *(to put pen or pencil to paper)*
   He did not charge me the **right** amount.   *(correct)*

Examples:

   Take this road **to** the mall.   *(toward)*
   Those pants are **too** long for me.   *(more than needed)*
   This shirt is large, **too**.   *(also)*
   I will buy **two** new sweaters.   *(a number)*

Guided Practice

A. **Choose the homophone in parentheses ( ) to complete each sentence.**

   Example: (write|right) They will _____ the store's address on a card.   *write*

   1. (write|right) The clerk will _____ the price on tags.
   2. (write|right) The owner will make sure the prices are _____.
   3. (to|too|two) These _____ items are the same price.
   4. (to|too|two) This item is _____ expensive.
   5. (to|too|two) Take it _____ the back room.

Vocabulary Power

en•ter•prise
[en′tər•prīz′] *n.* An activity set up to earn money.

Independent Practice

B. Complete each sentence with the correct homophone in parentheses (). Write each sentence.

Example: (to|too|two) I want _____ make money. *to*

6. (write|right) We should _____ down our ideas for a new business.

7. (to|too|two) The _____ of us can buy what we need to make candy.

8. (to|too|two) We can take the candy _____ a store.

9. (write|right) If I am _____, we can sell lots of candy.

10. (to|too|two) Someone should take the money we make _____ the bank.

11. (to|too|two) I will put my savings in the bank, _____.

12. (to|too|two) There are _____ banks in our town.

13. (write|right) I will _____ to them both.

14. (to|too|two) Let's go _____ the candy sale.

15. (to|too|two) This costs _____ much!

Remember

that homophones are words that sound alike but have different meanings and different spellings.

Writing Connection

Art Connection What is your favorite store? Make a poster advertising the store. Show the products it sells and what is on sale. Write a sentence across the bottom of the poster to tell what makes the store special and why people should shop there. Try to use these words in your poster: *write, right, to, too, two*.

More Homophones

You know that homophones are words that sound alike but have different meanings and different spellings.

Here are some more homophones. Look at their different meanings and spellings.

Examples:
The children sold **their** toys.   *(belonging to them)*
You will find the prices listed **there**.   *(tells where)*
They're looking for the new shop.   *(they are)*
You can start **your** own enterprise.   *(belonging to you)*
You're old enough to have a paper route.   *(you are)*
The store opens **its** doors early.   *(belonging to it)*
It's good to use a shopping list.   *(it is)*

Guided Practice

A. Choose one of the homophones in parentheses () to complete the sentence.

Example: (your|you're) Is _____ business making money?   *your*

1. (their|there|they're) Hank wants to open a store over _____.
2. (its|it's) He has some money, but _____ not enough.
3. (your|you're) He wants to borrow some of _____ money.
4. (its|it's) Then you can share in _____ profits.
5. (Your|You're) _____ going to be glad you helped.

Independent Practice

B. Complete each sentence with the correct word in parentheses ( ). Write each sentence.

Example: (Your|You're) ____ going to have a job this summer. *You're*

6. (their|there|they're) Mr. and Mrs. Harker invited us to help on ____ farm.
7. (their|there|they're) The Harkers have an office ____.
8. (Their|There|They're) ____ going to show us the business side of farming.
9. (their|there|they're) The farmers send ____ crops to stores far away.
10. (their|there|they're) We can help with ____ business.
11. (Your|You're) ____ going to help send bills to the stores.
12. (its|it's) Check each bill to make sure ____ correct.
13. (its|it's) A business should keep ____ records in a file.
14. (your|you're) Mr. Harker will mail ____ pay for the work.
15. (your|you're) How will you spend ____ money?

Writing Connection

Real-Life Writing: Survey With a partner, write three survey questions to ask classmates about their favorite stores. Try to use some of these words in your questions: *their, there, they're, its, it's, your, you're.*

GRAMMAR-WRITING CONNECTION

Homographs and Other Homophones

Homographs are spelled the same but have different meanings. Notice that some homographs do not sound the same.

Examples:
Our class is taking a **trip**.   *(a journey)*
Be careful not to **trip**.   *(to stumble)*

It is in the **bow** of the ship.   *(front of a boat)*
The singers **bow** at the end of the show.   *(to bend at the waist)*
I have a **bow** and arrow.   *(tool used in archery)*

You know that homophones sound alike but have different meanings and spellings.

Examples:
Did you **see** the sign?   *(take in with the eyes)*
It shows a picture of the **sea**.   *(body of water)*

Do you **know** her name?   *(to understand)*
No, I do not.   *(opposite of yes)*

Guided Practice

A. Tell the meaning of each underlined homograph.

Example: Gentlemen sometimes bow to one
another.   *to bend at the waist*

1. Dad is going on a hunting <u>trip</u>.
2. On the ship, he will <u>bow</u> to the captain.
3. His luggage will be stored in the <u>bow</u>.
4. No one will <u>trip</u> over his archery equipment.
5. He is taking his <u>bow</u> and arrows.

Independent Practice

B. Write each sentence, using the correct word from the box.

| see   sea   trip   know   no   bow |

Example: I ——— that fishing is an important enterprise.   *know*

6. People catch fish from the _____.
7. We _____ them go out each day.
8. The ship's _____ holds the equipment.
9. Usually the fishing _____ is very short.
10. It is important to _____ about changes in the weather.
11. The workers on the boat _____ their heads when the wind blows.
12. A storm may come with _____ warning.
13. Sometimes they _____ storm clouds.
14. Workers keep the deck clear so no one will _____.
15. _____, there will not be any fishing today.

Writing Connection

Writer's Journal: Record Responses
Ask some classmates the questions that you wrote about favorite stores in your community. Record their answers on a chart. Check all the responses for homographs and homophones. Be sure you wrote them correctly in your chart.

Extra Practice

A. Complete each sentence with the correct word in parentheses ( ). Write each sentence. *pages 346-347*

Example: We can (write|right) a list of ways to earn money.   *write*

1. Yolanda has a list, (to|too|two).
2. She came up with (to|too|two) different enterprises.
3. A dog-walking service seems like the (write|right) idea.
4. She won't charge (to|too|two) much.
5. She will (write|right) an ad.

B. Complete each sentence with the correct word in parentheses ( ). Write each sentence. *pages 348-349*

Example: What is (your|you're) idea for a new product?   *your*

6. (Their|There|They're) thinking of ideas.
7. (Its|It's) not easy to create a new product.
8. Think about what things are already out (their|there|they're).
9. (Your|You're) going to think about buyers.
10. What are (their|there|they're) interests?
11. Talk about (your|you're) idea with others.
12. (Their|There|They're) thoughts are important.
13. Build your product over (their|there|they're).
14. What is (its|it's) name?
15. Be proud of (your|you're) idea!

For more
activities with
easily confused
words, visit
The Learning Site:
www.harcourtschool.com

352

C. Complete each sentence with the correct word from the box. Write each sentence. *pages 350-351*

see, sea   know, no   trip   bow

Example: Do you —— what kind of job you want to do?   *know*

16. My mom is going on a business ____.
17. She is going across the ____.
18. She will sleep in a cabin in the ____ of the ship.
19. There is ____ other place to sleep.
20. I will ____ her when she gets home.
21. Don't ____ over her suitcase!
22. I ____ that I will have a job like hers someday.
23. I will ____ different parts of the world.
24. People ____ when they say "Hello" in some countries.
25. I ____ my mom works hard.

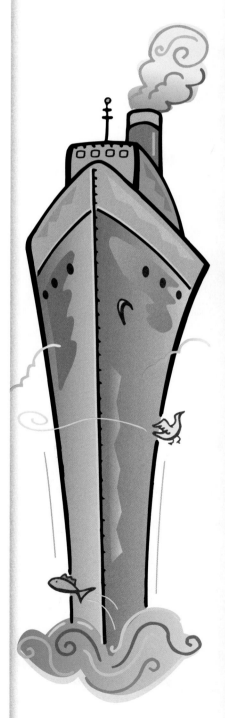

Writing Connection

Writer's Craft: Summarize Look at the chart you made about your classmates' favorite stores. With a partner, write a paragraph summarizing what you learned from your classmates' answers. Then trade papers with another group and check the paragraph for easily confused words.

Chapter Review

Choose the word that belongs in each space in the paragraph below. Write the letter for your answer.

> Do you want to go on a (1) _____? Do you (2) _____ how to plan a vacation? Many people (3) _____ to me for advice on where to visit. I might say they should go (4) _____ another country. I tell them what they should (5) _____. I have had (6) _____ unhappy customers. (7) _____ all planning to travel with me again. I can help you plan (8) _____ vacation.

TIP When you cannot answer a question right away, skip it and go on. Then come back to it after you have finished answering the other questions.

1 A trip
 B sea
 C see
 D right

2 F trip
 G bow
 H know
 J no

3 A write
 B right
 C see
 D you're

4 F your
 G to
 H too
 J two

5 A no
 B trip
 C see
 D sea

6 F its
 G it's
 H know
 J no

7 A Their
 B There
 C They're
 D see

8 F your
 G you're
 H know
 J no

**For additional test preparation, visit *The Learning Site:*
www.harcourtschool.com**

Troublesome Words

Not all easily confused words are homophones or homographs. Some words sound so much like each other that they are often misused.

Examples:

Isabela **set** her book on the table.   *(to place)*

She will **sit** down to do her homework.   *(to rest)*

set

sit

Her assignment is to draw a **picture**.   *(an image)*

This **pitcher** of water is a good subject.   *(a container)*

picture

pitcher

YOUR TURN

What are some word pairs that you find confusing? These words can be homophones, homographs, or words that sound like each other.

1. **Make a list of at least four words.**

2. **Use a dictionary or a grammar book to find the definition of each one.**

3. **Use each word in a sentence.**

TIP When using words that are easily confused, be sure to speak clearly so that others can understand you.

Writing Workshop

You know that a research report gives facts about a subject. The writer uses different sources to find facts. In this research report, Gail Gibbons writes about lighthouses. As you read, notice the facts she gives about the history of lighthouses.

Beacons of Light
LIGHTHOUSES
by Gail Gibbons

Lighthouses help guide ships and boats safely from one place to another. They warn of dangerous rocks and ledges, hidden points of land, sandbars, and narrow entrances to harbors.

The first guiding lights were huge bonfires that burned brightly from the tops of hills. In some places, sailors watched for landmarks, such as volcanoes, glowing in the night. For thousands of years, light signals didn't change very much. When lighthouses were built, they were often stone towers with fires burning at the top.

The first lighthouse in North America was the Boston Light, built in 1716. From Little Brewster Island, it guided sailing vessels in and out of Boston harbor. Over the next hundred years, many more lighthouses were built. Most were round and narrowed off at the top to resist wind and stormy seas. The light was placed high to be seen at a distance.

Boston Light

These early lighthouses used wick lamps as a source of light, burning whale oil or fish oil for fuel. The lighthouse keepers learned to increase the lamps' brightness by placing reflectors behind them.

In 1782, a Swiss scientist, Aimé Argand, developed a brighter lamp. It had a circular wick. When whale oil became scarce, colza (a form of vegetable oil), lard (from animal fat), and, later, kerosene were used. At that time, signals from lighthouses were visible only a few miles, even on a clear night.

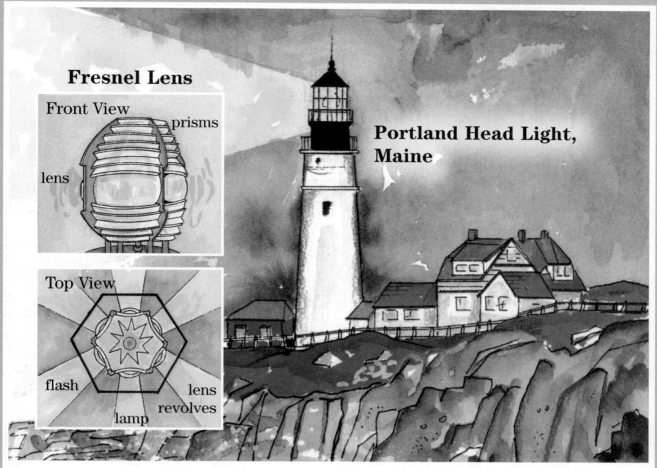

Fresnel Lens

Front View

prisms

lens

Top View

flash

lamp

lens revolves

Portland Head Light, Maine

Then, in 1822, the first modern lighthouse lens was invented by a Frenchman named Augustin Fresnel, who found a way to increase the light by using prisms. The prisms of the lens bent the light beam and concentrated it, making the light visible for many miles. In 1841, the Fresnel lens was installed for the first time in a lighthouse in the United States. Its beam could be seen twenty miles away at night.

The top of a lighthouse is like a giant lantern. Usually, a winding staircase goes to the top. Years ago, the lighthouse keeper made many trips up and down the stairs, doing chores. The burned lamp wick had to be *trimmed*—or adjusted and cut off—to keep the lamp from smoking. Lighthouse keepers were sometimes called *wick trimmers* or *wickies*.

lighthouse

kerosene

fog bell

fuel house

barn

house

Lighthouse keepers and their families were kept busy cleaning and polishing the lenses, shining all the brass in the lighthouse, and cleaning soot off the tower windows. The keeper's house stood near or was attached to the base of the lighthouse. Sometimes, the keeper lived right inside the lighthouse. Often, there were a number of other structures around the lighthouse, called outbuildings. Everything in and around the lighthouse was kept tidy. All of these buildings had to be maintained and frequently painted. It was hard work.

Today, lighthouses are powered by electricity. There are very few lighthouse keepers needed. Some lights stay on all the time. Others go on and off automatically.

electric lamp

boat house

They are maintained by the Coast Guard. Although they have changed over the years, lighthouses are still beacons of light to guide and warn of danger and to remind us of the past.

Vocabulary Power

vis·i·ble [vi'zə·bəl]
adj. Able to be seen.

Analyze THE *Model*

1. What is the topic of this research report? How far do you have to read to find out?

2. What facts does Gail Gibbons give about the first lighthouse in North America?

3. What facts does she give about today's lighthouses?

4. Why do you think Gail Gibbons included facts about the history of lighthouses in this piece of writing?

READING — WRITING CONNECTION

Parts of a Research Report

Gail Gibbons researched lighthouses and told the facts she learned about them. Read this research report that a student named Lita wrote. Pay attention to the parts of a research report.

MODEL

**introduction|
main topic**

subtopic

**supporting
facts|details**

subtopic

**supporting
facts|details**

Helping Boys and Girls

There are over 1,200 Boys & Girls Clubs in the United States, Puerto Rico, and the Virgin Islands. Communities organize the clubs to provide safe, caring places for young people to go. It does not cost much to belong to these clubs, so almost any boy or girl can join.

The clubs offer activities after school for students whose parents work. Boys and girls can play sports and make crafts at the clubs. They can also learn about finding careers and helping their communities. The skills boys and girls learn at the clubs can help them lead successful lives.

The clubs have grown over the years. The first clubs were started in the 1860's and were for boys only. Later, girls were allowed to join. Today, the clubs help about 1 1/2 million young people.

Though they have changed in some ways, Boys & Girls Clubs continue to help young people to be ready for the future. These clubs are in many communities, from big cities to small towns. Maybe there is one near you!

conclusion

Analyze THE Model

1. Who do you think is Lita's audience? What is her writing purpose?

2. What facts does Lita mention to introduce her topic?

3. What facts about the history of Boys & Girls Clubs did Lita find in her research?

Summarize THE Model

Use an outline to list the important facts that Lita included in her report. Look back at Chapter 27 if you need to review outline format. Include a main point on your outline for each paragraph in Lita's report. Then, list the facts in each paragraph under the correct main point. When your outline is complete, use it to write a summary of Lita's report.

Topic:
I. Introduction
   A.
   B.
II.
   A.
   B.

Prewriting

Purpose and Audience

You can learn more about a topic by doing research. In this chapter, you will share what you learn about a career by writing a research report.

WRITING PROMPT Write a research report to share with your classmates about a career that is important to the community. Begin with a paragraph that introduces your topic. Your report should include at least two subtopics with supporting details. Make sure your report also has a concluding paragraph.

Before you begin, think about your purpose and audience. What parts should your report include? Who will your readers be?

MODEL

Lita chose the Boys & Girls Clubs for her topic. Then she did research. She put the facts she found into an outline to organize her ideas. Here is the first part of her outline:

Topic: Boys & Girls Clubs
I. Introduction
   A. 1,200 clubs
   B. Communities organize
   C. Safe places
   D. Low cost of membership
II. Activities

Strategies Good Writers Use

- Decide on your audience.
- Decide on the purpose of your report.
- Include facts that will inform your audience.

YOUR TURN

Choose the job that you will write about. Research the job in one or more books. Take notes on important information. Then use an outline to organize your notes.

Organization and Elaboration

Follow these steps to help you organize your report:

STEP 1 Introduce the Topic
Introduce your main topic in the first paragraph.

STEP 2 Organize the Subtopics
Decide how to order the subtopics you researched.

STEP 3 Add Supporting Facts and Details
Add facts and details that support your subtopics.

STEP 4 End with a Summary
Summarize your main points in the last paragraph.

MODEL

Here is the first paragraph of Lita's research report. What interesting facts does she include?

> There are over 1,200 Boys & Girls Clubs in the United States, Puerto Rico, and the Virgin Islands. Communities organize the clubs to provide safe, caring places for young people to go. It does not cost much to belong to these clubs, so almost any boy or girl can join.

YOUR TURN

Now draft your research report. Follow the steps above. Use the outline you made.

Strategies Good Writers Use

- Introduce your topic with interesting facts.
- Use other facts to support your subtopics.
- End with a strong concluding paragraph.

Use a computer to write your draft. You can use the delete key to take out sentences that you decide to rewrite.

Revising

Organization and Elaboration

Reread your draft and think about these questions:

- How could I make my beginning more interesting?
- Does the order of my subtopics make sense?
- What facts could I add to better support my subtopics?
- How might I make my ending stronger?

Strategies Good Writers Use

- Include facts that will interest your audience.
- Replace weak words with exact ones.

Use the cut and paste feature to reorganize your facts.

MODEL

Here is another part of Lita's research report. Notice that she used some more precise words. She also added a sentence with more examples to support her subtopic.

The clubs offer activities after school for students whose parents work. Boys and girls can play sports and make crafts things at the clubs. They can also learn about finding careers and helping their communities. The skills boys and girls learn at the clubs can help them lead successful good lives.

YOUR TURN

Now revise your research report. Think about facts you might add to tell more about your subtopics.

Checking Your Language

Proofreading helps you find and correct mistakes in grammar, spelling, punctuation, and capitalization. It will be easier for your readers to understand your report if it has no mistakes.

MODEL

After Lita revised her research report, she proofread it. Here is another part of her report. What spelling mistakes did she correct? What other kinds of mistakes did she correct?

> The clubs have ~~grone~~ *grown* over the
> ~~yaers~~. The first clubs ~~are~~ *were* started in
> the 1860's and ~~are~~ *were* for boys only.
> Later, girls were ~~allowd~~ *allowed* to join.
> today, the clubs help about 1 1/2
> million young people.

Strategies Good Writers Use

- Look up words if you are not sure how to spell them.
- Watch out for easily confused words, such as to, two, and too.

YOUR TURN

Now proofread your revised research report. You may want to ask another writer to proofread it, too. Look for

- **grammar mistakes.**
- **spelling mistakes.**
- **mistakes in capitalization and punctuation.**

Editor's Marks

℘	take out text
∧	add text
∂	move text
¶	new paragraph
≡	capitalize
/	lowercase
○	correct spelling

367

Research Report

Publishing

Sharing Your Work

Now you will share your research report with your audience. Use the following questions to help you decide how to publish your work:

1. Who is your audience? How can you present your research report so your audience will enjoy it and learn from it?

2. Should you type your report on a computer or write it by hand? Should you use manuscript or cursive writing?

3. Would a multimedia presentation be an interesting way to present your research report? To give a multimedia presentation, follow the steps on page 369.

USING YOUR
Handbook

• Use the rubric on page 500 to evaluate your research report.

Reflecting on Your Writing

 Using Your Portfolio What did you learn about your writing in this chapter? Write your answer to each question below.

1. How did prewriting help you write a better research report?

2. What kinds of mistakes did you correct after proofreading your writing?

Place your answers and your research report in your portfolio. Take time to look through your portfolio and read your work. Write one or two sentences telling how your writing has improved.

Technology: Giving a Multimedia Presentation

A *multimedia* presentation involves several different means of communication, such as pictures, videos, music, or drama. After thinking about it, Lita decided to share her report with the class as a multimedia presentation. You can do the same. Use these steps:

STEP 1 Decide which multimedia aids might help your audience better understand your report. Can you use photos, drawings, videos, or music? Can you act out part of the information in your report?

STEP 2 Get permission to use any equipment you need, such as an audiotape or videotape player. If you need "actors," ask classmates to help.

STEP 3 Plan when you will use multimedia aids in your presentation. Prepare them ahead of time.

STEP 4 Organize your presentation. Write notes of what you will say. Practice your presentation.

STEP 5 At the end of your presentation, answer any questions your classmates ask.

Strategies for Multi-Media Presentations

- Choose multimedia aids that your whole audience can see and hear.
- Learn how to operate any equipment you need ahead of time. Practice using the equipment.
- Make sure that the equipment you plan to use works properly.

Unit 5
Grammar Review

CHAPTER 25

More About
Adjectives
pages 308–317

Articles pages 308–309

A. Write the correct article in parentheses ( ) for each sentence.

1. Calves are born in (the, an) spring.
2. (A, An) veterinarian comes to check the newborns.
3. The doctor brings (a, an) helper.
4. (The, A) new calves are healthy.
5. The birth was quite (a, an) adventure.

Adjectives That Compare

pages 310–311

B. Write the correct adjective that compares in parentheses ( ) for each sentence.

6. The farm down the road is (larger, largest) than our farm.
7. This is the (better, best) crop we have ever had.
8. Our machine works (faster, fastest) than theirs.
9. The rainy season was (heavier, heaviest) this year than last year.
10. It was the (baddest, worst) rainy season of all.

Avoiding Incorrect Comparisons pages 312–313

C. Write the correct form of the adjective in parentheses ( ) for each sentence.

11. (Few) sheep were born this year than last year.
12. Our sheep produce the (beautiful) wool in the county.
13. Their fleece is (soft) than anything else.
14. These lambs seem (active) than those lambs.
15. They are (playful) than the other lambs.

Adverbs   *pages 318–319*

A. Write the adverb that tells *how* in each sentence.

1. My kitten quickly raced out the door.
2. It easily climbed up on the roof.
3. It meowed loudly for help.
4. My neighbor, Mr. Kwan, softly called for the kitten.
5. It eagerly jumped into his arms.

More About Adverbs   *pages 320–321*

B. Write the adverb that tells *when* or *where* in each sentence.

6. Lindsay often visits the library.
7. She enjoys going there with her best friend.
8. They look everywhere for good books.
9. Soon they find three interesting stories.
10. Lindsay is now ready to go.

Comparing with Adverbs

pages 322–323

C. Write the correct form of the underlined adverb.

11. The car was traveling <u>fast</u> than the others.
12. The patrol officer went after the speeding car <u>quickly</u> than the other officers.
13. His siren sounded <u>loudly</u> than the patrol car behind him.
14. He drove the <u>carefully</u> of all.
15. He was the <u>more</u> praised officer of the year.

Adjective or Adverb? *pages 336–337*

A. Write whether each underlined word is an adjective or an adverb. Then write the noun or verb it describes.

1. I went to the new museum <u>early</u>.
2. The paintings were shown <u>beautifully</u>.
3. I chose <u>some</u> gifts from the gift shop.
4. The <u>old</u> museum was much smaller.
5. "Come back again," the tour guide said <u>cheerfully</u>.

Adverb Placement in Sentences *pages 338–339*

B. Add the adverb in parentheses ( ) to each sentence. Try to put the adverb in a different place in each sentence.

6. (regularly) Visitors come to our city.
7. (especially) They like the new science museum.
8. (everywhere) There are interesting sites in our city.
9. (now) The new museum is open.
10. (soon) More visitors will come.

Using *Good* and *Well, Bad* and *Badly* *pages 340–341*

C. Write *good, well, bad,* or *badly* to complete each sentence.

11. There is a _____ park near my home.
12. The park _____ needs cleaning.
13. I will do a _____ deed and help clean up the park.
14. We _____ need other volunteers.
15. We will clean the park _____.

Homophones *pages 346–347*

Unit 5
Grammar Review
CHAPTER 29

Easily Confused
Words
pages 346–355

A. **Complete each sentence with the correct word in parentheses ().**

1. (write/right) Mom was _____ about the many kinds of stores in the mall.

2. (to/too/two) I want _____ look in that hobby shop.

3. (write/right) I like to _____ letters decorated with rubber stamps.

4. (to/too/two) The hobby shop has _____ different rubber stamps for sale.

5. (to/too/two) We plan to visit the pet store, _____.

More Homophones *pages 348–349*

B. **Complete each sentence with the correct word in parentheses ().**

6. (Your/You're) _____ coming with us to the grocery.

7. (its/it's) I think _____ the store down on the corner.

8. (your/you're) Is this where _____ family shops?

9. (its/it's) This store has _____ own fresh vegetable section.

10. (their/there/they're) They have fresh fish _____.

Homographs and Other Homophones *pages 350–351*

C. **Complete each sentence with the correct word from the box.**

see	know	trip (n.)	bow (n.)
sea	no	trip (v.)	bow (v.)

11. We traveled to a village on our _____.

12. I wanted to _____ all the fishing boats.

13. I _____ a lot about fishing.

14. I got to stand on the _____ of a fishing boat.

15. _____ two boats were alike.

Oral History

What is your neighborhood like? What was it like many years ago? How has it changed? Find a neighbor who has lived in your neighborhood a very long time. With the permission of your parent or guardian, interview your neighbor. You could learn many things about your neighborhood's history. The steps below will help you.

Find a Neighbor to Interview

- Ask family members to help you decide on someone to interview.

- Arrange an interview with your neighbor. Set a date and time.

- Plan to take notes during the interview. Ask permission if you want to tape the interview.

Ask Your Neighbor Questions About Your Neighborhood

- What did our neighborhood look like when you first lived here?

- Who used to live in our neighborhood? What jobs did they have?

- What types of businesses and houses used to be here?

- What big changes have happened in our neighborhood?

- How has our neighborhood stayed the same?

Make a Report About Your Neighborhood

- Use notes from your interview to write a report. Tell something about the neighbor you interviewed. Explain what he or she said.

- Publish your report in a class newsletter or on your class website. E-mail it to people from your neighborhood.

Books to Read

Back Home
by Gloria Jean Pinkney
HISTORICAL FICTION
Ernestine visits the country town where her mother grew up. Although everything seems different from the city she knows, Ernestine still hopes to become friends with her cousin Jack.
ALA Notable Book; Notable Social Studies Trade Book

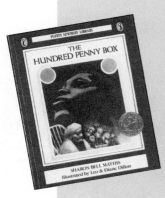

The Hundred Penny Box
by Sharon Bell Mathis
REALISTIC FICTION
Michael's great-great-aunt Dew has one penny for every year of her life and a story for every penny.
Newbery Honor; ALA Notable Book; Notable Social Studies Trade Book

Unit 6

Grammar — Usage and Mechanics

Writing — Expressive Writing

CHAPTER 31
Negatives 378

CHAPTER 32
Commas 388

CHAPTER 33
Writer's Craft: Elaboration
Writing a Character Study 398

CHAPTER 34
Quotation Marks 406

CHAPTER 35
Titles 416

CHAPTER 36
Writing Workshop
Writing a Story 426

Space Ride
by Tonya Jackson

The day of Rosa's first ride
into space was foggy and cold.
She was worried that the engines
on the spaces...

Negatives with *No* and *Not*

The words *no* and *not* are negative words.

Negative words such as *no* and *not* change the meaning of a sentence. *No* is often used as an adjective.

> **Example:**
> I think **no** subject is more important than science.

Not is an adverb. It makes the meaning of a verb negative.

> **Example:**
> We would **not** have electricity without science.

Remember that a contraction can sometimes be formed by joining a verb and the word *not*. A verb becomes a negative word when it is made into a contraction with *not*.

> **Example:**
> Scientific facts **aren't** opinions.

Some Negative Contractions

do not	don't
can not	can't
will not	won't
have not	haven't
was not	wasn't
is not	isn't

Vocabulary Power

in•ves•ti•gate
[in•ves′tə•gāt′] *v.*
To study thoroughly in order to learn facts or details.

Guided Practice

A. Tell the negative word in each sentence.

> **Example:** Some people do not know what science involves.
> *not*

1. Science is not about just one thing.
2. No book could tell everything about science.
3. Science gives us answers we didn't have before.
4. Science hasn't explained everything.
5. Some things are not easy to understand.

Independent Practice

B. Write the negative word in each sentence.

Example: Wasn't Thomas Edison a great inventor?
Wasn't

6. Thomas Edison did not do well in school.
7. His mother wasn't concerned, and she taught him everything she knew.
8. As a child, Edison couldn't stop reading science books.
9. Experimenting did not frighten him.
10. Even hearing problems didn't discourage young Edison.
11. One of his first inventions was not used.
12. However, Edison didn't give up.
13. Most homes had no electricity when Edison first invented the electric light.
14. I can't imagine life without electric power!
15. Edison's favorite invention was the phonograph, not the electric light.

Writing Connection

Writer's Journal

Writer's Journal: Story Ideas Think of a character for a story about a scientist. Write the name of your character in the center of a web. Then think of six sentences that describe the character, using negatives such as "She does not make wild guesses." Write these sentences on branches of the web. Use the ideas on your web to write a description of your character. Include at least three contractions made from a verb and the word *not* in your description.

Other Negatives

No one, nobody, nothing, none, nowhere, never, and *hardly* are also negative words.

Like *no* and *not*, each of these negative words changes the meaning of a sentence. Notice how the meaning of the sentence below changes when a negative word is used instead of a positive word.

Example:

(positive) We **always** do experiments.

(negative) We **never** do experiments.

Here are more negative and positive word pairs.

Negative Words	Positive Words
no one	everyone, someone
nothing	everything, something
none	one, all, some
hardly	almost

Guided Practice

A. Tell the negative word or words in each sentence.

Example: Before the Wright brothers, nobody could travel by plane. *nobody*

1. Nothing could stop the inventors from their dream of learning how to fly.
2. Orville and Wilbur Wright never grew tired of experimenting.
3. At first, nobody paid much attention to their work.
4. No one believed that a machine could fly.
5. Never before in history had anyone been able to fly in a machine.

Independent Practice

B. Make each sentence a true statement by replacing the underlined positive word with a negative word. Write the new sentence.

> **Example:** <u>Always</u> work alone in the science lab.
> *Never work alone in the science lab.*

6. Wait if <u>someone</u> can help you.
7. Sometimes, you need <u>something</u> but your eyes to study science.
8. You <u>always</u> know what you will find to study.
9. <u>Many</u> tools are needed to observe a plant.
10. You may notice something <u>everyone</u> else has observed.
11. <u>Always</u> pass up a chance to investigate nature.
12. <u>Somebody</u> has to tell you that science is fun.
13. You can use a book on experiments if <u>everyone</u> can help you.
14. You can <u>always</u> tell what interesting science facts you will find in a science book.
15. <u>Something</u> is more fun than learning.

Writing Connection

Writer's Craft: Point of View Choose an object to observe as a scientist might. Describe it using the following sentence starters:

> Everybody would say this object is _____.
> Nobody would say this object is _____.
> This object is always _____.
> This object is never _____.

Then write a descriptive paragraph about the object.

USAGE AND MECHANICS

Avoiding Double Negatives

When you use two negative words in one sentence, you are using a double negative.

Never use double negatives. They make the meaning of a sentence positive instead of negative and confuse readers. To correct a sentence with a double negative, delete one negative word or change one of the negative words to a positive word.

> **Examples:**
>
> Incorrect: I have <u>not never</u> studied chemistry.
>
> Correct: I have <u>never</u> studied chemistry.
>
> Correct: I have <u>not ever</u> studied chemistry.

Guided Practice

A. The sentences below are incorrect because they have double negatives. Name the double negative in each sentence.

Example: We had not never learned about George Washington Carver. *not never*

1. There was hardly no reason to believe Carver would become a famous scientist.
2. He didn't have no easy childhood.
3. There was not nothing he could do except investigate plants and animals.
4. He didn't have no one to help him study.
5. He hardly never had any free time to go to school.

Independent Practice

B. Each sentence has a double negative. Rewrite each sentence to correct the double negative.

> **Example:** Hardly no colleges would admit Carver.
> *Almost no colleges would admit Carver.*

6. Carver didn't never give up.
7. He wouldn't let nothing keep him from earning his science degree in 1896.
8. He couldn't never have become a famous inventor without studying hard in school.
9. Carver knew farmers wouldn't grow nothing because of poor soil.
10. Carver found there wasn't nothing better than peanuts and sweet potatoes for Alabama's soil.
11. Farmers didn't know nothing about these.
12. George Washington Carver wasn't never afraid to work hard to help people.
13. Because of him, Southern farmers wouldn't never grow only cotton in their fields.
14. George couldn't never stop there.
15. If it wasn't never for Carver, it would be much harder to be a farmer.

Remember

that you should never use two negative words in one sentence.

Writing Connection

Real Life Writing: Advertisement Write an advertisement for a product that a scientist might find useful. Include three incorrect sentences that include double negatives. Then trade papers with a partner and correct the double negatives in each other's advertisements. Read your corrected advertisement to your class.

Extra Practice

A. Write the negative word or words in each sentence. *pages 378–381*

> **Example:** Don't you know about the scientist Eloy Rodriguez? *Don't*

1. Eloy Rodriguez wasn't from a rich family.
2. Nothing could stop him from becoming a scientist.
3. He never stopped studying hard.
4. He learned from his family that medicines aren't the only things that cure people.
5. Dr. Rodriguez knows that plants called chiles can help people who are not well.

B. Write the negative word from the box that best completes each sentence. *pages 378–381*

wasn't	not	never	no	won't	couldn't

> **Example:** You may _____ have heard of the scientist Clever Fox.
> *not*

6. Clever Fox _____ go to school until he was nine.
7. He wasted _____ time once he got to school.
8. He _____ afraid to study hard to become a scientist.
9. Clever Fox has _____ gone into space, but his experiments have gone up in spaceships.
10. He wants to find a type of power that _____ hurt the earth.

Remember

that negative words change the meaning of a sentence. *No, not, no one, nobody, nothing, none, nowhere, never,* and *hardly* are all negative words. A verb becomes a negative word when it is made into a contraction with *not.*

For more activities with negatives, visit *The Learning Site:*

www.harcourtschool.com

C. Rewrite each sentence to correct the double negative. *pages 382–383*

Example: Robert Jones couldn't not stop asking questions when he was a boy.
Robert Jones couldn't stop asking questions when he was a boy.

11. He didn't hardly mind making his own science experiments.
12. However, he invented things that no one else had never imagined.
13. He didn't never quit in college.
14. Jones never doubted that he would not become a scientist.
15. Nothing has never interested Jones as much as investigating better ways to grow crops.
16. Inventors aren't hardly very different from scientists.
17. Many inventions couldn't hardly have been made without scientific thinking.
18. Inventors can't never forget about science facts.
19. They can't not settle for the way things are.
20. They don't never quit looking for new ideas.

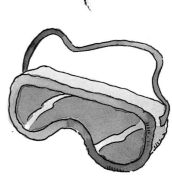

Writing Connection

Science Imagine that you are a scientist and you've just invented a new kind of shoe that helps people go places faster. Describe what worked and didn't work as you did your experiments. Use several negative words in your description. When you proofread, make sure there are no double negatives to confuse your readers.

Chapter Review

Read the paragraph. Choose the best way to rewrite each underlined section, and mark the letter for your answer. If the underlined section needs no change, mark the choice *No mistake*.

(1) <u>Haven't you never</u> thought about all the inventions around you? An invention starts with an idea, but it (2) <u>doesn't never</u> end there. Lots of hard work goes into inventing new things. (3) <u>Not all</u> inventors work in fancy labs. Some work on kitchen tables or in their basements. A few inventions make lots of money right away. Others (4) <u>do not</u>.

There have been some inventions, like cars, that (5) <u>aren't hardly</u> popular right away. Later, people accept the idea. There are other inventions that (6) <u>no one never</u> wants. One example is glasses for chickens, invented in 1903.

TIP Read the directions carefully. Be sure you know exactly what you are supposed to do.

1 A Have you not never
  B Haven't you ever
  C Have you never not
  D No mistake

2 F doesn't never ever
  G doesn't
  H doesn't not
  J No mistake

3 A Not no
  B Hardly no
  C Not hardly no
  D No mistake

4 F hardly never
  G don't never
  H never don't
  J No mistake

5 A are not hardly
  B are hardly not
  C aren't
  D No mistake

6 F no one ever
  G not nobody
  H no one don't
  J No mistake

For additional test preparations, visit *The Learning Site:*
www.harcourtschool.com

Comparing Images

Sometimes artists draw pictures to help show what a writer's words mean. When choosing pictures for a story, it's important to select ones that best fit the story or the characters.

Imagine that a writer has created a funny story about a scientist. The scientist loves his work, but he is always making mistakes. The reason he makes mistakes is that he does everything backward.

If you were the writer, you might want to compare the pictures below and then decide which one fits your story best. Follow these three steps to compare the drawings:

1. List what is the same about the drawings.

2. List what is different about each drawing.

3. Look at the completed lists. Decide which picture best fits the way the character is described in the story.

YOUR TURN

Write a short paragraph about a scientist. Create three quick drawings of the person you have imagined. Then exchange with a partner your pictures and the paragraphs you wrote. Use the steps above to compare the pictures your partner has drawn. Then choose the picture that best fits your partner's paragraph. Tell your partner why you made this choice.

TIP
Remember that readers need to know how the characters act and feel, not just how they look. Be sure to look for these things when you read and when you compare drawings of characters.

Commas

A **comma** (,) separates parts of a sentence and helps make the meaning clear.

Three or more similar words listed together are called a **series**. In a series of three or more similar words, put a comma after each item except the last one. The last comma should be before *and* or *or*.

Example:

Mountains, valleys, and islands are three natural landforms on Earth's surface.

When a sentence is addressed to someone directly, put a comma after the person's name. Also use commas after the words *yes*, *no*, and *well* at the beginning of a sentence.

Examples:

Lilly, will you pack my lunch for the hike?

Yes, a diamond is a mineral.

Vocabulary Power

min•er•al
[min′ər •əl] *n*. A natural material that does not come from a plant or an animal.

Guided Practice

A. Tell where commas are needed in each sentence. Be ready to explain why.

Example: I am meeting Sue Paul and Emily.
I am meeting Sue, Paul, and Emily.

1. Yes I have been to the museum before.
2. The museum has information about plants animals and Earth.
3. Rickie let's make sure we take notes.
4. Well we should see the movie about minerals.
5. It will show uses for minerals like diamonds quartz and iron.

Independent Practice

B. Write the sentence. Add a comma or commas where they are needed.

> **Example:** I rowed toward the island with Dad Mr. Omerjee and Elena.
>
> *I rowed toward the island with Dad, Mr. Omerjee, and Elena.*

6. We sang whistled and hummed as we rowed.

7. Yes the sandy island seemed far away.

8. Dad how is the sand formed?

9. It is made of minerals and rocks that are sharp round and very small.

10. Well we passed a beach with lots of sand.

11. Mr. Omerjee how did the sand get there?

12. Wind sun and rain can change rocks into sand.

13. We could see sand wood and shells on the shore.

14. Dad I think the sand will feel hot on my toes.

15. Sand can be found on the shores of islands rivers lakes and oceans.

Writing Connection

Writer's Journal

Writer's Journal: Taking Notes Talk with a classmate about the kinds of rocks you have seen in your neighborhood. Then make a list of these different rocks. Choose two rocks on your list, and write a sentence about each one. In your sentences, use exact words to give three details about each rock's look and feel. Make sure to use commas correctly.

More About Commas

Commas are used in letters, dates, and addresses.

Commas follow both the greeting and the closing of a letter. Use a comma after greetings such as *Dear Grandmother* in a letter and after the closing words such as *Thank you*, *Love*, and *Good-bye*.

Examples:

Greeting

Dear Grandmother,
I had a wonderful vacation.
Love,
Sean

Closing

A comma belongs between the name of the city and the state. A comma is also placed between the day and the year.

Examples:
Heading in a Letter

27 North 4th Street
Olean, New York 14760
June 16, 2000

Guided Practice

A. Tell where a comma is needed in each sentence or letter part.

Example: Sincerely Mom   *Sincerely, Mom*

1. Your friend Ahmad
2. My baby brother was born on March 24 1999.
3. Many cars are made in Detroit Michigan.
4. Dear Aunt Rita
5. Love Mama and Dad

Dear Ron,
I'm having fun panning for gold with Aunt Kim.
Love,
Alice

Ron Chen
3 Harbor Dr.
San Diego, CA
92015

Independent Practice

B. Write the letter in the box. Add commas where they are needed.

Example:

> 28 Rockford Street
> Los Angeles, California 91107
> August 9, 2001

Dear Grandpa,

    I miss you and wish you were here in Los Angeles, California. You could see my great fossil collection. I will show it to you when you visit.

> Love,
> Susan

6. 253 Lee Street
   Alexandria Virginia 22206
7. December 25 2001
8. Dear Aunt Annie
9. Thank you very much for the great book on rocks. My science class took a field trip to Charlottesville Virginia. I hope you are having a happy winter! I'll see you on January 1 2001!
10. Miss you
    Leah

Writing Connection

Art Pretend that you know where a hidden mine can be found. Draw a map to show the mine's location. Then write a paragraph that tells how to find the mine and what is in it. Remember to use commas in the paragraph as you mention locations and dates.

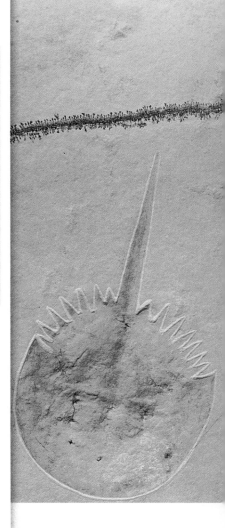

USAGE AND MECHANICS

Combining Sentences with Commas

Commas are used to help separate parts of a sentence.

When you join two simple sentences with the word *and*, *or*, or *but*, the new sentence is called a compound sentence. Use a comma before the word *and*, *or*, or *but* in compound sentences.

Examples:

I like emeralds. Ruth likes diamonds.

I like emeralds, but Ruth likes diamonds.

My mom likes opals. My dad gave her one.

My mom likes opals, and my dad gave her one.

Guided Practice

A. Tell where a comma is needed in each sentence.

Example: Our class likes hiking and we go on nature walks together.   *hiking, and*

 1. Marisol climbed Mount Red and she hiked in River Park.
 2. She looks for new kinds of birds and once she saw a blue heron.
 3. I like birds but I hope to find some neat insects on my hike.
 4. Joshua looks for striped rocks but they are hard to find.
 5. Sasha walked along a mountain path and he found animal tracks in the snow.

Independent Practice

B. Combine the sentences to form a compound sentence using *and* or *but*. Add commas where they are needed.

Example: We've been to Crater Lake. We loved it
We've been to Crater Lake, and we loved it.

6. Crater Lake is in Oregon. It is at the top of a mountain.

7. The mountain is a volcano. It has not erupted for a long time.

8. The lake is in the crater of the volcano. There is an island in the lake.

9. Crater Lake is beautiful. I want to swim in it.

10. I plan to go back next year. I don't know who will come with me.

Remember

to use a comma before *and, or,* or *but* when joining two sentences in a compound sentence.

DID YOU KNOW
Crater Lake used to be called Deep Blue Lake because of its dark blue color. No streams flow into or out of the lake. It gets all its water from rain and snow.

Writing Connection

Writer's Craft: Personal Voice Pretend that you and a partner are fossils. Decide what plant or animal you used to be. Write a paragraph about the changes you have gone through. For example, are you a dinosaur's footprints? Did some rocks cover you? Using commas correctly, combine some of your sentences into compound sentences.

Extra Practice

A. Write the sentence. Add commas where they are needed. *pages 388–389*

Example: It took two days to drive from St. Louis to Denver Colorado. *Denver, Colorado*

1. We went on a vacation to Death Valley California.
2. It was 100 degrees at midnight and that's hot!
3. Well if it's that hot at midnight, I would not want to be outside in the afternoon!
4. Tina did you know that Death Valley is a desert?
5. It is hot dry and rocky in many places.

B. Combine the sentences to form a compound sentence using *and* or *but*. Add commas where they are needed. *pages 392–393*

Example: We will go to the large caves. We will look for pictures on the walls.
We will go to the large caves, and we will look for pictures on the walls.

6. Some cave paintings are handprints. Some pictures of animals.
7. I read about cave paintings in France. They are pictures of horses and bulls.
8. Many cave paintings show lions. Only one painting is a panther.
9. Some caves form on the sides of hills. They are all sizes and shapes.
10. Caves by the sea are called sea caves. They are formed by waves hitting cliffs on the shore.

For more activities with commas, visit *The Learning Site:* www.harcourtschool.com

C. Read the parts of the letter. Then write the letter and add commas where they are needed. *pages 390–391*

11. 131 Winthrop Road
    Topeka Kansas 66616
12. April 19 2001
    Dear Uncle Jasper,
13. Will you be able to come to our school farm picnic on May 1 2001?
14. It will be held in Kansas City Kansas.
15. Your nephew,
    Sidney

D. Write each sentence, adding a comma or commas where they are needed. *pages 388–391*

16. My family visited the Luray Caverns on June 19 2000.
17. They are near Luray Virginia.
18. We arrived at about 9:30 A.M. and then we went through the caves.
19. My favorite places were Giant's Hall Dream Lake and the Stalacpipe Organ.
20. I had a wonderful time at the cavern and I hope to go back.

Writing Connection

Writer's Craft: Sentence Variety Write a paragraph about different kinds of rocks you have seen. Vary the kinds of sentences that you use. Make some sentences short and some compound. Write at least one sentence that has a series of items. Be sure to use commas correctly in your paragraph.

For additional test preparation, visit *The Learning Site:*

www.harcourtschool.com

TIP Read the whole sentence before deciding how to punctuate it correctly.

Chapter Review

Read the letter. Some sections are underlined. Choose the best way to write each section and mark the letter for your answer. If the underlined section needs no change, mark the choice "No mistake."

---

89 Cherry Lane

(1) <u>Menlo Park. CA</u> 94025
(2) <u>May 26 2002</u>

Dear Latrell,

   We just got back. (3) <u>Latrell we had fun</u> in (4) <u>Boston, but im glad</u> to be home. I saw (5) <u>fish birds and shells</u> at the beach.

(5) <u>Your cousin</u>
Andrea

---

1 A Menlo Park! CA

  B Menlo Park, CA

  C Menlo Park CA

  D No mistake

2 F May 26, 2002

  G May, 26, 2002

  H May 26. 2002

  J No mistake

3 A Latrell, we had fun

  B Latrell. we had fun

  C Latrell we had fun,

  D No mistake

4 F Boston, but I'm glad

  G Boston? but I'm glad

  H Boston but, I'm glad

  J No mistake

5 A fish birds and shells,

  B fish, birds, and shells

  C fish, birds and shells

  D No mistake

6 F Your, cousin

  G Your cousin,

  H Your cousin.

  J No mistake

Listening Outside the Classroom

People who give directions use special words. They name directions, distance, and landmarks. A landmark is a place, like a big building, a river, or a hill. Notice these kinds of words as you listen to directions.

Directions	Distance	Landmarks
left, right	block, mile	Go beyond the bridge . . .
east	near, far	When you see the big
straight ahead		white house . . .

Here are some ways to help you follow directions:

- Picture in your mind what you are supposed to do.
- Ask the person giving the directions to repeat them.
- Say the directions back to the person who gave them.
- On a map, follow any instructions you are given.
- Write down the directions.

YOUR TURN

With a partner, choose a place in your classroom where you want your classmates to go. Then draw a map of the route.

- **Label landmarks in the room, such as windows, cabinets, or desks.**
- **Make an *X* on the starting point and an *X* at the ending point.**
- **Draw a line that shows the path people should take from the starting point to the ending point.**

Exchange directions with another team, and see if your classmates can follow your directions.

TIP Try out one or two of the ideas listed as you do YOUR TURN. Find out which one works best for you.

Writer's Craft

Elaboration

Suppose you want to write to express an idea or a feeling. This kind of writing is called expressive writing. A character study is a special form of expressive writing that describes a person.

Read the following passage from the book *Back Home*. Look at how the writer describes a character in the story.

LITERATURE MODEL

Ernestine recognized Uncle June Avery right away. She remembered Mama saying, "He'll probably bring you flowers." He also had the same sparkling eyes and apple-dumpling cheeks as Grandmama Zulah in Mama's old photograph.

He was waiting on the platform as the Silver Star slowly pulled into Robeson County Depot. When he caught a glimpse of Ernestine peering through the window, his face lit up in a broad smile.

—from *Back Home*
by Gloria Jean Pinkney

Analyze THE Model

1. What character is the author describing?
2. How did Ernestine recognize him?
3. What kind of person do you think he is? Why do you think so?

Using Elaboration

Using elaboration means using ideas and words that help your readers picture in their minds the person you are describing. Study the chart on the next page.

Vocabulary Power

e·lab·o·ra·tion
[i·lab′ə·rā′shən] *n.*
Developing and expanding a topic by adding details and reasons.

Strategies to Use for Elaboration	How to Use Strategies	Examples
Use figurative language.	• Figurative language describes something by comparing it to something else.	• apple-dumpling cheeks • hair as white as snow
Use exact words.	• Choose words that say exactly what you mean.	• "he **caught a glimpse** of Ernestine **peering** through the window."

YOUR TURN

THINK ABOUT ELABORATION Work with two or three classmates. Look at some stories and find examples of how writers describe different characters. Discuss the examples with your group.

Answer these questions:

1. What character is the writer describing?
2. How does the writer help you see in your mind a picture of the character?
3. Does the writer make comparisons to describe the character? If so, explain the comparisons.
4. How does the writer use exact words to describe?

Using Figurative Language

A. Read each sentence. On your paper, name the items that the writer compares in each sentence.

1. Jody's eyes sparkled like diamonds.
2. Dad's arms were as strong as steel.
3. Her long hair was a banner flying in the wind.
4. Willie runs like a spider on his long, thin legs.
5. The children's voices were little bells jingling with laughter.
6. The blanket was as soft as a kitten.
7. Excitement spread like wildfire.
8. He was the apple of his father's eye.
9. Mom's pleasure shone through her eyes like a moonbeam.
10. This scent smells like fresh flowers.

B. Choose a word from the box to complete each comparison. Write the completed sentences on your paper.

> **birds   garden   roses
> sunshine   thundercloud**

11. The baby's cheeks were as red as _____.
12. Grandfather's frown was a _____.
13. Mrs. Henderson's colorful hat looks like a _____ on her head.
14. His smile is as warm as_____.
15. Her hands are fluttering _____ looking for a place to land.

Using Exact Words

C. Choose a more exact word from the box to replace the underlined word in each sentence. Write the revised sentence on your paper.

wade	basket	friendly	switch
hammer	hike	enjoyable	bounced

1. Peter has a <u>nice</u> smile.
2. We had a very <u>nice</u> time at the party.
3. They had to <u>walk</u> a long way up the mountain.
4. Kelly likes to <u>walk</u> in the shallow water at the beach.
5. Put the trash in that green <u>thing</u>.
6. Where is the <u>thing</u> to turn on the light?
7. Dad used a <u>tool</u> to pound in these nails.
8. I need <u>something</u> to hold these picnic supplies.
9. Skating is a very <u>good</u> form of exercise.
10. The ball <u>went</u> down the steps.

Writing ᴀɴᴅ Thinking

Write to Record Reflections We use figurative language every day. For instance, you may say that something is as blue as the sky or that someone runs like the wind. Why do people enjoy using, hearing, and reading figurative language? Write your reflections in your Writer's Journal.

Character Study

Gloria Jean Pinkney wrote a description of Uncle June Avery. Paul decided to write a character study of his mother's Aunt Jessie. As you read what Paul wrote, look at how he used elaboration in his description.

MODEL

figurative
language
exact words

figurative
language

> The first time I met my mother's Aunt Jessie, I didn't know what to think of her. Aunt Jessie is as thin as a stick. She frowned at me and muttered, "So you're Paul, are you?"
>
> "Yes, Aunt Jessie," I replied politely.
>
> Suddenly she let out a lion's roar of a laugh. "We're going to be great friends, Paul," she declared.
>
> I didn't know it then, but Aunt Jessie was right.

Analyze THE Model

1. Does Paul's description give you a clear picture of Aunt Jessie? Why or why not?
2. How does Paul use figurative language to elaborate his description?
3. How does Paul use exact words to elaborate his description?
4. What kind of person do you think Aunt Jessie is? Why do you think so?

YOUR TURN

WRITING PROMPT Choose an interesting character that you have seen in a movie or a video. Write a character study to describe the character to your classmates. Use elaboration to make your description interesting and exact.

STUDY THE PROMPT Ask yourself these questions:

1. What is your purpose for writing?

2. Who is your audience?

3. What is your subject?

4. What writing form will you use?

USING YOUR

Handbook

- Use the Writer's Thesaurus to find interesting and exact words to use in your character study.

Prewriting and Drafting

Plan Your Character Study Choose a character whom you would like to describe. Think of details you can tell your readers to help them imagine the character. Use a web like this one to organize your ideas.

what the character looks like

personality traits

character's name

actions that show what kind of person the character is

Editor's Marks

ℐ   take out text

∧   add text

ↄ   move text

¶   new paragraph

≡   capitalize

/   lowercase

◯   correct spelling

Editing

Reread the draft of your character study. Do you want to add or change anything? Use this checklist to help you revise your work.

☑ Do you give your reader a clear picture of the character?

☑ Are there details you can add to describe the character better?

☑ Can you add figurative language to help the reader understand your description?

☑ Have you used exact words?

Use this checklist as you proofread your paragraph.

☑ I have begun my sentences with capital letters.

☑ I have used the correct end marks for my sentences.

☑ I have used negatives correctly and avoided double negatives.

☑ I have used commas and colons correctly.

☑ I have used a dictionary to check my spelling.

Sharing and Reflecting

Writer's Journal

Make a final copy of your character study. Share it with a partner. Discuss how each of you can use elaboration to make your writing better. Write your reflections in your Writer's Journal.

Looking at Fine Art

In a character study, a writer uses words to describe someone. An artist may draw or paint a picture to show what a person looks like. Details in the drawing or painting can help you understand the subject's personality, too.

Look at this painting. It is called *Woman with a Cat*. It was painted by a famous artist named Pierre-Auguste Renoir.

YOUR TURN

Discuss *Woman with a Cat* in a group with two or three classmates. Talk about these questions:

- Why do you think the artist decided to include the cat in this picture?

- What can you tell about the woman from the way she holds the cat?

- What other details do you notice in this painting?

- How can you describe the woman in words? Use exact words and examples of figurative language.

- How else could the artist have shown you the kind of person this woman was?

Detail, National Gallery of Art, Washington, Gift of Mr. and Mrs. Benjamin E. Levy

Direct Quotations

Someone's exact words are called a direct quotation.

Use quotation marks (" ") to show the exact words of a speaker. Quotation marks should be placed around all of the speaker's words.

Examples:

Maria said, "I found out what causes heat."

"It has to do with energy," she explained.

"Everything is made of matter," she added.

Guided Practice

A. Tell whether or not each sentence has a direct quotation.

> **Example:**   "Matter is made of particles," Maria told us.
> *direct quotation*

1. She added that it takes energy for the particles to move.
2. Kareem stated, "The particles move all the time."
3. "When something is hot, it has a lot of energy," Marsha said.
4. She explained that the hotter something is, the faster its particles are moving.
5. "Do particles in my soup move faster than particles in my sandwich?" Robert asked.

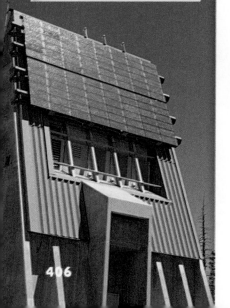

Independent Practice

Remember to put quotation marks around direct quotations.

B. Write the sentences. Put quotation marks where they are needed.

> **Example:** Today we are going to learn about thermometers, Ms. Jefferson said.
>
> *"Today we are going to learn about thermometers," Ms. Jefferson said.*

6. She said, A thermometer measures heat.

7. Most thermometers are tubes with special liquid, she explained.

8. What do thermometers do? Joseph asked.

9. The teacher told him, A thermometer can tell us what the temperature is outside.

10. She added, It can also tell us how warm it is inside.

11. Thermometers have numbers printed on them, Ms. Jefferson explained.

12. She told us, The numbers show the temperature.

13. Lydia said, Water boils at 100° Celsius.

14. That is right! Ms. Jefferson exclaimed.

15. She asked, Did you know that paper burns at 184° Celsius?

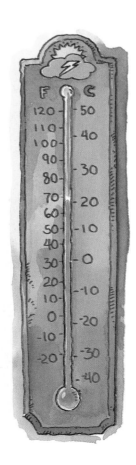

Writing Connection

Real-Life Writing: Comic Strip With a partner, create a comic strip that shows how people are affected by hot and cold temperatures. Put your characters' words in quotation marks to show exactly what they are saying.

More About Quotation Marks

When using quotation marks, you must be sure to use correct punctuation and capitalization.

Use a comma (,) to separate a speaker's words from the other words in a sentence. Capitalize the first word of a quotation.

Examples:

"The sun provides much of Earth's energy," our teacher said.

She explained, "Earth has lots of energy."

Put the end mark inside the second set of quotation marks. Do not use a comma when there is an exclamation point or a question mark.

Examples:

"The sun provides heat," she added.

"The sun is stronger than a heater!" exclaimed Todd.

Guided Practice

A. Tell how you would fix the punctuation or capitalization mistake in each sentence.

Example: "Light is a kind of energy" Mr. Nadal said.
"Light is a kind of energy," Mr. Nadal said.

1. "Light gives things their colors" he said.
2. "Wow, that's neat" Thomas shouted loudly.
3. "what do you see in a mirror?" Mr. Nadal asked.
4. Jesse answered "I see myself."
5. "Your reflection is light bouncing off the mirror, he said.

Independent Practice

B. **Each sentence has one or more mistakes in capitalization or punctuation. Write the sentence, correcting the mistake.**

Example: Callie said, "Earth spins around like a top.
Callie said, "Earth spins around like a top."

6. "Earth's movement is called rotation" she said.

7. Jerome added, "Earth rotates once each day"

8. "do you know why we have light in the daytime?" Callie asked.

9. "I do! I do" Francesca shouted.

10. She explained, It is daytime when our part of Earth faces the sun."

11. He asked, "how can it be day here and night somewhere else"

12. Callie explained As Earth rotates, one part of Earth is facing the sun and one isn't"

13. "it's daytime on the part of Earth that is facing the sun, she noted.

14. She added "It is night on the side of Earth that is facing away from the sun.

15. I get it! Warren cried.

Remember

to use correct punctuation and capitalization with quotation marks.

Writing Connection

Writer's Journal

Writer's Journal: Recording Ideas

Talk to a partner about why stories that take place at night can be scary. Are stories that are set during the day always happy stories? Write three sentences about what you and your partner discuss. Use quotation marks to include the exact words you and your partner say.

Punctuating Dialogue

Dialogue is conversation between two or more speakers.

Dialogue uses direct quotations to show a person's exact words. Dialogue also uses a noun or a pronoun with words such as *said, replied, asked, added,* and *shouted* to tell who the speaker is.

Example:

"I love early mornings!" exclaimed Ellen.

When the part of the dialogue that identifies the speaker divides a direct quotation, you need two commas.

Examples:

"I know," explained Marc, "that Earth circles the sun."

"I love learning about science," he said, "because you can see it all around you."

Guided Practice

A. **In each sentence, identify the words that tell who is speaking and how you know.**

Example: "Each circle around the sun," Marc told us, "is called a revolution." *Marc told us*

1. "How does that relate to the seasons?" asked Paula.
2. "It's very interesting!" Marc exclaimed.
3. He continued, "Each revolution around the sun takes one year."
4. Sam added, "Earth also tilts."
5. "You are right," Marc said with a smile.

Independent Practice

B. Identify the speaker in each sentence.

Example: "What causes shadows?" asked Melanie.
Melanie

6. "Yes," said Paul, "sunlight causes shadows."
7. He added, "In the morning, trees cast long shadows."
8. "As Earth rotates, the shadows grow shorter," Juanita said.
9. Kim replied, "At noon, the shadows are short."
10. "Later in the day," he went on, "the shadows grow longer again."

C. Each sentence contains errors in capitalization or punctuation. Write each sentence, correcting the errors.

Example: How many seasons are there?" Jon asked.
"How many seasons are there?" Jon asked.

11. There are four seasons," Claire answered.
12. "My favorite season" Joy shouted, "is spring"
13. "How do the seasons change" asked Pierre.
14. "The seasons change, explained Tim, "because Earth spins and tilts on an axis."
15. I said, "It is warm when Earth tilts toward the sun.

Remember to use quotation marks when you are writing dialogue. Use a comma to separate a direct quotation from the words that tell who is speaking.

Writing Connection

Technology Work with a partner to write a dialogue between two people discussing the seasons. Write your sentences on a computer or on paper. Use correct capitalization and punctuation in your quotations.

Remember

to use quotation marks to show a speaker's exact words. Be careful to use correct capitalization and punctuation with quotation marks.

Extra Practice

A. Write each sentence. Add quotation marks where they are needed. *pages 406–407*

Example: Eliza told us, The sun's energy can change the air pressure on Earth.
Eliza told us, "The sun's energy can change the air pressure on Earth."

1. That change in air pressure causes storms, she went on.
2. Do you mean storms can be caused by the sun? Alex asked.
3. Yes, and so was last month's snow, Eliza told him.
4. She explained, Some of the sun's energy isn't good for us.
5. The sun's rays can give you a sunburn, she said.

B. Each sentence contains mistakes in punctuation or capitalization. Write each sentence, correcting the errors. *pages 406–411*

Example: Channa said "The center of the sun is called the core.
Channa said ‚ "The center of the sun is called the core."

6. "The core is small compared with the size of the sun, she told us.
7. Do you know how hot it is" she asked.
8. She said it is about 27 million degrees!"
9. "that's hot Frank shouted.
10. Channa said, it is the hottest part of the sun"

For more activities about quotation marks and punctuation, visit *The Learning Site:*
www.harcourtschool.com

C. For each sentence, identify the words that tell who is speaking and how. *pages 410–411*

Example: Ishiro explained, "A sunspot is a cool spot on the sun."
Ishiro explained

11. "Because it is cooler, it looks darker," he said.
12. Tony said, "There are many sunspots."
13. "Sometimes," Ishiro added, "a sunspot can cause a burst of energy."
14. "What is that energy called?" asked the teacher.
15. "It is called a flare," the two boys said together.

D. Write each sentence, correcting the errors.
pages 406–411

Example: "Many sunspots are larger than Earth" stated Ms. Smith.
"Many sunspots are larger than Earth," stated Ms. Smith.

16. "Did you know that a solar flare can cause wind on the sun" asked the teacher.
17. "The wind is a stream of particles, she said.
18. "what happens then" asked Daniel.
19. "Then" the teacher told him, "the wind can reach Earth."
20. She added, "This wind makes our radios sound funny"

Writing Connection

Writer's Craft: Time-Order Words Write a dialogue between two students who are describing Earth's movement around the sun. Use time-order words such as *first, next, then,* and *finally.*

Chapter Review

Read the dialogue and decide which type of mistake, if any, appears in each line. Choose the letter that best describes the type of mistake, or choose *No mistake*.

(1) "There are many ways to produce energy, said Ms. Masterson.

(2) My sister, Kammy, sead, "One way is by burning fuel."

(3) "that is right," said Ms. Masterson.

(4) "But how do people use energy" I asked.

(5) "Well" she answered, "we use energy to cook food."

(6) "we also use energy to keep us warm," added Shirley.

(7) "I think," she added, "that energy heats the water we use to wash our faces

(8) "Wow!" exclaimed Ms. Masterson. "You reely do understand how energy works."

TIP Remember to read all answer choices carefully before making your selection.

1 A Spelling
  B Capitalization
  C Punctuation
  D No mistake

2 F Spelling
  G Capitalization
  H Punctuation
  J No mistake

3 A Spelling
  B Capitalization
  C Punctuation
  D No mistake

4 F Spelling
  G Capitalization
  H Punctuation
  J No mistake

5 A Spelling
  B Capitalization
  C Punctuation
  D No mistake

6 F Spelling
  G Capitalization
  H Punctuation
  J No mistake

7 A Spelling
  B Capitalization
  C Punctuation
  D No mistake

8 F Spelling
  G Capitalization
  H Punctuation
  J No mistake

Test-Taking Strategies

You know that you must study before a test in order to do your best on it. There are also strategies you can use during a test that will help you. The chart below lists several test-taking strategies and how they can help you when taking a test. Have you used any of these strategies before?

Strategy	What It Does
Read directions and questions carefully.	It helps you understand exactly what to do on the test.
Look for key words in the directions.	It helps you quickly identify the type of question you must answer.
Budget your time.	It helps you finish the test on time.
Read all of the choices before you choose your answer.	It helps you choose the right answer.
Eliminate choices you know are wrong.	It helps you focus on the most likely choices.
Go back to make sure all questions are answered.	It keeps you from losing points for skipped questions.

YOUR TURN

Go back to the Chapter Review test on page 414. Using the test-taking strategies you've just learned, take the test again. Did the strategies help?

Underlining Titles

A title is the name of something.

Underline the titles of books, magazines, and newspapers. Proper punctuation of titles keeps your readers from being confused.

> **Examples:**
>
> The book **Forces Around Us** says that a force is what pushes and pulls objects.
>
> An article in **Science for Kids** magazine says force makes things speed up or slow down.
>
> A report in **Science Times** newspaper describes gravity as an invisible force.

Vocabulary Power

in•vis•i•ble
[in•viz′ə•bəl] *adj.*
Not able to be seen.

Guided Practice

A. Identify the title in each sentence. Name the words that should be underlined.

> **Example:** The Science Book of Forces has a picture of someone hammering to show force.
> *The Science Book of Forces*

   1. Isabel Carillo wrote an article for Science Works magazine.
   2. I read about muscle power in the book Forces, Forces, Forces.
   3. An article in The Journal says that some forces can pull and push at the same time.
   4. The book Moving talks about pushing and pulling in the game tug-of-war.
   5. An article in Science Fun magazine says that force can stretch things into different shapes.

Independent Practice

B. Write each sentence. Underline the title of the book, magazine, or newspaper.

> **Example:** Motion and Force discusses friction.
> _Motion and Force_

6. An article in Science and Nature explains that friction makes things slow down.
7. The newspaper Elementary Science for Kids says sports shoes create lots of friction.
8. The book Motion Everywhere shows how skates glide on ice.
9. The book Push and Pull says that air can also slow down objects.
10. Young Scientist's Book of Motion defines _drag_ as the "force that slows things down."
11. The magazine Experiment shows you how to measure the force of your muscles.
12. Pushing and Pulling tells how to measure friction.
13. I read an article in Bird Watcher magazine.
14. An experiment in the book Kitchen Science shows that oil is more slippery than water.
15. A drawing in Force and Motion shows how force changes the shape of things.

Writing Connection

Science Think about how some of the machines in your house came to be invented. Choose three machines and write a letter to a friend including titles of imaginary books about each one.

Quotation Marks with Titles

Place **quotation marks** around the titles of stories, poems, magazine articles, newspaper articles, and songs.

Examples:

Rishi created a clever song about gravity called **"Gravity Rap."**

The story **"The Talented Seal"** is about a seal that uses gravity to balance a ball.

Tonya's poem is titled **"Moon Path."**

Guided Practice

A. Identify the title in each sentence. Tell where quotation marks need to be added.

Example: The Thrill of Sky Diving is a poem about the feeling a diver gets when gravity pulls her into the pool.

"The Thrill of Sky Diving"

1. Because you can't see gravity, Tom called his story about an invisible man Gravity Man.
2. Drifting is a song about falling leaves.
3. Hold on Tight is a true story about a roller coaster.
4. The Life of Newton is an article about the discoveries of Isaac Newton.
5. Same Speed is a funny poem about how all things fall to Earth at the same speed.

Independent Practice

B. Write the sentences. Put quotation marks around the titles of stories, songs, articles, and poems.

Example: Greater Force is a Greek myth.
"Greater Force" *is a Greek myth.*

6. The poem Mighty Machine says that machines increase people's power to do work.

7. People use ramps to build pyramids in the story The Age of the Pyramids.

8. The sound of the wheel is repeated in the poem Potter's Wheel.

9. The magazine article Pedal Power explains how bicycles work.

10. The story An Apple a Day tells how a falling apple helped Isaac Newton figure out gravity.

11. Fighting Friction is an exciting story about a man who works with race cars.

12. The poem Forces of Nature is about a woman fighting the forces of wind and water.

13. World in Motion is an article about movement.

14. The Push and Pull is a song about machines.

15. Waterwheel is a song about a water-powered machine used long ago.

Remember

to use quotation marks around the titles of stories, poems, magazine articles, newspaper articles, and songs.

Writing Connection

Writer's Journal: Story Titles You probably have ideas for a story or a poem, but what about a title? A title should grab the reader's attention. Brainstorm titles for a story or a poem. Be sure to write them correctly.

USAGE AND MECHANICS

Capitalizing Words in Titles

Capitalize the first word, last word, and every important word in a title.

Capital letters are used to let readers know a group of words is a title. Be sure to capitalize all verbs, including all forms of the verb *be*, such as *is* and *are*. Also capitalize all pronouns, including *he*, *she*, and *it*. Small words, such as *and, or, but, the, a, of, to, for,* and *with* are not capitalized unless they are the first or last word in a title.

Examples:

Building with Machines

"The World of Machines"

"Machines at Work"

Guided Practice

A. Tell how you would capitalize each title correctly.

Example: Machines to make Work Easier
Machines to Make Work Easier

1. "simple tools"
2. the lever
3. "Using a pulley"
4. the invention of the wheel
5. "hammering without hitting your thumb"

Independent Practice

Remember to capitalize the first, last, and all other important words in a title.

B. Write each title, using correct capitalization.

Example: "Machine force"
"Machine Force"

6. ramps and planes
7. "what is a drill?"
8. The story of scissors
9. "the uses of axles"
10. Ropes Plus Wheels equal Pulleys

C. Read each title. If it is capitalized correctly, write *correct*. If it is capitalized incorrectly, write it correctly.

Example: "How the wheel changed The world"
"How the Wheel Changed the World"

11. "Playground Machines"
12. Gentle and Steep Slopes
13. Lighten The Load
14. "Tools for less Friction"
15. Invisible Forces

Writing Connection

Real-Life Writing: Advertisement Create an advertisement for a product. You may use the machine you invented, or you may choose a different product. Your ad can tell what the product does and where to buy it. Make a list of real or imaginary magazines where your ad might appear. Make sure to underline the magazine titles and to use correct capitalization.

Extra Practice

A. Write the sentences. Underline each book, magazine, and newspaper title. Place quotation marks around the titles of stories, poems, articles, and songs. *pages 416–419*

Example: The book Doing Work explains that work is the force that moves objects.
The book <u>Doing Work</u> *explains that work is the force that moves objects.*

1. The book Work and You tells about machines that move things.
2. We sang the song Climbing Higher.
3. A Science Kids article says that some wheels have teeth called cogs.
4. An article in Atlanta Weekly says that there are levers in people's bodies.
5. The poem Easy Walk is about a hike.
6. My song Stepping Stairs is about how steps make it easier to climb slopes.
7. The book Force and Work explains how wheels were invented.
8. An article titled What Is Physics? says that physics is the study of force and motion.
9. The story Free of Gravity is about space.
10. Kevin wrote a poem called No Up or Down.

B. Write the titles, using correct capitalization.
pages 420–421

Example: <u>skiers and gravity</u>
<u>Skiers and Gravity</u>

11. <u>What a Slope Means To A Skier</u>
12. "Heavy Object, big force"
13. <u>Friction And Fire</u>
14. "rolling and sliding"
15. <u>machines with muscles</u>

C. Read the titles below. If the title is correct, write *correct*. If the title is incorrect, write it correctly. *pages 420–421*

Example: <u>Smoothing Forces</u>
correct

16. "No one Falls up"
17. <u>force and everyday objects</u>
18. "Bicycle Experiments with Motion"
19. <u>Skateboarding ramps</u>
20. <u>Rollers To Wheels</u>

D. The following sentences contain titles with punctuation and capitalization errors. Write each sentence, correcting the errors.
pages 416–421

Example: My teacher read the story Push, Push, Push.
My teacher read the story "Push, Push, Push."

21. Super Force is the title of my story.
22. My science book, Our World, says that force is what pushes and pulls objects.
23. I also decided to include some ideas from an article in Science World.
24. There was a picture of a man lifting weights to show force in The Book Of Forces.
25. My next poem will be called Favorite forces.

Writing Connection

Writer's Craft: Choosing a Form Look in your Writer's Journal for an idea you wrote about in an earlier chapter. Then, rewrite the idea as a story or in another form. Create a title for the story, and use correct capitalization.

Chapter Review

The underlined words in each sentence contain mistakes in punctuation and capitalization. Choose the answer that is the correct way to write the underlined section of the sentence.

TIP Be sure to read all the choices carefully before selecting an answer.

1 The song <u>Work With Wheels</u> tells how wheels make it easier to do work.
   A The song "Work with wheels"
   B The song <u>Work with Wheels</u>
   C The song "Work with Wheels"

2 An article in <u>the Magazine Fun with History</u> says wheels were invented more than 6,000 years ago.
   F the magazine <u>Fun with History</u>
   G the magazine "Fun With History"
   H the magazine <u>Fun With History</u>

3 The book <u>"Inventors of the Past"</u> says no one knows who invented wheels.
   A The book <u>Inventors of the Past</u>
   B The book <u>Inventors Of The Past</u>
   C The book "Inventors Of The Past"

4 The article <u>Ball Bearings</u> explains how ball bearings are used in bicycles.
   F <u>Ball Bearings</u>
   G "Ball Bearings"
   H "Ball bearings"

5 In the book <u>Mystery at the Ranch,</u> a pulley is a clue to figuring out the mystery.
   A In the book "Mystery At The Ranch"
   B In the book <u>Mystery at The Ranch</u>
   C In the book <u>Mystery at the Ranch</u>

For additional test preparation, visit *The Learning Site:*
www.harcourtschool.com

Interpreting a Picture

When you look at a picture, you should ask yourself the following questions:

1. **What is the artist trying to say?** Sometimes pictures can inform or explain. Often, artists want to say something in their work. What is the main idea of the picture? How does he or she say it?
2. **What details do you notice?** Look at the details and think about how they communicate the main idea.
3. **What do the details mean?** Sometimes the details in a picture can have more than one meaning. For example, besides being a bird, a dove can mean peace.

TIP Look for the elements of art in a picture. These include line, shape, color, and space. Notice how the artist uses these elements to tell a story or express a mood.

YOUR TURN

Look carefully at this painting. Answer the three questions above. Then tell what you think about the painting. Explain your reaction to it.

425

Writing Workshop

Stories can be fun to read and write because they involve characters, settings, and plots. Remember that characters can be real or imaginary. When reading this story by Alma Flor Ada, follow the events that happen to the characters, and notice where the author uses elaboration to help tell the story.

Half-Chicken

by Alma Flor Ada
illustrated by Kim Howard

One day on a Mexican ranch, a chick is born that has only one eye, one leg, one wing, and only half as many feathers as the other chicks. The ranch animals decide to call him "Half-Chicken," and they give this special chick lots of attention!

One day he overheard the swallows, who traveled a great deal, talking about him: "Not even at the court of the viceroy in Mexico City is there anyone so unique."

Then Half-Chicken decided that it was time for him to leave the ranch. Early one morning he said his farewells. Then *hip hop hip hop*, off he went, hippety-hopping along on his only foot.

Half-Chicken had not walked very far when he found a stream whose waters were blocked by some branches.

"Good morning, Half-Chicken. Would you please move the branches that are blocking my way?" asked the stream.

Half-Chicken moved the branches aside, but when the stream suggested that he stay awhile and take a swim, he answered:

"I have no time to lose.
I'm off to Mexico City
to see the court of the viceroy!"

Then *hip hop hip hop*, off he went, hippety-hopping along on his only foot.

A little while later, Half-Chicken found a small fire burning between some rocks. The fire was almost out.

"Good morning, Half-Chicken. Please, fan me a little with your wing, for I am about to go out," asked the fire.

Half-Chicken fanned the fire with his wing. It blazed up again, but when the fire suggested that he stay awhile and warm up, he answered:

"I have no time to lose.
I'm off to Mexico City
to see the court of the viceroy!"

Then *hip hop hip hop*, off he went, hippety-hopping along on his only foot.

After he had walked a little farther, Half-Chicken found the wind tangled in some bushes.

"Good Morning, Half-Chicken. Would you please untangle me, so that I can go on my way?" asked the wind.

Half-Chicken untangled the branches. When the wind suggested that he stay and play, and offered to help him fly here and there like a dry leaf, he answered:

"I have no time to lose.
I'm off to Mexico City
to see the court of the viceroy!"

Then *hip hop hip hop*, off he went, hippety-hopping along on his only foot. At last he reached Mexico City.

"Good afternoon," said Half-Chicken to the guards in fancy uniforms who stood in front of the palace. "I've come to see the viceroy."

One of the guards began to laugh. The other one said, "You'd better go in around the back and through the kitchen."

So Half-Chicken went, *hip hop hip hop*, around the palace and to the kitchen door.

The cook who saw him said, "What luck! This chicken is just what I need to make a soup for the vicereine." He threw Half-Chicken into a kettle of water that was sitting on the fire.

When Half-Chicken felt how hot the water was, he said, "Oh, fire, help me! Please, don't burn me!"

The fire answered, "You helped me when I needed help. Now it's my turn to help you. Ask the water to jump on me and put me out."

Then Half-Chicken asked the water, "Oh, water, help me! Please jump on the fire and put him out, so he won't burn me."

The water answered, "You helped me when I needed help. Now it's my turn to help you." He jumped on the fire and put him out.

When the cook returned, he saw that the water had spilled and the fire was out.

"This chicken has been more trouble than he's worth!" exclaimed the cook.

He picked Half-Chicken up by his only leg and flung him out the window.

When Half-Chicken was tumbling through the air, he called out: "Oh, wind, help me, please!"

The wind answered, "You helped me when I needed help. Now it's my turn to help you."

The wind blew fiercely. He lifted Half-Chicken higher and higher, until the little rooster landed on one of the towers of the palace.

"From there you can see everything you want, Half-Chicken, with no danger of ending up in the cooking pot."

From that day on, weathercocks have stood on their only leg, seeing everything that happens below, and pointing whichever way their friend the wind blows.

Vocabulary Power

vice•roy [vīs´roy] *n.* A person who helps rule a country, colony, or province.

Analyze THE Model

1. How does Alma Flor Ada use elaboration in the first paragraph to give the reader more details about the swallows?

2. Give at least two examples of figurative language or exact words that the author uses to describe a character, the setting, or the plot.

3. What characters did Half-Chicken help on his way to Mexico City?

4. How does Half-Chicken rely on these characters to solve his own problem?

READING — WRITING CONNECTION

Parts of a Story

Alma Flor Ada told her readers a story that showed characters helping each other. Study the story below, written by a student named Ruth. Pay attention to how she uses elaboration.

MODEL

setting/ characters

figurative wording character/ event

event

event

dialogue/ problem

event/ dialogue/ solve problem

Lost and Found

The ticket agent explained, "Go to Gate 48 for Flight 233 to Houston." Dad, Mom, and Tasha carried their bags to the security machine to be x-rayed. Then they walked to Gate 48.

Time dragged on in the gate area. A tall man with gray hair used the pay phone nearby. Later, the gate agent announced, "Flight 233 will be two hours late."

Mom and Tasha went to the pay phone to tell Grandpa. As Mom returned to her seat, Tasha yelled, "Mom, you forgot your keys!"

"Those aren't mine," Mom answered.

Tasha thought of the tall man with the gray hair. Tasha walked over to him and asked, "Are these your keys?" The man felt in his left pocket.

"Yes, thank you." The man introduced himself as Mr. Fellows.

At last the gate agent called Flight 233. Tasha reached for her backpack, but it wasn't there. Then she remembered she had put it on the floor at the security gate. Mr. Fellows heard Tasha telling her parents. He said, "I can go look. You helped me when I needed help."

Soon Tasha saw Mr. Fellows returning with the backpack. Her roller skates were safe!

elaboration

problem

event

dialogue

event
solve problem

Analyze THE Model

1. What is Ruth's purpose? Explain your answer.

2. What does Ruth tell about the setting?

3. How does dialogue make the story seem real?

Summarize THE Model

Use a flowchart like the one shown to help summarize Ruth's story. Name the setting, main characters, and important events in the story.

Title of Story

Characters

Setting

Events

Writer's Craft

Elaboration Ruth used elaboration to help tell her story. Tell what exact or figurative words she used to help you understand what happened in the story. Then, rewrite three sentences from Ruth's story that give more detail about a character.

Prewriting

Purpose and Audience

You have read many kinds of stories. In this lesson, you will write a story to share with younger students.

WRITING PROMPT Write a story for younger students about a trip. Have your main character leave a familiar place and travel to a new place. He or she should meet strangers and solve a problem.

Before you begin, think about your audience and purpose. Who will your readers be? What kind of story would they enjoy?

MODEL

Ruth began thinking about her story. She decided who the characters would be and where the story would take place. Then she imagined what could happen to her characters.

Title

Characters: Mom, Tasha, Dad, Mr. Fellows

Setting: the airport

Events

Family checks in and flight's late

Tasha returns Mr. Fellows' keys

Mr. Fellows returns Tasha's backpack

YOUR TURN

Decide what your story will be about. Use a web to organize your ideas.

Organization and Elaboration

Follow these steps to help you organize your story.

STEP 1 **Get Your Audience's Attention**
Write about an event or use dialogue that will interest your reader.

STEP 2 **Give the Events in Time Order**
Tell the events in the order that they happen.

STEP 3 **Solve the Problem**
Have your main character figure out a way to solve the problem.

MODEL

Read the first paragraph of Ruth's story. How does she get the reader's attention? What words does she use to help you see the setting?

> The ticket agent explained, "Go to Gate 48 for Flight 233 to Houston." Dad, Mom, and Tasha carried their bags to the security machine to be x-rayed. Then, they walked to Gate 48.

YOUR TURN

Now draft your story. Look back at your prewriting web for ideas. Reread the stories by Alma Flor Ada and Ruth to see how they used elaboration.

Strategies Good Writers Use

- Use elaboration to give details about the characters.
- Use exact words to tell about the problem or problems that the main character has to solve.

Use a computer to draft your story. You can use the Delete key to erase parts that you want to change.

Revising

Organization and Elaboration

Reread your draft. Think about these questions.

- Is my beginning interesting?
- Are the events in an order that makes sense?
- How well do details show the setting?
- Does the character solve the problem?

MODEL

Here is part of Ruth's story. Notice the exact words and dialogue she uses to make the action seem like real life.

¶Time dragged on
They sat in the gate area. A tall man
with gray hair
used the pay phone nearby. Later, the gate agent announced,
the woman who worked for the
airlines said that "Flight 233 will be two hours
late,"

Mom and Tasha went to the pay phone to tell Grandpa. As Mom
returned to her seat, Tasha yelled, "Mom,
You forgot your
she had forgotten her keys," but she ¶"Those
aren't mine," Mom answered.
said they weren't hers.

YOUR TURN

Revise your story. Look for places where you can use exact or figurative words to help the reader better "see" the setting, characters, and events.

Checking Your Language

You look for mistakes in grammar and spelling when you proofread. You also check for errors in punctuation and capitalization. Readers may not understand your story if you do not correct mistakes.

MODEL

Below is another part of Ruth's story. Look at how Ruth corrected mistakes in punctuation. What else did she fix?

> At last the gate ~~agint~~ *agent* called Flight 233. Tasha reached for her backpack, but it wasn't there. Then she ~~remembred~~ *remembered* she had put it on the floor at the ~~securty~~ *security* gate. Mr. Fellows hear^d Tasha telling her parents. He said, "I can go look, you helped me when I needed help."

Strategies Good Writers Use

- Make sure you have not left out any words.
- Check for correct spelling of similar words.
- Use quotation marks in your dialogue.

Editor's Marks

- ℘ take out text
- ∧ add text
- ○ move text
- ¶ new paragraph
- ≡ capitalize
- / lowercase
- ○ correct spelling

YOUR TURN

Proofread your revised story. Reread it several times to
- **check grammar and spelling**
- **check punctuation**
- **check capitalization**

Publishing

Sharing Your Work

It is now time to publish your story. Think about the audience you chose. Answer these questions to help you choose the best way to share your story.

1. Who is your audience?

2. Would pictures help your audience understand the story?

3. Can your audience read your story? Will you have to read the story to them? Use the information on page 439 for a read-aloud story.

USING YOUR
Handbook

• Use the rubric on page 501 to evaluate your story.

Reflecting on Your Writing

 Using Your Portfolio What did you learn about your writing from this chapter? Write your answer to each of these questions:

1. Would a reader be able to correctly describe your main character? Why or why not?

2. Was the problem in your story clear? Why or why not?

3. Look at the rubric in your Handbook. How would you score your writing? Explain your answer.

Add your answers and your story to your portfolio. Compare this story to your writing for Chapters 6, 21, and 33. Write a few sentences to explain how well you met your goals and how you can do better.

Teamwork

You have been reading stories about people helping others. Now you have an opportunity to work with a classmate and help him or her make a presentation. Ruth and a friend decided to read Ruth's story to a first-grade class. You and a partner can present a story in the same way. Follow these steps:

STEP 1 Print your story on poster board. Write in large letters. Then first graders can follow along as you read. Leave space for pictures.

STEP 2 Have your partner help proofread the story.

STEP 3 With the help of your partner, add pictures to the story.

STEP 4 Practice reading your story aloud to your partner. Decide if you will point to the pictures.

STEP 5 Have your partner help you set up the poster board. Read the story to the children. Each of you can read the words of different characters.

Strategies for Listening and Speaking

These strategies will help you become a better storyteller:

- Learn your story well so you don't have to read every word as you present it. Then you will be less likely to lose your place.
- Vary the sound of your voice to match what is happening in the story. For example, you might want to sound excited, scared, or happy.
- Say the dialogue as if you are the character.

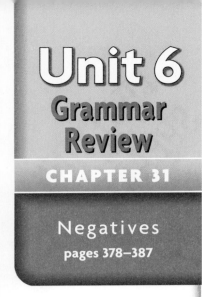

Unit 6
Grammar Review

CHAPTER 31

Negatives
pages 378–387

Negatives   *pages 378–379*

A. Write the negative word in each sentence.

1. I couldn't stop reading a book about Thomas Edison, the inventor.
2. I didn't know he had invented the light bulb.
3. Homes hadn't any electricity until then.
4. That did not stop him from inventing other things.
5. Edison's inventions will not be forgotten.

No, Not, and Other Negatives   *pages 380–381*

B. Use the correct word from the box to fill in the blank in each sentence.

no	none	no one	nowhere
not	never	nobody	nothing

6. It seems there is _____ left to learn about Earth.
7. Yet scientists _____ stop learning about it.
8. There is almost _____ new for scientists to go.
9. Yet we always find life forms that were _____ known about before.
10. _____ knows everything about the world.

Avoiding Double Negatives

pages 382–383

C. Each sentence has a double negative. Write each sentence with only one negative word.

11. I don't like no subject as much as science.
12. I can't never get enough of it.
13. There isn't nothing I like as much as learning about nature.
14. I can't hardly wait for science class each day.
15. I won't never stop studying science.

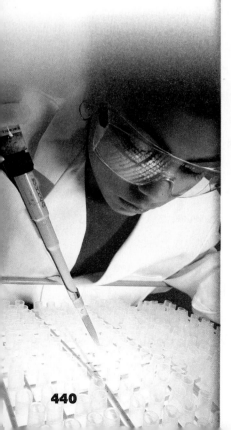

440

Commas   *pages 388–389*

A. Write each sentence. Add commas where they are needed.

  1. Miguel did you know that people used flint to make tools many thousands of years ago?

  2. Well they needed tools to prepare animal hides.

  3. The adze was a tool made from flint wood and leather.

  4. Flint tools could cut scrape and chop.

  5. Yes flint was a very useful kind of rock.

More About Commas   *pages 390–391*

B. Add a comma to each letter part where it is needed.

  6. Manchester New Hampshire

  7. December 14 2001

  8. Dear Uncle Hideo

  9. I found the best rocks near Portland Maine.

10. Your nephew Deepak

Combining Sentences Using Commas   *pages 392–393*

C. Combine each pair of sentences with the word *and* or *but*. Write the new sentence, adding a comma where it is needed.

11. The coal we burn is rock now. It began many years ago as plants in wet forests.

12. The plants rotted. They became buried over time.

13. More plants rotted. They became heavy.

14. The weight of the plants pressed out the water. The bottom layers became hard.

15. These layers turned into coal. People mine the coal for fuel.

Unit 6
Grammar Review

CHAPTER 34

Quotation
Marks

pages 406–415

Quotation Marks in Direct Quotations   pages 406–407

A. Rewrite each sentence. Put quotation marks where they are needed.

1. Carol said, We do not heat our pool.
2. Pedro asked, Why not?
3. Carol explained, We want to save energy.
4. Baker asked, Is it really cold?
5. Carol answered, The sun warms it up.

More About Quotation Marks

pages 408–409

B. Write each sentence, using the correct capitalization and punctuation with the quotation marks. If the sentence is correct as is, write _Correct_.

6. "Can you swim in your pool all year" asked Pedro.
7. "it is not warm enough in the winter," said Carol.
8. Carol explained "The trees shade the pool when the sun is low in the sky.
9. "The sun is low in winter," Carol added.
10. "may I swim in the pool?" asked Pedro.

Punctuating Dialogue   pages 410–411

C. If a sentence has mistakes in punctuation, write it correctly. If a sentence has no mistakes, write _Correct_.

11. Derek, I saw a rainbow yesterday, said Jameela.
12. "Was the rainbow colorful?" asked Derek.
13. "It was made up of many colors said Jameela.
14. Rainbows seem high when the sun is low" added Derek.
15. He said "Sometimes the rainbow goes across the whole sky.

Underlining Titles   *pages 416–417*

A. Underline the book, magazine, or newspaper title in each sentence.

1. Robin read Gravity, by Tess Gerrit, for her report.
2. Just for fun, she read Bowled Over: The Case of the Gravity Goof-Up.
3. She gave Andy a copy of Balloons in the Pool.
4. In the Brereton Daily News, José read about being without gravity in space.
5. He also learned some interesting facts in a magazine called Highlights on the Sky.

Quotation Marks with Titles   *pages 418–419*

B. Place quotation marks around the titles of stories, articles, or songs in each sentence.

6. Danielle taught her little brothers the song The Wheels on the Bus.
7. She made up another song and called it Gravity Gets Me Down.
8. Rob wrote a song called Set Me Free, Oh Gravity.
9. He wrote an article called The Force of Gravity for the school paper.
10. Danielle and Rob want to write a story called The Day Gravity Stopped Working.

Capitalizing Words in Titles   *pages 420–421*

C. Write each title, using correct capitalization.

11. "Gravity: simple experiments for Young Scientists"
12. newton and gravity
13. The laws of gravity
14. "The Lighter Side Of Gravity"
15. Motion And Gravity

An Inventor's Story

Most inventions are created to solve problems. With a group of classmates, research a famous inventor from the past. Write a story that shows how he or she tried to solve a problem by inventing something. Follow the steps below.

Research the Inventor's Story

- What did the inventor do? When and where did he or she live? Did others help him or her?

- What problem did the inventor want to solve?

- How did the invention work? Did it solve the problem?

- What happened to the inventor later?

Write the Story

- Use the facts you found in your research to create your story.

- Make sure your story has a beginning, a middle, and an ending.

- Part of the story can be told by a narrator, but make sure to include dialogue between the characters.

- Illustrate your story. Draw pictures or use computer drawing software.

Publish Your Story

- Display your story on the bulletin board in your classroom.

The Gadget War
by Betsy Duffey
REALISTIC FICTION
Kelly, a third-grade inventor, faces competition as the class inventor when a new student joins her class.
Award-Winning Author

Five Notable Inventors
by Wade Hudson
BIOGRAPHY
This book tells the stories of five important African American inventors. It also describes what they invented and how their inventions improved society.
Award-Winning Author

A Picture Book of Thomas Alva Edison
by David A. Adler
BIOGRAPHY
Thomas Edison loved to solve problems and invented many items, such as the light bulb, that are still used today.
Award-Winning Author

Sentences pages 24–27

Write each sentence. Label it *statement*, *command*, *question*, or *exclamation*.

1. The piano recital was held on Wednesday.
2. Kate played a piece by Beethoven.
3. Did you like her performance?
4. She was so great!
5. Listen carefully to the next piece.

Subjects and Predicates

pages 34–37, 52–55

Write each sentence. Draw one line under the complete subject and two lines under the complete predicate. Then circle the simple subject and the simple predicate.

6. Naomi's father is an architect.
7. Her father designed the family's new home.
8. Naomi's friends watched with interest.
9. Naomi's family moved in last month.
10. The family is very happy with the new house.

Complete Sentences pages 62–65

Rewrite each group of words to make it a complete sentence. If the group of words is already a complete sentence, write *complete sentence*.

11. I went to an opera called *Hansel and Gretel*.
12. It is a fairy tale set in modern times.
13. The singers' words appeared above the stage.
14. Was beautiful, and the costumes were great.
15. Some of the scenes scary, but I knew it would end happily.

Common and Proper Nouns

pages 92–95

Replace the underlined words with proper nouns. You may make up names of people, places, and things for this activity.

1. This <u>girl</u> sleeps eight hours a day.
2. That <u>boy</u> needs nine hours of sleep.
3. Our <u>local college</u> did a study on sleep.
4. Some <u>professors</u> were in charge of the study.
5. The <u>professors</u> found that some people need ten hours of sleep each day.

Singular and Plural Nouns

pages 102–107

Write the plural form of each noun in parentheses ( ).

6. Lisa eats many healthful (food).
7. She likes to eat (vegetable) and (fruit) at The Sprout, a local restaurant.
8. Her favorite foods are (cherry), (radish), and (orange).
9. She also eats (bean) and (nut) to stay healthy.
10. She eats different (cheese), (bread), (cracker), and (fish), too.

Possessive Nouns *pages 120–123*

Write the possessive form of each underlined noun.

11. <u>Charlie</u> father works at a construction site.
12. He is in charge of the <u>workers</u> safety.
13. Construction <u>workers</u> hard hats protect them.
14. <u>Charlie</u> <u>father</u> job is very important.
15. Each <u>person</u> life is in his hands.

Main Verbs and Helping Verbs
pages 166–169

Choose the correct helping verb in parentheses ( ) to complete each sentence. Then underline the main verb.

1. Yolanda's class (is, are) worried about the garbage in Decatur Park.
2. They (has, have) planned to clean up the park.
3. Yes, the class (do, does) use donated garbage bags.
4. The Civic Association (is, are) helping them.
5. The park (has, have) never looked better.

Verb Tenses *pages 176–179, 194–197*

Write each sentence. Write whether the verb is *present tense*, *past tense*, or *future tense*.

6. Lina's family lived in Russia years ago.
7. Her great-grandfather traveled to New York City.
8. From there he moved to a town in Wisconsin.
9. Now Lina's whole family lives in Wisconsin.
10. They will visit Russia again one day.

Irregular Verbs *pages 204–207*

Choose the correct word in parentheses ( ) to complete each sentence.

11. Our senator (came, comed) to our school.
12. He (rided, rode) from his office in a taxi.
13. The senator (gived, gave) a speech about how important it is to vote.
14. He (said, sayed) that every citizen should vote.
15. We (writed, wrote) him a letter thanking him for coming.

Subject and Object Pronouns

pages 234–237, 242–245

Write a pronoun to take the place of the underlined words in each sentence.

1. <u>The oceans</u> are important to <u>my friends and me</u>.
2. <u>You and I</u> get food of all kinds from the sea.
3. <u>The sea</u> gives us fish and seaweed to eat.
4. <u>These foods</u> are important parts of many people's diets.
5. <u>Scientists</u> study the oceans and ocean life.

Possessive Pronouns *pages 262–265*

Write each sentence. Draw one line under the possessive pronoun. Then draw two lines under the antecedent.

6. We watched a shower of shooting stars from our backyard.
7. I looked through my telescope.
8. Pablo's sister tried to take a picture of one with her camera.
9. Pablo took a picture with his camera.
10. Pablo and Maria are proud of their pictures.

Adjectives *pages 272–277*

Write each sentence. Underline each adjective.

11. The penguins at the aquarium are funny.
12. They waddle around on their short, unsteady legs.
13. In the water, they are graceful and quick.
14. They can pop out of the water like little corks.
15. They make loud honking noises.

Articles and Adjectives That Compare pages 308–313

Rewrite each sentence. Use the correct article and adjective that compares in parentheses ( ).

1. (A, The) Potters have the (bigger, biggest) goat farm in the area.
2. They have a (larger, largest) selection of goats than (an, the) others do.
3. (The, An) goat cheese they make is (popularer, more popular) than anyone else's.
4. Our (favorite, favoritist) goat cheese is sold at (a, an) local market.
5. It is (a, the) (tastier, tastiest) cheese of all.

Adverbs pages 318–321

Write the sentence. Underline each adverb.

6. The Gardiners recently moved from the city.
7. They quickly bought a house in the country.
8. Their son now goes to our school.
9. He runs faster than anyone else in school.
10. He easily won the race last week.

Using *Good* and *Well*, *Bad* and *Badly* pages 340–341

Write each sentence using the correct word in parentheses ( ).

11. Our town (bad, badly) needed a new supermarket.
12. Everyone thought it was a (good, well) idea.
13. The store did very (good, well).
14. The produce was (better, best) than anywhere else.
15. This was the (goodest, best) thing to happen to our town in years.

Negatives pages 378–381

Write the sentence. Use a word from the box to fill in the blank.

| nobody   never   no   not   nothing |

1. I _____ saw a rainbow until recently.
2. I did _____ know that they had so many colors.
3. There was _____ warning before it came.
4. _____ could believe how clear the colors were.
5. In a few minutes, there was _____ left to see.

Commas pages 388–391

Write each sentence, placing commas where they are needed.

6. An earthquake shook California Arizona and Nevada.
7. Manuel the earthquake hit in the morning.
8. It woke people up and they felt the ground shaking.
9. No there weren't any injuries.
10. Highway 113 Main Street and Cramer Avenue were closed.

Quotation Marks pages 406–409

Write each sentence, placing quotation marks and punctuation marks where they are needed.

11. How cold is it?" asked Jane.
12. Mrs. Fenice said "It is ten degrees above zero.
13. "Wow! Jane cried We'd better dress warmly."
14. Wear your boots," Mrs. Fenice said.
15. "Don't stay outside too long Mrs Fenice warned, "or you might get frostbite."

Language Use

Read the passage and decide which type of mistake, if any, appears in each underlined section. Mark the letter for your answer.

"How does a thermometer <u>work," asked James?</u> Ms.
(1)
Perry gave him an article <u>called "Measuring heat."</u> It
(2)
said <u>"that a thermometer contains a thin glass tube."</u>
(3)
The tube is partly filled with liquid. The liquid may be
<u>alcohol colored red, or it may be mercury.</u> When the
(4)
liquid gets warmer, it <u>expands and risses</u> up the tube.
(5)
<u>"Thats simple,"</u> James said.
(6)

1 **A** Spelling
   B Capitalization
   C Punctuation
   D No mistake

2 **F** Spelling
   G Capitalization
   H Punctuation
   J No mistake

3 **A** Spelling
   B Capitalization
   C Punctuation
   D No mistake

4 **F** Spelling
   G Capitalization
   H Punctuation
   J No mistake

5 **A** Spelling
   B Capitalization
   C Punctuation
   D No mistake

6 **F** Spelling
   G Capitalization
   H Punctuation
   J No mistake

Written Expression

Use this paragraph to answer questions 1–4.

> Dutch settlers settled my town in the 1600s. They traveled up the Hudson River in ships. They built houses. They built churches. Many of their houses are still standing. My town is called Mount Kill. Next year I'm moving to a different town. Many people think "Kill" is a strange name for a town, but it really means "stream."

1 Choose the best opening sentence to add to this paragraph.

   A My town is one of the oldest in the area.

   B Some towns were settled by the English.

   C My town is on the Hudson River.

2 Which sentences can best be combined?

   F 2 and 3

   G 5 and 6

   H 3 and 4

3 Choose the best concluding sentence to add to this paragraph.

   A Some of the settlers returned to Holland.

   B The old buildings are still standing.

   C Mount Kill is very proud of its Dutch heritage.

4 Which of these sentences does not belong in the paragraph?

   F Dutch settlers settled my town in the 1600s.

   G They built houses.

   H Next year I'm moving to a different town.

Extra Practice

A. Write whether each sentence is a statement, a question, a command, or an exclamation.
pages 26–27

 1. Dave likes vacation time.
 2. What does he enjoy most?
 3. He likes to go fishing with his Uncle Freddie.
 4. He also rides his bicycle along the river.
 5. Wow, he saw some cranes!

B. Write each sentence. Add the correct end mark. *pages 28–29*

 6. Once he saw a big fish along the river bank
 7. Did he try to catch it by hand
 8. Guess what happened
 9. Wow, he got wet
 10. What happened on your vacation

C. Read each group of words. Put the words in an order that makes sense. Make the kind of sentence shown. Use correct end marks.
pages 24–29

 11. Command—your line cast water into the
 12. Exclamation—fish huge wow a what
 13. Question—you do what do now
 14. Command—tight line the keep
 15. Command—fish the bring land to
 16. Statement—eat fish the we'll later
 17. Statement—to I don't cook like
 18. Question—campfire you do how start a
 19. Exclamation—hungry I'm wow really
 20. Command—soon eat let's

Extra Practice

A. Write each sentence. Underline the complete subject. Then circle the simple subject. *pages 34–35*

  1. The class is planning a school event.

  2. Many students offered ideas.

  3. One idea was to collect pennies.

  4. The pennies will buy school equipment.

  5. One student is in charge of the project.

B. Write the noun in each subject. *pages 36–37*

  6. Many students brought in pennies.

  7. The teacher made a big yardstick to show the number of pennies collected.

  8. The yardstick was placed in the hall.

  9. The principal contributed pennies.

10. This school project was a big success.

C. Combine each group of sentences into one sentence that has a compound subject. Write the new sentence. *pages 38–39*

11. Parents brought in pennies. Children brought in pennies. Teachers brought in pennies.

12. The principal counted the pennies. Her student helper counted the pennies.

13. The students received small ice cream cones. Their teachers received small ice cream cones.

14. Basketballs were bought with the money. Tumbling mats were bought with the money.

15. Davon hoped we'd have another school event soon. I hoped we'd have another school event soon.

Extra Practice

A. Write each sentence. Underline the complete predicate once. Underline the simple predicate twice. *pages 52–53*

1. Weather changes often in many places around the world.
2. Hawaii has nice weather all the time.
3. I plan vacations to warm islands.
4. Some places have cold weather outdoors and swimming pools inside.
5. Some people like skiing and sledding.

B. Write the verb in each sentence. *pages 54–55*

6. People talk about the weather every day.
7. Children fly kites in windy spring weather.
8. Children and adults swim in the summer.
9. The breeze becomes cooler in the fall.
10. The sky is often gray in winter.

C. Read the sentences in each group. Then write one sentence with a compound predicate. *pages 56–57*

11. The sky is blue. The sky has many fluffy white clouds.
12. A weather station watches for weather changes. A weather station warns about storms.
13. Some people plan for big storms. Some people have flashlights. Some people store bottled water.
14. Some bad storms roar like a train. Some bad storms pass quickly.
15. Farmers plant their seeds in good weather. Farmers hope rain will water their seeds.

Extra Practice

A. Write *complete sentence* if the group of words is a complete sentence. If it is not, make a complete sentence. *pages 62–63*

  1. Bob and Ishiro play baseball after school.
  2. Meet at the park near their home.
  3. All their friends on the diamond.
  4. Three players are pitchers.
  5. During the game.

B. Write whether each sentence is a simple sentence or a compound sentence. *pages 64–65*

  6. The batter swung at a bad pitch.
  7. Bob hit a home run, and his team won the game.
  8. A teacher helps coach the team.
  9. Darkness ends most games.
  10. Pablo is a good batter, and Jessica likes to pitch.

C. Use the word shown to combine each pair of sentences into a compound sentence. *pages 66–67*

  11. Marta plays first base. Sometimes she plays right field. *and*
  12. Johnny is a great pitcher. He's a fast runner, too. *and*
  13. Rishi is a good hitter. He's an even better fielder. *but*
  14. Our team made it to the play-offs. We didn't win. *but*
  15. Next year we'll practice harder. Maybe we'll win the championship. *and*

Extra Practice

A. Write each noun in the sentence.
pages 92–93

1. Good readers enjoy books that are written well.
2. The class listed exciting stories on the board.
3. A good story does not have to be long.
4. Will the knight rescue the queen from the beast?
5. My teacher reads the class a mystery.

B. Rewrite each sentence. Capitalize each proper noun. *pages 94–95*

6. Mr. johnson says that books are full of facts.
7. Dr. yoon says there are astonishing ideas in books.
8. Are you a visitor to discovery park library?
9. My friend roberto is eager to learn and chooses lots of books.
10. Some people buy books at the blue butterfly book market.

C. Write the abbreviation for each underlined word or words. *pages 96–97*

11. We completed the book by 11:30 (<u>before noon</u>).
12. At 1:00 (<u>after noon</u>) we recorded ideas on tape.
13. We each had three <u>minutes</u> for our message.
14. In <u>November</u> our classes shared these tapes.
15. At Copper <u>Road</u> School, everybody discovers new books.

Extra Practice

A. Write each plural noun in the sentence. Then write the singular form of each.

pages 102–103

1. Many boys and girls like animals.
2. Tom's hamsters have several food bowls.
3. Wet dogs make their fur shake after baths.
4. Cats like to explore holes and chase toys.
5. Snakes and lizards make interesting pets.

B. Form a plural noun from the underlined singular noun. *pages 104–105*

6. There are special combs and <u>brush</u> for horses.
7. The farmer keeps horse harnesses in <u>box</u>.
8. One of the farm animals ate some <u>berry</u>.
9. The rooster made <u>scratch</u> in the dirt.
10. The farmer has two <u>pony</u>.

C. Write the plural noun in each sentence. Then write the singular form.

pages 106–107

11. Do sheep have wool that is soft and curly?
12. Thirsty deer drink at the farm's water tank.
13. Geese are swimming in the lake.
14. Did you hear mice in the barn?
15. There are three trout in that pond.
16. My feet got wet near the pond.
17. Those women gave me a blanket.
18. Later, I'll try to catch some fish.
19. I won't catch any salmon, though.
20. My teeth start to chatter when it gets cold.

Extra Practice

A. Write the possessive form of each singular or plural noun. *pages 120–123*

1. teacher
2. seasons
3. Todd
4. sister
5. presidents

B. Write whether the underlined possessive noun is singular or plural. *pages 120–123*

6. The <u>company's</u> picnic includes children.
7. Each <u>guest's</u> child will receive a prize.
8. All the <u>pumpkins'</u> seeds are roasted.
9. The <u>winners'</u> prizes will be announced.
10. The <u>storyteller's</u> story was funny.

C. Complete each sentence. Choose the correct word in parentheses ( ). *pages 120–123*

11. We celebrate our (countrys', country's) birthday on the Fourth of July.
12. We always have fun at our (neighborhoods, neighborhood's) Fourth of July picnic.
13. My (dad's, dads') tie has white stars on it.
14. My (sisters, sister's) dress is red, white, and blue.
15. Everyone loves my (mom's, moms) cookies.

D. Rewrite each sentence using a possessive noun. *pages 124–125*

16. The lights of the city are beautiful.
17. Some people like the flame of a candle.
18. Others like the sparkle of fireworks.
19. The hug of a grandparent is special.
20. The rules of the games are fair.

Extra Practice

A. Write each sentence. Underline the verb in each sentence. *pages 130–131*

1. The automobile is one way of traveling.
2. The Model T took early drivers many places.
3. Those early motor cars were all black.
4. Now automobiles are many colors.
5. What color is your car?

B. Write each sentence. Underline the action verb in each sentence. *pages 132–133*

6. Today pilots jet around the world easily.
7. Airplanes fly overhead day and night.
8. Some carry cargo only.
9. Airports handle a lot of luggage.
10. Children visit grandparents by plane.

C. Write the verb in each sentence. Tell whether it is an action verb or a form of the verb *be*. *pages 132–135*

11. Some people go places by train or boat.
12. Trains plow slowly through snow.
13. They climb up steep hills.
14. Some people travel aboard a passenger ship.
15. It is fun on the deck of a ship.

D. Write each sentence, using the correct form of the verb *be* in parentheses ( ). *pages 134–135*

16. Some people (is, are) happy to exercise.
17. I (am, are) in a tennis tournament.
18. My dad (is, are) always in his car.
19. My mom and dad (is, are) walking more.
20. My friends (am, are) on the soccer team.

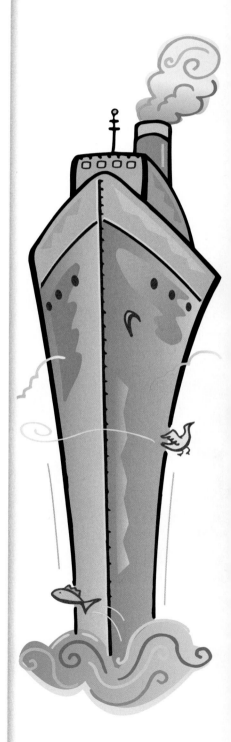

Extra Practice

A. Write each sentence. Circle the helping verb and underline the main verb. *pages 166–169*

1. The new girl in school is smiling at everyone.
2. We are welcoming her to our class.
3. Have you made new friends before?
4. Are you sitting next to her at lunch?
5. Do not forget her name.

B. Make a chart with two columns. Label the first column *Helping Verbs* and the second column *Main Verbs*. Write each underlined verb in the correct column. *pages 166–169*

6. The new girl <u>does</u> not <u>know</u> anyone at our school.
7. She <u>has</u> <u>moved</u> here from New Jersey.
8. We <u>were</u> <u>talking</u> about her old school.
9. She <u>is</u> <u>hoping</u> other children will talk to her.
10. She <u>was</u> <u>smiling</u> so that the class would know she is friendly.

C. Write each sentence, using a contraction for the underlined words. *pages 170–171*

11. <u>Do not</u> worry if it takes a few days for children to talk to you.
12. You <u>are not</u> someone they know well yet.
13. It <u>is not</u> unusual for new students to be shy at first.
14. I <u>should not</u> forget that it takes time to make friends.
15. I <u>have not</u> forgotten how exciting it is to go to a new school.

Extra Practice

A. Write each sentence, and underline the verb. Write whether the verb shows action that is happening in the present, happened in the past, or will happen in the future. *pages 176–177*

1. Jeff likes history.
2. He learned a lot from older people.
3. They told him about the difference between their early years and now.
4. Jeff will study ancient Rome soon.
5. He will use books from the library.

B. Choose the correct present-tense verb in parentheses ( ). *pages 178–179*

6. The class (study, studies) American history.
7. Each student (dress, dresses) in clothing from colonial days.
8. Jeff (wear, wears) an army uniform.
9. Some of the girls' skirts (touch, touches) the floor.
10. Jeff's friends Jake and Alberto (own, owns) costumes of famous men.

C. For each sentence, tell whether the subject is singular or plural. Then write the sentence, using the correct verb in parentheses ( ). *pages 180–181*

11. Jeff (learn, learns) a lot from a history channel on television.
12. The channel (has, have) old news stories.
13. Paintings (show, shows) the days before cameras.
14. Internet searches (find, finds) some interesting facts.
15. These books (explain, explains) the history of the Civil War.

Extra Practice

A. Write the verb in each sentence. Label each verb *past tense* or *future tense*.
pages 194–195

1. A famous writer will visit our school.
2. The writer will bring his books.
3. Jim and Maki wrote him a letter.
4. The writer sent us a poster for the school library.
5. We will invite a different author to our school next year.

B. Write each sentence, using the verb in parentheses ( ). Form the tense that is given at the end of the sentence. *pages 196–197*

6. We (promise) our teacher to give the author a warm welcome. (past)
7. The mayor (honor) the author with a special visitor's ribbon. (future)
8. His fan club (meet) him at the airport. (future)
9. The teachers (plan) a class activity. (past)
10. We (purchase) his books for the library so everyone could read his stories. (past)

C. Write the correct form of the verb in parentheses ( ) for each sentence. *pages 198–199*

11. On the day of the program, we (hurries, hurried) to school.
12. After greeting the writer, our teacher (disappears, disappeared) behind the curtain.
13. The crowd (cheers, cheered) for him when he arrived.
14. All the rest of the year we (remembers, will remember) his visit.
15. I (will decide, decided) he is my new hero.

Extra Practice

A. Write the sentence. Choose the correct verb in parentheses ( ) to complete each sentence. *pages 204–207*

1. He (saw, seen) the beautiful meadow.
2. He (say, said) it was filled with flowers.
3. He (drew, drawn) a picture of a beehive.
4. The sound of the bees (growed, grew) louder.
5. He (rode, rided) home with no stings at all and a beautiful picture.

B. Write the past-tense form of the verb in parentheses ( ) to complete the sentence.
pages 204–207

6. Long ago, children from this village _____ beans, peas, and carrots. (grow)
7. They _____ the packages of seeds outside. (take)
8. They _____ lines in the dirt. (draw)
9. The leaky hose _____ enough water for the garden. (give)
10. Helpers, parents, and friends _____ the ripe vegetables. (eat)

C. Write the verb in parentheses ( ) that completes each sentence correctly.
pages 208–209

11. The flower garden (lies, lays) between the house and the river.
12. Gardeners (teach, learn) others about plants.
13. Spring flowers start to bloom when the temperature (raises, rises).
14. Gardeners (teach, learn) from nature, too.
15. Elena (lies, lays) her garden tools on a shelf in the shed.

Extra Practice

A. Write each pronoun in the sentence. Write _S_ if the pronoun is singular or _P_ if the pronoun is plural. *pages 234–235*

1. Brian smiled as he fed the turtles.
2. Maki was silent and just looked at him.
3. She didn't want to touch the turtles.
4. Maki doesn't like them as much as she likes hamsters.
5. Brian thinks you should have lots of different pets.

B. Write the pronoun that can take the place of the underlined noun or nouns. *pages 236–237*

6. <u>Maki and Brian</u> both have dogs.
7. They like to walk <u>the dogs</u> in the park.
8. <u>Maki</u> has a beagle.
9. <u>Maki's dog</u> is white, brown, and black.
10. <u>Brian</u> has a spaniel that plays catch with <u>Brian</u>.

C. Write the antecedent from the first sentence for each underlined pronoun. *pages 238–239*

11. My hamsters run fast. <u>They</u> could be track stars.
12. Their wheel turns a lot. <u>It</u> lets me know they want to race.
13. Brian looked at the hamsters. <u>He</u> thought <u>they</u> were cute, soft, and furry.

14. Maki and Brian talked about the animals. <u>They</u> decided to have a pet show.
15. Isabel could bring her pets, too. <u>She</u> has many of <u>them</u>.

Extra Practice

A. Write each sentence, using the correct pronoun in parentheses ( ). *pages 244–249*

1. (I, Me) like Nidia's parents' store.
2. (She, Her) thinks it is wonderful, too.
3. The customers often call (she, her) by name.
4. Her parents give (we, us) treats.
5. (They, Them) know we like to help, too.

B. Write *subject pronoun* or *object pronoun* to name the underlined word in each sentence.

pages 244–247

6. <u>She</u> enjoys Saturdays best.
7. The empty shelves make a lot of work for <u>us</u>.
8. <u>You</u> came in last Saturday with your husband.
9. <u>He</u> found some tires in back that were just right.
10. Mr. Ramos put them on for <u>you</u>.

C. Rewrite each sentence. Replace the underlined words with a pronoun. *pages 244–247*

11. <u>My friend and I</u> built a tool display.
12. <u>The tool display</u> is popular.
13. People smiled at <u>my friend and me</u>.
14. <u>A man</u> took a picture of it.
15. The story in the newspaper surprised <u>her parents</u>.

Extra Practice

**A. Write each possessive pronoun in the
sentence.** *pages 262–263*

1. I think Missy has taken her baggage to the
airport by now.
2. Its handles are silver.
3. My suitcase has wheels on it.
4. Put your suitcase next to my backpack.
5. At least our bags will start the trip next to
each other.

**B. Write the possessive pronoun that belongs
in each space.** *pages 264–265*

6. Since Missy likes pink bags, the pink bag
is _____.
7. The blue one is _____.
8. They are renting a cabin, and _____ windows
look over a lake.
9. When are you taking _____ vacation?
10. _____ vacation next year will be at my
grandmother's house.

**C. Underline the contraction in each sentence.
Write the two words that were used to make
the contraction.** *pages 266–267*

11. We're not going anywhere this year.
12. I'm helping my dad repair a house in
my neighborhood.
13. We'll volunteer every year to help out a
family in need.
14. They've always helped other people in
our community.
15. You get a special feeling when you've helped
someone else.

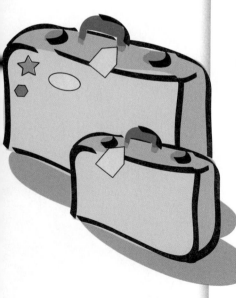

Extra Practice

A. For each sentence, write the adjective that tells _how many_. *pages 274–275*

1. Most people enjoy birthdays.
2. Do you have a party each year?
3. Some people have birthdays on the same day.
4. Several people are twins.
5. Two cousins in my family were born on the same day.

B. Complete each sentence with an adjective that tells _how many_. The answer may or may not be an exact number. *pages 274–275*

6. I know_____thing about getting older.
7. _____ people have birthdays.
8. Triplets celebrate _____ birthdays at the same time.
9. _____ birthdays are in the summer.
10. This year I will be_____years old.

C. Read each sentence. Write each adjective that tells _what kind_. *pages 276–277*

11. Birthday cakes usually have candles.
12. Cakes can be round or flat.
13. There are red roses on the cake for my mother.
14. Is that a tiny nibble on the corner of the cake?
15. This chocolate cake is delicious!

Extra Practice

A. Write each sentence, using the correct article in parentheses ( ). *pages 308–309*

1. Have you been to (a, an) airport?
2. Some airports will give you (a, an) tour.
3. Usually you take baggage to the main desk of (a, an) airline.
4. You may need (a, an) baggage cart.
5. (An, The) metal detector alarm may ring.

B. Write each sentence, using the correct form of the adjective that compares in parentheses ( ). *pages 310–311*

6. First-class seats are (expensive) than coach seats.
7. First-class seats are (large) than coach seats.
8. First-class passengers get (good) service than coach passengers.
9. My pilot was the (friendly) of all the pilots.
10. Chicago is one of the (busy) airports.

C. Write each sentence, using the correct form of the adjective that compares shown in parentheses ( ). *pages 310–313*

11. Some people think that the takeoff is (more exciting, excitinger) than the landing.
12. Pretend you are the (more adventurous, most adventurous) person in the world.
13. You rise above the earth like the (most biggest, biggest) bird in the world.
14. The clouds today are (puffier, most puffy) than the clouds yesterday.
15. This jet is (more powerful, most powerfulest) than that one.

Extra Practice

A. Write the adverb in each sentence. Write whether it tells *how, when,* or *where*. Then write the verb it describes. *pages 318–321*

1. I go inside to cook.
2. Sometimes I make cookies from my favorite cookbook.
3. I never bake cookies without asking my mom.
4. Measure your flour correctly by the cup.
5. Carefully mix the other dry items with the flour.
6. Finally, pour the wet mix into the dry mix.
7. Stir steadily with a wooden spoon until all the lumps are gone.
8. Drop the mixture gently by spoonfuls onto the cookie sheet.
9. Always check your baking time.
10. Stay downstairs when you eat your cookies.

B. Write each sentence. Choose the correct word or words in parentheses ( ). *pages 322–323*

11. Cookies bake _____ than cakes. (quickly, more quickly)
12. The cake rose _____ than the cookies. (higher, more high)
13. This mix bakes _____ than a recipe made from scratch. (more faster, faster)
14. Which of these two cookies tastes _____ to you? (more delicious, most delicious)
15. We eat cookies _____ during the holidays. (most often, most oftener)

Extra Practice

A. Write whether the underlined word is an adjective or an adverb. *pages 336–337*

1. <u>Regular</u> exercise helps keep your body healthy.
2. Running <u>fast</u> expands your lungs.
3. Your <u>many</u> leg muscles also get a workout.
4. A <u>mountain</u> bicycle is fun to ride.
5. Ride <u>carefully</u> along the trail.

B. Write each sentence. Include the adverb in parentheses ( ). Put it in the best place. *pages 338–339*

6. (skillfully) The children played soccer at the picnic.
7. (often) The score was tied.
8. (later) They shot baskets.
9. (peacefully) Some people canoed on the river.
10. (rapidly) Others hiked through the woods.

C. Rewrite each sentence, using the correct word in parentheses ( ). *pages 340–341*

11. Your class did (good, well) in the school fitness test.
12. Most of the students had a (good, well) heart rate.
13. The teachers felt (bad, badly) for the children who never exercise.
14. The weather was (good, well) on the day of the test.
15. My friend was ill, so he thought he would do (bad, badly) on the test.

Extra Practice

A. Write each sentence, using the correct word in parentheses ( ). *pages 346–347*

1. Sally plans a trip (to, too, two) Japan.
2. She will stay for (to, too, two) weeks.
3. She will (write, right) postcards each day.
4. She would not feel (write, right) if she did not keep in touch.
5. Do you feel that way, (to, too, two)?

B. Write each sentence, using the correct word in parentheses ( ). *pages 348–349*

6. (Their, There, They're) thinking of places to go.
7. (Its, It's) exciting to plan trips for other people.
8. You have to know (their, there, they're) likes and dislikes.
9. (Your, You're) the one who presents the ideas.
10. Make certain they want to go (their, there, they're).

C. Write each sentence, using the correct words from the box. *pages 350–351*

sea	know	trip (v.)	bow (n.)
see	no	trip (n.)	bow (v.)

11. If you don't _____ well, you might _____ .
12. Be especially careful if you are taking a _____ across the _____ to Japan.
13. I _____ how to _____ to my Japanese host.
14. I _____ where a gift with a _____ is hidden.
15. He will _____ that I am polite.

Extra Practice

A. Write each sentence, and underline the negative word or words. *pages 378–381*

1. Sonja told her sister she wouldn't get lost.
2. No one could change her mind about going.
3. She never stopped planning the adventure.
4. Friends didn't believe she would go.
5. Nobody wanted to go with her.

B. Choose a negative word from the box to best complete each sentence. *pages 378–381*

nowhere	never	nothing	not	none

6. _____ of this bothered Sonja.
7. _____ was standing in her way.
8. She knew there was _____ else for her to go.
9. _____ a person came to say good-bye.
10. She is going to a place I _____ heard of.

C. Rewrite each sentence to correct the double negative. *pages 382–383*

11. I couldn't not be as brave as Sonja.
12. I don't have no plans for a big adventure.
13. She wasn't never worried to leave her family behind.
14. I will never not go alone when I take a trip.
15. It won't be no fun to travel without you.
16. Tom didn't never think about the farm.
17. Lucy wasn't going not far to visit him.
18. Her mother knew nobody not in the city.
19. She couldn't write not one letter.
20. She didn't have no pens or pencils.

Extra Practice

A. Write the sentence. Add commas where they are needed. *pages 388–389*

1. Manuel took his camera and went hunting for people birds and wild animals.
2. What can you find in Santa Rosa California?
3. He found lizards hamsters and friends.
4. Manuel will your friends at school smile when you take their picture?
5. Yes they love to have their pictures taken!

B. Rewrite the letter. Add commas where they are needed. *pages 390–391*

6. Chicago Illinois
7. April 19 2002
   Dear Mr. Fuentes
8. I have some wonderful pictures of wildlife in Santa Rosa California.
9. They will be in the show on May 2 2002.
10. Sincerely
    Manuel

C. Combine each group of sentences to form a compound sentence, using *and* or *but*. Add commas where they are needed. *pages 392–393*

11. Manuel took his camera to school. His teacher let him take pictures of the class pet.
12. Crows flew into the schoolyard at recess. Manuel had his camera ready.
13. He wanted to get several pictures of lizards. They rushed away.
14. Some friends brought their pet lizards to school. Manuel got great shots of them.
15. Manuel took his film to the store. The pictures were great.

Extra Practice

A. Write each sentence, adding quotation marks where they are needed. *pages 406–407*

1. We expect everybody to be part of our community volunteer program, said the mayor.
2. Do you mean even us? Ryan asked.
3. Yes, and even the rest of your family, the mayor told him.
4. She explained, Some of the families who live here will make a great difference in our community.
5. The helpers will meet next week to get started, she said.

B. Write the sentence, correcting each error in punctuation and capitalization. *pages 406–409*

6. "The group is small, she told us.
7. Do you know how large the neighborhood is" she asked.
8. Betsy shouted Farther than I can walk
9. "That's so big exclaimed Frank.
10. The mayor said, It is a key part of the city.

C. Write each sentence and underline the words that tell who is speaking and how.
pages 410–411

11. "That's why it is important for us to clean it up as an example for others," she continued.
12. Ryan exclaimed, "It will be so much work!"
13. "Yes," Betsy said, "but we can do it."
14. "What questions do you have?" asked the mayor.
15. "When do we start?" Betsy and Ryan asked together.

Extra Practice

A. Write the sentence. Underline each book, magazine, or newspaper title. *pages 416–417*

1. The main characters in the book Charlotte's Web are a pig and a spider.
2. Ranger Rick magazine had a story with facts about spiders.
3. The Evening Tribune told about a pet pig named Wilbur.
4. Have you read the book Mr. Popper's Penguins?
5. My sister wrote a review of that book for the Woodland Middle School News.

B. Write each sentence. Place quotation marks around the titles of stories, poems, articles, and songs. *pages 418–419*

6. Where the Sidewalk Ends is a famous poem in a book with the same name.
7. I read an article about poetry called Other Dangers of Poetry Writing.
8. An unusual song is Grandma Wore Her Nightcap to Work in the Garden.
9. Peter Rabbit is a great children's story.
10. I wrote a poem called The End.

C. Rewrite each title, using correct capitalization. *pages 420–421*

11. "Going on a bear hunt"
12. A child's garden of verses
13. "Jack and the beanstalk"
14. "singing in the rain"
15. folktales of Texas

Handbook

Contents

Writing Models **480**

Writing Rubrics **496**

Study Skills and Strategies **502**

Spelling Strategies **524**

Commonly Misspelled Words **527**

Handwriting Models **528**

Thesaurus **530**

Glossary **548**

Vocabulary Power **560**

Writing Models

Personal Narrative

A **narrative** is a story. A **personal narrative** is a story about a writer's own experiences.

How to Write a Personal Narrative

- Write from your **point of view**. Use the pronouns *I*, *me*, and *my*.
- Tell about an **event** that happened to you.
- Include **details** to help your readers picture the event.
- Express how you felt about the event.

writer's viewpoint using *I* and *my*

beginning/ details

middle/ details

end/details

writer's viewpoint

The One That Didn't Get Away

I am just crazy about my cat, Creamy. My mom and dad gave her to me on my sixth birthday. She sleeps on my bed every night and wakes me up every morning.

Last summer, though, I thought I'd lost her forever. My family moved to a new house about a mile away. Creamy got scared by the noise of the furniture being moved, and she ran off. We could not find her anywhere. I didn't want to leave, but we had to go to our new house without her.

Every day, I got sadder and sadder. Then one morning, about ten days after we moved, I heard scratching and meowing at the door. It was Creamy! She had found us on her own. I always knew cats were smart. I'll never let Creamy get lost again!

How-to Essay

A **how-to essay** gives directions that tell how to do something. These directions are given in order.

How to Write a How-to Essay

- Write an opening paragraph that tells what you will explain how to do.
- List all the materials needed.
- Write sentences that tell the steps in order.
- Use sequence words such as *first*, *next*, *then*, and *last* to show the correct order.

It can be fun to decorate the table for a party. One way is to make animals from vegetables and fruits. Suppose you want to make a horse. Here are some steps that can help you. — **opening paragraph**

You will need the following items:
- fruit (berries, bananas, or other colorful fruits)
- vegetables (green and red peppers, cucumbers, carrots, and lettuce)
- toothpicks

— **materials the reader will need**

First, choose a large fruit or vegetable to use for the body, such as a banana or a cucumber. Next, cut long pieces of carrot for the legs. Then, choose a small pepper for the head. Use berries for the eyes and pieces of red pepper for the ears. Attach them to the head with toothpicks. Next, slice lettuce for the mane and tail. Finally, attach the legs, head, mane, and tail to the body with toothpicks. — **steps in order/ sequence words**

Persuasive Essay

A **persuasive essay** tells how a writer feels about a topic. The writer tries to persuade the reader to agree.

How to Write a Persuasive Essay

- Write a topic sentence that tells how you feel about the topic.
- Give reasons that support how you feel. Add details to make your reasons clearer.
- List your strongest reason last.
- At the end of your essay, tell how you feel about the topic again. Ask your audience to take action.

topic sentence that gives opinion

Many people like to play and watch different sports. I think that baseball is the best sport of all. Everyone who likes to play sports should learn how to play baseball.

reasons and details

Baseball is a great sport to play. When you play baseball a lot, you make the muscles in your arms and legs strong. You also learn how to run fast. Baseball teaches you how to work with other team players. It's really fun when your team wins. The best part is that your teammates make good friends!

call to action

Baseball is my favorite sport. It provides exercise and helps players work together and make friends. Find out about baseball leagues in your neighborhood and join up.

Advantages and Disadvantages Essay

An essay that tells **advantages and disadvantages** explains the good and bad things about a topic.

> ### How to Write an Advantages and Disadvantages Essay
>
> - Get your readers' interest with your introduction.
> - Write one paragraph about the disadvantages and one about the advantages of the topic.
> - Use detail sentences and clear examples.
> - Summarize your thoughts in a concluding paragraph.

Summer Visitors

My cousins come to visit every summer. I always look forward to their visits because I like them very much. There are also some things I do not like about their visits. — *introduction*

There are some disadvantages to my cousins coming to visit. For example, one of my cousins gets to sleep in my bed at night, so I sleep on the floor. I also have to share my things with my cousins. Sometimes, one cousin leaves dirty fingerprints on my books. — *disadvantages and details about them*

We always have a lot of fun during their visits, though. That is the biggest advantage. For example, we get to go to special places, like the water park and a baseball game. My cousins are also really fun friends for me to play with. — *advantages and details about them*

When my cousins go home, I miss them a lot. So, even though there are some bad things about my cousins' visits, I'm always excited to see them again the next year. — *conclusion*

title

Research Report

A **research report** gives information about a topic. Writers gather facts from different sources, such as books or magazines. They take notes to remember the facts, and they make outlines to organize the facts. Then they write their reports.

How to Write a Research Report

- Write an interesting paragraph to introduce your topic.
- Use your notes to write detailed paragraphs about each main topic in your outline. Remember to use your own words when you write.
- Write a concluding paragraph to end your report.

title

introduction/
main topic

subtopic and
details

Tiny Helpers

Ants are not just tiny insects. They are very interesting creatures. They make their own homes, work together, and are helpful to nature and humans.

Ants live everywhere on Earth except in very cold areas. They live together in communities called colonies. Each colony may have as few as a dozen or as many as a million ant members. Most ants make homes in underground tunnels. Some ants, however, live inside trees or other plants.

An ant colony is very organized. Each ant has a special purpose in the colony. Most of the ants are female worker ants. These ants build and protect the nest. They also find food for the colony and care for the young ants. Each colony has at least one queen ant whose main job is to lay eggs. Male ants live in the colony part-time.

subtopic and details

Ants are very important in nature. They help keep things in balance on Earth. By eating other insects, ants help keep the insect population from getting too big. Ants are also helpful to humans. When they dig tunnels, ants help farmers by breaking up hard-packed soil. What helps farmers is good for all of us, since farmers produce much of our food.

subtopic and details

Many people think ants are just pests because they get into buildings where people do not want them. Ants are actually very hard workers that are very important to the world. Maybe you will think of ants differently next time you see one of these tiny helpers!

concluding paragraph

Short Story

A **short story** tells about characters solving a problem. A short story has a beginning, a middle, and an end.

How to Write a Short Story

- Write a beginning. Name the story characters, and tell where the story takes place. Give the characters a problem to solve.
- Write the middle of the story. Tell what the characters do to try to solve the problem.
- Write the end. Tell how the problem is solved.
- Write a title for the story.

title —

beginning: characters, setting, problem —

The Jaguar and the Monkeys

It was morning in the rain forest. The sun shone through the canopy of trees and onto the forest floor. A stream flowed quietly over the rocks, and even the birds were asleep. In fact, everything in the forest was asleep except the monkeys, because the monkeys never seem to sleep. They are always busy swinging from limb to limb and having a good time. This morning, the monkeys started howling and yelling back and forth.

Not far away, a sleepy jaguar woke up when he heard the monkeys' noise. He stretched his back and growled. He was in a terrible mood.

"I have to make those monkeys be quiet," said the jaguar. "I need my sleep."

So the jaguar went to the banana trees. He picked bunches and bunches of bananas. Then he went to the mango trees. He picked buckets and buckets of mangoes. The giant cat took the bananas and mangoes to the other side of the forest.

middle

When the jaguar returned home, he spoke to the monkeys. "There is a surprise for you on the other side of the forest," he said. "Go there soon before someone else finds it!"

The monkeys ran off as fast as they could. The tired jaguar then climbed back into bed. Finally, he would be able to sleep for as long as he wanted.

end

Descriptive Paragraph

A **descriptive paragraph** is writing that describes an object, a feeling, an event, or anything else a person is writing about.

How to Write a Descriptive Paragraph

- Use vivid words to describe how things look, sound, taste, or feel.
- You may express your personal viewpoint, telling the reader how you feel about the subject.

vivid words

personal viewpoint

> The rose garden was a rainbow of dancing colors. Every shrub was covered with crowds of flowers. There were tiny roses painted with soft shades of pink and yellow. Near them were the bigger flowers. Those were fire-engine red and royal purple. They seemed to say to me, "Look at us! Aren't we beautiful?" They were too lovely to pick, so I just breathed in the sweet smell.

Book Review

A **book review** tells what a book is about. It tells what the writer thinks about the book.

How to Write a Book Review

- Write the title of the book and the author's name in the first sentence.
- Tell about the most important characters and the main idea.
- Then tell about the important events.
- Include interesting details, but do not tell the ending.
- Give your opinion of the book and tell why someone might or might not like to read it.

Miss Spider's Tea Party, by David Kirk, is a make-believe story in rhyme about a spider who is lonely. When she sees insects flying by, she invites them to have tea with her. None of the insects will come because they don't want to be the spider's next meal. Instead, Miss Spider tries to have tea with rubber insects, but they are no fun. Then, Miss Spider tries to find another way to get the real insects to visit her for tea.

I liked the book because it is written in rhyme and because the pictures are so pretty. I really liked the ending because it made me want to be Miss Spider's friend.

title and author's name

most important character and main idea

important events/ details

opinion of the book

Paragraph That Compares

A **paragraph that compares** tells how two or more people, places, or things are alike.

How to Write a Paragraph That Compares

- Write a topic sentence. Name the subjects and tell how they are alike.
- Write detail sentences that give clear examples.
- In the detail sentences, list the two subjects in the same order you used in the topic sentence.

---

topic sentence

Parakeets and macaws are alike because they are the same colors, they live in pairs, and they eat the same things. Both birds' feathers can be blue, red, yellow, and green.

detail sentences

Parakeets and macaws like to live in pairs, and you can see them gather in larger groups at night. Parakeets and macaws eat nuts, berries, and seeds. One interesting thing that both parakeets and macaws eat is clay. Each morning you can see up to 500 parakeets and macaws eating lumps of clay near the riverbank!

Paragraph That Contrasts

A **paragraph that contrasts** tells how two or more people, places, or things are different.

How to Write a Paragraph That Contrasts

- Write a topic sentence. Name the subjects and tell how they are different.
- Write detail sentences that give clear examples.
- List the two subjects in the same order you used in the topic sentence.

parakeets   macaw

Parakeets and macaws are different sizes and make different noises. Parakeets are small, slender birds. They are seven to eleven inches long. Macaws are very large birds and can be thirty to forty inches long. Parakeets can chirp loudly, but not as loudly as macaws. Macaws can make a loud screeching noise that would scare any animal that might want to eat them.

topic sentence

detail sentences

Friendly Letter with Envelope

A **friendly letter** is a letter you write to someone you know well. Friendly letters include a heading, greeting, body, closing, and signature.

A **thank-you note** is one kind of friendly letter. A thank-you note thanks someone for giving a gift or for doing something.

How to Write a Friendly Letter
• Include a heading that gives your address and the date.
• In the greeting, include the name of the person to whom you are writing.
• In the body, tell why you are writing to the person.
• Include an appropriate closing before your signature.
• Write your signature at the bottom.

Thank-You Note

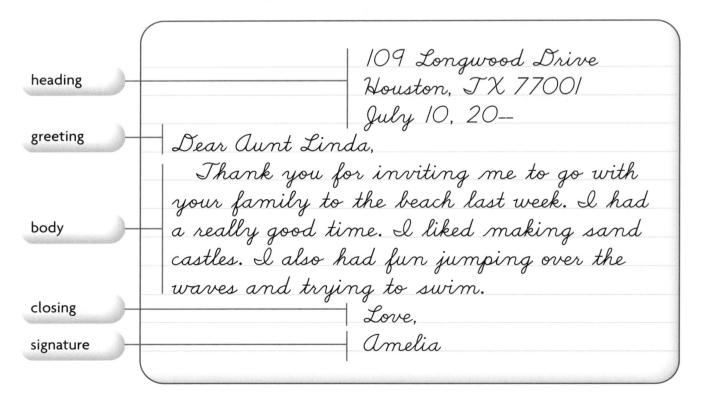

heading
: 109 Longwood Drive
Houston, TX 77001
July 10, 20--

greeting
: Dear Aunt Linda,

body
: Thank you for inviting me to go with your family to the beach last week. I had a really good time. I liked making sand castles. I also had fun jumping over the waves and trying to swim.

closing
: Love,

signature
: Amelia

Envelope

After you have written your friendly letter, you can mail it. Be sure to write the correct information on the envelope.

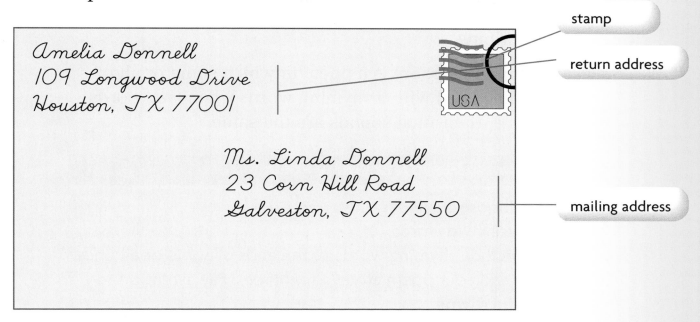

Amelia Donnell
109 Longwood Drive
Houston, TX 77001

stamp

return address

Ms. Linda Donnell
23 Corn Hill Road
Galveston, TX 77550

mailing address

The mailing address is the address of the person who receives the letter. It is written in the center. The return address is the address of the person who writes the letter. It is written in the upper left corner.

Both the mailing address and the return address will include a postal abbreviation, or a shorter form of the state name. They will also include a ZIP code, a special number that helps the post office deliver the letter.

Your envelope must have a stamp as payment for sending the letter. The stamp is placed in the upper right corner of the envelope.

Postal Abbreviations

Alabama AL	Idaho ID	Missouri MO	Pennsylvania PA
Alaska AK	Illinois IL	Montana MT	Rhode Island RI
Arizona AZ	Indiana IN	Nebraska NE	S. Carolina SC
Arkansas AR	Iowa IA	Nevada NV	S. Dakota SD
California CA	Kansas KS	New Hampshire NH	Tennessee TN
Colorado CO	Kentucky KY	New Jersey NJ	Texas TX
Connecticut CT	Louisiana LA	New Mexico NM	Utah UT
Delaware DE	Maine ME	New York NY	Vermont VT
District of	Maryland MD	North Carolina NC	Virginia VA
Columbia DC	Massachusetts MA	North Dakota ND	Washington WA
Florida FL	Michigan MI	Ohio OH	W. Virginia WV
Georgia GA	Minnesota MN	Oklahoma OK	Wisconsin WI
Hawaii HI	Mississippi MS	Oregon OR	Wyoming WY

Poems: Rhymed and Unrhymed

A **poem** is one way for a writer to describe something or to express feelings about a subject. Poets use vivid words to help readers picture what they are describing.

A **rhyming poem** is a poem in which some or all of the lines end with a rhyming word. When two words rhyme, their final sounds are the same.

How to Write a Rhyming Poem

- Choose a subject.
- Use vivid words.
- Include rhyming words at the ends of some or all lines.
- Read your poem aloud a few times. Pay attention to the rhyme.

Here are two rhyming poems about a pet:

My Dog
He sniffles and snuffles and snoozes all day.
He's old and he's tired, but he likes to play.

rhyming words

A Good Friend
My dog is my buddy.
My dog is my friend.
Now that I've said it,
My poem will END!

rhyming words

Writing Unrhymed Poems

Poems do not always rhyme. **Unrhymed poems** are not like stories, though. They look and sound different, and they use special language.

How to Write an Unrhymed Poem

- Choose a subject.
- Use vivid words.
- Use repetition of words and sounds.

One kind of poem that does not use a regular rhythm or rhyme is a **free-verse poem**. Notice the vivid words in the poem below. Also notice the repetition of the "b" sound and of the phrase "But Bo doesn't yell."

My Basketball Buddy

Dribbling the ball down the court,
I feel so good that I forget to pass,
But Bo doesn't yell, "BALL HOG!"

I put up a shot from the 3-point line,
It slams BAM! *hard off the backboard . . .*
But Bo doesn't yell, "BRICK!"

Because he's my basketball buddy.

Expressive Writing: *Personal Narrative*

The best personal narratives show all the points on the checklist below. Here is how you can use it:

Before writing Look at the checklist to remind yourself of how to make your personal narrative the best it can be.

During writing Check your drafts against the list to see how you can make your personal narrative better.

After writing Check your work against the list to see if it has all the points of the best personal narratives.

SCORE OF 4 ★★★★

- The story fits the purpose for writing. The audience it was written for would enjoy it. The ideas are interesting.

- The story has a clear beginning that tells the problem, a middle that tells events in order, and an ending that gives the solution to the problem.

- The story has description and rich details that help the reader visualize the events.

- The story has interesting words and phrases, such as specific nouns, vivid verbs, sensory words, and comparisons. It shows the writer's feelings.

- The sentences are written in a variety of ways to make the writing interesting to read.

- The story has few errors in spelling, grammar, and punctuation.

What else is important in a personal narrative?

Informative Writing: *How-to Essay*

The best how-to essays show all the points on the checklist below. Here is how you can use it:

Before writing Look at the checklist to remind yourself of how to make your how-to essay the best it can be.

During writing Check your drafts against the list to see how you can make your how-to essay better.

After writing Check your finished work against the list to see if it shows all the points of the best how-to essays.

SCORE OF 4 ★★★★

- The essay fits the purpose for writing well. The audience it was written for would understand it.

- The essay has a clear beginning that introduces the topic, a middle that gives facts or directions about the topic in a logical order, and an ending that summarizes or draws a conclusion. The topic is interesting.

- The essay has description and rich details that add information about the facts or directions.

- The essay has interesting words and phrases, especially specific nouns. It shows the writer's style.

- The sentences are written in a variety of ways to make the writing interesting to read.

- The essay has few errors in spelling, grammar, and punctuation.

What other points are important in a how-to essay?

Persuasive Writing: *Persuasive Paragraph*

The best persuasive essays show all the points on the checklist below. Here is how you can use it:

Before writing Look at the checklist to remind yourself of how to make your persuasive essay the best it can be.

During writing Check your drafts against the list to see how you can make your persuasive essay better.

After writing Check your finished work against the list to see if it shows all the points of the best persuasive essays.

SCORE OF 4 ★★★★

★ The essay was well written to persuade a particular audience.

★ The essay has a clear statement of opinion at the beginning, a middle that gives good reasons that support the opinion, and an ending that restates the opinion and calls for action. The writer cares about the topic.

★ The essay has details, description, or examples that give more information about the reasons.

★ The essay has interesting words and phrases, such as specific nouns, vivid verbs, emotional language, and comparisons.

★ The sentences are written in a variety of ways to make the writing interesting.

★ The essay has few errors in spelling, grammar, and punctuation.

What else is important in a persuasive essay?

Informative Writing: *Advantages and Disadvantages Essay*

The best advantages and disadvantages essays show all the points on the checklist below. Here is how you can use it:

Before writing Look at the checklist to remind yourself of how to make your advantages and disadvantages essay the best it can be.

During writing Check your drafts against the list to see how you can make your essay better.

After writing Check your finished work against the list to see if it shows all the points of the best essays.

SCORE OF 4 ★★★★

★ The essay fits the purpose for writing well. The audience it was written for would understand it. The writer cares about the topic.

★ The essay has a clear beginning that introduces the topic, a middle that explains information and ideas about the topic, and an ending that summarizes or draws a conclusion.

★ The essay has description and rich details that add information about the topic.

★ The essay has signal words and phrases that help the reader understand how the ideas are related.

★ The essay has few errors in spelling, grammar, and punctuation.

What else is important in this kind of essay?

Informative Writing: *Research Report*

The best research reports show all the points on the checklist below. Here is how you can use it:

Before writing Look at the checklist to remind yourself of how to make your research report the best it can be.

During writing Check your drafts against the list to see how you can make your research report better.

After writing Check your finished work against the list to see if it shows all the points of the best research reports.

SCORE OF 4 ★★★★

★ The research report fits the purpose for writing well. The audience it was written for would understand it.

★ The report has a clear beginning that introduces the topic. The middle sections explain information and interesting ideas about the topic. The ending summarizes or draws a conclusion.

★ The report presents ideas and information from a variety of sources in the writer's own words.

★ The report has description, rich details, or narrative parts that add information about the topic.

★ The report has signal words and phrases that help the reader understand how the ideas are related.

★ The sentences are written in a variety of ways.

★ The report has few errors in spelling, grammar, and punctuation.

Expressive Writing: *Story*

The best stories show all the points on the checklist below. Here is how you can use it:

Before writing Look at the checklist to remind yourself of how to make your story the best it can be.

During writing Check your drafts against the list to see how you can make your story better.

After writing Check your finished work against the list to see if it shows all the points of the best stories.

SCORE OF 4 ★★★★

★ The story fits the purpose for writing well. The audience it was written for would enjoy it.

★ The story has developed characters and a setting. The characters solve a problem by the end of the story.

★ The story has description and rich details that help the reader visualize the events. The ideas are interesting.

★ The story has interesting words and phrases, such as specific nouns, vivid verbs, sensory words, and comparisons. It shows the writer's feelings.

★ The sentences are written in a variety of ways to make the writing interesting to read.

★ The story has few errors in spelling, grammar, and punctuation.

What other points do you think are important in a story?

Study Skills and Strategies

Skimming and Scanning

Skimming is a way to look at a book or story quickly. Skimming helps you learn the main ideas that are in a book or in a story. It can also help you decide whether you want to read the book or story.

Scanning is a way to read quickly to find information about a subject. When you are scanning a book or story, look for key words about your subject. Key words may be in titles, headings, or the text of the book or story itself.

Here are some tips for skimming:

How to Skim a Book

1. Read the **chapter titles** in the **table of contents** at the beginning.
2. Look at the **index** to find main topics.
3. Read the **beginning** to decide whether you want to read the whole book or chapter.

Wildlife Photos

by Celia Coburn

Suppose you want to know more about taking photos. Scan the selection below to learn what one person who takes photos does and where he works. Before you begin, think about what kinds of words might be key words for this topic.

David Jones is a (wildlife photographer), a person who takes pictures of animals. Sometimes he takes (pictures underwater). He says that finding the best place to take pictures is important.

At each photo shoot, Jones finds the best place to put his camera, so that he can get the most interesting picture. Sometimes he takes pictures of sunrises over (beaches). Sometimes he takes pictures in the deep, dark (sea). He has even gone to the ice-covered (Arctic) to take pictures of walruses.

This first paragraph answers your questions.

The circled words are the key words you should notice when you scan.

This paragraph gives you more information.

The beauty of nature.

Using Book Parts

Books have special parts that help you find information.

Front of the Book

The **title page** tells you
- the title of the book.
- the name of the author.
- the name of the company that made, or published, the book.
- the city or cities where the company is located.

The **copyright page** tells you
- what year the book was made.

The **table of contents** lists
- the different parts, or chapters, in the book.
- the title of each chapter.
- the page on which each chapter begins.

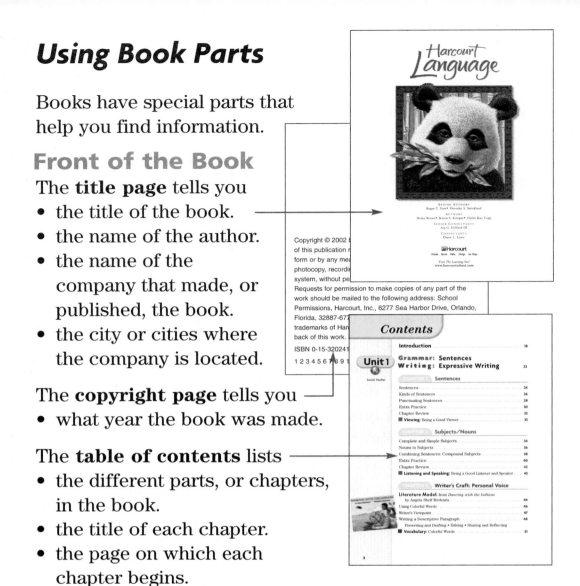

Back of the Book

The **glossary**
- gives the meanings of important words in the book.
- is arranged in alphabetical order.

The **index** shows what topics are in a book.
- An **entry** is a main topic in the book.
- Page numbers tell where in the book you can find information on the entry.
- A **cross-reference** tells you about another entry that has more information.

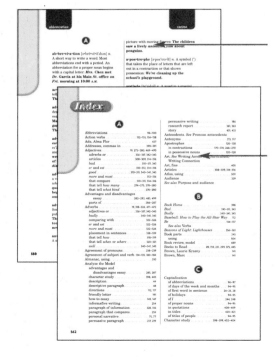

Using a Dictionary

A dictionary tells you the meaning of words and how to say them.

Words in a dictionary are arranged in alphabetical order. The **guide words** at the top of every page name the first word and the last word on the page. To find a word, use the guide words to decide which page contains the word.

Each word defined in a dictionary is called an **entry word**. The entry word is printed in dark type.

A special spelling of the word comes right after the entry. This special spelling shows the word's **pronunciation**, or how to say it aloud.

goo [goo] *n. U.S. slang* Any sticky substance.

goo·ber [goo′bər] *n. U.S.* A peanut. *Goober* may come from *nguba*, an African Bantu word for *peanut*.

good [good] *adj.* better, best **1** Having the proper qualities; admirable. **2** Skillful: a *good* pianist.

The **definition** tells the meaning of the word. When a word has more than one meaning, the definitions are numbered.

The letter or letters after the pronunciation tell the **part of speech**. Most dictionaries use abbreviations.

A **pronunciation key** appears on every other page. The key shows the letters and symbols used, and gives sample words to tell how to pronounce each sound.

a	add	i	it	ŏŏ	took	oi	oil
ā	ace	ī	ice	ōō	pool	ou	pout
â	care	o	odd	u	up	ng	ring
ä	palm	ō	open	û	burn	th	thin
e	end	ô	order	yōō	fuse	th	this
ē	equal					zh	vision

ə = { a in *above*   e in *sicken*   i in *possible*
        o in *melon*   u in *circus*

763

505

Using the Internet

Most computers can be connected to the **Internet**. The Internet can be used to get information, to do work, or to have fun.

When you connect your computer to the Internet, you are **online**. This means your computer can communicate with other computers on the Internet.

Information on the Net is found at **websites**. Every website has its own **address**. The ending of the address tells you what kind of site it is.

> *.gov* means this is a government site.
> *.org* means this is an organization's site.
> *.com* means this is a person's or a business's site.

Sometimes you may not know what website you want. You can use a **search engine** to help you. You can type in keywords, and the search engine will find websites that have information about those words.

You can also communicate with people you know. One common way of communicating is through **e-mail**. E-mail is a lot like regular mail, but much faster. You can send someone a note, a picture, or even a song. All you need is the e-mail address. An e-mail address works like a home address.

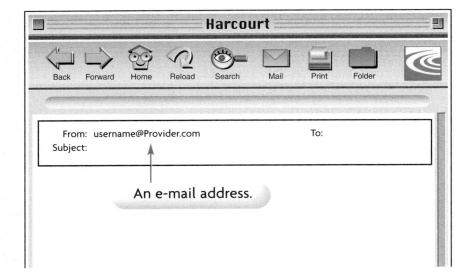

An e-mail address.

Using an Encyclopedia

An **encyclopedia** is a set of books with information on many different topics. Each **volume**, or book, has one or more letters on its spine. The letters go from A to Z. Sometimes there is also a number for each book.

Encyclopedia topics are arranged in alphabetical order. If you wanted to learn about stagecoaches, you would look in Volume 10, *S-T*.

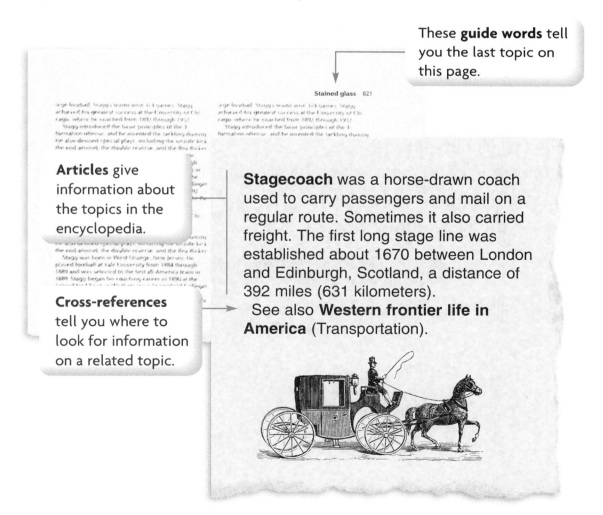

These **guide words** tell you the last topic on this page.

Stained glass   821

Articles give information about the topics in the encyclopedia.

Cross-references tell you where to look for information on a related topic.

Stagecoach was a horse-drawn coach used to carry passengers and mail on a regular route. Sometimes it also carried freight. The first long stage line was established about 1670 between London and Edinburgh, Scotland, a distance of 392 miles (631 kilometers).

See also **Western frontier life in America** (Transportation).

Using Periodicals and Newspapers

Newspapers and other **periodicals**, such as magazines, can be sources of information for all sorts of topics. A newspaper tells about current events in your neighborhood and around the world. Magazines have reports and photos about special topics. Knowing the parts of a periodical will help you find information.

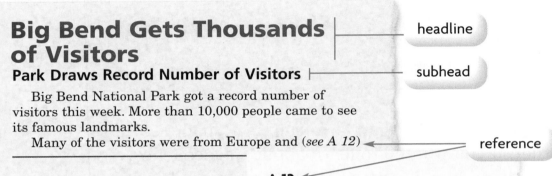

Big Bend Gets Thousands of Visitors
Park Draws Record Number of Visitors

headline

subhead

Big Bend National Park got a record number of visitors this week. More than 10,000 people came to see its famous landmarks.

Many of the visitors were from Europe and (*see A 12*)

reference

A 12
Asia, though most of the visitors were from Texas.

Some people who came to the park played games and hiked there.

The table of contents lists the articles in a periodical. You will find the table of contents near the front, usually on the first or second page. The table of contents tells you

- the title of each article or feature.
- the page number where it begins.

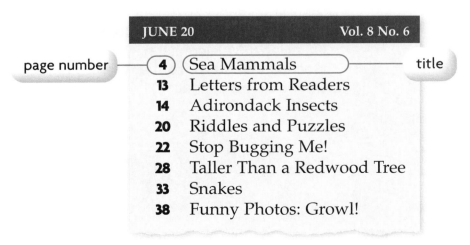

JUNE 20		Vol. 8 No. 6

page number

		title
4	Sea Mammals	
13	Letters from Readers	
14	Adirondack Insects	
20	Riddles and Puzzles	
22	Stop Bugging Me!	
28	Taller Than a Redwood Tree	
33	Snakes	
38	Funny Photos: Growl!	

Using an Atlas

An **atlas** is a book of maps. A world atlas has maps of every country in the world. Some atlases have maps of only one country. Different kinds of maps show different facts about places.

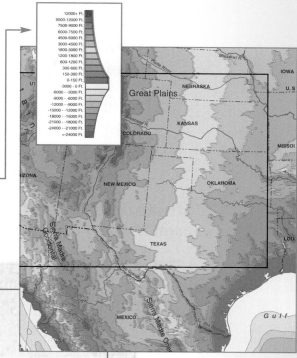

Map colors are used to show how high the land is. The **legend** tells you what the colors mean. On this map the color brown shows high mountain areas. The color blue shows water.

TEXAS

- El Paso
- Fort Worth
- Dallas
- ☆ Austin
- San Antonio
- Houston
- Corpus Christi

```
0        100 Miles
0        100 KM
Parallel scale at 29°N 0°E
```

```
0        100 Miles
0        100 KM
Parallel scale at 33°N 0°E
```

★ State capital
  Metropolitan area

This map shows the names of cities in Texas. The legend, or **map key**, tells you that the star shows the state's capital. On the map the star is next to the name of the state capital, Austin.

Using an Almanac

An **almanac** is a book of facts. It has information about people, places, weather, sports, history, and important events. Most almanacs also have facts about different countries. A new almanac is published every year.

Every almanac has an **index**, which lists all of the subjects in the almanac. The index tells you the page on which you can find the facts you want.

United States of America
Farm Products from Texas

TYPE	AMOUNT PRODUCED
Corn	201,600,000 bushels
Cotton	4,345,000 bushels
Hay	7,815,000 tons
Oats	3,400,000 bushels
Soybeans	7,020,000 bushels
Wheat	75,400,000 bushels

Spain

Area: 195,364 square miles **Number of People:** 39,167,744 (1999) **Language:** Spanish **Capital:** Madrid **Major Crops:** olives, wine grapes, grain **Major Factories and Businesses:** clothes, shoes, steel, cars, ships

An almanac may show facts in maps, tables, or charts.

Using a Map

A **map** is a drawing that shows what a place would look like from above. A map can show a large part of the world, an entire country, a city, or a smaller place like a shopping mall. Maps can also help people find their way from one place to another.

This is a map of Grand Canyon National Park. It has some features found on many maps.

The **compass rose** tells you which way is north (*N*), south (*S*), east (*E*), or west (*W*).

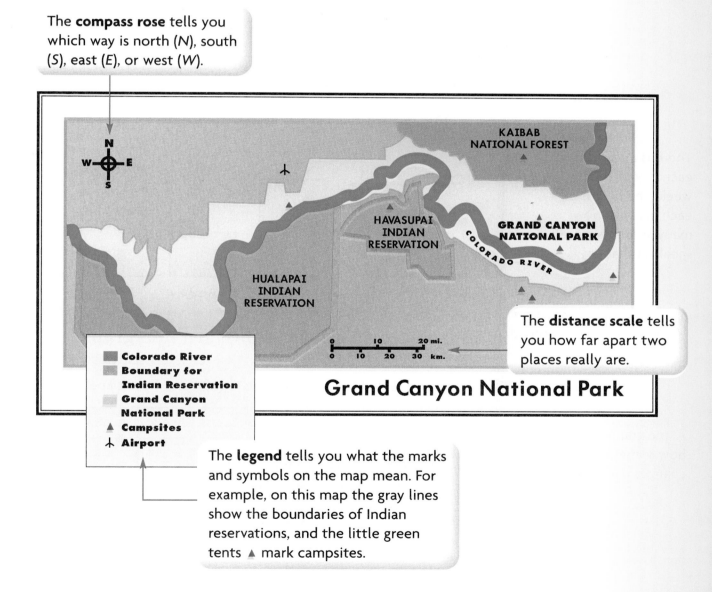

Grand Canyon National Park

Colorado River
Boundary for Indian Reservation
Grand Canyon National Park
▲ Campsites
✈ Airport

The **distance scale** tells you how far apart two places really are.

The **legend** tells you what the marks and symbols on the map mean. For example, on this map the gray lines show the boundaries of Indian reservations, and the little green tents ▲ mark campsites.

Using Graphs

Graphs are used to show information in a way that is easy to understand. Graphs compare information that is measured with numbers.

Suppose a student counted the number of her classmates who wore sneakers to school. She did this every day for a week and recorded this information.

Third-Grade Students Who Wore Sneakers to School

Day	Count
Monday	23
Tuesday	21
Wednesday	22
Thursday	10
Friday	25

This information can be shown in a **bar graph**.

There is a bar for each day of the week. The height of each bar tells how many students wore sneakers that day.

The information could also be shown in a **line graph**.

A line graph shows how something changes over time.

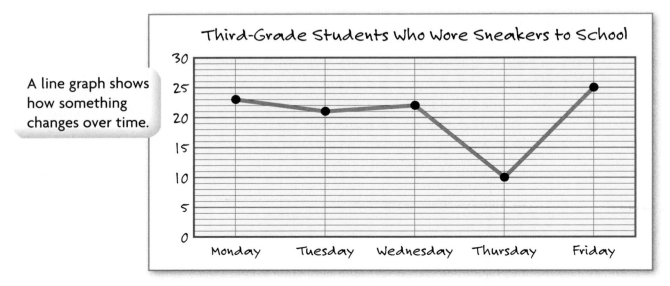

Using Tables

A **table** is a way to present a lot of facts in a form that is easy to use.

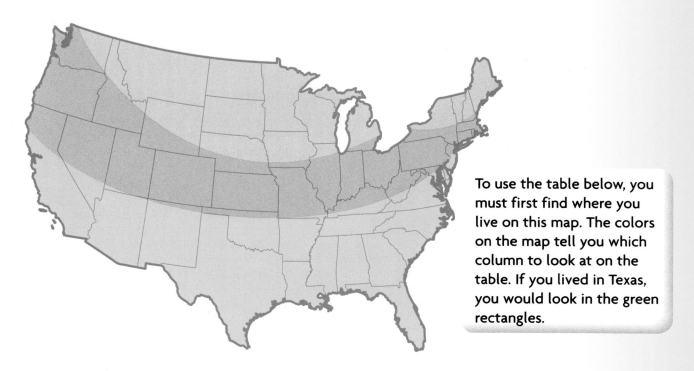

To use the table below, you must first find where you live on this map. The colors on the map tell you which column to look at on the table. If you lived in Texas, you would look in the green rectangles.

This table tells the best time to plant certain plants in different parts of the country.

Cucumbers	May 7 to June 20	April 7 to May 15	March 7 to April 15
Lettuce	May 15 to June 30	March 1 to March 31	February 15 to March 7
Squash	May 15 to June 15	April 15 to April 30	March 15 to April 15
Sweet Potatoes	May 15 to June 15	April 21 to May 2	March 23 to April 6
Watermelon	May 15 to June 30	April 15 to May 7	March 15 to March 28

Gardeners in Texas should plant cucumbers between March 7 and April 15.

row

column

Find what you want to plant at the left. Then move to the right until you get to the column that matches your area on the map.

Using Charts

A **chart** is a picture that shows information. Some charts are arranged in columns. This one tells you how much food to give a dog. To use this chart, find your dog's weight in the left column. The right column tells how much to feed him or her each day.

How Much Food to Give Your Dog	
Dog's Weight	Amount of Food
3 – 10 pounds	1/3 to 3/4 cup
10 – 20 pounds	3/4 to 1 1/4 cups
20 – 30 pounds	1 1/4 to 1 1/2 cups
30 – 40 pounds	1 1/2 to 1 3/4 cups
40 – 60 pounds	1 3/4 to 2 1/3 cups
60 – 80 pounds	2 1/3 to 2 3/4 cups
80 – 100 pounds	2 3/4 to 3 1/3 cups

fats, oils, and sweets

milk, yogurt, and cheese group

meat, poultry, fish, dry beans, eggs, and nuts group

vegetable group

fruit group

bread, cereal, rice, and pasta group

The **food pyramid** is also a kind of chart. It defines the different food groups.

Pie Charts

A **pie chart** is a good way to show parts of a whole. By looking at the size of the pieces of this pie, you can tell what a typical third grader does in a day.

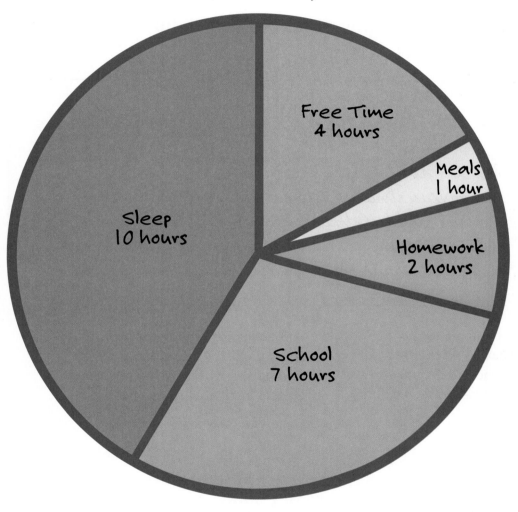

What I Do in Twenty-Four Hours

Sleep
10 hours

Free Time
4 hours

Meals
1 hour

Homework
2 hours

School
7 hours

Note-Taking

Taking notes helps you remember what you read. You can look at your notes, whenever you need to, to check your facts when writing a report or studying for a test.

A good way to take notes is on cards. Make a separate card for each main idea. This lets you put the cards in order in different ways. This can be helpful if you are writing a report.

Write on the card the title and author of the book where you found the information. If your source has numbered pages, include the page number.

Gail Gibbons, Weather Words and What They Mean

What kinds of clouds are there?
1. cumulus clouds (puffy clouds)—fair weather
2. cirrus clouds (streaky clouds high in the sky)—fair weather
3. stratus clouds (low, gray clouds)—rain or snow

Write the main idea of the information on the card. Sometimes it helps to write the main idea as a question.

Write the most important facts and details. Put the information in your own words. Write in phrases instead of sentences.

Note-Taking with Graphic Organizers

Sometimes it helps to use a **graphic organizer** when you are taking notes. A **K-W-L chart** is a good chart for taking notes. The chart has three columns.

- Before you read, write what you already **know** about the subject in the **K** column.
- Think about what you **want** to find out. Write those questions in the **W** column.
- As you are reading, write what you **learn** in the **L** column.

Clouds		
K	W	L
Moisture in the air causes clouds. Rain comes from clouds.	What kinds of clouds are there? What makes clouds release their moisture?	cumulus (puffy clouds) cirrus (streaky clouds) stratus (low, gray clouds)

A **web** can also be helpful when you are taking notes. A web is a good way to show how facts or ideas are connected.

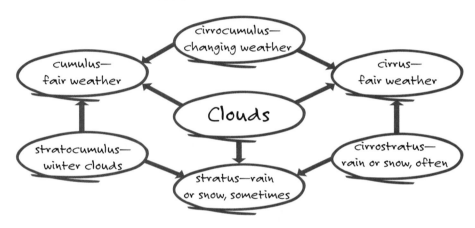

A **Venn diagram** helps you compare two things. This Venn diagram shows what is alike and what is different about rain and snow.

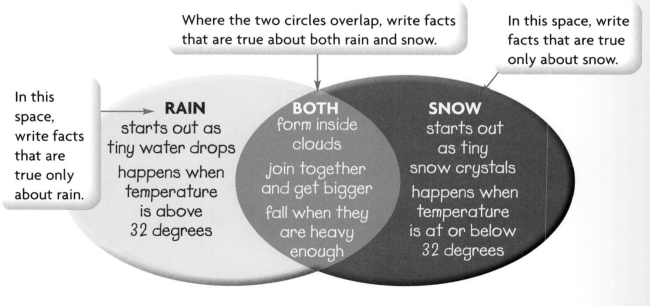

In this space, write facts that are true only about rain.

Where the two circles overlap, write facts that are true about both rain and snow.

In this space, write facts that are true only about snow.

RAIN
starts out as tiny water drops

happens when temperature is above 32 degrees

BOTH
form inside clouds

join together and get bigger

fall when they are heavy enough

SNOW
starts out as tiny snow crystals

happens when temperature is at or below 32 degrees

Summarizing

A **summary** is a brief explanation in your own words that includes

- the main idea of the work.
- the most important details that support the main idea.

Writing a summary is a good way of making sure you understand what you have read. A summary can also help you remember something later.

Read the paragraphs below. Look for the main idea and the most important supporting details. Then read the summary. Notice that it tells only the most important details.

Giant pandas and red pandas look very different. Giant pandas are huge black-and-white animals. They are shaped like bears. Giant pandas have round heads and chubby bodies. They measure between five and six feet long. They also have short tails and can stand on their hind legs. Adult giant pandas may look cuddly, but they are not lightweights! They usually weigh between 200 and 300 pounds. Bai-yun, a panda at the San Diego Zoo, weighed 600 pounds after she had her cub (a baby panda). Giant pandas eat up to eighty-five pounds of bamboo a day!

The red panda, on the other hand, is much smaller. Weighing about eleven pounds, red pandas are usually about two feet long (tails not included). They have long reddish-brown fur and pale faces with red markings under each eye. Red pandas are not active most of the day. However, they are great climbers. Like raccoons, they use their front paws for grasping. They sleep away most of the day in trees. They do not go looking for food except at dawn and dusk. Also, unlike the giant pandas, red pandas will eat something besides bamboo. They sometimes will eat fruit and berries.

Summary

Giant pandas and red pandas are different. Giant pandas are much bigger than red pandas. Red pandas climb a lot and eat more different kinds of foods than do giant pandas.

How would you summarize the paragraphs in one sentence?

Outlining

Outlining is a way to understand information. It will help you see the main ideas and the details of an article or book you read. You can also use an outline to help plan your own writing.

Tips for Outlining

- Make an outline before you write.
- Write the topic of your outline at the top as your title.
- The most important ideas are called main ideas.
- Write main ideas after Roman numerals and periods.
- Supporting details follow each main idea.
- Write each detail after a capital letter and a period.

This outline uses words and phrases for main ideas and supporting details. You can also create a **sentence outline**, in which all the items are complete sentences.

Woodchucks

I. Name
  A. Where the name came from
  B. Other name for woodchuck (groundhog)
II. Where Woodchucks Live
  A. Northeastern United States and Canada
  B. In woods and on farms
  C. In backyards
III. The Woodchuck's Habits
  A. Active during the day
  B. Sleeps underground
  C. Sleeps all winter long
  D. Wakes up on Groundhog Day
  E. If sees shadow, goes back to sleep
  F. Sleeps for another six weeks until spring comes

Here is the report about woodchucks that was written using the outline. Compare the outline and the report.

Woodchuck

The name woodchuck looks like a compound word, but it isn't. Woodchuck comes from the Native American word otchek or otchig. Woodchucks are also called groundhogs, because they are round like hogs and they dig holes in the ground.

*The first paragraph tells about the woodchuck's **name**.*

Woodchucks can be found all over the northeastern United States and Canada. They live in the woods and on farms. They are happy in backyards, too.

*The second paragraph tells about **where woodchucks live**.*

Woodchucks move around during the day. At night, they sleep underground. They sleep all winter long. They usually wake up on, or around, February 2. This is called Groundhog Day. According to legend, if the woodchuck sees its shadow, it goes back to sleep. It sleeps for another six weeks, which is when spring comes.

*The third paragraph tells about the woodchuck's **habits**.*

Test-Taking Strategies

Follow these test-taking tips for all kinds of tests.

In class:
- Listen carefully. Write down important facts.
- Ask questions.

The night before the test:
- Study in a quiet place with good light.
- Skim your textbook and reread your notes.

Multiple-Choice Tests

A multiple-choice test asks you to choose the correct answer from several possible answers.

Here are some tips for taking multiple-choice tests:
- Answer the easy questions first.
- Read each choice and cross out the ones you know are wrong.
- Double-check your answers.

Here is a sample test question:

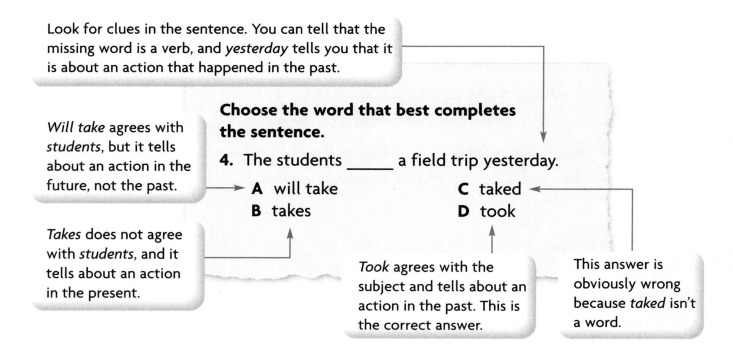

Look for clues in the sentence. You can tell that the missing word is a verb, and *yesterday* tells you that it is about an action that happened in the past.

Will take agrees with *students*, but it tells about an action in the future, not the past.

Choose the word that best completes the sentence.

4. The students _____ a field trip yesterday.
   A will take   **C** taked
   B takes   **D** took

Takes does not agree with *students*, and it tells about an action in the present.

Took agrees with the subject and tells about an action in the past. This is the correct answer.

This answer is obviously wrong because *taked* isn't a word.

Essay Tests

An **essay test** asks you to write answers in the form of sentences or paragraphs.

Understanding Essay Test Questions

As in all writing, think about your purpose and audience when taking an essay test. Are you being asked to inform or persuade your audience? Are you being asked to compare or contrast something?

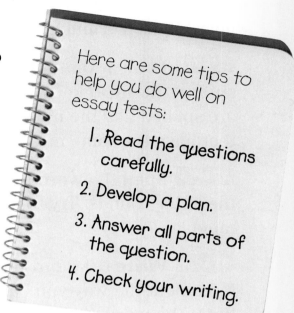

Here are some tips to help you do well on essay tests:

1. Read the questions carefully.
2. Develop a plan.
3. Answer all parts of the question.
4. Check your writing.

Tell the main point clearly at the beginning. Use many details to tell about the main ideas. Use the writing steps you learned in the writing chapters—prewrite, draft, revise, proofread, and publish.

Here are several kinds of essay questions:

Explain When you explain something, you tell more details about it.

Compare When you compare two or more things, you write about how the things are like each other.

Contrast When you contrast two or more things, you write about how the things are different from each other.

Describe When you describe something, you give details about it. You might tell how it looks or sounds or what it does.

Solve a Problem Some questions give information and then ask you to solve a problem. Think about the problem, and read the information several times. Underline important words in the question. Then explain your solution in your answer.

Spelling Strategies

Use these five steps to learn a new word.

STEP 1 **Say** the word. Remember times you have heard it used. Think about what it means.

STEP 2 **Look** at the word. Find prefixes and suffixes that you know. Think about words that are spelled like the new word. Think of words that have the same meaning.

STEP 3 **Spell** the word to yourself. Think about the letter sounds. Try to picture the word in your mind.

STEP 4 **Write** the word while you are looking at it. Look at the way you have formed your letters. Write the word again if you did not write it clearly or correctly.

STEP 5 **Check** your learning. Cover the word and write it again. If you did not spell the word correctly, repeat these steps.

Vowel Sounds

Short Vowel Sounds

- The **short vowel sounds** are usually spelled with one letter but not always.

/**a**/ is spelled **a**, as in *tap*
/**e**/ is spelled **e**, as in *ten*
/**e**/ is spelled **ea**, as in *bread*
/**i**/ is spelled **i**, as in *pit*
/**o**/ is spelled **o**, as in *lot*
/**u**/ is spelled **u**, as in *run*

Long Vowel Sounds

- Here are five ways to spell the /ā/ sound.

  a-consonant-e, as in *date*

  ai, as in *maid*

  ay, as in *say*

  ey, as in *obey*

  eigh, as in *sleigh*

- Here are four ways to spell the /ē/ sound.

  ea, as in *bean*

  ee, as in *feel*

  e, as in *me*

  y, as in *happy*

- Here are five ways to spell the /ī/ sound.

  i-consonant-e, as in *time*

  i, as in *climb*

  igh, as in *night*

  y, as in *my*

  uy, as in *buy*

- Here are four ways to spell the /ō/ sound.

  o-consonant-e, as in *rope*

  oa, as in *loaf*

  o, as in *colt*

  ow, as in *show*

- Here are two ways to spell the /o͞o/ or /yo͞o/ sound.

  u-consonant-e, as in *tube*

  u, as in *music*

Letter Combinations

- The letter *i* usually comes before *e* when these two letters are written together in a word. If the letters follow *c*, or if they make the /ā/ sound, they are written *ei*.

piece

receive

weigh

- Here are two ways to spell the /ər/ sound.

er, as in *cover*

ar, as in *sugar*

- Here are two ways to spell the /əl/ sound.

le, as in *middle*

el, as in *barrel*

Commonly Misspelled Words

again

another

anything

before

bought

boy's

brought

caught

decided

everybody

everyone

everything

field

finally

getting

girl's

guess

happened

heard

it's

kept

knew

let's

maybe

missed

outside

practice

really

scared

sometimes

stopped

suddenly

surprise

than

that's

their

thought

threw

through

tomorrow

too

trouble

trying

until

upon

we're

what's

where

whole

won't

Handwriting Models

Cursive Alphabet

A B C D E F G H

I J K L M N O P

Q R S T U V W

X Y Z

a b c d e f g h

i j k l m n o p

q r s t u v w

x y z

D'Nealian Cursive Alphabet

A B C D E F G H

I J K L M N O P

2 R S T U V W

X Y Z

a b c d e f g h

i j k l m n o p

q r s t u v w

x y z

Using a Thesaurus

A **synonym** is a word that has almost the same meaning as another word.

An **antonym** is a word that means the opposite of another word.

A thesaurus is an important tool because it can help you find just the right word to use. If you were writing about the weather in this picture, you might say it is cold. If you wanted a word that means *very, very cold*, you could check a thesaurus for synonyms for the word *cold*. One synonym you could choose is *frosty*. *Frosty* may be a much better word to describe the weather in this picture. *Frosty* may be better because it is a vivid and exact word. An *exact* word is one that has just the right meaning. *A vivid* word is one that helps bring the scene to life.

> The weather is *cold*.
> The weather is *frosty*.

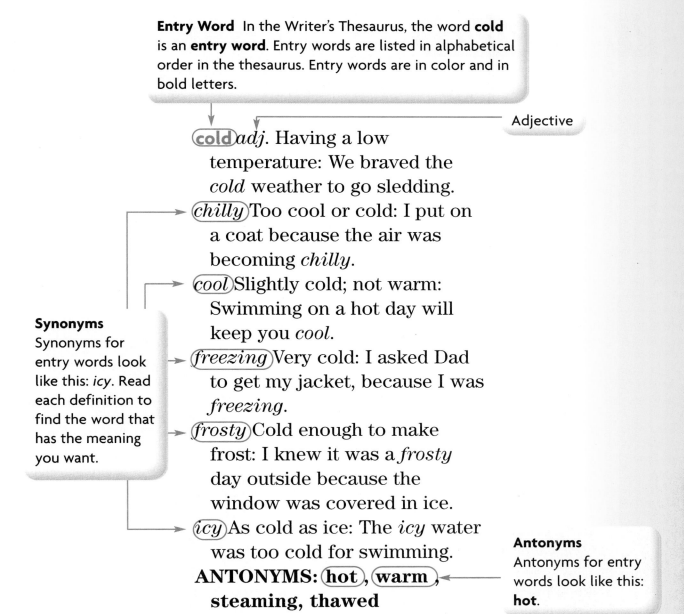

Adjective

cold *adj.* Having a low temperature: We braved the *cold* weather to go sledding.

chilly Too cool or cold: I put on a coat because the air was becoming *chilly*.

cool Slightly cold; not warm: Swimming on a hot day will keep you *cool*.

freezing Very cold: I asked Dad to get my jacket, because I was *freezing*.

frosty Cold enough to make frost: I knew it was a *frosty* day outside because the window was covered in ice.

icy As cold as ice: The *icy* water was too cold for swimming.

ANTONYMS: **hot**, **warm**, **steaming, thawed**

You can also look in the index of a thesaurus to find antonyms and synonyms for entry words.

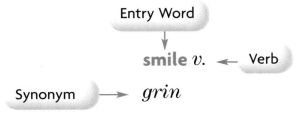

Entry Word

smile *v.* ← Verb

Synonym → *grin*

The index shows that *grin* is listed as a synonym for smile. If you wanted another word for *grin*, you would look up *smile* in the thesaurus.

A

afraid *adj.* Filled with fear; feeling frightened: My dog is *afraid* of thunder and lightning.

anxious Worried: Andrea was *anxious* about her first day at school.

fearful Expecting danger or a bad outcome: My little sister is *fearful* of spiders.

frightened Suddenly scared; startled: The *frightened* birds scattered when the car drove by them.

terrified Having great fear; filled with terror: The *terrified* cat ran away from the barking dog.

ANTONYMS: bold, unafraid, confident

angry *adj.* Feeling or showing rage or annoyance: The *angry* little girl stamped her feet.

furious Very angry: Chin was *furious* when her dog ate her homework.

mad Feeling hurt or unhappy: I was *mad* at my brother for messing up my room.

upset To feel bothered by someone or something: I was *upset* at first when we moved to our new home.

ANTONYMS: calm, pleased

ask *v.* To request; to invite: I can *ask* the teacher if I don't understand.

explore To think about; to examine: The students *explore* the causes of fog.

inquire To seek information: My mother *inquired* about the tickets for tonight's concert.

question To ask in a challenging way: The news reporters *question* the mayor about the new law.

ANTONYMS: answer, explain, reply, respond

B

bad *adj.* Not good; unkind or unsafe: It is a *bad* idea to lie to a friend.

harmful Causing damage: Eating too many sweets can be *harmful* to your health.

mean Selfish or nasty: The *mean* person said awful things about Jo.

poor Not good: The air is *poor* today because of the smog.

severe Causing damage or hardship: There is a *severe* storm forming over the ocean.

unpleasant Not pleasing; not fun: Being sick with the flu is an *unpleasant* experience.

ANTONYMS: good, pleasant, all right

big *adj.* Of great size: The box was too *big* for me to carry.

enormous Much larger in size than usual: The circus elephant was *enormous*.

giant Huge or great: The *giant* basketball player towered over the little boy.

grand Large and wonderful: Everyone admired the *grand* library building.

great Large; important: The *great* oak tree was the tallest and oldest tree in the town.

huge Of very great size: *Huge* machines called cranes are used to build skyscrapers.

ANTONYMS: little, ordinary, small, tiny

break *n.* A short rest from an activity: Fasal took a *break* from studying and ate a snack.

holiday A day when many offices and schools are closed; a national or religious festival: Independence Day is my favorite *holiday*.

recess A break from work for rest or play: The students will have *recess* outside after lunch.

vacation A longer break from work or school; a pleasure trip: We visited my grandparents on our *vacation*.

broken *adj.* Not in good condition; not working; damaged: The *broken* cup lay in many pieces.

cracked Broken but not completely falling apart: The *cracked* mirror still hung on the wall.

crushed Broken completely by being pressed between two things: A *crushed* tomato was at the bottom of the grocery bag.

ANTONYMS: fixed, mended, repaired

C

call *v.* To speak in a loud voice: The teacher will *call* us in from the playground.

bellow To say something in a very loud voice: Sergeants *bellow* orders to their troops as they march across the field.

greet To welcome someone, using friendly words: The teachers *greet* the students at the door on the first day of school.

roar To make a very loud and deep sound in pain, excitement, or anger: The fans *roar* every time their favorite team scores a point.

scream To make a loud, sharp sound because of fright: Viewers *scream* during the scary parts of the movie.

shout To say loudly: The conductor had to *shout* to be heard over the noise of the train.

telephone To call by telephone: I will *telephone* my friend.

yell To shout, scream, or roar: The outfielder had to *yell* to the catcher.

carry *v.* To take from one place to another: Many students *carry* their homework in a backpack.

cart To carry a weight or burden: Every week I have to *cart* the trash cans out to the curb.

haul To carry a heavy load: A moving truck will *haul* the furniture to our new home.

move To carry from one place to another: When it gets cold, I will *move* some of the plants inside the house.

remove To carry or take away: Please *remove* your dirty boots from the kitchen.

ANTONYMS: drop, leave behind

catch *v.* To take hold of a moving object: The children *catch* butterflies with a net.

capture To catch by force, with skill, or by surprise: The cat tried to *capture* the mouse.

clutch To hold tightly: The little girl will *clutch* her mother's hand when crossing the street.

grasp To take hold of firmly: Grandmother must *grasp* the handrail as she walks down the stairs.

trap To catch by using a trick: Spiders *trap* insects in their webs.

ANTONYMS: drop, let go, miss, release, throw

cold *adj.* Having a low temperature: We braved the *cold* weather to go sledding.

chilly Quite cool or cold: I put on a coat because the air was becoming *chilly*.

cool Slightly cold; not warm: Swimming on a hot day will keep you *cool*.

freezing Very cold: I asked Dad to get my jacket, because I was *freezing*.

frosty Cold enough to make frost: I knew it was a *frosty* day outside because the window was covered in ice.

icy As cold as ice: The *icy* water was too cold for swimming.

ANTONYMS: hot, warm, steaming, thawed

cook *v.* To heat food: We had to *cook* the oatmeal before we could eat it.

bake To cook in an oven: *Bake* the cake for twenty-five minutes.

boil To heat until it is hot and bubbling: My mother will *boil* water to fix rice for dinner.

fry To cook in hot oil: Restaurants *fry* potato sticks in hot oil to make french fries.

prepare To put together or make ready: After we *prepare* dinner, we will sit down and eat it.

steam To cook in the hot mist that rises from boiling water: We *steam* carrots until they are soft.

cut *v.* To divide or break into parts: *Cut* the cake into ten pieces.

carve To cut up or slice: My uncle will *carve* the turkey.

chop To cut with a sharp tool: I asked him to *chop* some tomatoes for my salad.

clip To cut short; to cut out with scissors: I asked the barber to *clip* my hair.

crack To split apart: To eat the nut, you will have to *crack* open its shell.

slice To cut into thin pieces: Dad asked Alex to *slice* cucumbers for the salad.

split To cut from end to end: A lightning bolt *split* the tree down the middle.

trim To cut just a little: I hope she will only *trim* my hair and not cut it too short.

ANTONYMS: repair, combine, join

draw *v.* To make pictures with a marker or pencil: I like to *draw* horses.

design To draw plans for something that can be made: Judy will *design* our tree house before we build it.

sketch To draw quickly to give a general idea: He will first *sketch* his idea for the poster.

ANTONYM: erase

eat *v.* To take in food: You must *eat* a variety of food to stay healthy.

chew To bite up and down many times: You should *chew* your food carefully before you swallow it.

dine To eat a meal: We will *dine* at a Chinese restaurant on my mother's birthday.

feast To eat a large and special meal: Every Thanksgiving we *feast* on turkey and other foods.

gobble To eat quickly and greedily: The dog will *gobble* down the food as soon as you put it in the dish.

gulp To drink in large swallows: The thirsty basketball players *gulp* water after each game.

munch To eat happily and with a crunching sound: I like to *munch* on popcorn during a movie.

nibble To take small bites: The small birds *nibble* on bits of crackers.

swallow To pass something from one's mouth to one's stomach: Be sure to *swallow* your cold medicine.

F

fast *adj.* Moving with speed: The team needs *fast* runners to win races.

quick Taking little time: The goalkeeper's *quick* movement prevented a goal.

swift Moving easily and with speed: He picked up the ball and threw it to first base in one *swift* move.

ANTONYMS: slow, sluggish

find *v.* To come upon by surprise; to look for and discover: I cannot go outside until I *find* my jacket.

discover To find out; to come upon before anyone else; to know about: Students *discover* new words by looking in a thesaurus.

locate To find the place where something is: When I saw a flag on the building, I was able to *locate* the post office.

search To look for someone or something: I will *search* until I find my sneakers.

uncover To take the cover or covering off; to make known: They move the pile of newspapers and *uncover* a litter of kittens.

ANTONYMS: bury, cover, hide, lose

funny *adj.* Causing people to laugh or smile: Everyone laughed at the *funny* joke.

amusing Funny in a quiet way: The *amusing* story made the reader smile.

entertaining Funny in an interesting way: He always has *entertaining* stories to tell.

silly Funny in a foolish way: In the cartoon a *silly* bear bumps into a tree.

witty Funny in a clever way: A *witty* comic makes us laugh and think about things in a new way.

ANTONYMS: serious, sad

G

good *adj.* Not bad; helpful: Giving toys to a sick child is a *good* idea.

excellent Very good: He gave an *excellent* review of the movie.

kind Good-hearted: A *kind* student made friends with the new third grader.

right Behaving by the rules: Both runners started at the same time, which was the *right* thing to do.

worthy Having worth, value, or honor: A *worthy* person can be trusted with a secret.

ANTONYMS: bad, evil, mean, unfair, unworthy

grow *v.* To get larger in size, older in age, or greater in amount: If you water the seed, it will *grow*.

develop To grow in stages: You must exercise to *develop* strong muscles.

gain To increase in size or amount; to grow better, stronger, or more skillful:

Basketball practice will help you *gain* skills in passing and shooting.

raise To bring up or to help grow: Parents work hard to *raise* their children.

sprout To begin to grow: In spring the park is filled with new plants just starting to *sprout*.

ANTONYMS: decrease, die, shrink, wither

happy *adj.* Full of joy: The *happy* little girl clapped and giggled as she ran under the sprinkler.

cheerful Happy; joyous; bright and pleasant: Party balloons and colored streamers make our classroom look *cheerful*.

excited Having strong, lively feelings about something: The *excited* camper jumped up and down when he caught his first fish.

jolly Full of fun; merry: The *jolly* singers sang holiday songs on our doorstep.

joyful Showing much happiness: The friends felt *joyful* when they saw each other again on the first day of school.

merry Full of fun and laughter; joyous: My family had a *merry* time together during the holidays.

pleased Having good feelings about something: The teacher was *pleased* that everyone passed the test.

ANTONYMS: gloomy, sad, depressed, upset

healthy *adj.* Feeling and being well; free from disease: Exercise helps us feel *healthy*.

fit In good physical shape: The soccer player is *fit*.

hearty Healthy and strong: The mountain climber is a *hearty* person.

normal Not ill: The doctor said that my skin looks *normal*.

well In good health: When you are *well* again, you may play outside.

ANTONYMS: ailing, ill, sick, unhealthy, unwell

hot *adj.* Having a high temperature: It was 100 degrees on that *hot* summer day.

boiling Having such a high temperature that liquid bubbles: The *boiling* water in the pot bubbled.

burning Being covered by fire: We could smell the *burning* hot dogs all over the camp.

sizzling Having such a high temperature that a crackling sound is made: We heard the *sizzling* bacon cooking on the stove.

steaming Having such a high temperature that a gas is created: When I saw the *steaming* cup, I knew the hot chocolate would warm me.

warm Comfortably hot: The heavy blanket kept her *warm* on cold nights.

ANTONYMS: cold, freezing, chilly, nippy

interesting *adj.* Holding the attention: We learned about the weather by watching an *interesting* video.

entertaining Holding the attention by being enjoyable: The book was so *entertaining* that I kept reading until late at night.

exciting Causing strong, lively feelings: Their first ride in an airplane was very *exciting*.

fascinating Causing amazement: In her report, Leah told us many *fascinating* facts about pyramids.

ANTONYMS: uninteresting, boring, dull

jump *v.* To move up quickly from the ground to the air: My dog can *jump* over that fence.

bounce To jump or leap suddenly: If a player falls, he needs to *bounce* right up again.

hop To make short jumps or leaps: The birds *hop* around picking up seeds.

leap To make a big jump; to rise free of the ground: I had to run and then *leap* to get over the large puddle in the street.

skip To move by stepping, hopping, and sliding on each foot in turn: It is more fun to *skip* to school than to walk.

spring To make a quick jump from one spot to another: If a deer is scared, it may *spring* away from the danger.

land *n.* Solid surface of the earth: We could see the ocean and the *land* from our airplane.

earth The dry surface of our planet; dirt or soil: We planted flower seeds in the *earth* in our backyard.

ground The part of the Earth's surface that is solid: The *ground* looked very far away when we flew in an airplane.

ANTONYMS: air, water, sky

little *adj.* Not big in size, amount, or importance: I was not hungry, so I ate only a *little* slice of pizza.

puny Small and feeble: The *puny* kitten fit inside a teacup.

short Small in height: Compared to a giraffe, a human being is *short*.

small Not large in size or amount: We paid a *small* price for that jigsaw puzzle at the garage sale.

skinny Thin: Because the dog was so *skinny*, we named him Stringbean.

teeny Very, very small: I have *teeny* pots and pans in my dollhouse.

tiny Very small: I saw a *tiny* bug crawling on a leaf.

ANTONYMS: big, great, huge, large, mighty, giant

make *v.* To put together; to bring into being: We will *make* a castle out of sand.

build To make by putting parts or materials together: They *build* computers by fitting together many small parts.

complete To make whole with no parts missing: She will *complete* her story as soon as she thinks of an ending.

create To make, using imagination or skill: Because he draws so well, he can *create* wonderful pictures.

form To make something by shaping it: The artist will *form* a clay pot with her hands.

produce To grow or manufacture: These farmers *produce* the best corn I ever tasted.

put together To connect two or more parts: To make a model airplane, you must *put together* many small parts.

ANTONYMS: destroy, smash, take apart, undo

mix *v.* To put together or combine different things: The directions say to *mix* the ingredients well.

add To put one thing with another: The artist will *add* red paint to white and make pink.

beat To mix something by stirring it hard: *Beat* the cake batter until it is smooth.

blend To mix two or more things together: To make chili, the cook will *blend* meat, beans, and spices.

combine To put or mix two or more things together: *Combine* water, flour, and salt to make paste.

mingle To bring or come together: We wanted to *mingle* with the guests at the party.

stir To mix, using a spoon or stick: The chef must *stir* the soup.

ANTONYMS: divide, separate, unravel

new *adj.* Just made, started, or arrived: The *new* teacher introduced himself to the class.

current Taking place now: The *current* school year is half over.

fresh Unused; clean; not spoiled: Ginny turned to a *fresh* page in her notebook.

latest Most recent: The *latest* space mission took place a month ago.

modern In the present time; up-to-date: Computers are a *modern* invention.

original Not copied: The song is based on an *original* poem.

ANTONYMS: old, used, worn

nice *adj.* Pleasant; enjoyable: It's a *nice* day for a walk in the park.

attractive Likable; pleasing to the eye: The new gymnastics uniforms are very *attractive*.

friendly Showing kindness: Our *friendly* neighbors visited us when we moved in.

good Admired; well-behaved or helpful; of high quality: Angelo is a *good* athlete.

kind Helpful; gentle; generous: The *kind* student stayed to help.

pleasant Likable, enjoyable: We had a *pleasant* time at the party.

pleasing Giving pleasure: Taking a long walk outdoors is a *pleasing* way to spend a fall afternoon.

ANTONYMS: mean, nasty, rude, unpleasant

old *adj.* Having lived or existed for a long time: The stone tools in the museum are very *old*.

ancient From times long past: *Ancient* tribes hunted animals with bows and arrows.

used Made use of already; not new: Gary bought a *used* bike for twenty dollars.

worn Damaged by use: Her favorite jeans were badly *worn*.

ANTONYMS: current, modern, new, young, fresh, unused

Ⓟ

part *n.* A portion of a whole: He saved *part* of the melon for me.

fraction A part of a whole; a small amount: The dog ate only a *fraction* of its food.

piece A section of something; a part taken from a whole: A *piece* of the broken plate is still missing.

scrap A small or unwanted piece, as of paper, food, or metal: Oscar wrote the information on a *scrap* of paper.

section A division of something; a part of an area: The downtown *section* of my city is beautiful.

ANTONYMS: whole, all

person *n.* A man, woman, or child; a single human being: A bicycle is made for one *person*.

child A young girl or boy; a son or daughter: The *child* enjoyed playing on the swings.

human A human being: That footprint was made by a *human*.

man An adult male human being: The *man* and his son sat together.

woman An adult female human being: The *woman* in the red coat is my sister.

pretty *adj.* Nice to look at: The shiny blue and silver fish was *pretty*.

beautiful Especially pleasant to look at or listen to: The singer had a *beautiful* voice.

handsome Having pleasing looks, especially in a noble or dignified way: My grandfather was a *handsome* man.

lovely Having a pleasing appearance or effect: A *lovely* breeze cooled us on the hot afternoon.

ANTONYMS: plain, unattractive

pull *v.* To move something toward you: *Pull* the chain to turn on the light.

draw To pull forward: Two horses *draw* the cart along the road.

haul To carry by pulling; to pull with difficulty: Lucia agreed to *haul* her little brother up the hill in her wagon.

tow To pull something behind a vehicle: We used our car to *tow* the boat to the dock.

tug To pull hard: If you *tug* the loose thread, you may make a hole in your sweater.

ANTONYMS: push, shove, thrust

put *v.* To set or lay something: *Put* your dirty shoes outside.

lay To place in a certain order or position: Please *lay* that blanket on the bed.

place To move a thing carefully or on purpose: Let's *place* the flowerpot on the kitchen table.

spread To stretch out; to cover with something: Jake likes to *spread* peanut butter on his toast.

sprinkle To scatter something over a surface: Many people *sprinkle* sugar on cereal.

quiet *adj.* With little or no noise; calm: The classroom was *quiet* during the test.

calm Quiet; peaceful; still; not upset: You can see your face in the *calm* water of the lake.

peaceful Pleasantly calm and quiet: After the boys went outside to play, the house was *peaceful*.

silent With no noise at all: *Silent* movies have pictures but no sound.

still Without noise or movement: Please keep *still* during the concert.

ANTONYMS: loud, noisy, upset

R

rest *v.* To take a break from activity: Josie will *rest* after playing tennis.

nap To sleep for a short time, usually during the day: I like to *nap* in the car when we go on long trips.

relax To become less tense; to rest: Nell likes to *relax* by reading.

sleep To rest the body and mind with the eyes closed: Most people dream when they *sleep*.

snooze To sleep lightly for a short time: Cats like to *snooze* in sunny places.

ANTONYM: wake

road *n.* A wide path made for traveling: The *road* to our house is bumpy.

avenue An especially wide road in a town or city: The parade will take place on the main *avenue*.

highway A main road: The *highway* is busy at rush hour.

lane A narrow road or street: The swimmers walked down the *lane* to the lake.

path A narrow way, especially for walking or bicycling: Teresa rides to school on the bike *path*.

route A road or course leading from one place to another: We always take the shortest *route* to the beach.

street A road in a town or city, usually lined with buildings: All my friends live on the same *street*.

run *v.* To move by using steps that are faster than walking: Hideo can *run* farther than I can.

dash To run a short distance quickly: Naomi must *dash* to her locker between classes.

race To move quickly, as in a contest to see who is fastest: The sisters *race* each other home.

scramble To rush or struggle to reach a goal: We sometimes *scramble* to get the best seats.

ANTONYMS: walk, crawl, creep

sad *adj.* Feeling unhappy or low: Rainy days make some people *sad*.

sorry Feeling sadness for someone; feeling regret for something you have done: Tony was *sorry* he had hurt his friend's feelings.

unhappy Without joy: The team was *unhappy* when they lost the game.

ANTONYMS: glad, happy, pleased, joyful

say *v.* To put something into words: Rebecca is shy and does not *say* much.

describe To tell about: Can you *describe* the picture to me?

mention To say something in passing: Did she *mention* what time we will leave?

recount To tell in great detail: He is eager to *recount* his adventure.

whisper To speak in a soft tone: We should *whisper* so we don't wake up the baby.

see *v.* To use your eyes; to notice something: Did you *see* the sunset?

glimpse To see something for a short time: I hope we get to *glimpse* the baby eagles.

observe To look at something carefully: Dana likes to *observe* insects.

view To look at something: They will *view* the fireworks tonight.

smart *adj.* Fast in thinking or learning: The *smart* math student subtracted the numbers in his head.

bright Having a quick, clever mind: The *bright* girl was the first one to raise her hand for every question.

clever Good at learning and solving problems; skillful: The *clever* boy fixed the broken computer.

quick Swift to learn or understand: The *quick* boy figured out the answer right away.

sharp Fast in thinking; lively and alert; quick to notice: Denny is *sharp* when dealing with an emergency.

wise Showing good judgment: He made a *wise* decision to tell the truth.

ANTONYMS: foolish, senseless, stupid

smile *v.* To express joy or pleasure by curving the corners of your mouth upward: It is friendly to *smile* at others.

grin To give a large smile: Sometimes people *grin* when they do something silly.

laugh To show pleasure by making sounds: Cartoons can make children *laugh*.

ANTONYMS: frown, scowl

stop *v.* To come to an end; to prevent something from going or moving: The new traffic light will *stop* the cars at this busy corner.

end To be over or done: The meeting will *end* at 9:30.

finish To complete something; to come to an end: You must *finish* the assignment by tomorrow.

halt To stop: The guard at the gate asked the driver to *halt*.

quit To stop doing something: Carlos plans to *quit* the team at the end of the season.

ANTONYMS: begin, continue, go, start

strong *adj.* Having great force or power: Running every day will help make your legs *strong*.

mighty Having great force: The *mighty* storm brought heavy winds.

powerful Having great physical strength or force: The soccer player has *powerful* legs.

sturdy Solid or well built: The chair was *sturdy* and not easily broken.

ANTONYMS: fragile, weak, delicate, frail, sickly

talk *v.* To put ideas into words: She likes to *talk* about horses.

chatter To talk a lot; to talk about silly things: The teacher does not allow students to *chatter* during class.

discuss To talk about a topic: We will *discuss* our homework after dinner.

gossip To talk about other people's business: It is not polite to *gossip*.

think *v.* To form ideas in your mind; to have an opinion: *Think* carefully before you mark your answer.

consider To think about something: *Consider* your choices carefully.

imagine To picture something in one's mind: Can you *imagine* living under the ocean?

ponder To think about carefully: He wanted to *ponder* his decision calmly for a while.

reflect To think about something carefully: I sometimes *reflect* on things that happened in the past.

throw *v.* To send something through the air: *Throw* the ball to Francis.

hurl To throw with great force: Peter tried to *hurl* the heavy rock into the water.

pitch To throw: Some baseball players can *pitch* a ball at ninety miles an hour.

toss To throw lightly: Please *toss* me that magazine.

town *n.* A small city: Camille lives in a small *town* in West Texas.

city A large town: The *city* has many tall office buildings.

community A group of people who live in the same area or share an interest: Our *community* has a parade every Fourth of July.

village A small town: The *village* has only one traffic light.

trouble *n.* A bad or dangerous situation; something that causes worry: Stormy weather can cause *trouble* for farmers.

bother Something that is annoying: Driving you home will be no *bother*.

difficulty Something that causes worry and must be figured out: The math question gave Sam *difficulty*.

problem A difficulty: Barry was stumped by the *problem* with his computer.

worry Nervousness; something that causes nervousness: Her tooth decay was a *worry* to her dentist.

ANTONYMS: comfort, joy, pleasure

very *adv.* To a great degree; much or most: My family is *very* proud of me.

awfully Very much: I'm *awfully* glad it did not rain on my birthday.

extremely Much more than usual: Be *extremely* careful when you cross the street.

greatly In a big way; importantly or wonderfully: The students were *greatly* moved by the soldier's story.

terribly Extremely: They were all *terribly* happy about winning the spelling bee.

ANTONYMS: barely, hardly, merely

wait *v.* To stay idle until something happens; to look forward to something: We had to *wait* all afternoon for our guest to come.

delay To put something off until later; to cause someone or something to be late: We will *delay* the start of school because of the snow.

pause To stop for a short while: The crowd will *pause* for a moment of silence.

remain To stay in one place; to continue to be: The Steins will *remain* in their old house until the new one is built.

ANTONYM: hurry

walk *v.* To move, using the legs: Some of the children are able to *walk* to school.

hike To walk a long distance, especially in the country: Sharon likes to *hike* in the hills.

march To walk together in formation; to walk in a determined way: The school band will *march* in the parade.

stroll To walk slowly and casually: Visitors often *stroll* through the garden.

win *v.* To finish first in a race or contest: Who will *win* the soccer game tonight?

succeed To reach a goal; to do well: Jason will surely *succeed* in his new job.

triumph To win a victory: The team hopes to *triumph* in the finals.

ANTONYMS: fail, lose

Thesaurus Index

A

add mix *v.*

afraid *adj.*

ailing healthy *adj.*

air land *n.*

all part *n.*

all right bad *adj.*

amusing funny *adj.*

ancient old *adj.*

angry *adj.*

answer ask *v.*

anxious afraid *adj.*

ask *v.*

attractive nice *adj.*

avenue road *n.*

awfully very **adv.**

B

bad *adj.*

bad good *adj.*

bake cook *v.*

barely very *adv.*

beat mix *v.*

beautiful pretty *adj.*

begin stop *v.*

bellow call *v.*

big *adj.*

big little *adj.*

blend mix *v.*

boil cook *v.*

boiling hot *adj.*

bold afraid *adj.*

boring interesting *adj.*

bother trouble *n.*

bounce jump *v.*

break *n.*

bright smart *adj.*

broken *adj.*

build make *v.*

burning hot *adj.*

bury find *v.*

C

call *v.*

calm angry *adj.*

calm quiet *adj.*

capture catch *v.*

carry *v.*

cart carry *v.*

carve cut *v.*

catch *v.*

chatter talk *v.*

cheerful happy *adj.*

chew eat *v.*

child person *n.*

chilly cold *adj.*

chilly hot *adj.*

chop cut *v.*

city town *n.*

clever smart *adj.*

clip cut *v.*

clutch catch *v.*

cold *adj.*

cold hot *adj.*

combine cut *v.*

combine mix *v.*

comfort trouble *n.*

community town *n.*

complete make *v.*

confident afraid *adj.*

consider think *v.*

continue stop *v.*

cook *v.*

cool cold *adj.*

cover find *v.*

crack cut *v.*

cracked broken *adj.*

crawl run *v.*

create make *v.*

creep run *v.*

crushed broken *adj.*

current new *adj.*

current old *adj.*

cut *v.*

D

dash run *v.*

decrease grow *v.*

delay wait *v.*

delicate strong *adj.*

depressed happy *adj.*

describe say *v.*

design draw *v.*

destroy make *v.*

develop grow *v.*

die grow *v.*

difficulty trouble *n.*

dine eat *v.*

discover find *v.*

discuss talk *v.*

divide mix *v.*

draw *v.*

draw pull *v.*

drop carry *v.*

drop catch *v.*

dull interesting *adj.*

E

earth land *n.*

eat *v.*

end stop *v.*

enormous big *adj.*

entertaining funny *adj.*

entertaining interesting *adj.*

erase draw *v.*

evil good *adj.*

excellent good *adj.*

excited happy *adj.*

exciting interesting *adj.*

explain ask *v.*

explore ask *v.*

extremely very *adv.*

F

fail win *v.*

fair good *adj.*

fascinating interesting *adj.*

fast *adj.*

fearful afraid *adj.*

feast eat *v.*

find *v.*

finish stop *v.*

fit healthy *adj.*

fixed broken *adj.*

foolish smart *adj.*

form make *v.*

fraction part *n.*

fragile strong *adj.*

frail strong *adj.*

freezing cold *adj.*

freezing hot *adj.*

fresh new *adj.*

fresh old *adj.*

friendly nice *adj.*

frightened afraid *adj.*

frosty cold *adj.*

frown smile *v.*

fry cook *v.*

funny *adj.*

furious angry *adj.*

G

gain grow *v.*

giant big *adj.*

giant little *adj.*

glad sad *adj.*

glimpse see *v.*

gloomy happy *adj.*

go stop *v.*

gobble eat *v.*

good *adj.*

good bad *adj.*

good nice *adj.*

gossip talk *v.*

grand big *adj.*

grasp catch *v.*

great big *adj.*

great little *adj.*

greatly very *adv.*

greet call *v.*

grin smile *v.*

ground land *n.*

grow *v.*

gulp eat *v.*

H

halt stop *v.*

handsome pretty *adj.*

happy *adj.*

happy sad *adj.*

hardly very *adv.*

harmful bad *adj.*

haul carry *v.*

haul pull *v.*

healthy *adj.*

hearty healthy *adj.*

hide find *v.*

highway road *n.*

hike walk *v.*

holiday break *n.*

hop jump *v.*

hot *adj.*

hot cold *adj.*

huge big *adj.*

huge little *adj.*

human person *n.*

hurl throw *v.*

hurry wait *v.*

I

icy cold *adj.*

ill healthy *adj.*

imagine think *v.*

interesting *adj.*

J

join cut *v.*

jolly happy *adj.*

joy trouble *n.*

joyful sad *adj.*

joyful happy *adj.*

jump *v.*

K

kind good *adj.*

kind nice *adj.*

L

land *n.*

lane road *n.*

large little *adj.*

latest new *adj.*

laugh smile *v.*

lay put *v.*

leap jump *v.*

leave behind carry *v.*

let go catch *v.*

little *adj.*

little big *adj.*

locate find *v.*

lose find *v.*

lose win *v.*

loud quiet *adj.*

lovely pretty *adj.*

M

mad angry *adj.*

make *v.*

man person *n.*

march walk *v.*

mean bad *adj.*

mean good *adj.*

mean nice *adj.*
mended broken *adj.*
mention say *v.*
merely very *adv.*
merry happy *adj.*
mighty little *adj.*
mighty strong *adj.*
mingle mix *v.*
miss catch *v.*
mix *v.*
modern new *adj.*
modern old *adj.*
move carry *v.*
munch eat *v.*

N

nap rest *v.*
nasty nice *adj.*
new *adj.*
new old *adj.*
nibble eat *v.*
nice *adj.*
nippy hot *adj.*
noisy quiet *adj.*
normal healthy *adj.*

O

observe see *v.*
old *adj.*
old new *adj.*
ordinary big *adj.*
original new *adj.*

P

part *n.*
path road *n.*
pause wait *v.*
peaceful quiet *adj.*
person *n.*
piece part *n.*
pitch throw *v.*
place put *v.*

plain pretty *adj.*
pleasant bad *adj.*
pleasant nice *adj.*
pleased angry *adj.*
pleased happy *adj.*
pleased sad *adj.*
pleasing nice *adj.*
pleasure trouble *n.*
ponder think *v.*
poor bad *adj.*
powerful strong *adj.*
prepare cook *v.*
pretty *adj.*
problem trouble *n.*
produce make *v.*
pull *v.*
puny little *adj.*
push pull *v.*
put *v.*
put together make *v.*

Q

question ask *v.*
quick smart *adj.*
quick fast *adj.*
quiet *adj.*
quit stop *v.*

R

race run *v.*
raise grow *v.*
recess break *n.*
recount say *v.*
reflect think *v.*
relax rest *v.*
release catch *v.*
remain wait *v.*
remove carry *v.*
repair cut *v.*
repaired broken *adj.*
reply ask *v.*
respond ask *v.*

rest *v.*
right good *adj.*
road *n.*
roar call *v.*
route road *n.*
rude nice *adj.*
run *v.*

S

sad *adj.*
sad funny *adj.*
sad happy *adj.*
say *v.*
scowl smile *v.*
scramble run *v.*
scrap part *n.*
scream call *v.*
search find *v.*
section part *n.*
see *v.*
senseless smart *adj.*
separate mix *v.*
severe bad *adj.*
serious funny *adj.*
sharp smart *adj.*
short little *adj.*
shout call *v.*
shove pull *v.*
shrink grow *v.*
sick healthy *adj.*
sickly strong *adj.*
silent quiet *adj.*
silly funny *adj.*
sizzling hot *adj.*
sketch draw *v.*
skinny little *adj.*
skip jump *v.*
sky land *n.*
sleep rest *v.*
slice cut *v.*
slow fast *adj.*

sluggish fast *adj.*
small big *adj.*
small little *adj.*
smart *adj.*
smash make *v.*
smile *v.*
snooze rest *v.*
sorry sad *adj.*
split cut *v.*
spread put *v.*
spring jump *v.*
sprinkle put *v.*
sprout grow *v.*
start stop *v.*
steam cook *v.*
steaming cold *adj.*
steaming hot *adj.*
still quiet *adj.*
stir mix *v.*
stop *v.*
street road *n.*
stroll walk *v.*
strong *adj.*
stupid smart *adj.*
sturdy strong *adj.*
succeed win *v.*
swallow eat *v.*
swift fast *adj.*

T

take apart make *v.*
talk *v.*
teeny little *adj.*
telephone call *v.*
terribly very *adv.*
terrified afraid *adj.*
thawed cold *adj.*
think *v.*
throw *v.*
throw catch *v.*
thrust pull *v.*
tiny big *adj.*

tiny little *adj.*
toss throw *v.*
tow pull *v.*
town *n.*
trap catch *v.*
trim cut *v.*
triumph win *v.*
trouble *n.*
tug pull *v.*

U

unafraid afraid *adj.*
unattractive pretty *adj.*
uncover find *v.*
undo make *v.*
unfair good *adj.*
unhappy sad *adj.*
unhealthy healthy *adj.*
uninteresting interesting
  adj.
unpleasant bad *adj.*
unpleasant nice *adj.*
unravel mix *v.*
unused old *adj.*
unwell healthy *adj.*
unworthy good *adj.*
upset angry *adj.*
upset happy *adj.*
upset quiet *adj.*
used new *adj.*
used old *adj.*

V

vacation break *n.*
very *adv.*
view see *v.*
village town *n.*

W

wait *v.*
wake rest *v.*
walk *v.*
walk run *v.*

warm cold *adj.*
warm hot *adj.*
water land *n.*
weak strong *adj.*
well healthy *adj.*
whisper say *v.*
whole part *n.*
win *v.*
wise smart *adj.*
wither grow *v.*
witty funny *adj.*
woman person *n.*
worn new *adj.*
worn old *adj.*
worry trouble *n.*
worthy good *adj.*

Y

yell call *v.*
young old *adj.*

Using the Glossary

Like a dictionary, this glossary lists words in alphabetical order. It contains the Vocabulary Power words, grammar terms, and writing forms covered in this book. To find a word, grammar term, or writing form, look it up by the first letter of the word.

To save time, use the **guide words** at the top of each page. These show you the first and last entry words on the page. Look at the guide words to see if your entry word falls between them alphabetically.

Here is an example of a glossary entry:

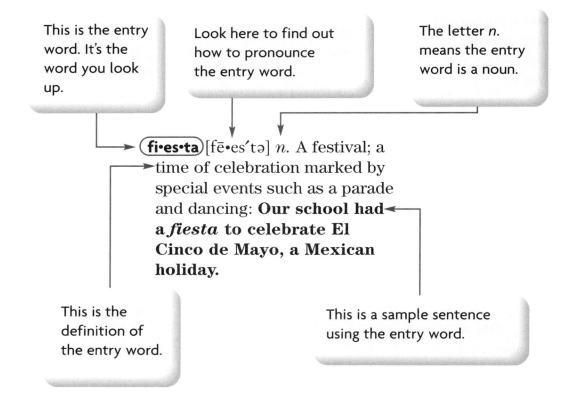

This is the entry word. It's the word you look up.

Look here to find out how to pronounce the entry word.

The letter *n.* means the entry word is a noun.

fi•es•ta [fē•es′tə] *n.* A festival; a time of celebration marked by special events such as a parade and dancing: **Our school had a *fiesta* to celebrate El Cinco de Mayo, a Mexican holiday.**

This is the definition of the entry word.

This is a sample sentence using the entry word.

Pronunciation

The pronunciation in brackets [ ] is a respelling that shows how the word is pronounced.

The **pronunciation key** explains what the symbols in a respelling mean. A shortened pronunciation key appears on every other page of the glossary.

Pronunciation Key*

a	add, map	m	move, seem	u	up, done
ā	ace, rate	n	nice, tin	û(r)	burn, turn
â(r)	care, air	ng	ring, song	yo͞o	fuse, few
ä	palm, father	o	odd, hot	v	vain, eve
b	bat, rub	ō	open, so	w	win, away
ch	check, catch	ô	order, jaw	y	yet, yearn
d	dog, rod	oi	oil, boy	z	zest, muse
e	end, pet	ou	pout, now	zh	vision, pleasure
ē	equal, tree	o͝o	took, full	ə	the schwa, an
f	fit, half	o͞o	pool, food		unstressed vowel
g	go, log	p	pit, step		representing the
h	hope, hate	r	run, poor		sound spelled
i	it, give	s	see, pass		*a* in *above*
ī	ice, write	sh	sure, rush		*e* in *sicken*
j	joy, ledge	t	talk, sit		*i* in *possible*
k	cool, take	th	thin, both		*o* in *melon*
l	look, rule	t̶h̶	this, bathe		*u* in *citrus*

Other symbols
- separates words into syllables
- ' indicates heavier stress on a syllable
- ' indicates lighter stress on a syllable

Abbreviations: *adj.* adjective, *adv.* adverb, *conj.* conjunction, *interj.* interjection, *n.* noun, *prep.* preposition, *pron.* pronoun, *syn.* synonym, *v.* verb

* This Pronunciation Key, adapted entries, and the Short Key that appear on the following pages are reprinted from *HBJ School Dictionary*. Copyright © 1990 by Harcourt, Inc. Reprinted by permission of Harcourt, Inc.

A

ab·bre·vi·a·tion [ə·brē·vē·ā′shən] *n.* A short way to write a word. Most abbreviations end with a period. An abbreviation for a proper noun begins with a capital letter: *Mrs.* **Chen met** *Dr.* **Garcia at his Main** *St.* **office on** *Fri.* **morning at 10:00** *A.M.*

ac·tion verb [ak′shən vûrb] *n.* A verb that tells what the subject of a sentence does: **The girl** *ran* **on the playground.**

ad·jec·tive [aj′ik·tiv] A word that describes a noun. Some adjectives tell *how many.* Other adjectives tell *what kind:* **Ms. Ling buys** *five* **bags of soil for her garden. I jog** *several* **times a week. The** *large, brown* **dog is playful.**

ad·van·tag·es and dis·ad·van·tag·es es·say [ad·van′tij·iz and dis′əd·van·tij·iz es′ā] *n.* An essay that explains the good and bad points about a topic: **Roberto wrote about the good and bad parts of winter in his** *advantages and disadvantages essay.*

ad·verb [ad′vûrb] *n.* A word that describes a verb. An adverb may tell *how, when,* or *where* an action happens: **We walk** *quickly* **to the theater. The movie begins** *soon.* **The theater is** *near* **our home.**

ad·ver·tise·ments [ad·vûr·tīz′mənts] *n.* Things that are made known to the public, especially by paid announcement: **The TV** *advertisement* **said that your teeth would be whiter if you used the new toothpaste.**

an·i·ma·ted film [an′ə·mā·tid film] *n.* A series of drawings shown as a motion picture with moving figures: **The children saw a lively** *animated film* **about penguins.**

a·pos·tro·phe [ə·pos′trə·fē] *n.* A symbol (') that takes the place of letters that are left out in a contraction or that shows possession: *We're* **cleaning up the** *school's* **playground.**

ar·ti·cle [är′ti·kəl] *n.* A word in a special group of adjectives that includes *a, an,* and *the*: **We saw** *a* **gorilla,** *an* **elephant, and many other animals at** *the* **zoo.**

as·tron·omy [ə·stron′ə·mē] *n.* The study of stars, planets, and other objects in the sky: **We learned a lot about Earth and Mars in our** *astronomy* **class.**

au·di·ence [ô′dē·əns] *n.* The people who are reached by books, programs, and so on: **A writer's** *audience* **is made up of his or her readers.**

B

blus·ter·y [blus′tər·ē] *adj.* Stormy and noisy; very windy: **The leaves fly through the air on a** *blustery* **autumn day.**

book re·view [book ri·vyoo′] *n.* An article that tells what a book is about. It also tells what the writer thinks about the book: **Pablo's** *book review* **on** *Wolves* **said that he enjoyed the book.**

C

ca·nine [kā′nīn] *adj.* Like a dog; belonging to a group of animals that includes dogs, foxes, and wolves: **The wolf is a *canine* animal.**

ca·reer [kə·rir′] *n.* A person's lifework or profession: **E.B. White, the author of *Charlotte's Web,* made writing his *career*.**

car·pen·ter [kär′pən·tər] *n.* A person who uses wood to make, build, or repair things: **The *carpenter* built a table and some chairs.**

cav·i·ty [kav′i·tē] *n.* A small hole, caused by decay in a tooth: **Tommy went to the dentist to get his *cavity* filled.**

col·or·ful words [kul′ər·fəl wûrdz] *n.* Interesting words that help the reader picture what the writer is describing: ***Enormous* and *scurry* are examples of *colorful words*.**

com·bin·ing sen·ten·ces [kəm·bīn′ing sen′tən·səz] *n.* Putting related ideas and information together in one sentence instead of in two or three: *(separated)* **The day is snowy. The day is windy.** *(combined)* ***The day is snowy and windy.***

com·ma [kom′ə] *n.* A punctuation mark (,) that separates parts of a sentence, tells readers where to pause, and helps make the meaning clear: **Yes, I like carrots, broccoli, and celery. I like cucumbers, but I like tomatoes better. We're having a health fair on August 5, 2001, in Denver, Colorado.**

com·mand [kə·mand′] *n.* A kind of sentence that gives an order or a direction.

Use a period (.) at the end of a command: **Help me feed the ducks.**

com·mon noun [kom′ən noun] *n.* A noun that names any person, animal, place, or thing. A common noun begins with a lowercase letter: **The *farmer* fed *hay* to the *horses*.**

com·mu·ni·ty [kə·myoo′nə·tē] *n.* All the people living in a place; the place, district, or area where people live: **The people in my *community* organized a neighborhood watch group.**

com·plete pred·i·cate [kəm·plēt′ pred′i·kit] *n.* All the words that tell what the subject of the sentence is or does: **The student *finished his homework at 8 P.M.***

com·plete sen·tence [kəm·plēt′ sen′təns] *n.* A group of words that has a subject and a predicate and expresses a complete thought: *Elena missed the school bus today.*

com·plete sub·ject [kəm·plēt′ sub′jikt] *n.* The simple subject and all the other words in the subject that describe it: *My younger sister* **takes ballet lessons.**

com·pound pred·i·cate [kom′pound pred′i·kit] *n.* Two or more predicates that have the same subject. The word *and* or *or* is usually used to join the predicates: **Her brother *dances and sings.* Before bed, we *watch TV or play checkers.***

a add	e end	o odd	o͞o pool	oi oil	th this	
ā ace	ē equal	ō open	u up	ou pout	zh vision	ə =
â care	i it	ô order	û burn	ng ring		
ä palm	ī ice	o͝o took	yo͞o fuse	th thin		

{ *a* in *above*
e in *sicken*
i in *possible*
o in *melon*
u in *circus*

com·pound sen·tence [kom′pound sen′təns] *n.* A sentence made up of two or more simple sentences. The sentences are connected with a comma (,) and the word *and, or,* or *but*: **Sarah met her friends, *and* they played jump rope together.**

com·pound sub·ject [kom′pound sub′jikt] *n.* Two or more subjects that have the same predicate. The word *and* or *or* is usually used to join the subjects: ***Janet and Davon*** **went to the store. *My mother, my brother, or I* cook breakfast.**

con·fi·dence [kon′fə·dəns] *n.* Firm belief or trust: **Because Yoko studied hard for the test, she has *confidence* that she will do well on it.**

con·trac·tion [kən·trak′shən] *n.* A short way to write two words. When a contraction is made, one or more letters are left out. An apostrophe (′) takes the place of the missing letters: ***I'm*** **happy that *you're* in my class this year. *We'll* be able to work together.**

co·op·er·ate [kō·op′ər·āt] *v.* To work with one person or others for a common purpose: **Diego and Sam were able to finish their project together after they learned how to *cooperate*.**

de·scrip·tive par·a·graph [di·skrip′tiv par′ə·graf] *n.* Writing that gives details about something. A descriptive paragraph may describe an object, a feeling, an event, or any other subject: **In my *descriptive paragraph*, I gave lots of details about the weather.**

de·tail [dē′tāl] *n.* A fact or an example that helps explain a topic: **Rishi gave many *details* about the foods farm animals eat in his story about growing up on a farm.**

dou·ble neg·a·tive [dub′əl neg′ə·tiv] *n.* Two negative words in one sentence. Double negatives make the meaning of a sentence unclear and should never be used: *(Incorrect)* **You *shouldn't never* do that.** *(Correct)* **You *should never* do that.**

draft [draft] *adj.* Used or adapted for pulling loads: **The *draft* horses pulled the heavy cart.**

e·col·o·gy [i·kol′ə·jē] *n.* The relationship of plants and animals to their surroundings and to one another: **We are studying the *ecology* of the rain forest in our science class.**

ef·fec·tive sen·ten·ces [i·fek′tiv sen′tən·siz] *n.* Sentences that give information in a clear and interesting way: **John's paragraph had *effective sentences* that were filled with vivid verbs and adjectives.**

e·lab·o·ra·tion [i·lab′ə·rā′shən] *n.* Developing and expanding a topic by adding details and reasons: **The author's use of *elaboration* in describing Alaska showed us how weather, transportation, animal life, and the fishing industry affect the people who live there.**

end marks [end märks] *n.* Punctuation marks that come at the end of a sentence:

Did you see my new dog? Yes, she's really cute*!* I wish I had a dog.

en·er·gy [en′ər·jē] *n.* The ability to do work or give power; electric or heat power: **After eating a healthful snack, LaToya had the *energy* to finish her chores.**

en·ter·prise [en′tər·prīz] *n.* An activity set up to earn money: **Manny's newest *enterprise* is a lemonade stand.**

ev·er·green [ev′ər·grēn] *adj.* Trees or shrubs that have green leaves throughout the year: **The *evergreen* tree looks pretty when its needles are covered with snow.**

ex·act words [ig·zakt′ wûrdz] *n.* Words that are very specific instead of general: **The teacher asked us to use *exact words,* such as *panther* instead of *animal.***

ex·cla·ma·tion [eks·klə·mā′shən] *n.* A kind of sentence that shows strong feeling. Use an exclamation point (!) at the end of an exclamation: ***What a great electric light show!***

ex·cla·ma·tion point [eks·klə·mā′shən point] *n.* An end mark (!) that follows an exclamation: **Wow, what a great idea!**

ex·pe·ri·ence [ik·spir′ē·əns] *n.* Something one has gone through; knowledge or skill gained by doing something: **Paco got a lot of job *experience* by working during the summer in his dad's shop.**

Fahr·en·heit scale [far′ən·hīt skāl] *n.* A temperature scale showing 32 degrees as the freezing point of water and 212 degrees as the boiling point: **The average temperature last summer was 75 degrees on the *Fahrenheit scale.***

fan·ta·sy [fan′tə·sē] *n.* Imagination; a creation, as a story, that is different from reality: **The story about Babe the talking pig is a *fantasy.***

fed·er·al [fed′ər·əl] *adj.* Having to do with the central government of the United States: **When Gina's family visited Washington, D.C., they toured several of the *federal* buildings and learned a lot about the U.S. government.**

fi·es·ta [fē·es′tə] *n.* A festival; a time of celebration marked by special events such as parades and dancing: **Our class had a *fiesta* to celebrate El Cinco de Mayo, a Mexican holiday.**

fig·ur·a·tive lan·guage [fig′yər·ə·tiv lang′gwij] *n.* Words that are used in an unusual way to create a vivid description: **Mitchell used *figurative language* to compare a firefly to a blinking flashlight.**

friend·ly let·ter [frend′lē let′ər] *n.* A letter written in a conversational style to someone the letter writer knows well. Its purpose is to exchange news or send greetings: **Josh sent a *friendly letter* about his vacation to his best friend, José.**

a add	e end	o odd	o͞o pool	oi oil	t̶h̶ this	zh vision		ə =	a in *above*
ā ace	ē equal	ō open	u up	ou pout					e in *sicken*
â care	i it	ô order	û burn	ng ring	th thin				i in *possible*
ä palm	ī ice	o͝o took	yo͞o fuse						o in *melon*
									u in *circus*

fu·ture-tense verb [fyōo′chər tens vûrb] *n.* A verb that shows action that will happen at a later time. To form the future tense of a verb, use the helping verb *will* with the main verb: **Bryan *will buy* some grapes at the supermarket.**

help·ing verb [help′ing vûrb] *n.* A verb that works with the main verb to tell about an action. The helping verb always comes before the main verb: **Jennifer *has* written an answer to her friend Sue's letter. She *did* enjoy the jokes Sue sent!**

hom·o·graph [hom′ə·graf] *n.* A word that sounds like another word and is spelled the same but has a different meaning: **Did you see Miguel *trip* over the hose? Mary took a *trip* to San Diego.**

hom·o·phone [hom′ə·fōn] *n.* A word that sounds like another word but has a different meaning and a different spelling: **Please *write* me a letter while you're on vacation. Tara was proud that she knew the *right* answer.**

how-to es·say [hou tōo es′ā] *n.* An essay that gives step-by-step directions that explain how to do or make something: **Marina's *how-to essay* gave steps for making a hot-fudge sundae.**

il·lu·mi·nate [i·lōo′mə·nāt] *v.* To brighten with light: **After dark they *illuminate* the playing field so that players can see.**

in·stru·ment [in′strə·mənt] *n.* A tool for making music: **My favorite musical *instrument* is the guitar.**

in·ves·ti·gate [in·ves′tə·gāt] *v.* To study thoroughly in order to learn facts or details: **The police officer had to *investigate* the crime scene in order to solve the crime.**

in·vis·i·ble [in·viz′ə·bəl] *adj.* Not able to be seen: **You can't see the oxygen in the air because it is *invisible*.**

in·vi·ta·tion [in′və·tā′shən] *n.* A form of writing used to invite someone to a party or other event: **Marty sent out *invitations* to his ninth birthday party.**

ir·reg·u·lar noun [i·reg′yə·lər noun] *n.* A noun that has a special plural form or that stays the same in the plural form: **The *women* and *children* saw some *sheep* at the petting zoo.**

ir·reg·u·lar verb [i·reg′yə·lər vûrb] *n.* A verb that does not end with *ed* to show past tense: **A child *ran* down the aisle at the movie theater. Mom has *written* a check for the groceries.**

main verb [mān vûrb] *n.* The most important verb in the predicate. It comes after the helping verb: **Jennifer is *reading* a letter from a friend. The letter was *sent* last Tuesday.**

min·er·al [min′ər·əl] *n.* A natural material that does not come from a plant or an animal: **Rocks, metals, jewels, and oil are all *minerals* that come from the earth.**

neg·a·tive [neg′ə·tiv] *n.* A word that means "no." Some negatives are *never, no, nobody, not, nothing,* and *nowhere.* Contractions with *not* are also negatives: **No other nation was larger than the Soviet Union. The United States is *not* larger than Canada. India *doesn't* have as many people as China.**

noun [noun] *n.* A word that names a person, an animal, a place, or a thing: **That *woman* is cheerful. The *horse* runs and jumps over a high, white *fence.***

nu·tri·ent [noo′trē·ənt] *n.* A substance in food that helps people, animals, and plants stay healthy: **Vegetables and fruits are good for you because they're rich in *nutrients.***

ob·ject pro·noun [ob′jikt prō′noun] *n.* A pronoun that follows either an action verb or a word such as *about, at, for, from, near, of, to,* or *with.* The words *me, you, him, her, it, us,* and *them* are object pronouns: **Our teacher tells *us* about volcanoes. We are very interested in *them.***

out·line [out′līn] *n.* A way of organizing information into main parts and details: **We made an *outline* to plan our writing.**

par·a·graph·ing [par′ə·graf·ing] *n.* The division of information or ideas into paragraphs, or groups of sentences about one main idea: ***Paragraphing* is important in organizing information for a research report.**

par·a·graph that com·pares [par′ə·graf t̶h̶at kəm·pârz′] *n.* A paragraph that tells how two or more people, places, or things are alike: **Nancy's *paragraph that compares* was about the similarities between frogs and toads.**

par·a·graph that con·trasts [par′ə·graf t̶h̶at kən·trasts′] A paragraph that tells how two or more people, places, or things are different: **Chin wrote a *paragraph that contrasts* about the differences between butterflies and moths.**

past-tense verb [past tens vûrb] *n.* A verb that shows action that happened in the past. Add *ed* or *d* to most present-tense verbs to make them show past tense: **Josh *walked* to the park. Then he *hiked* up the hill.**

pe·ri·od [pir′ē·əd] *n.* A punctuation mark (.) used with an abbreviation and at the end of a statement or command: ***Tues.* is the abbreviation for *Tuesday.* Please take turns.**

per·son·al nar·ra·tive [pûr′sən·əl nar′ə·tiv] *n.* A true story about a writer's own experiences: **I wrote about my summer vacation when we were asked to write a *personal narrative.***

a	add	e	end	o	odd	o͞o	pool	oi	oil	t̶h̶	this			
ā	ace	ē	equal	ō	open	u	up	ou	pout	zh	vision		*a* in *above*	
â	care	i	it	ô	order	û	burn	ng	ring			ə =	*e* in *sicken*	
ä	palm	ī	ice	o͝o	took	yo͞o	fuse	th	thin				*i* in *possible*	
													o in *melon*	
													u in *circus*	

per·son·al voice [pûr′sən·əl vois] *n.* A person's own special way of expressing himself or herself through words and ideas: **Renaldo found his *personal voice* when he began writing poetry.**

per·sua·sive es·say [pər·swā′siv es′ā] *n.* A type of writing that shows how a writer feels about a topic. The writer tries to persuade the reader to agree: **Angela's *persuasive essay* encouraged readers to exercise at least three times a week.**

plu·ral noun [ploŏr′əl noun] *n.* A noun that names more than one person, animal, place, or thing. Add *s* to most singular nouns to form the plural: **The *students* took their *books* to the library.**

plu·ral pos·ses·sive noun [ploŏr′əl pə·zes′iv noun] *n.* A noun that shows ownership by more than one person or thing: **The *players'* uniforms are red and blue. All of the *books'* covers are new.**

plu·ral pro·noun [ploŏr′əl prō′noun] *n.* A pronoun that takes the place of a plural noun or of two or more nouns. The words *we, you, they, us,* and *them* are plural pronouns: **The children put stamps in a book. *They* put *them* in a book. Carlos gave stamps to Brandon and me. Carlos gave stamps to *us*.**

po·em [pō′əm] *n.* A form of writing in which a writer uses vivid or unusual words to describe something or to express feelings about a subject. A poem often has rhyme or rhythm: **Our class wrote a *poem* about how we felt on the first day of school.**

pos·ses·sive noun [pə·zes′iv noun] *n.* A noun that shows ownership. An apostrophe (') is used to form a possessive noun: **The *girl's* soccer ball is new. The *tractor's* wheels are huge.**

pos·ses·sive pro·noun [pə·zes′iv prō′noun] *n.* A pronoun that shows ownership, taking the place of a possessive noun. One type of possessive pronoun is used before a noun. The other type of possessive pronoun stands alone: ***My* dog is bigger than *yours*.**

pre·cau·tion [pri·kô′shən] *n.* A measure taken to avoid possible harm or danger; care taken ahead of time: **As a *precaution* against sunburn, we used sunscreen lotion at the beach.**

pred·i·cate [pred′i·kit] *n.* The part of a sentence that tells what the subject of the sentence is or does. The predicate usually comes after the subject: **My family *went to the festival on Saturday*.**

pre·sent-tense verb [prez′ənt tens vûrb] *n.* A verb that tells about action that is happening now: **He *brings* a towel to the pool. She *swims* in the pool. Water *splashes* on the lifeguard.**

pro·noun [prō′noun] *n.* A word that takes the place of one or more nouns: **Luis collects stamps. *He* collects stamps. Michael and Chan trade stamps. *They* trade stamps.**

pro·noun an·te·ce·dent [prō′noun an·tə·sēd′ənt] *n.* The noun or nouns to which a pronoun refers. A pronoun must agree with its antecedent in number and gender: ***Laurie* practices *her* jump shot every day. *Laurie and Ron* play basketball in *their* backyard.**

prop·er noun [prop′ər noun] *n.* A noun that names a particular person, animal, place, or thing. People's titles and the names of holidays, days of the week, and months are also proper nouns: *Jason visited the Statue of Liberty last Tuesday.*

pur•pose [pûr′pəs] *n.* A reason for doing something, such as writing: **The *purpose* of my research report is to inform my readers about working dogs.**

ques•tion [kwes′chən] *n.* A sentence that asks something. Use a question mark (?) at the end of a question: *How many ducks are in the pond?*

ques•tion mark [kwes′chən märk] *n.* An end mark (?) used after a sentence that asks a question: **Did you water the plants?**

quo•ta•tion marks [kwō•tā′shən märks] *n.* Punctuation marks (" ") used to show the exact words a speaker says or to identify the title of a story, poem, or song: *"I love to read poetry,"* said Emma. Emma's favorite poem is Robert Frost's *"Birches."*

reg•is•ter [rej′is•tər] *v.* To enter one's name in an official record, such as a list of voters: **When Maria turned eighteen, she *registered* to vote in the presidential election.**

reg•u•lar verb [reg′yə•lər vûrb] *n.* A verb that ends with *ed* in the past tense: **We *walked* to the library and picked out our books.**

re•search re•port [rē′sûrch ri•pôrt′] *n.* A type of writing that gives information about a topic. Writers gather facts from several sources, such as books or magazines: **Helen went to the library to get information for her *research report* about dolphins.**

rur•al [rŏŏr′əl] *adj.* A person or thing belonging to or happening in the country: **Photographs of country churches and other *rural* scenes are very popular in calendars.**

sen•tence [sen′təns] *n.* A group of words that tells a complete thought. A sentence begins with a capital letter, ends with an end mark, and has a subject and a predicate: *The ducks live near the pond. Is the water cold? Yes, it's freezing!*

sen•tence va•ri•e•ty [sen′təns və•rī′ə•tē] *n.* A way of making writing interesting by combining different types of sentences: **This story is fun to read because it has *sentence variety.***

se•quence words [sē′kwəns wûrdz] *n.* Words that tell the reader the order of steps or ideas: **The writer's *sequence words* included *first, then, next,* and *last.***

a	add	e	end	o	odd	oo͞	pool	oi	oil	t͟h	this		
ā	ace	ē	equal	ō	open	u	up	ou	pout	zh	vision		*a* in *above*
â	care	i	it	ô	order	û	burn	ng	ring			ə =	*e* in *sicken*
ä	palm	ī	ice	ŏŏ	took	yoo͞	fuse	th	thin				*i* in *possible*
													o in *melon*
													u in *circus*

shim·mer·ing [shim′ər·ing] *adj.* Shining with a reflected light; glimmering: **The metal beads had a *shimmering* glow in the sun.**

sim·ple pred·i·cate [sim′pəl pred′i·kit] *n.* The main word or words in the complete predicate. The simple predicate is always a verb: **Amy *ran* around the track. Misha *has played* the piano all morning.**

sim·ple sen·tence [sim′pəl sen′təns] *n.* A sentence that has a subject and a predicate and expresses one complete thought: **Sarah walked to school. Maki found a quarter.**

sim·ple sub·ject [sim′pəl sub′jikt] *n.* The main word in the complete subject of the sentence: **My *father* works in the garden.**

sin·gu·lar noun [sing′gyə·lər noun] *n.* A noun that names one person, animal, place, or thing: **The *girl* lives near me. The *lake* is deep. That *boat* is fast.**

sin·gu·lar pos·ses·sive noun [sing′gyə·lər pə·zes′iv noun] *n.* A noun that shows ownership by one person or thing. Add an apostrophe (') and *s* to a singular noun to form the possessive: **A *firefighter's* helmet is heavy. The *sun's* rays are hot.**

sin·gu·lar pro·noun [sing′gyə·lər prō′noun] *n.* A word that takes the place of a singular noun. The words *I, me, you, he, she, him, her,* and *it* are singular pronouns: **Ashley gives Hideo a stamp from Mexico. *She* gives *him* a stamp from Mexico. The stamp shows an eagle and a sun. *It* shows an eagle and a sun.**

spe·cif·ic noun [spi·sif′ik noun] *n.* A noun that names a particular thing instead of a whole group of things: ***Pear* is a *specific noun,* but *fruit* is not.**

state·ment [stāt′mənt] *n.* A sentence that tells something. Use a period (.) at the end of a statement: **Ducks lay eggs in the spring.**

sto·ry [stôr′ē] *n.* A type of writing that has a setting, a plot, and characters. A story is made up and has a beginning, a middle, and an ending: **The *story* we read in class today is about a pig that wants to win a prize at the county fair.**

sub·ject [sub′jikt] *n.* The part of a sentence that names the person or thing the sentence is about. The subject is usually at the beginning of a sentence: ***Rocco* went to the grocery store. *The cats* ran outside.**

sub·ject pro·noun [sub′jikt prō′noun] *n.* A word that takes the place of one or more nouns in the subject of a sentence. The words *I, you, he, she, it, we,* and *they* are subject pronouns: ***I* will be nine years old in October. *You* are older than my sister is.**

sub·ject-verb a·gree·ment [sub′jikt vûrb ə·grē′mənt] *n.* The form of the verb in a sentence must match, or agree with, the subject of the sentence: **She *drinks* orange juice for breakfast. Oranges *grow* in warm places.**

tense [tens] *n.* The verb form that tells the time of the action. It tells whether the action is happening now, has happened in the past, or will happen in the future: **Sandy *sends* an e-mail to Pepe. Pepe *spoke* to Sandy yesterday. Tomorrow they *will see* each other at school.**

thank-you note [thangk yoo not] *n.* A form of writing used to thank someone for a gift or for doing something: **You should always write a *thank-you note* after you receive a gift.**

ti•tle [tīt′əl] *n.* The name of something such as a book, magazine, or newspaper. Titles of long works such as books and newspapers are underlined or italicized. Titles of shorter works such as poems and stories are placed in quotation marks: **Did you read The Story of Little Tree? I'm reading a poem called "The Owl and the Pussycat."**

tra•di•tions [trə·dish′·ənz] *n.* Customs that are passed on from parents to children: **Ricardo and his family celebrate many Spanish *traditions*.**

vac•cine [vak·sēn′] *n.* Medicine that puts germs of a certain kind into the body to prevent illness: **Children can be given a *vaccine* to protect them against mumps.**

verb [vûrb] *n.* The main word in the predicate of a sentence. It tells what the subject of the sentence is or does: **The boy *rides* a bike. His bike *is* new.**

vice•roy [vīs′roy] *n.* A person who helps a king rule a country, colony, or province: **The *viceroy* told the king that the people in the kingdom wished him well.**

vis•i•ble [vi′zə·bəl] *adj.* Able to be seen: **On sunny days, the mountains are *visible* from my window.**

viv•id verb [viv′id vûrb] *n.* A strong verb that describes action in an interesting way: **Instead of the verb *hurry*, use a *vivid verb* such as *bolt*, *speed*, or *zoom*.**

word choice [wûrd chois] *n.* Choice of words and phrases to give the effect that the writer intends: **The writer's *word choice* makes it clear that he loves dogs.**

writ•er's view•point [rī′tərz vyoo′point] *n.* The way a writer expresses himself or herself to let the reader know how he or she feels about the subject: **The *writer's viewpoint* is that summer is her least-liked season.**

a add	e end	o odd	o͞o pool	oi oil	t̶h̶ this	{ a in *above*
ā ace	ē equal	ō open	u up	ou pout	zh vision	e in *sicken*
â care	i it	ô order	û burn	ng ring	ə =	i in *possible*
ä palm	ī ice	o͝o took	yo͞o fuse	th thin		o in *melon*
						u in *circus*

Vocabulary Power

advertisements If the **advertisements** are true, this shampoo will make your hair shiny and beautiful.

animated film Do you like **animated films** such as *The Lion King* and *Toy Story*?

astronomy My brother is studying **astronomy** and learning about Mars.

blustery The trees were bending in the wind on the cold, **blustery** day.

canine Dogs and wolves are members of the **canine** family.

career Marta wants to play on a pro soccer team so she can have a **career** in sports.

carpenter The **carpenter** hammered nails into the desk he was building.

cavity Jimmy had a **cavity** in his tooth filled by the dentist.

community People in my **community** decided to have a neighborhood picnic.

confidence Our coach has **confidence** in our team because we practice very hard.

cooperate If you and your sister **cooperate**, you will work well together.

draft Farms in the past used **draft** horses to pull heavy loads.

ecology Rishi is learning about animals and their environment in his study of **ecology**.

elaboration Mrs. Diaz said that using **elaboration** in our stories would explain more about our characters.

energy If you eat healthful foods, you will have the **energy** to run the race.

enterprise Elena set up a baby-sitting **enterprise** to earn money for camp.

evergreen An **evergreen** tree is green even in winter.

experience Yoko has a lot of **experience** with animals because she lives on a farm.

Fahrenheit scale Water boils at 212 degrees on the **Fahrenheit scale**.

fantasy Jen wrote a story that is a **fantasy** about a trip to Pluto.

federal Paul's father is a **federal** worker who works for the government.

fiesta We enjoyed a parade, music, and dancing during a **fiesta** to celebrate Mexican independence.

illuminate Lights **illuminate** the tennis courts so that people can play after dark.

instrument Mary's favorite musical **instrument** is the piano.

investigate The detective **investigated** the area where the burglar was last seen.

invisible Carlos couldn't read the message because it was written in **invisible** ink.

mineral Coal is a **mineral** used as a fuel.

nutrient Vitamin C is a **nutrient** you get when you eat oranges.

precaution Check the battery in your home fire alarm as a safety **precaution**.

register All students **register** for class on the same day.

rural There is not as much traffic in **rural** areas as there is in a city.

shimmering The sun shines on the icicles, giving them a **shimmering** glow.

traditions One of our **traditions** is to break a piñata filled with candy at a birthday party.

vaccine A **vaccine** helps protect children against disease.

viceroy The **viceroy** told the people in the kingdom that taxes would be cut.

visible The stars are not **visible** in the sky tonight because it is too cloudy.

Index

A

Abbreviations 96–100
Action verbs 132–133, 136–138
Ada, Alma Flor 427
Addresses, commas in 390–391
Adjectives 272–280, 469–470
    adverbs or 336–337, 342–343
    articles 308–309, 314–316
    bad 310–311, 340–341, 343
    er and *est* 310–312, 314–316
    good 310–311, 340–341, 343
    more and *most* 312–316
    that compare 310–311, 314–316
    that tell *how many* 274–275, 278–280
    that tell *what kind* 276–280
Advantages and disadvantages
    essay 282–292, 483, 499
    parts of 286–287
Adverbs 318–326, 471–472
    adjectives or 336–337, 342–343
    badly 340–341, 343
    comparing with 322–326
    er and *est* 322–326
    more and *most* 322–326
    placement in sentences 338–339
    that tell *how* 318–319
    that tell *when* or *where* 320–321
    well 340–341, 343
Agreement of pronouns 238–239
Agreement of subject and verb . 134–135, 180–184
Almanac, using 510
Analyze the Model
    advantages and
      disadvantages essay 285, 287
    character study 398, 402
    description 44
    descriptive paragraph 48
    directions 112, 117
    friendly letter 191
    how-to essay 145, 147
    informative writing 254
    paragraph of information 328, 333
    paragraph that compares 258
    personal narrative 75, 77
    persuasive paragraph 217, 219
    persuasive writing 186
    research report 361, 363
    story 431, 433
Antecedents. *See* Pronoun antecedents
Antonyms 213, 317
Apostrophes 120–128
    in contractions 170–174, 266–270
    in possessive nouns 120–128
Art. *See* Writing Across the Curriculum;
    Writing Connection
Art, fine 405
Articles 308–309, 314–316
Atlas, using 509
Audience 329
See also Purpose and audience

B

Back Home 398
Bad 310–311, 340–341, 343
Badly 340–341, 343
Baseball: How to Play the All-Star Way . . . 112
Be 134–138
    See also Verbs
Beacons of Light: Lighthouses 356–361
Book parts 243
    using 504
Book review, model 489
Books to Read 89, 159, 231, 299, 375, 445
Brown, Laurie Krasny 141
Brown, Marc 141

C

Capitalization
    of abbreviations 96–97
    of days of the week and months 94–95
    of first word in sentence 24–25, 28
    of holidays 94–95
    of *I* 244, 248
    of proper nouns 94–95
    in quotations 408–409
    in titles 420–421
    of titles of people 96–97
Character study 398–399, 402–404

Charts
 K-W-L..516
 understanding.................................101
 using.......................................514–515
Churchman, Deborah.......................283
Coaching Ms. Parker................215–217
Colorful words..51
 using...45–46
Combining sentences........66–67, 255, 257
 using commas.............................392–393
 with compound predicates..............56–57
 with compound subjects..................38–39
Commands.......................................26–31
Commas.............................388–396, 475
 in addresses..............................390–391
 before combining words..................66–67
 combining sentences using..........392–393
 in compound predicates.................56–60
 in compound sentences...................64–70
 in compound subjects.....................38–42
 in dates....................................390–391
 in direct address........................388–389
 with introductory words................388–389
 in letters...................................390–391
 in quotations.............................408–414
 in series...................................388–389
Commonly misspelled words..........526–527
Commonly misused verbs..............208–211
Common nouns.................................94–95
Compare and contrast
 paragraph that compares....258–260, 490
 paragraph that contrasts....................491
 writing and speaking..........................261
 writing to compare.....................254–260
Complete predicates...................52–53, 58
Complete sentences......................62–63, 68
Complete subjects...........................36–37
Compound predicates................56–57, 59
Compound sentences...64–65, 68–69, 392–393, 457
Compound subjects, combining
 sentences with................................38–39
Computers. *See* Technology
Context clues......................................271
Contractions
 with *not*....................170–171, 378–379
 with pronouns..........................266–270

D

Dancing with the Indians....................44
Dates, commas in.........................390–391
Days of the week, capitalization of.....94–95
Description.....................................44–45
Descriptive paragraphs...........48–50, 488
Details..113–114
Dialogue, punctuating...............410–411
Dictionary, using.......................175, 505
Direct address, commas in.........388–389
Direct quotations..........406–407, 410–411
Directions
 giving spoken......................119, 397
 writing..............................116–118
Double negatives...................382–385
Drafting..................................19
 advantages and
  disadvantages essay..................289
 character study..........................403
 descriptive paragraph....................49
 directions................................117
 friendly letter...........................191
 how-to essay.............................149
 paragraph of information..............333
 paragraph that compares..............259
 personal narrative.......................79
 persuasive paragraph...................221
 research report..........................365
 story.....................................435

E

E-mail.............................199, 506
Editing.................................20
 See also Revising
 character study.......................404
 descriptive paragraph..................50
 directions..............................118
 friendly letter........................192
 paragraph of information.............334
 paragraph that compares.............260
Editor's marks.........50, 81, 118, 151, 192, 223, 260, 291, 334, 367, 404, 437
Effective sentences................254–257

Elaboration 398–404
   advantages and
      disadvantages essay 289–290
   how-to essay 149–150
   personal narrative 79–80
   persuasive paragraph 221–222
   research report 365–366
   story 435–436
Encyclopedia, using 507
End marks 24–25, 28–29
   with quotations 408–409
Envelope 493
er and *est* 310–315, 322–325
Essay
   advantages and
      disadvantages 282–292, 483, 499
   how-to 481, 497
   persuasive 482, 498
   research report 484–485, 500
Exact words 399, 401
Exclamation points 28–32
   with quotations 408–409
Exclamations 26–31
Expressive writing
   character study 398–404
   descriptive paragraph 44–50
   personal narrative 72–82, 496
   story 426–438, 501

F

Facts 203
Figurative language 399–400
Friendly letter 190–192, 492
Future-tense verbs 194–202

G

General nouns 193
Gibbons, Gail 357
Glossary 243, 504, 548–559
Good 310–311, 340–341, 343
Grammar
   action verbs and *be* 130–138

adjectives 272–280, 336–344, 472
adverbs 318–326, 336–344, 471–472
articles 308–309, 314
easily confused words 346–354, 473
irregular verbs 204–212
main verbs and helping verbs 166–174
nouns 92–100, 102–110, 455, 458–460
past-tense and future-
   tense verbs 194–202
possessive nouns 120–128
predicates 52–60
present-tense verbs 176–184
pronouns 234–242, 262–270, 466–468
sentences 24–32, 454
simple and compound sentences . 62–70, 457
singular and plural nouns 102–110
subject and object pronouns 244–252
subjects and nouns 34–42
verbs 52–60, 456, 461–465
Graphic organizers, note-taking with . 516–517
Graphs, using 512
Guide words 175

H

Half-Chicken 426–431
Handbook
   commonly misspelled words 527
   glossary 548–559
   handwriting models 528–529
   spelling strategies 524–525
   study skills and strategies 502–503
   thesaurus 530–547
   writing models 480–495
Handwriting models 528–529
Health. *See* Writing Across the
   Curriculum
Helping verbs 166–174, 196–197, 206–207
Heymsfeld, Carla 215
Holidays, capitalization of 94–95
Homographs 350–351, 353
Homophones 346–353
Horsepower: The Wonder of
   Draft Horses 328
How to Be a Friend 140–145

How-to essay 140–152, 481, 497
   parts of 146–147

I

I. See Pronouns

Information. *See also* Informative writing
   organizing 328–331
   paragraphs of 332–334

Informative writing
   advantages and disadvantages
      essay 282–292, 499
   directions 112–118
   how-to essay 140–152, 481, 497
   paragraph that compares 258–260, 490
   paragraph that contrasts 491
   paragraph of information 328–334
   research report 356–368, 500

Internet 506
   See also Technology

Interviewing 345

Irregular plural nouns 106–110

Irregular verbs 204–212
   commonly misused 208–211

J

Jin, Sarunna 73

Journal. *See* Writing Connection,
   Writer's Journal

K

K-W-L chart 516

Key words 253, 502

L

Letter
   commas in 390–391
   friendly 190–192, 492

Listening and Speaking
   acting out a story 83
   being a good listener and speaker 43
   comparing writing and speaking 261
   facts and opinions 203
   giving spoken directions 119
   listening outside the classroom 397
   making a video 293
   making an oral presentation 153, 225
   teamwork 439

Literature models
   advantages and
      disadvantages essay 282–285
   character study 398
   description 44
   directions 112
   how-to essay 140–145
   informative writing 112, 254
   paragraph of information 328
   personal narrative 72–75
   persuasive paragraph 214–217
   persuasive writing 186
   research report 356–361
   story 426–431

Log's Life, A 254

M

Main verbs 166–174

Maps 509
   reading 111
   using 511

Me. See Pronouns

Mechanics
   abbreviations and titles 96–100
   capitalizing words in titles 420–421
   combining sentences 38–42, 66–70, 392–396
   contractions 170–174, 266–270, 378–379
   punctuating dialogue 410–411
   punctuating sentences 28–29

Medearis, Angela Shelf 44

Months, capitalization of 94–95

More and *most* 312–316, 322–325

Multimedia presentation 369

My First American Friend 72–75

N

Names. *See* Nouns; Proper nouns
Negative words 378–385, 474
   double negatives 382–385
Newspapers, using 508
No. See Negative words
Not. See Contractions; Negative words
Notetaking 327, 335, 516–517
   with graphic organizers 516–517
Nouns 36–37, 92–100, 455, 458–460
   adjectives with 272–273
   common 94–95, 98–100
   general 193
   irregular plural 106–110
   plural 102–110
   plural possessive 122–123, 126–128
   possessive 120–128
   proper 94–100
   singular 102–103, 108–110
   singular possessive 120–121, 126–128
   specific 187, 189, 193, 219
   in subjects 34–35, 40–42

O

Object pronouns 246–252
Opinions 203
Oral presentation 83, 119, 153, 225
Organization
   advantages and
      disadvantages essay 289–290
   how-to essay 149–150
   personal narrative 79–80
   persuasive paragraph 221–222
   research report 365–366
   story 435–436
Organizing information 328–331
Outlining 327, 329–330, 520–521

P

Paragraphing 112–115, 147
Paragraphs 112
   descriptive 48–50, 488
   of information 332–334
   persuasive 214–224
   that compare 258–260, 490
   that contrast 491
Past-tense verbs 194–202, 204–207, 210–212
Periodicals, using 508
Periods 24–32
   with abbreviations 96–100
   at end of sentences 24–25, 28–32
   with quotations 408–414
Personal narrative 72–82, 480, 496
   acting out a 83
   parts of 76–77
Personal voice 44–50, 77
Persuasive essay 482, 498
Persuasive paragraph 214–224
   parts of 218–219
Persuasive writing 186–192, 214–224, 498
Peterson, Cris 328
Pfeffer, Wendy 254
Pictures, interpreting 425
Pinkney, Gloria Jean 398
Plural nouns 102–105, 108–110
   irregular 106–110
   possessive 122–123, 126–128
Plural pronouns 236–237, 240–242
Poems, rhymed and unrhymed 494–495
Point of view 45, 47
Portfolio 21
   advantages and disadvantages essay . . 292
   how-to essay 152
   personal narrative 82
   persuasive paragraph 224
   research report 368
   story 438
Possessive nouns 120–128
   plural 122–123, 126–128
   revising sentences using 124–125
   singular 120–121, 126–128
Possessive pronouns 262–265, 268–270

Predicates 52–60, 62–63
   complete 52–53, 58–60
   compound 56–57, 59–60
   with compound subject 38–39
   simple 52–53, 58–60
   verbs in 54–55, 58–60, 130–131,
                     136–138, 166–167, 172–174
Prefixes 185
Present-tense verbs 176–184
Prewriting 19
   advantages and disadvantages essay . . 288
   character study 403
   descriptive paragraph 49
   directions 117
   friendly letter 191
   how-to essay 148
   paragraph of information 333
   paragraph that compares 259
   personal narrative 78
   persuasive paragraph 220
   research report 364
   story 434
Pronoun antecedents 238–241, 262
Pronouns 234–235, 240–242, 466–468
   agreement of 238–242
   contractions with 266–270
   I and *me* 248–252
   object 246–252
   plural 236–237, 240–242
   possessive 262–265, 268–270
   singular 236–237, 240–242
   subject 244–245, 248–252
Proofreading
   advantages and disadvantages essay . . 291
   how-to essay 151
   personal narrative 81
   persuasive paragraph 223
   research report 367
   story 437
Proper nouns 94–95, 98–100
   abbreviations of 96–97, 98–100
Publishing 19
   See also Sharing
   advantages and disadvantages essay . . 292
   how-to essay 152
   personal narrative 82

persuasive paragraph 224
research report 368
story 438
Punctuating sentences 28–32
Punctuation
   apostrophes 120–128, 170–174, 266–270
   commas 38–42, 56–60, 64–70,
                  388–396, 408–414, 475
   of dialogue 410–414
   end marks 24–25, 28–32, 408–414
   exclamation points 28–32, 408–409
   periods 24–25, 28–31, 96–97, 408–409
   question marks 28–31, 408–409
   quotation marks 406–414, 418–419
   sentences 28–29
   underlining 416–417
Purpose 329
   See also Purpose and audience
Purpose and audience 331
   how-to essay 148
   personal narrative 78
   persuasive paragraph 220
   research report 364
   story 434

Q

Question marks 28–31
   with quotations 408–409
Questions 26–31
Quotation marks 406–414
   with titles of written works 418–419
Quotations
   capitalization in 408–409, 422–424
   direct 406–407, 410–411
   punctuating 408–409

R

Ramona and Her Mother 186
Reading strategies 502–503
Reflecting
   advantages and disadvantages essay . . 292
   character study 404

descriptive paragraph 50
directions 118
friendly letter 192
how-to essay 152
paragraph of information 334
paragraph that compares 260
personal narrative 82
persuasive paragraph 224
research report 368
story 438
Research report 356–368, 484–485, 500
parts of 362–363
Revising. *See also* Editing
advantages and disadvantages essay . . 290
how-to essay 150
personal narrative 80
persuasive paragraph 222
research report 366
story 436
Rhymed and unrhymed poems 494–495

S

Scanning 502–503
Science. *See* Writing Across the
Curriculum; Writing Connection
Search engine 253, 506
Sentences 24
adverb placement in 338–339, 342–343
agreement in 134–135, 180–181, 238–239
combining 38–42, 56–60, 66–70,
255, 257, 392–393
commands 26–32
complete 62–63, 68–69
compound 64–65, 68–69, 392–393, 457
effective 254–257
exclamations 26–32
kinds of 26–27
punctuating 28–29
questions 26–32, 456
revising with possessive nouns 124–125
simple 64–65, 68–69, 457
statements 24–31, 454
subject of 52–53, 62–63, 455
subjects in 34–35
topic 113–114

variety in 255–256, 287
word order in 24–25
Sequence words 113, 115
Series, commas in 388–389
Science. *See* Writing Across the
Curriculum; Writing Connection
Sharing
advantages and disadvantages essay . . 292
character study 404
descriptive paragraph 50
directions 118
friendly letter 192
how-to essay 152
paragraph of information 334
paragraph that compares 260
personal narrative 82
persuasive paragraph 224
research report 368
story 438
Short story. *See* Story
Simple predicates 52–53, 58
Simple sentences 64–65, 68–70, 457
Simple subjects 36–37
Singular nouns 102–103, 108–109
Singular possessive nouns 120–121
Singular pronouns 236–237, 240–241
Skimming 502–503
Social Studies. *See* Writing Across the
Curriculum; Writing Connection
Speaking. *See* Listening and Speaking
Specific nouns 187, 189, 193, 219
Spelling
commonly misspelled words 527
strategies 524–525
Statements 24–32, 454
Story 426–438, 486–487, 501
acting out a 83
parts of a 432–433
Strategies Good Writers Use 78–81,
148–151, 220–223, 288–291, 364–367, 434–437
Study Skills
almanac 510
atlas 509
book parts 243, 504
charts 514–515
dictionary 175, 505

encyclopedia 507
graphs 512
Internet 506
maps 511
note-taking 327, 335, 516–517
outlining 327, 329–331, 520–521
periodicals and newspapers 508
reading tips 71
skimming and scanning 502–503
and strategies 502–523
summarizing 518–519
tables 513
test-taking strategies 415, 522–523
thesaurus 213
Subject pronouns 244–245, 248–251
Subjects 34–42
agreement with verb 134–135, 180–181
complete 36–37
compound 38–39
nouns in 34–35
plural 178–181
of a sentence 52–53, 62–63
simple 36–37
singular 178–181
Subject-verb agreement 134–135, 180–181
Suffixes 185
Summarizing 518–519
Synonyms 213, 317

T

Tables, using 513
Taking notes. *See* Note-taking
Teamwork 439
Technology
exploring websites 253
giving a multimedia presentation 369
interviewing to learn about your
community 345
making a video 293
Teirstein, Mark Alan 112
Tenses. *See* Verbs
Test-taking strategies 415, 522–523
for essay tests 523
for multiple-choice tests 522
Thank-you note 492–493

Thesaurus 532–547
using 213, 530–531
writer's 532–547
Titles 416–424, 477
abbreviations of 96–100
capitalization in 94–95, 420–421
quotation marks with 418–419
underlining 416–417
Topic, identifying your 113–114
Topic sentence 113–114

U

Underlining titles of written works . . . 416–417
Usage
adjectives 276–277, 312–313
adverbs 322–323
agreement of pronouns 238–239
agreement of subject and verb 180–181
be 134–137, 461
choosing verb tenses 198–199
commonly misused verbs 208–209
easily confused words 346–354, 473
irregular plural nouns 106–107
negative words 382–383, 474
using *good* and *well, bad*
and *badly* 340–341
using *I* and *me* 248–249

V

Verbs 52–60, 130–131, 136–137, 456, 461–465
action 132–133, 136
agreement with subject 134–135, 180–181
be 134–137
commonly misused 208–211
contractions with *not* 170–171
future-tense 194–202
helping 166–174, 196–197, 206–207
irregular 204–212
main 166–174
past-tense 194–202, 204–207
in predicates 54–55
present-tense 176–184

tenses of 176–177, 198–199
vivid 187–188, 219
Verb tenses. *See* Verbs
Video, making a 293
Viewing
  being a good viewer 33
  comparing images 387
  interpreting a picture 425
  looking at fine art 405
  understanding charts 101
Viewpoint, expressing your 45, 47
Vivid verbs 187–188, 219
Vocabulary. *See also* Vocabulary Power
  categorizing words 139
  colorful words 51
  context clues 271
  dictionary, using a 175
  general and specific nouns 193
  prefixes and suffixes 185
  synonyms and antonyms 317
  troublesome words 355
  words from many places 61
Vocabulary Power
  advertisements 186
  animated film 24
  astronomy 234
  blustery 254
  canine 272
  career 318
  carpenter 52
  cavity 120
  community 204
  confidence 217
  cooperate 145
  draft 328
  ecology 262
  elaboration 398
  energy 406
  enterprise 346
  evergreen 285
  experience 75
  Fahrenheit 244
  fantasy 62
  federal 194
  fiesta 336
  illuminate 112
  instrument 34

investigate 378
invisible 416
mineral 388
nutrient 102
precaution 92
register 176
rural 308
shimmering 44
traditions 166
vaccine 130
viceroy 431
visible 361

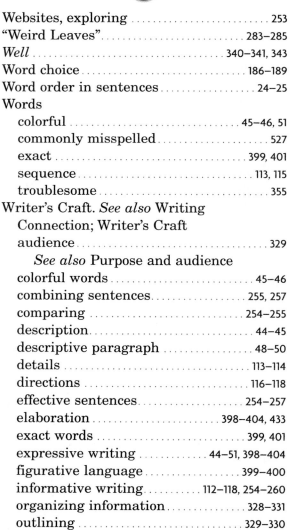

Websites, exploring 253
"Weird Leaves" 283–285
Well 340–341, 343
Word choice 186–189
Word order in sentences 24–25
Words
  colorful 45–46, 51
  commonly misspelled 527
  exact 399, 401
  sequence 113, 115
  troublesome 355
Writer's Craft. *See also* Writing
Connection; Writer's Craft
  audience 329
    See also Purpose and audience
  colorful words 45–46
  combining sentences 255, 257
  comparing 254–255
  description 44–45
  descriptive paragraph 48–50
  details 113–114
  directions 116–118
  effective sentences 254–257
  elaboration 398–404, 433
  exact words 399, 401
  expressive writing 44–51, 398–404
  figurative language 399–400
  informative writing 112–118, 254–260
  organizing information 328–331
  outlining 329–330
  paragraphing 112, 147

paragraph of information 332–334
paragraph that compares 258–260
personal voice 77
persuasive writing 186–192
purpose 329
    See also Purpose and audience
research report 356–368
sentence variety 255–256, 287
sequence words 113, 115
specific nouns 187, 189, 219
topic sentence 113–114
vivid verbs 187–188, 219
word choice 186–189
writer's viewpoint 45, 47
Writer's Thesaurus 532–547
Writing Across the Curriculum
  Art and Creativity 88
  Health 158
  Science 298, 444
  Social Studies 230, 374
Writing and Thinking 47, 115, 189, 257, 331, 401
Writing Connection
  Art 29, 135, 205, 249, 263, 309, 325, 347, 391
  Music 35
  Real-Life Writing 25, 67, 97, 107, 127, 131,
                  173, 181, 201, 207, 237, 251, 277,
                  315, 319, 343, 349, 383, 407, 421
  Science 103, 123, 267, 275, 385, 417
  Social Studies 167, 211, 323, 341
  Technology 31, 53, 59, 95, 183, 199,
                         241, 269, 411
  Writer's Craft 27, 41, 55, 65, 69, 99, 109,
            121, 133, 169, 179, 197, 209, 239, 247,
            265, 273, 311, 321, 339, 353, 381,
            393, 395, 413, 423
  Writer's Journal 39, 47, 57, 63, 93, 105,
           115, 125, 137, 171, 177, 189,
           195, 235, 245, 257, 279, 313,
        331, 337, 351, 379, 389, 401, 409, 419

Writing models 480–495
  advantages and disadvantages essay . . 483
  book review 489
  descriptive paragraph 488
  friendly letter with envelope 492–493
  how-to essay 481
  paragraph that compares 490
  paragraph that contrasts 491
  personal narrative 480
  persuasive essay 482
  poem 494–495
  research report 484–485
  story 486–487
Writing process
  advantages and
    disadvantages essay 288–292
  character study 402–404
  descriptive paragraph 48–50
  directions 116–118
  friendly letter 190–192
  how-to essay 148–152
  paragraph of information 332–334
  paragraph that compares 258–260
  personal narrative 78–82
  persuasive paragraph 220–224
  research report 364–368
  understanding 19
Writing rubrics
  expressive writing:
    personal narrative 496
  expressive writing: story 501
  informative writing: advantages
    and disadvantages essay 499
  informative writing: how-to essay 497
  informative writing: research report . . . 500
  persuasive writing: persuasive essay . . 498

Acknowledgments

For permission to reprint copyrighted material, grateful acknowledgment is made to the following sources:

Boyds Mills Press, Inc.: Cover illustration by Maryann Cocca-Leffler from *Wanda's Roses* by Pat Brisson. Illustration copyright © 1994 by Maryann Cocca-Leffler. From *Horsepower: The Wonder of Draft Horses* by Cris Peterson, cover photograph by Alvis Upitis. Text copyright © 1997 by Cris Peterson; photograph copyright © 1997 by Alvis Upitis.

Delacorte Press, a division of Random House, Inc.: From *Half-Chicken* by Alma Flor Ada, illustrated by Kim Howard. Text copyright © 1995 by Alma Flor Ada; illustrations copyright © 1995 by Kim Howard.

Dial Books for Young Readers, a division of Penguin Putnam Inc.: From *Back Home* by Gloria Jean Pinkney, cover illustration by Jerry Pinkney. Text copyright © 1992 by Gloria Jean Pinkney; cover illustration copyright © 1992 by Jerry Pinkney.

HarperCollins Publishers: From *Ramona and Her Mother* by Beverly Cleary, cover illustration by Alan Tiegreen. Text and cover illustration copyright © 1979 by Beverly Cleary. From *Beacons of Light: Lighthouses* by Gail Gibbons. Copyright © 1990 by Gail Gibbons.

Holiday House, Inc.: Cover illustration by John and Alexandra Wallner from *A Picture Book of Benjamin Franklin* by David A. Adler. Illustration copyright © 1990 by John and Alexandra Wallner. Cover illustration by John and Alexandra Wallner from *A Picture Book of Thomas Alva Edison* by David A. Adler. Illustration copyright © 1996 by John and Alexandra Wallner. Cover illustration from *Dancing With the Indians* by Angela Shelf Medearis, cover illustration by Samuel Byrd. Text copyright © 1991 by Angela Shelf Medearis; illustration copyright © 1991 by Samuel Byrd.

Henry Holt and Company, Inc.: Cover illustration by Megan Lloyd from *Cactus Hotel* by Brenda Z. Guiberson. Illustration copyright © 1991 by Megan Lloyd.

Little, Brown and Company (Inc.): From *How to Be a Friend* by Laurie Krasny Brown and Marc Brown. Copyright © 1998 by Laurene Krasny Brown and Marc Brown. Cover illustration from *Dinosaurs Alive and Well!* by Laurie Krasny Brown and Marc Brown. Copyright © 1990 by Laurie Krasny Brown and Marc Brown. Cover illustration from *Arthur Writes a Story* by Marc Brown. Copyright © 1996 by Marc Brown. Cover illustration from *Recycle!* by Gail Gibbons. Copyright © 1992 by Gail Gibbons. Cover illustration from *Click! A Book about Cameras and Taking Pictures* by Gail Gibbons. Copyright © 1997 by Gail Gibbons.

National Wildlife Federation: "Weird Leaves" by Deborah Churchman from *Ranger Rick* Magazine, October 1999. Text copyright 1999 by the National Wildlife Federation.

Puffin Books, a division of Penguin Putnam Inc.: Cover illustration by Janet Wilson from *The Gadget War* by Betsy Duffey. Illustration copyright © 1991 by Janet Wilson.

Scholastic Inc.: Cover photograph from *What Food Is This?* by Rosmarie Hausherr. Copyright © 1994 by Rosmarie Hausherr. Cover illustration by Ron Garnett from *Great Black Heroes: Five Notable Inventors* by Wade Hudson. Illustration copyright © 1995 by Ron Garnett. HELLO READER! and CARTWHEEL BOOKS are registered trademarks of Scholastic Inc.

Simon & Schuster Books for Young Readers, an imprint of Simon & Schuster Children's Publishing Division: From *Coaching Ms. Parker* by Carla Heymsfeld, cover illustration by Jane O'Conor. Text copyright © 1992 by Carla Heymsfeld; illustration copyright © 1992 by Jane O'Conor. From *A Log's Life* by Wendy Pfeffer, cover illustration by Robin Brickman. Text copyright © 1997 by Wendy Pfeffer; illustration copyright © 1997 by Robin Brickman. Cover illustration from *A Desert Scrapbook: Dawn to Dusk in the Sonoran Desert* by Virginia Wright-Frierson. Copyright © 1996 by Virginia Wright-Frierson.

Steck-Vaughn Company: From *My First American Friend* by Sarunna Jin, cover illustration by Shirley V. Beckes. Text and cover illustration copyright © 1992 by Steck-Vaughn Company; text and cover illustration copyright © 1991 by Raintree Publishers Limited Partnership. From *Baseball: How to Play the All-Star Way* by Mark Alan Teirstein, cover photograph by Frank Becerra, Jr. Text and cover photograph © copyright 1994 by Steck-Vaughn Company.

Viking Penguin, a division of Penguin Putnam Inc.: Cover illustration by Leo and Diane Dillon from *The Hundred Penny Box* by Sharon Bell Mathis. Illustration copyright © 1975 by Leo and Diane Dillon.

Walker Publishing Company: Cover illustration by Barbara Bash from *Tiger Lilies and Other Beastly Plants* by Elizabeth Ring. Illustration copyright © 1984 by Barbara Bash.

Photo Credits

Page Placement Key: (t)-top (c)-center (b)-bottom (l)-left (r)-right (fg)-foreground (bg)-background.
Photos by Richard Hutchings/Harcourt: Page 47, 59, 64, 81, 83, 131, 169, 180, 189, 222, 223, 225, 289, 293, 367, 368, 415, 437.
Other:
Abbreviations for frequently used stock photo agencies:
PR - Photo Researchers, NY; SM -The Stock Market NY; TSI -Stone.
Unit One:
22-23 Bernard Boutrit/Woodfin Camp & Associates; 24 Daudier/Jerrican/PR; 25 Index Stock Photography; 28 The Granger Collection; 33 Harcourt; 34 Harcourt; 35 Prof. J.H. Nkatia, University of California, Los Angeles, Ethnomusicology Dept.; 37 PhotoDisc; 39 Joe Sohm/SM; 52 Walter Hodges/TSI; 53 Mark Joseph/TSI; 55 Phil Jude/Science Photo Library/PR; 62 Joseph Nettis/TSI; 67 Sean Ellis/TSI; 69 The Granger Collection, New York; 84 Cathlyn Melloan/TSI; 85 Howard Kingsnorth/TSI; 86 Jay S. Simon/TSI; 87 The Granger Collection; 88-89 I. Burgum/P. Boorman/TSI.
Unit Two:
90-91 Susan Leavines/PR; 92 Lori Adamski Peek/TSI; 93 Rob Downey/Harcourt; 95 Carl Scofield/Index Stock Photography; 102 Tom Martin/SM; 103 Bo Zaunders/SM; 105 Index Stock Photography; 109 Harcourt; 120 Chip Henderson/TSI; 121 Bachmann/PR; 123 Harcourt; 125 Pete Saloutos/SM; 130 NIBSC/Science Photo Library/PR; 154 Harcourt; 155 Laurence Monneret/TSI; 156 Weronica Ankerorn/Harcourt; 158-159 Charles Krebs/SM.

Unit Three:
164-165 Chris McLaughlin/SM; 166 Cameramann International; 167 Index Stock Photography; 171 Kevin Horan/Stock, Boston; 176 Bachmann/PR; 177 Bob Daemmrich/Stock, Boston; 179 Ed Young/Science Photo Library/PR; 181 Dana White/PhotoEdit; 194 Ed Pritchard/TSI; 195 (t) D. B. Owen/Black Star; 195 (b) Karl Schumacher/The White House; 196 Peggy and Ronald Barnett/SM; 197 AFP/Corbis; 199 Ross Ressmeyer/Corbis; 201 David Phillips/Harcourt; 204 Randy Wells/TSI; 205 Index Stock Photography; 207 J. Faircloth/Transparencies; 230-231 Harcourt.
Unit Four:
232-233 Lois Moulton/TSI; 234 David Parker/Science Photo Library/PR; 235 NASA; 237 NASA; 239 Jerry Schad/PR; 245 H.A. Miller/PR; 246 Bob Daemmrich/Stock, Boston; 247 (l) Harcourt; 247 (r) Hans Strand/TSI; 249 Steve Terrill/SM; 251 John Callahan/TSI; 262 Art Wolfe/TSI; 264 Francois Gohier/PR; 265 Renee Lynn/PR; 267 F. Gohier/PR; 272 Tom Brakefield/SM; 273 Renee Lynn/PR; 274 Gerard Lacz/Peter Arnold, Inc.; 275 Tim Davis/PR; 279 Daniel J. Cox/TSI; 282 (t) Robert & Linda Mitchell; 282 (b) Uniphoto; 283, 284 (t), (c), (b) J. H. (Pete) Carmichael/Nature Photographics; 285 (b) Lori Franzen; 285 (t) Derek Fell; 294 Kevin Kelley/TSI; 296 Charles Krebs/TSI; 298-299 Sonny Senser/Harcourt; 306-307 Benelux Press/Index Stock Photography.
Unit Five:
308 Larry Lefever from Grant Heilman Photography; 309 Adam Jones/PR; 311 B. Seitz/PR; 313 Renee Lynn/PR; 319 James Strachan/TSI; 321 David Madison/TSI; 325 Grantpix/PR; 336 Bob Daemmrich Photography; 337 David L. Brown/The Picture Cube/Index Stock Photography; 339 Myron Taplin/TSI; 340 David Stoecklein/SM; 343 Robert E. Daemmrich/TSI; 346 Rich Franco/Harcourt; 347 Harcourt; 349 Zane Williams/TSI; 351 Richard Pasley/Stock, Boston; 370 Larry Lefever from Grant Heilman Photography; 371 Weronica Ankerorn/Harcourt; 373 Murray & Associates/Picturesque Stock Photo; 374-375 Tom Sobolik/Black Star/Harcourt.
Unit Six:
376-377 Kevin Kelley/TSI; 378 Michal Heron/Woodfin Camp & Associates; 379 National Park Service, Edison National Historic Site; 381 Photo, (1905 Wright Bros. Flyer10/04/05 Simms Station Huffman Prairie) Wright State University Special Collections & Archives (Dayton, OH), The Wright Bros. TradeMark, Licensed by The Wright Family Fund, Represented by The Roger Richman Agency, Inc.; Beverly Hills, CA 90212 (www.wrightbrothers2003.com); 382 Harcourt Photo Library; 383 Bonnie Sue/PR; 388 Roberto De Gugliemo/Science Photo Library/PR; 389 David N. Davis/PR; 390 Art Wolfe/TSI; 391 James Martin/TSI; 393 John M. Roberts/SM; 395 Vanessa Vick/PR; 405 (detail) Gift of Mr. and Mrs. Benjamin E. Levy © 2000 Board of Trustees, National Gallery of Art, Washington, DC; 406 Richard R. Hansen/PR; 410 Paul Souders/TSI; 411 Index Stock Photography; 413 Stocktrek/SM; 416 Jim Corwin/TSI; 417 World Perspectives/TSI; 419 Wolfgang Kaehler; 421 Tony Freeman/PhotoEdit; 423 L.L.T. Rhodes/TSI; 440 I. Burgum/P. Boorman/TSI; 441 Art Wolfe/TSI; 442 Michael Giannechini/PR; 443 NASA; 444-445 L. P. Winfrey/Woodfin Camp & Associates.
Extra Practice:
454 Paul Souders/TSI; 455 Harcourt; 456 Michael Giannechini/PR; 459 Renee Lynn/PR; 462 Harcourt; 463 Sean Ellis/TSI; 464 Joseph Nettis/TSI; 465 Index Stock Photography; 467 Zane Williams/TSI; 471 Don Mason/SM; 474 Jose Fuste Raga/SM.
Handbook:
488 Lee Snider/The Image Works; 491 (l) Chris Warbey/TSI; 491 (r) Francois Gohier/PR; 502-503 Michele Burgess/SM; 530 Tom Benoit/TSI.

Art List

Harcourt, 23; Elizabeth Wolf, 27; Nathan Young Jarvis, 29; Claude Martinot, 31; Myron Grossman, 36; Harcourt, 37 (Left); Myron Grossman, 38; Elizabeth Wolf, 40; Nathan Young Jarvis, 41; Harcourt, 43; Jane Winsor, 54; Claude Martinot, 56; Nathan Young Jarvis, 65-66; Harcourt, 69 (bottom); Ilya Bereznickas, 71; Stacey Schuett, 72-75; Karen Pritchett, 77-78, 80; Harcourt, 85, 91; Andy Levine, 94; Ilya Bereznickas, 96; Andy Levine, 99; Harcourt, 101; Donna Turner, 103 (bottom), 104 (left), 104 (right), 106; Alexi Natchev, 107; Ken Batleman, 111; Claude Martinot, 122; Illya Berezmickas, 124; George Ulrich, 127; Andy Levine, 129, 132; Myron Grossman, 133; Christine Mau, 134; Andy Levine, 137; Christine Mau, 139; Karen Pritchett, 153; Elizabeth Wolf, 157; Harcourt, 165; Elizabeth Wolf, 168; Andy Levine, 170; Myron Grossman, 173; Tamara Petrosino, 178; Alexi Natchev, 183; Andy Levine, 193 (ALL); Claude Martinot, 196, 198; Elizabeth Wolf, 203; Tamara Petrosino, 206; Myron Grossman, 208, 211; Ilene Robinette, 214-217; Nathan Young Jarvis, 218; Tammara Petrosino, 226-227; Christine Mau, 228; Tamara Petrosino, 229; Harcourt, 230-231, 233; Myron Grossman, 236; Nathan Young Jarvis, 241(right); Harcourt, 241 (bottom); Christine Mau, 243; Nathan Young Jarvis, 244; Harcourt, 247 (Snowflake), 248; Andy Levine, 253; Claude Martinot, 263, 266, 268; Jane Winsor, 269; Andy Levine, 271; Donna Turner, 273 (bottom); Karen Pritchett, 276; Donna Turner, 277; Harcourt, 281, 307; Myron Grossman, 310; Karen Pritchett, 312; Patricia Fila, 315; Myron Grossman, 317 (Top), 317 (Bottom); Nathan Young Jarvis, 319; Elizabeth Wolf, 320, 322- 323; Ezra Tucker, 338; Alexi Natchev, 341; Myron Grossman, 342; Nathan Young Jarvis, 345; Ilya Bereznicka, 348; Harcourt, 350; Andy Levine, 353; Tamara Petrosino, 355 (All); Harcourt, 369; Myron Grossman, 372, 377; Karen Pritchett, 385; Tamara Petrosino, 387; Elizabeth Wolf, 392; Christine Mau, 397; Myron Grossman, 407; Nathan Jarvis, 408-409; Christine Mau, 418; Andy Levine, 420; Alexi Natchev, 425; Karen Pritchett, 439; L.P Winfrey/Woodfin Camp And Associates, 444-445; Janet Wilson, 445 (top book); Ron Garnett, 445 (middle book); John and Alexander Wallner, 445 (bottom book); L.P Winfrey/Woodfin Camp And Associates, 445; Janet Wilson, 445 (top book); Ron Garnett, 445 (middle book)